AN IRREGULAR LIFE

Being The Adventures &
Memoirs
Of A Fortunate Sherlockian

Chronicled by

MARK F. McPHERSON, BSI

Something old,
something new,
something borrowed...

(hope you enjoy it.

xo
M

Hardcover ISBN 978-1-78705-952-8
Paperback ISBN 978-1-78705-953-5

Published by MX Publishing
335 Princess Park Manor, Royal Drive,
London, N11 3GX
www.mxpublishing.com

Cover compiled by Brian Belanger

"I suppose that one could say that Gerald Middleton had taken life a bit too easily."

She cocked her head, bird-like, on one side, as if considering her words.

"Don't you think so?" she asked Sir Edgar. The old man got up from the red American leather couch.

"I could imagine someone who barely knew him at all saying so" he said.

—Angus Wilson, Anglo-Saxon Attitudes

"It is all true, or it ought to be; and more and better besides."

—Winston Churchill

"The strongest beings are those who sing themselves into existence."

—Lakota Sioux Proverb

"May the words of my mouth and the meditation of my heart be pleasing to your sight, O Lord."

—Psalms 19:14

TABLE OF CONTENTS

The author and Dame Jean Conan Doyle

The "Apiary"
Downsland, near Eastborne

My Dear Watson:

I am in receipt of the rather curious manuscript which you have forwarded for my comments. Initially I was surprised to find that the work at hand was not your own. More so perhaps, to discover that you are apparently lending your talents in these latter days toward the business of a literary agent. Truth to tell, I might have thought that your prior experiences with Dr. Conan Doyle would have sated such rash or impulsive urges.

However as you have requested, I have begun a perusal of "An Irregular Life: The Adventures and Memoirs of a Fortunate Sherlockian." Given its vaguely Doylean provenance, is not this title a bit presumptuous? Worse yet, as your enclosed note states, this is obviously the author's cleverly double entendre, if not his intentional homage to myself. Quite frankly, I must begin with the question of what, if anything to make of any of this?

Certainly the passing years have witnessed an upsurge of clubbable, social worship for such literary lights as Shakespeare, Dickens and Edgar Allan Poe. While in theory such ventures may be deemed acceptable, you know my thoughts about the notion of strangers gathering in some formalized worship of any public figure, be he an author, artist, or dare I suggest it, a consulting detective. Many years ago I believe we discussed the formation of that singular set of gentlemen in New York who promoted their "irregular" bacchanalian celebrations of my casework. For this I did then and do now lay the blame upon the threshold of your own sensationalized treatments of my work. Likewise, the matter of the present "homage" does I think present certain perils of a similar nature.

An initial perusal of the enclosed pages finds me unable to pronounce any sort of verdict on Mr. Mark McPherson's slender memoir. This however is not to say that his life has appeared to be uneventful. Quite the contrary, for that matter. Nor may I be so churlish as to deny his claim that I in any way may have motivated him in his youth or even dotage.

Nevertheless, this comparatively younger man has seemingly known his share of personal exploits. Further, from what I have seen thus far he seems fairly apt in the art of observation and its employment. Also to his credit, I think, he appears to have possessed common sense enough to eschew such organizational, or "scion" activities as have been cast in my name. In a related sense, I find that his desire to avoid the fawning herds if only to pursue his solitary course is in its way praiseworthy.

So then I will proceed as you have asked me, to punctuate the enclosed ms copy with my thoughts. Whether or not they might affect or improve it is scarcely the point. I suspect, doctor, that you may harbor some deeper motivation. With that said, it is pleasant to once again state that I have yet to get your limits.

Therefore your request shall be honoured by your colleague and faithful sounding board, who has the pleasure to remain

Very sincerely yours,
Sherlock Holmes

AN IRREGULAR LIFE
Being THE ADVENTURES & MEMOIRS
of A FORTUNATE SHERLOCKIAN

AN AUTHORIAL INTRUSION

Last week and while being driven to school by their mother, my two grandchildren rang me from Nashville. That call to me now seems somewhat prophetic. The reason for it also reflects upon the fact that five years ago and upon publication of the First Edition of this memoir, I dedicated its contents to those podlings--with the caveat, "when it is time."

But now hearing their inquiry of "Grandpa, can you tell us about the Loch Ness Monster?" I thought to myself, "Well perhaps that time has arrived. After all, they're getting older and so am I. And what after all is the point of having had an adventurous life if you can't share it?" That at least was the advisement of Isabella and Christian's grandmother those years ago as I contemplated the notion of writing a memoir.

So yes, my dears, I can indeed tell you about "Nessie." If not about a catalogue of the curious and quaint; of ghoulies and ghosties, haunted houses, if not a hundred other unsolved mysteries. And why? Simply because long before you were born, your grandfather-as-he-was-yet-to-be decided to pursue mysteries for a living. And in that sense he became, for no better way to put it, a kind of historical detective.

Which now finds me here, however briefly, back within the Present. Equipped with more than any being's fair share of memories, suddenly I once again feel disposed to no longer study the Tardis standing in the corner of my library sanctum, but to re-enter it.

And if by so doing this poor man's Doctor Who can better illumine what he strove to describe half a decade ago, then well and good. Better yet, and with a suddenly renewed zest to share those recollections, memory itself may offer even more.

For you see, I am blessed (or tormented) much like the Great Detective in Billy Wilder's abridged cinematic masterpiece "The Private Life of Sherlock Holmes." To wit, I remain possessed of a fly-paper-like memory still chock-a-block with "a staggering amount of data, mostly useless."

Well as for the "useless" claim, that may be an overstatement. All here depends upon time, place, and the reminiscer's own intention, don't you think? At any rate, for now my point relates to one writer with stories enough to tell, and hopefully, a prospective audience to hear them.

Here then am I prepared once again to re-visit my past. Moreover and encouraged by my new publisher to do so, I am excited to reach into my sea-chest of Yesteryears for the sake of conjuring up not a few things which never made the First Edition pages of An Irregular Life. Also and if only for the sake of having that privilege, allow me to also admit that I'm actually a bit chuffed, as my Brit friends say, to set sail on an all-too-familiar journey.

Moreover and with miles already travelled, "time, tide, and buttered eggs" (in John Masefield's words) now compel me to navigate from the comfort of my armchair—or at least, my writer's seat. That in itself is quite an admission, given the fact that I've spent most of my prime time "in the field." So it goes.

And while I'm at it, this "revisitation" might be a fine opportunity to tidy a few of those dusty mental shelves which continue to sag with the weight of years. Harsh words hastily employed are always dangerous. So too are estimations which mays give way to certain retrospective understandings.

Lastly, I recall upon originally writing the sense of pausing, shaking my graying head and feeling decidedly as if I were some voyeur intruding upon another being's private existence. In other words: as if I were peering over a high fence and into some familiar stranger's rather antiquated mansion.

But now I realize a good deal more than I did before. To begin with, that "mansion" I allude to is a two-fold element. First off, it represents the physical base from which I have realized so much inspiration. This is "Gray Gables," my residence built in 1849 seated on the island of Grosse Ile, Michigan. It is here that I share my life with my wife Dori and canine "Dr. Watson," Bradbury.

Secondly however, the mansion in question also represents my figurative Palace of Memory, as the Italian sage Ricci once put it. And inside its mazery of rooms, corridors and vast and dusty attics are the repository for what my late friend Ray Bradbury used to describe as his "metaphors." Just so here, indeed.

For jam-packed within my lofty-ceilinged brain-box are a cornucopia of oddments, relics and reminders. Maps, an Alexandrian Library's-worth of rare volumes, bladed weaponry, portraiture, carvings, relics, statuary and a good deal more, both real and figurative. Ergo, like one or many of those old "museums of curiosities," my own repository differs only from Bradbury's now vanished basement word-laboratory in the most minor of ways. Yet very like his formerly creative subterranean retreat, my sanctum sanctorum is without a doubt a sort of Rorschach Test for its owner-curator-creator.

So here I stand, once again prepared to overlook those curious corners of my existence in a double entendre fashion. And the paradox here? Even as I say, I plan to "look over" the chain of years in a survey-like fashion, I must do so with the aim of very little being "overlooked."

But here too "there be dragons," as the nautical charts used to say.

First off, this endeavor demands an understanding that as time passes much we have done and remembered may seem to recede and fade, if not to vanish entirely from sight and mind. Friends and colleagues take their leaves. And like those "little gray cells" Hercule Poirot speaks of, dusty files, photos, clippings and their scrapbooks may crumble to dust. Here then perhaps the only stop-gap is in their preservation. In other words, some form of drastic recourse. But in aid of what? Well perhaps for the dubious service of recording one's sins, deeds, and if we're lucky, our rarified good works.

Or to put it another and more artful way, and as an old Lakota Sioux adage has it, sometimes one simply needs to "sing himself into existence." On reflection I suppose, I've been unwittingly embarked on just such a mission for quite a while. So then, are you prepared to share one man's rather sentimental journey? Then "let's away!"

Mark McPherson
"Gray Gables"
Spring-time, 2021

PREFACE TO THE PRESENT EDITION

Within the end-flap of the 2016 edition of *An Irregular Life,* its author was quoted in dubbing it to be "the first and last of my memoirs."

Well, he lied. Or at least, and without prevarication, he had no way of envisioning the fast-altering shape of his world, if not his own small place within it.

Which now brings us to 2021. Amid "wars and rumors of wars," the Pandemic has wrought a global dysfunction untold since H.G. Wells suggested an alien invasion which threatened every phase of human existence.

And just so now. New strains of viral contagion. Also a polemic fascism which threatens to compete as the newest, most lethal virus of all. Add in international stirrings. Moreover, a nation torn asunder and seeming to be rehearsing for a new civil war.

And if that weren't bad enough, the American government's recent admission that "we are not alone" in the cosmos. And that yes, those seemingly extra-terrestrial objects in our skies were and have been in fact "up there" all along. Shades of Mr. Wells.

Here then, on a ten-mile-long battle-shaped island seated between the U.S. and Canada, a retired writer sits down again to re-pen and review a score of his lifetime's recollections. And why? Simply because some five years back he was persuaded that largely on account of one of his most abiding literary influences, he ought to share it with an untold audience of other mavens, aficionados, specialists and dilletantes who revel yet in the name of Sherlock Holmes the Great Solver of Mysteries.

Therefore and despite the question of whether such a *raison d'être* is sufficient inspiration for more than five hundred pages of reminiscence, there is this question: does not the writing of one's memoirs smack of a certain level of presumption? Moreover, and by virtue of doing so, must not an author presume that something he has thought or done is now worthy of being recorded?—or better yet, read?

So then, hardly rich and not quite famous, I regard my life, as perceived within certain "Sherlockian" or better, "Doylean" terms, has put me in the way of the famous, the infamous, the marvelous, the serendipitous, the frightening, the elemental, the splendid, and the spiritual. In other words, I believe I have been blessed more than a score of others embarked upon their quests. If only for the sake of that, then, have I been persuaded to share it, even as it has chanced to happen.

Accordingly, I have grappled with this matter and finally decided to give in. I do so as if by the urging of another scribe—this one both famous and infamous by the name of Giacomo Casanova.

Yes, Casanova, whose surname stands as synonymous and as a trope for that archetypally and sybaritically roguish lover-adventurer of the 18th century. In fact, and while I have always felt more empathy with his successor, Lord Byron, something of late compelled me to assess the two volumes of Casanova's *Memoirs* which had gathered dust in my library. Some of this may have had to do with their translator, in the person of Arthur Machen, the dean of 19th century British horror tales. Author of *The Great God Pan, The Bowman,* and his classic chiller *The Three Impostors.* Today Machen's work is either well-known and loved or entirely forgotten by readers.

But apart from the *cachet* of Machen's translation of Casanova's exploits, I was initially piqued by the *Preface* to his narrative. There he stated, in part,

"By recollecting the pleasures I have had formerly, I renew them, I enjoy them a second time, while I laugh at the remembrance of troubles now past, which I no longer feel. A member of this great universe, I speak to the air, and I fancy myself rendering an account of my administration, as a steward is wont to do before leaving his situation. For my future I have no concern, and as a true philosopher I never would have any, for I know not what it may be; as a Christian, on the other hand, faith must believe without discussion, and the stranger it is, the more it keeps silent. I know that I have lived because I have felt, and, feeling giving me the knowledge of my existence, I know likewise that I shall exist no more when I shall have ceased to feel."

As for yours truly, while I cannot claim a roster of Casanovan conquests, I too may often have "spoken to the air," and hold no one accountable for my foibles save myself. And as for the spiritual precept that "faith must believe without discussion," I fear I have violated that by engaging in an unending series of discourses on the Unseen World. These pages are in due part a reflection of that.

All of which then may or may not have necessitated the creative act of self-explanation you now find before you. And doubtless while there may be those who would state that the act of waxing on autobiographically ought to be a right, rather than an un-ending obligation, I carry on. For so long as both memories and feelings serve, there are stories queuing up and waiting to be told.

However and not unlike that fabled and swashbuckling cocksman of bygone days, I am able to freely state, here and now, that I too "know I have lived because I have felt, and, feeling giving me the knowledge of my existence." And while Casanova spoke of surrendering to the judgment of readers who might believe in his veracity, so too perhaps must I.

So accept if you will this authorial retraction concerning the former edition's disclaimer concerning his "last memoir." And believe if you will in its truth. Here I voluntarily fall back upon Winston Churchill's description of King Arthur's mytho-historical saga.

"It is all true, or it ought to be" wrote that 20th century knight, "and more and better besides."

Here then but in much less royal fashion is the story of one man's personal mythos, which in turn has been tempered by a retinue of others. And with that in mind, I hope you find yourself enjoying his journey.

1
The Time Machine

Now then, as for this business of writing one's "memoirs." I've discovered a couple of other interesting things along the way. First off, you *can* "go home again" through the power of the written word. That in itself is a form of time-travel.

Secondly, hopefully at one's disposal there exists the possible means of re-visiting the Past, replete as it is with its memories, songs, landscapes, if not its share of galloping ghosts. Some of them friendly, others not; some beloved, while others may drift past without managing to evoke more than the wispiest twinge of recognition.

But as for the "why?" behind this memoir, I was recently visited by a well-remembered cinematic wraith. That remains in keeping with the chronic manner that this "boy who was half a man and man who is half a boy" was nurtured by a slew of classic media images, and most of them on the Big Screen.

Therefore I think now of one of my favorite Steve McQueen films, "The Thomas Crown Affair" (1968). In it the protagonist is a wealthy man of business who chooses to rob a bank—not once, but twice. He does so for a number of reasons: atonement, regret, and undoubtably, *because he can.* Ergo, deciding on that unusually repetitive course and on the heels of being caught, he commits the second robbery.

And just so, dear reader, the volume before you is my second presentation of an essentially similar subject: it is a composite of my life, viewed through the lens of Arthur Conan Doyle and his greatest invention, Mr. Sherlock Holmes.

As things sometimes chance, the present memoir is in its second, if not altered edition. Here then, and perhaps like Thomas Crown's double robbery, I am re-presenting my life story through the courtesy of perhaps the world's best purveyor of "Sherlockian" lore, MX Publishing.

I do so as well in order to call some attention to my book. Sadly, its 2016 edition should never have seen the light. This, largely in terms of a rushed deadline schedule which precluded proper editing. Moreover, and perhaps blessedly, once the book appeared between its handsome cover, it speedily careened its way to obscurity. Here the reasons are many, but mostly to do with a non-existent campaign to promote or critically make *An Irregular Life* available to critics, no less a general readership, near or far. To wit then, and perhaps fortunately, the book was reviewed favorably, but only once in print, and its subscription list depended upon prospective purchasers enduring an expensive game of Chutes and Ladders to secure it.

But now however the volume before you has been corrected, redacted and measurably expanded. It is, for the record, a "better book," if only for the stalwart efforts of my British publisher, and before them, my loving wife Dori, who plowed through unfamiliar fields in quest of their author. For that, I will always be in her debt.

Finally, here is one man's memoir about what occurred, early and late when the Sherlockian/Holmesian game was "afoot." So then, and out of a sense of gladness, a lack of regret, if not a memory-keeper's own excited return to the Past, stands my dubious legacy. I have therefore chosen to set it down once again both while, and essentially because I can. Not exactly a "second robbery of the same bank" in a lucrative sense, it nonetheless remains a happy "return to the scene of the crime(s)."

Yet oddest of all perhaps in this endeavor, among those summonable wraiths I cite one might even encounter the livid shade of one's own former self. That in itself is a kind of surreal bonus. And why do you suppose? Well simply because when you come face to face with your younger reconjured incarnation, the exercise can be rather retroactively assuring.

For instance, I recall my initial reaction in "meeting myself" as if I were re-encountering an absent friend. Moreover, and courtesy of the agency of my fly-paper-like memory, I recall smiling and frowning, laughing, crying and sighing at the antics of one self-directed young fellow who seemed to find very little difficulty in assaying the distances between Fact and Fiction, Fantasy and Reality.

I believe much of this sense of almost filial, self-kinship may also have to do with what the great Sherlockian magus Christopher Morley once described as "The Man Who Made Friends With Himself." When I first discovered his book's title I liked it greatly. In fact, even before encountering that volume I'd already embraced its meaning. You see, years back this only child had chosen to stare back at the darkness to forestall its parade of nightmares. And charted from that moment he had developed a passion for the Unknown; enough so in fact to make it his business. And by doing so I suppose I became both Holmes and Watson; at least until I found some friend and confident in whom to confide my secrets.

Because of that self-wrought friendship I later found myself visited by an almost filial feeling for my youthful *alter ego*. Ultimately the two of us would share a slew of bisecting and diverging arteries leading to a set of factual, fictional, if not phantasmagorical destinations.

In effect then, I became a real-life fabulist. And as a friendly acquaintance once alleged, I'd begun to "make my fantasies real." Which, as I also tend to presume, may come as no surprise whatsoever to those who know me. Or think they do.

Spoiler Alert: If indeed there is a constant within the pages to follow, it must be the somewhat shadowy presence of another and most singularly elemental entity which has long-since assumed a familiarly lean and hawklike visage. Pipe in mouth, lens in hand, shoulders caped, and according to his archetype at least, deer-stalker cap resting upon his famous brain. I dare say many of you would probably recognize him at first glance. Even his name evokes an almost magical, incantatory effect: *Sherlock Holmes.*

And I too recognized him early on. Yes even long before I could suspect that that hawk-faced sleuth, if not his more genial creator, would both inveigle themselves deeply and unwittingly enough to become my own life models. *For thinking. For exploring. For imagining. And for adventuring.*

But here you may well ask, "why is any of this important?" Here perhaps the answer has greatly to do with my being asked *"what made you this way?"* The answer to that exists in a particularly enduring literary genre and what some have described as the game of Sherlockian Pursuit. Its players are many and diverse. They are serious and sardonic. They are both playful and often staid in their observation.

There is in fact an outright reverence for the Sherlockian/Holmesian "Sacred Canon" consisting of four novels and fifty-six shorter stories devised by their Doylean maker (who might, as many have also insisted, have actually been Dr. Watson's literary agent.) Yet regardless of their true and "only begetter," the Holmes saga has long possessed the ability to hold a legion of its beholders in its thrall. And among them, I confess, I include myself.

I suppose that the consequence or after-effect or primary symptom of having given one's self so chronically to Conan Doyle's immortal amateur reasoner has become for many something vaguely akin to a secular religion. And what does that mean? Well certain of our peculiar minority of acolytes have even striven to emulate Holmes by learning his methods and retracing his steps, if only as a curious means of offering him honour due.

This then is the story of one of those acolytes. Furthermore, and as Arthur Conan Doyle once described, as "a man who is half a boy and the boy who is half a man." That (and with respect too for the female followers of Holmes) covers the field, I think. But it also takes in my own Sherlockian navigations over the course of what may be conservatively gauged to be some sixty-odd years.

During the time in question I have often bilocated in Time and Space. Even as I have sometimes willingly traded my riverfront Michigan idyll for the vanished London world of Mr. Sherlock Holmes. Ergo I have vacated my own cluttered library if only to transport to the familiar precinct of that well-described and cluttered Victorian study with its Baker Street-side windows looking down upon a misty gaslit avenue. Then suddenly a moment later one finds himself prowling a fog-bound moor within sight of its haunted manor and the prospect of a phantom beast baying in the near distance. And advancing, upon the sigh of the wind one hears a chorus of spectral voices chanting from the Great Beyond.

So again, I now freely admit to being willingly claimed by such a strand of eldritch enchantment. Moreover, to not only observing, but actually having become a part of its *milieu*.

And as for the "how?" and "why?" of what I've described? That doubtless has much to do with a rather singular fact: *I have worked rather diligently to seek the means of retreating into time.* And the result of my quest? As you will hear down the pike, I believe I may have found the key.

But along the way I have managed to walk apace with a figure so eccentric, so solitary and so inordinately clever that for me he surpasses any other character who has "never lived and so can never die." That is the brief for believing in Sherlock Holmes: for to paraphrase Winston Churchill on the subject of King Arthur, "it is all true or it ought to be: and more and better besides."

For such reasons I have once again decided to travel back to my Yesterdays. To do so imagine being offered H.G. Wells's fabulous time-traveling machine for us to chronologically troll through those bygone ethers. Ideally the pages to follow will attempt to achieve just such an effect.

Meanwhile however and as I've sought to place people, things and places in their properly temporal cubby holes, I beg to be forgiven for the occasional short-fall. Notwithstanding the best of intentions, sometimes accuracy and order may fall prey to memory's glitches. As a consequence and as the narrator has occasionally discovered, he suddenly asks himself, *"does this bit belong to a year ago?"* or *"did that came much later?"* Or worse, *"did it actually occur at all?"*

It's also occurred to me rather after-the-fact that another strangeness of such an exercise as this is recalling one's own past-tense inability to realize certain things. But what do I mean by that?

Well one curious thought which has reoccurred over the years is how, at given times, I was positioned to, but restrained from seeing the future. Here then are a few examples. Moreover upon reviewing portions of my life, it's occurred to me that I might one day pen a small book entitled *"If I'd Only Known."*

The aforementioned book would largely consider one's inability to know what's to come, save in retrospect. And it's then I suppose the strangeness sets in. How, you might ask?

Here are three examples. The first of these involves two actors, one of them great and the other—yet even to aspire to set foot on stage. I'm

18

talking here of the great, if not legendary Henry Fonda, who was appearing in a Detroit's Fisher Theater production at a time when I happened to be working in an art gallery seated several floors above.

Anyway, I got the great idea of asking my chum in the Press Department at the Fisher "if Mr. Fonda would like to see our gallery?" Knowing that the actor was quite an artist and aficionado on his own, the notion made sense. And apparently it didn't fall on deaf ears, because shortly after my friend rang and said "pick him up at the theatre's lobby door."

Well I confess the message left me a bit gob-smacked, and even more so when I arrived on the dot to usher the star of "The Grapes of Wrath," "Mr. Roberts" and "On Golden Pond" (to cite but a few credits) up to the third floor.

I still recall the effect of feeling like Moses walking the path through the Red Sea as Henry Fonda and I made our way to the hallway elevator. But I also recall there was little bonhomie exchanged. In fact, Fonda barely broke a smile in the forty-five minutes or so that we were together. Polite when he got to the London Arts Gallery, he made a quick survey before noting he needed to return belowstairs to prepare for his matinee performance.

Well here's my point. Away back then, roughly the Nineteen Seventy-something, I knew things about Henry Fonda but not that much about myself. Not, say, that in the wake of the actor's classic appearance in John Ford's "My Darling Clementine" as a laconic Wyatt Earp, that one day I too, now the young gallery's dogsbody, would appear as old Wyatt myself, in a one-man-show on the storied stage of Tombstone's Schieffelin Hall Theater. But if I'd known any of that or could have informed my famous companion, would it have mattered?

A second example of nescience, or "un-knowing" came about in 1988. I was visiting my friend Richard Lancelyn Green at his home in Cheshire, for the sake of his vetting my script for "An Evening With Sir Arthur Conan Doyle." This was to be my initial foray onto any stage in this genre, and if asked, I would have said, "it's unlikely I'll ever try this again."

19

As it chanced however, I continued with Doyle, who was to be followed in his dramatically local, statewide, national and international wake by my renditions of Bernard Shaw, Charles Dickens, Wyatt Earp, Winston Churchill, Theodore Roosevelt, Mark Twain, and—wait for it—C.S. Lewis.

Now I place some emphasis on Professor Lewis, because about a decade after birthing my Doylean "Evening," I wrote and performed in a one-character, two-act drama about Clive Staples Lewis entitled "From Narnia, With Love."

And now, here as they say, comes the punch. For you see, unwittingly back in '88, I thought it only a nice curiosity that the bedroom I'd been given on my visit to Poulton Hall, the Lancelyn Green family home, had once been allotted to Clive Staples Lewis on his occasional visits. For you see, C.S.L. was an Oxford colleague of Richard's literary father Roger Lancelyn Green. In fact, his imprint on the author's series of books featuring Narnia and the great Lord of the Wood, Aslan, was major. For contrary to Lewis's other friend J.R.R. Tolkien, who criticized *The Lion, The Witch and The Wardrobe* as "ramshackle stuff," it was Green who encouraged Lewis not to give up on his proposed series. And it was also Roger Lancelyn Green who suggested the collateral title "The Narnian Chronicles," which Lewis used and is celebrated as such to this day.

So then, there I was in that fine old British manse in 1988, and offered C.S. Lewis's occasional digs. *But never suspecting that on one still-distant future day, I myself would "become" the creator of Narnia!* Add to this the fact that upon being driven to the Chester Station at weekend's end, it was Richard's mother June, wife of the late Roger, who took me to my train. Add insult to injury when I tell you that only later did I learn that June and Roger had spent the last holiday with Professor Lewis and his wife Joy. And had I known that? Well, think of what I might have asked my hostess. But could not, given my "state of un-knowing" for what the future had yet in store!

There are other examples afoot of my "Had I But Known Then"-styled experiences. However, no doubt the most resonating of them involves my future meeting with President Anwar Sadat in Egypt. That to my mind presents the most peculiar, realistically surreal, and possibly the most portentous example of my proposition. And like its fellows, this example depended principally upon my being "in the right place, at the right time." But the surreality of the thing also reflects the science fictional premise of whether in one's Past or Present they might be somehow equipped with knowledge beyond that moment. And if so, might they have somehow altered it? Which in a greater and imagined sense, is also the matter of whether one individual, capable of intruding upon the Past, could also affect the Yet-to-come?

As for the just-cited implication of my notion, *vis a vis* what I'll term The Sadat Incident, you may be the judge, should you succeed in wading through these pages to reach the chapter entitled "An Egyptian Odyssey."

But for now I hope you get the gist of what I'm busy suggesting; namely, *that there are things we cannot or possibly should not know at certain times, however interesting it might be to consider whether making use of such knowledge were possible.*

Further, and taking into consideration what we'll dub the Einsteinian and Wellsian Principles of Time, it's likely that one bit of wrong or anachronistic knowledge might conceivably set off a parade of collisions in terms of history or Reality as we tend to view it. So perhaps I ask myself, it's just as well to leave the Now to the Now?

Therefore and despite the pitfalls inherent to writing one's memoir, there may also be a few benefits as well. Just as when additional thoughts or memories suddenly decide to intrude as if to make themselves known, albeit in *ex post facto* fashion.

With the latter thought in mind, I find myself surprised by the league of specters who have since taunted me with the question, *"why did you forget or ignore me?"* Hopefully this new and addendum-laden edition will stand in part as my gesture of reparation to them.

Finally, here then is my "love letter" to Sir Arthur Conan Doyle's greatest invention. Also, my paean to Sherlockian "detectivism," both real and imagined. Moreover, of how in a happily viral fashion, such an influence has infected this writer for as long as he may recall.

On such basis I hope you will enjoy what amounts to my own "remembrance of things past" as it meanders down many a long and often shadowy passage. For it is there that my inquiries have at times been pointless, while other moments have offered up their share of incredible epiphanies. If nothing else, these experiences have allowed me the opportunity of seeking to pierce the veil of such things as normally go unsought, and more often which seem destined to remain unrevealed. But such I think is the Grail Seeker's Credo: *for to seek may be more important even than to find.*

So settle back as this Wellsian Traveller reaches for the crystal rod that will move us through three dimensions, and significantly, we hope, into that fourth where Past, Present, and Future are all relative.

This time around then, I'm looking forward to re-encountering that legion of people, places and things that figured so largely throughout my existence.

An image of the Legend"

2
L'OVERTURE

STAGE DIRECTION:
It is evening—the view is a vacant streetscape in London, England. The hour is late but indeterminate. The vision itself commences like a waking dream and the viewer's destination, he senses, is only a short distance away.

Walking down a lonely lane, mentally the observer rehearses the way ahead of him.

First there is Covent Garden and then the bustling Strand. Cross that busy artery and proceed to Craven Street, where once a Philadelphian named Franklin established Britain's first American Embassy. Passing this the traveler will continue moving toward the Thames, and ultimately Craven Passage. Upon reaching that point, close by as well stands Northumberland Avenue. And it is there that the public house awaits which is called THE SHERLOCK HOLMES.

But first.

In the nearing perspective stands the ghost of a legend. Covent Garden. Once a marketplace for poulterers, flower sellers and fruiteries, at present this place has given up its past to a grander plan. For today and tonight the simpler and rustic world of "the Garden" has been transformed, rendering it into a trendy mecca for emporia, street performers and tourist herds to watch them. No longer the barrows and shuttered stalls with their floral arrays and produce. Now in their place a legion of glittering shops or bars or assortments of theatrical entertainment.

But on this particular evening it is as if time itself has unexpectedly made a gentler retreat. And it begins with the shape of the approaching stranger. His nearly apparitional form seems to intrude upon the observer's sanctum musings even as he draws near, lit by the muted haloes of the intermittent streetlamps. Strangely, their glow lends a curious sense of light trying to become mist. And odder yet, the figure now framed in their aura is suddenly familiar.

24

As the observer and the stranger pass one another upon the pavement there is that about the second that which is at once startling. But not in a fearful fashion. But rather in a kind of magical yet somehow validating manner. For he is tall, wears a graying overcoat collared up, and on his head—wait for it—he wears that most iconic of literary headgear, the softly ear-flapped "deerstalker" cap.

Like hailing ships the two figures cross, but do not share currents with one another. As they do so however the man in the cap nods, as if to an acquaintance. And for the other? Later he does not recall nodding back, so astonished by the specter before him. But without a doubt he felt the sense of recognition. For he realizes that this stranger is the reason there for his own presence beyond the shadows of the lamp-post's glow. And for all of that, in that instant and in that place and upon this journey, he senses that somehow the stars have aligned, as if to say, "Yes, the magic is all real. And you have become a part of it."

3
An Unclubbable Man

Many years ago when God was younger and so was I, I remember a meeting of the Amateur Mendicant Society of Detroit. Apart from the normal hubbub such enclaves usually generated, on this particular occasion something rather extraordinary was afoot. It had to do with the notable attendance that evening of a long-ago member of the faithful corps. But tonight he is an unknown brother from a formative legion of Sherlock Holmes' admirers. Now he is here like a shade, materialized from a vanished world. Yet his presence is deemed all the more remarkable, given that the gentleman in question had been considerably "out of the loop" for decades. This fact, notwithstanding his provenance as an investitured Baker Street Irregular in official standing, and a member of the AMS, if not a brace of other scions over the course of many years. And then he had seemed suddenly to drop off the face of the Holmesian planet.

But through some adept bit of investigation the man of the moment had been tracked down, still alive, found living in some form of assisted care. I cannot speak to whether or not he had family, but we did learn he was quite on his own. When he was discovered and thereafter invited to participate in a modern-day evocation of his former Sherlockian sodality, he'd grudgingly agreed.

The gentleman whom I'll call here Dale Holermeyer (not his real name) seemed dazzled, if not dazed by the rampant *bonhomie* of the Mendicants do. Like a creature of the shadows brought back to the light, he no doubt felt a stranger among unmet friends. Nevertheless, he was coerced in gentle fashion, both before and after dinner to share a few memories of those olden times when giants such as Morley, Smith, Stout and Davis had presided where today a younger crop of devotees now stood. In understanding of that, only such veteran Mendicants as McLauchlin, Harris, or Rabe seemed to know what might have lurked in Mr. Holermeyer's mind.

There is not a great deal more to share, apart from the fact that even from my long ago perspective as a stripling in the group, I'd felt aware that afoot that evening was a certain degree of—how shall we say it?—*sotto voce* inquisitiveness concerning Dale Holermeyer's former days as a collector. *"What had become of his books?" "Did he keep any mementoes of those historic days? Manuscripts? Relics?"* I wondered too. And I also recall pondering at the time whether that old Irregular's true value was more as a relict specie than as the hopefully prospective conservator of some long-buried treasure chest full of Sherlockian doubloons?

The long and short of my story is this: when the dinner was over the aforesaid Dale Holermeyer was duly shuttled to the place he called home. And was never quite heard from or about again. Presumably then, there was no eventual bequest of first editions or rare holographs consigned to either Mendicant, or other safe-keeping. And he was gone. *A ghost returned to his shadows.*

I recalled this even-then-distant anecdote to an associate many years ago. The occasion of it was his inquiring, however diplomatically, why I no longer made a ritual practice of attending club meetings either locally or annually, in New York? In truth however, my comrade as he then was, already knew the answer. Also that I had longago earned my stripes in those convivial vineyards. I had made the toasts, played the quiz games, won my share of prizes, and even delivered my lot of *bon mots* and presentations. And then had come the decisive moment when a small clear, Scots-sounding voice in my cranium said, *"let's awa' from here."*

I even recall that penultimate occasion rather well. It had taken place on an autumn Sunday afternoon. The purpose was a scion gathering of the re-orchestrated Amateur Mendicant Society. The atmosphere bustled with many voices. Couples laughed and conspired and all in all the sodality of it all was pleasant enough.

Among the group however I was most struck by one little chap, rather rotund and in the noticeable cut of the late Oliver Hardy. Save of course for the fact that rather than a dark suit and derby, this gentleman was attired in a deerstalker cap and an Inverness cape. As I noted his approach toward me I also saw that he also clutched a framed picture in his portly fist hands. When he extended this to me like a rare, votive object, I saw that the preserved item contained two illustrations, each

27

seemingly snipped from some newspaper or magazine. But to my even greater surprise, there before me was my own countenance in a somewhat dated *Detroit Free Press* interview. At the chat's close I'd been photographed in my below-stairs version of "221B."

But more surprising as well was the fact that beneath the smudged glass of my companion's artifact, it was my image which shared that eight-by-ten-inch space with a young actress, whose name I believe, was Maren Jensen. And as the attached caption verified, this beauty in the skin-tight uniform was one of the cast members of the program "Battlestar Galactica."

I looked from the picture to its owner, wondering how and why he had chosen to confine me there with this gorgeous creature from the seeming future? Then I decided to beard the lion by stating, "This is nice. Do you wish me to sign it?" To which my soundless companion merely gave a kind of feral grunt, retrieved his item and returned to the crowd.

That meeting also had the distinction of culminating in a quiz-off challenge. The participants in this duel were myself and my respected and long-time Holmesian colleague, the accomplished author Loren Estleman.

At any rate, we were down to the wire with a final question designed to confer victory to whomsoever possessed the keenest memory for trivia, or maintained the best pneumonic devices for preserving such multi-part answers as Sherlockian queries often require.

And then came my turn to answer. I was correct. A loud flutter of applause ensued. I looked at Estleman and he at me, and both of us seemed to silently ask, *"what in the world are we doing here?"* I might have said as much, for I was also aware in that moment of something I'd often seen at such gatherings. Namely, the supposed discernment of the better, smarter, most-together Holmes aficionado, based purely upon his ability to simply come up with the right answer. Which may well reflect how so many members of a professional medical or legal bent were often the winners in such trivial pursuits. In other words, the trained ability to recall selective or minute details.

But for myself, the upshot of that afternoon, even as I collected my prize of a copy of Frank Thomas' volume, *Sherlock Holmes, Bridge Detective,* was a kind of fatigue. For you see, I suddenly realized that despite the fellowship and the commonality of our Sacred Trust, I was simply tired of being a known commodity who presumably (and often erroneously) seemed a "better" Sherlockian for anyone's particular reason. But the fact of the matter as I also well knew, was that there were many in that room who might be more avid in their ways. Many as well who had read the sixty "Canonical" works more times than I. None of which lent any irrevocable reason to believe that by virtue of a photo of you with pipe, club tie and vest, or via your ability to recall some obscure detail or other, that you were not only "better," but "best." Hardly that. But this awareness, I suppose, sealed an evolving compact which until then had not been fully realized. Yet upon that autumnal afternoon it did indeed become real, Moreover, and speaking to the point of my own self-made vow, I knew that if and whenever I had the opportunity to act upon my love of Sherlock Holmes, I would do so, rather than simply to join some convivial herd to talk about doing so. And in this resolve I then believed (as I do now) I would probably be in company with Drs. Doyle and Watson, if not their friend and colleague the Great Detective.

So like a bottle on a vast, uncharted ocean, I simply drifted away from the scion societal scene. I suppose in the eyes of some, I became an unclubbable man. And in similar but perhaps more amplified fashion, I ceased to rush to New York, either as a supposed escape from the wife or a chance to drink or smoke myself into a gleefully bachelor-based, week-ended stupor. Yes, I'd heard and seen those as the *raisons d'etre* of some. But not myself. So I instead simply acknowledged that I would honor my voluntary vow to "act" rather than "discuss," whenever possible. And for the others? God bless them in their own irregularities.

Which then returns me to the story about old "Dale Holermeyer." Also of my saying to my companion in that discussion, *"one of those days, I will become him. Out of the social loop. Undiscussed. Unrecognized. Unremembered. Or at least until I am no longer available for an interview or the occasional dinner.* In other words, *as good as gone,* save for my own faded clippings and memories.

I suppose the recalling of that little anecdote has served as a wake-up call of sorts. For it has reminded me that like the proverbial tree in the forest which may or may not have had someone to hear its fall, nevertheless it did exist. And in that regard, and apart from a few footnotes or the fading recollections of equally faded or now-extinct colleagues, or even the dusty pages of many common-place-like scrapbooks stored in the basement, *I too did exist.* That vainglorious presumption was kindled from ember to flame after a fashion I described at the start of this memoir. You may recall her urgings.

"You did so much!" Dori urged. "Don't you want your grandchildren to know about your life?"

Well I gave the matter much thought. I even attempted a cursory outline of my long-term Sherlockian activities. And then I decided. For indeed, as I realized, I had seen a great deal, met many people, great and small, and come closer to the golden glow of a magical world than a legion of others. *So what would be the harm of giving evidence of that fact?*

Which brings us back to the subject of magic. For indeed throughout the course of my life I have often savored such a premise: *magic can be real.* As for the how or why of it, I cannot say. Suffice it to state that I have been blessed in this fashion a hundred ways. Inexplicably as well, my journeys have often had much to do with my fervent desire to enter into any number of fantastical doorways. In theory I suppose, some would say that is the key. I cannot be certain.

But of this, be certain reminds a familiar inner voice. *The magic can be real.* I often think on that notion. And of the many strangenesses I've registered. Such as that night walking alone in London en route to the pub, and of seemingly coming face to face with the ghost of Sherlock Holmes. Impossible, you say? Upon reflection, that event reminded me of another encounter, longago recorded in the pages of *The Baker Street Journal.*

The *Journal* story's veracity was strengthened greatly by the provenance of its author, who claimed to have come upon an elderly figure in a park who seemed to represent the fantasies of both his youth and adulthood. Moreover, the stranger had a message of sorts for his younger companion: *"nothing is lost that is born of the heart."* And that message, dare I say it, was not lost upon the writer himself, who recalled it long after before choosing to write it down. But only after becoming part of the greater warp and weft of a legend himself, whether wittingly or not. By then however he had also sold his imaginative soul to a dream shared by millions of others. And that man's name? *Basil Rathbone. Verily, and much like my own somewhat spectral close encounter, he of all people had seemingly met Sherlock Holmes.*

So perhaps at least in part I have addressed the singular question which has haunted me since my decision to undertake this memoir: *Why?* But for an even fuller explanation I suppose the answer must hark back at least half a century or more from the present moment. Fortunately perhaps, in their aggregate form the course of those years and the people and places which adorned them remain fresh in my mind for their peculiarity or kindness. Or perhaps because, to paraphrase the world's greatest detective in the now iconic Billy Wilder film "The Private Life of Sherlock Holmes," "*my mind is like fly-paper, and stuck there are a staggering number of details, mostly useless.*"

But not in the fullest consideration, truly useless. For in point of fact those myriad details and labyrinthine corridors of these last seventy-some years have constituted the who and what of my becoming. And as to what, exactly that may be? Such territory, I think, may well be better suited to the sphere of my own prospective eulogists, or even that curious legion of persons who have presumed to know me. On the latter note I can't help but recall certain lines re-read fairly recently which struck me as apt. These come from one character speaking of the protagonist of Angus Wilson's novel, *Anglo Saxon Attitudes*. She remarks,

> "*In any case I suppose one could say that Gerald Middleton had taken life a bit too easily.*" *She cocked her head, bird-like, on one side, as though considering her words.* "*Don't you think so?*" *she asked Sir Edgar.*
> *The old man got up from the red American-leather couch.* "*I can imagine someone who hardly ever knew him at all saying so.*"

In other words, of those who believe they knew or remembered you, how many actually did?

But I would prefer to think that like actors, we are indeed the ultimate sum of our cumulative parts. One comes back to the story about the blind man trying to cipher out the shape of an elephant. And such perhaps, are the minefields of biography.

However among that crazy-quilt puzzle of fragments which have formed what I call Myself, I've no doubt that there are at least two literary figures which predominated from my most formative days. One of those happened to be Sir Arthur Conan Doyle's master detective Sherlock Holmes. And the other was Ian Fleming's immortal secret agent 007, *aka* James Bond.

I have a theory which I believe stands up concerning the heroes of young boys. To that end, I believe that such larger-than-life figures as Holmes and then Bond spoke to their imaginative younger generations. Ergo, doubtless many a lad (and lasses as well) thrilled to Conan Doyle's Sherlockian adventures in *The Strand Magazine* sufficiently to make them want to solve a mystery or two. Likewise, as a young American in the Sixties, it was only natural, I thought, to wish one day for a regimen like James Bond's. In other words, fast cars, beautiful women, exotic places, and adventures chock-full of derring do. And I am pleased at this point to happily inform you that if anything, most of those wishes came true.

So then, on one level I might agree with William Goldman's Henry Plantagenet in 'The Lion In Winter,' who says

"... *my life when it is written will read better than it lived.*"

I wonder however, if that is true?

For such reasons then, I would be the last to try and explain how I became doubly fortunate, *vis a vis* the subjects of Mssrs. Bond and Holmes. Which is only to say, how I came to come into such close contact with my fictional idols largely through the courtesy of their creators. But more of that after a bit. For now let us begin where most good biographies usually do: at the Beginning.

And there, as always, stands Sherlock Holmes.

Two Icons: Holmes and "007"

4

The Road To Baker Street

I am convinced that had the most famous resident of Baker Street not loomed large in the template of my life, I should never have made friends with myself in quite the same way. Or for that matter, attracted or repelled so many persons in my path. And a good deal of it comes from Holmes, whom I met for the first time at about age 13 or 14.

I was youthfully impressionable and imaginative as many boys who are only children might be. Shy to a degree and decidedly bookish by nature, I was first attracted to Sherlock Holmes the great detective by a Basil Rathbone film, either "The Adventures of Sherlock Holmes" or "The Hound of the Baskervilles." Also in my prideful and slowly growing collection of written works (for I always prized my books) I recall purchasing a *Classics Illustrated* comic book version of *The Sign of Four*, and ultimately supplementing it with the Doubleday *Complete Sherlock Holmes* which cost me nearly five dollars of my *Detroit Times* paper-route profits. I have that edition still, and it occupies a place of honor beside its countless companions. You may know it yourself; it's the one with Christopher Morley's Introduction and the photograph of 221B, Baker Street on its dust-jacketed back.

My Holmes Collection at that time also included a paperback of *The Adventures*, if not a few odd and vaguely Holmesian items, such as a large magnifying glass and ultimately, a deerstalker cap, procured by my loving parents, from some actual British emporium!

All in all that first juvenile attempt at museum-like curatorship occupied about a foot of space upon one of my bedroom's shelves. But before long other volumes would be added to that ever-growing literary regiment. And among them was one seminal item in particular, entitled *Sherlock Holmes of Baker Street* by William Stuart Baring-Gould. I have that first-edition, Clarkson Potter volume still, and am amazed upon reflection at that book's catalytic capabilities.

The year was 1962. I was fifteen years old. An only child then and now, my cerebral landscapes seemingly broadening by the week, I cannot say exactly when my bearings moved from the turreted terrains of Camelot to the grimier byways of Victorian London. But I can fix a benchmark of sorts. You see I'd learned of Mr. Baring-Gould's groundbreaking volume after reading an eye-catching book review of it in *The Royal Oak Daily Tribune*. Eye-catching, inasmuch as the writer's review was accompanied by yet another photographic view of Sherlock Holmes' London lair. Yes, and there in monochromatic newsprint detail was the fabled Sitting Room. Before my eyes once more was that shrine-like place where damsels and villains and even royalty had been drawn, if only to meet, solicit, or confront the world's greatest "consulting detective."

My eye had been riveted to the item in the *Tribune* at once. As I read and re-read the review countless times I also took note that the story's by-line identified its writer as W.T. Rabe, who was further identified as "*a member of the Baker Street Irregulars, Old Soldiers of Baker Street, Sherlock Holmes Klubben in Denmark, and editor of "Sherlockian Who's Who and What's What."*

The book review was headlined "*Shock for Sherlockians*" beneath which included the line "*The Real Holmes Is Brought to Life in Death.*"

Did they actually say "the real Holmes?" The words had made me tingle. For before me now was what appeared to be a review of an actual biography of a man I'd supposed had been an entirely fictional character. But how was that possible? *Unless...Sherlock Holmes was real!*

"*To the millions of Americans who remember the late Sir Arthur Conan Doyle the obituary and in fact, the entire book "Sherlock Holmes of Baker Street—A Life of the World's First Consulting Detective," will be another confusing item in the continuing stream of banter and scholarly debate inspired by the Men of Baker Street.*" So wrote the *Tribune's* suburban reviewer, as if for my eyes alone.

Confusing? Yes it all was, and news about this new biography of the World's First Consulting Detective served only to stir a pot which had been simmering inside me. For at fifteen I'd been compelled to admit that despite my awareness that Conan Doyle's great hawk-nosed, pipe smoking sleuth was imaginary, how could a real-life study of his existence exist? Better yet, how could there be a photograph of his fabled London consulting room?

Hardly the trauma many of us face upon gradually learning the supposed truth about Santa Claus, still I confess to you here that my newer worries about Sherlock Holmes came a close second. Moreover, given my relative youth and peripheral knowledge of the subject, I could not help but be perplexed and dazzled, if not willingly enmired in the many layered quicksand of what some had dubbed the "Sherlockian" subject.

But close at hand, I now felt, was a beacon of sorts. For in the person of W.T. Rabe, the author of "Shock for Sherlockians," perhaps I had found a kind of True North for reckoning out the mysteries, if not the hidden truths of Mr. Holmes?

Truthfully, I am uncertain of how precisely my plan was hatched, but after conferring with my mother I wrote a letter to Mr. W.T. Rabe, c/o *The Royal Oak Daily Tribune.* But would he reply? I had little more than a week to wait for my answer. It came by way of a postcard to our front porch mailbox. The card was addressed to me and the curt message thanked "Mr. McPherson" for my appreciative remarks. Even better yet the writer concluded by adding that if I would like to meet and see his Sherlock Holmes collection, I had but to call him at the enclosed telephone number.

Well that was the initial phase of the first act of a drama which none of us could then envision. In fact, as these words are written a seeming lifetime later, it has yet to see its curtain.

In any event, and after a bit of parental consultation, the telephone call was made. Nervously, I took the step, and then my mother spoke with W.T. "Bill" Rabe. Those giant paces achieved, suddenly we were all bent toward a meeting. It was arranged! And for me? Well to this day I think of that imminent summit as the beginning of the beginning. Within less than a week it all took shape one wintry evening when my father drove me to the address on Pinecrest Street in Ferndale, Michigan, which was perhaps half an hour away of our own suburb of Berkley.

36

There was a palpable magic about that night which has lingered. I remember being greeted at the door by Rabe's wife, Mary Anne, who in turn made the introduction of their young visitor to her even younger children. Accordingly, they were smaller and more silent than myself, and vaguely I recall that the boy, John Rabe, was probably not much older than five or six, if indeed hazy memory serves. I trust that should he read this, he will not be offended if my recollection of him proves faulty. Yet I also trust that he will accord me the simplest of explanations: I was there to meet his father, and that was a bit dazzling on its own.

As if in photographic fashion, I recall my first glimpse of and contact with W.T. Rabe. He was tall, not quite burley, with a close-cropped head of hair with a kind of widow's peak. Further conjure the image of a pair of bright but serious eyes piercing thick lenses. Below these a handsome nose and a mouth not quite concealed beneath the line of moustache and a slight, well-trimmed brownish beard. I believe he was casually attired. No Inverness cloak. And no deerstalker cap, thank God. Just a vee-necked sweater over a tee-shirt, casual pants and slippers.

The evening went by rapidly, but in colorful and exciting installments. I recall following my host upstairs to his small study. And there, arrayed in every corner were pieces of the True Cross, much as I might have deemed them then. Say instead that everywhere there were books and artifacts, a hat-rack with the proverbial fore-and-aft *chapeau* of its absent wearer, also walking sticks and maps and framed photographs. My eye eventually anchored upon one of those, depicting the American actor William Gillette, who as Bill Rabe explained had been chosen by Arthur Conan Doyle himself to portray Sherlock Holmes on stage. And then the other item. This one stopped me in my tracks, as I'm certain my host could see. It was a sizably framed and matted object containing a photo of Sir Arthur, and beside it an actual letter written by the hand which had penned the Sherlock Holmes stories!

I must have done my best open-mouthed, gob-smacked, golly-gosh presentation, even as Rabe introduced me to one item after another. By my tour's end I seem to recall studying a small fireplace mantle upon which were numerous items, including a jack-knife pinning some letters or whatever to its surface. *Yes, just as Sherlock Holmes had done at "221B!"*

I am pleased to think even now that I must have passed my audition on that long-distant night in Ferndale. For there without a doubt, I had made my first foray toward Baker Street. And when the time came for me to leave *Chez* Rabe, I made my departure on the heels of its owner's promise that we would talk and meet again soon. And as if to seal the compact, when I walked out to the snowy curb to where my father's car was idling, in my hands I held incredibly precious cargo. These took the form of gifts bestowed by my new friend. They came in the shape of three bound copies of *The Strand Magazine,* in which the Holmes saga had unfurled from the 1890's onward. Adding to my largesse were also a few rare editions of *The Baker Street Journal*, published a few years before my own nativity. One of those, as I was soon to discover, contained a story which described the "real" Baker Street quarters, as well as a grainy photograph of the actual room where the great Holmes had set to deducing!

Even now I ponder the level of Bill Rabe's kindness, if not great generosity to a lad only marginally older than his own young son. What had my arrival that snowy evening represented? Was I an echo of his own younger self? A precursor to his own son's passport to Baker Street? I still wonder. Furthermore I ask myself, under similar circumstances would I have been so kind to a stripling bathed in the gold of Conan Doyle's great invention? I hope so.

But the key to my relationship with Bill Rabe perhaps resided in something more than my age and youthful innocence. It had to do, I now believe, with the fact I was open-minded to the prospect of wonder. I'd like to believe that I was also clever enough to follow my older mentor and companion's lead. Moreover, his new and unwittingly young "Watson" hopefully presented Rabe with certain challenges akin to a parent's, but linked to a peculiar camaraderie as well.

On some level it's also occurred to me that perhaps my lengthy relationship with Bill Rabe was not so different than the way Dr. John Watson felt about Sherlock Holmes. In short, that it was a kind of honor to be tolerated by the likes of him. That in any event rapidly became my attitude, and one which lasted nearly two decades later, until…but again, let us not rush the point. Let us remain for the moment in those halcyon days of the mid-Sixties, which for me were formative years indeed. I began to think then, and to muse with a certainty which exceeded my earlier childhood fragility. Now too I was ready to embark upon an adventure, and courtesy of my sudden acquaintance with W.T. Rabe, I felt or hoped there would be many to follow. And indeed there were. Moreover, throughout most of those I was pleased to sign on as this man's under-age friend-and-confident. Which I believe I was on a regular basis. Most often such occasions were associated with Bill's job as the Director of Public Relations at the University of Detroit, a position he held until moving to Lake Superior State College in 1969.

But as staid as the position might sound, trust Rabe to have shaped it to his own eccentric contours. First as a professional PR man and flack. Then as someone who seemed to know everybody in town. After that as a gadfly and catalytic goad able to promote any number of oddball causes, ranging from U. of D.'s "Stamp Out The Beatles" movement to his later Unicorn Hunter's Society, World Sauntering Society, and outreach efforts to relieve the English language of certain of its most troublesome words. The latter trio were by-products of his eventual hiatus to Lake Superior State College. But such blades had been whetted in Detroit. And on the basis of his publicist's role, Bill Rabe had set many a laudable tone, if not garnered a fair share of inevitable press for himself as well as his causes. Little too did I know it at the time, but being close enough to watch the master at his craft, I was actually taking lessons for my own future.

As indeed was this gentleman's influence upon The Amateur Mendicant Society. As its sparking plug and chief promoter, he brought forth its lightning. For that and countless other feats of literary legerdemain. W.T.R. earned his later title as "Merchant of Whimsy" and "Prince of Nonsense."

It was during that period, circa 1962-65 that I apprenticed to W.T. Rabe. This often took the shape of merely lending some Watsonish companionship in conjunction with certain university business, and often concerning the luminaries who visited. Sadly in this regard I missed meeting Robert Frost by a hair's breadth, but was in time to carry Professor Edward Teller's bag, drive Ralph Nader into town, and sit down backstage at Olympia Stadium, in company with four young fellows from Liverpool named John, Paul, George and Ringo. And yes of course, let us not forget to mention meeting a man named Rathbone. I'll tell you that story before long.

From this chronological point my literary life changed as well. And like my once vacant bookshelves, now there was a voluminous accumulation of things not only to read, but to do. Beneath my feet I could feel the landscape tectonically shifting, as did my passion for all things Sherlock Holmes. And now as well, underpinning my earlier confusions over the reality of the world's greatest fictional character, I embraced the alternate premise which has served so many for so long.

To wit, I now gravitated to that road and place once described by Vincent Starrett, "where it is always 1895." More than a rationale, this became the *cri de coeur* for an army of young as well as old soldiers of Baker Street who breathed the notion that concerning Holmes and Watson, *"they never lived, so they can never die."* Neat. Taut. To the point. And an excellent explanation for wondering whether, or even why Reality and Fantasy could not trade places?

In just such fashion I discovered my evolving capacity to literally read the fifty-six short stories and four Holmes novels into life. Also in a distinctly literal sense, this endeavor was occasionally tempered by my attendance at a series of wonderful meetings conducted in the name of the Great Detective. Ergo, I was introduced to members of the Amateur Mendicant Society. In fact, I became a card-carrying member of that singular set of persons, as I did for the Old SOB's, or "Soldiers of Baker Street" and Moriarty's Allied Friends In America (THE TRUE NAPOLEONS OF ALL CRIME). I see no expiration upon any of those warrants, which presently repose beneath plastic pages in one of my several Commonplace Books. Ergo, I presume I am yet in "active" status.

The "AMS" had been established in Detroit in the Forties and like many of its peer groups, borrowed its name from one of the "canonical" tales. That aggregation was and would be comprised largely of men my father's age and older who jointly shared a passion for all things Sherlockian. Moreover, Mendicant meetings were headily atmospheric, if not fueled by the essence of pipe and cigar smoke, if not libations. Their enclaves as I knew them were often held in the

Detroit Press Club on Howard Street. There in an upper banqueting room the drill usually featured a garrulous dinner, preceded by a raucous cocktail hour in advance of the evening's official presentation. In the main these usually took the shape of some question or arguable detail within the "Sacred Canon." In other words, the Gospel According to Watson.

Then there were the Mendicant "topics of the evening" What, for instance, was the actual breed of the Hound of the Baskervilles? Or how did Colonel Sebastian Moran attempt to assassinate Holmes with Von Herder's air gun, propelled from the empty house across from 221B? And who was Aunt Clara and why did we never mention her name? You might get the picture. But such eccentric queries were not merely academically parsed. Often and by custom they were vividly demonstrated.

Vivid in my memory was the attempt one night to establish the canine provenance of the Baskerville Hound. Toward that end the case was empirically demonstrated courtesy of several panting, whining, barking exhibits from the local Armory Kennel Club Show.

Or then of course there was Colonel Sebastian Moran's attempt at the assassination of Sherlock Holmes. This was furthered by an exercise describing the villain's shooting trajectory in the "Adventure of the Empty House." Just so, that night in the upper dining room of the Press Club one had only to leave his chair and peer out across the lamplit Howard Street and over to the shadowy parking structure opposite. And *ces voila!* was that not the silhouette of a top-hatted man with a long-barreled weapon dimly visible against a drawn shade of the structure's window?

Detroit became a proud and regular host of such "Sherlockian" ("Holmesian" to our British friends) activities. My eventual scrapbooks would preserve not a few of those accounts. For instance, a column by Doc Greene, one of the Motor City's most prosaic and O. Henry-ish writers on the daily newspaper scene. One of his pieces was entitled "Echo of Hound of Baskerville." In it the scribe opined, *'A spent messenger arrived at the desk a couple of days ago bearing the photograph presented here, and two volumes of the copies of London's Strand magazine of the year 1901."* So began Doc's essay on an imminent Mendicants meeting to which the reporter was invited.

Moreover, the intriguing premise of the future enclave: "*To draw attention to the All-Breed Dog Show at the Artillery Armory Sunday, May 17.*" And why? Chiefly as a means, according to W.T. Rabe, of ascertaining the true doggy specie of the horrific Baskerville Hound, of course.

Or then there was daily columnist Jane Schermerhorn's opus: "Baker Street Boys Meet A Lady." In this she described how the usual regimen of males-only was expanded to accommodate Ms. S. *Archivist Bill Rabe presented us as 'the woman' and the gentlemen bowed graciously with a trace of the chill Sherlock Holmes reserved for women.*" And after that, Jane was treated to dinner and the evening's ceremonies, complete with toasts, constant recharging of glasses, as well as a program tailored to challenge the mad hatters in Larco's Restaurant, deerstalkered or not.

For a young fellow such as I, those meetings were, to quote C.S. Lewis, all "red meat and strong beer" for me. And while I never got beyond the former at the time, did I not long for the day that I would join Bill Rabe in lighting up a stogy, or perhaps methodically packing a briar pipe, just as Holmes himself? Indeed, a Sherlockian consummation devoutly to be wished.

Along the way there were a number of interesting, if not eccentric characters among the Mendicants I met in those fledgling Detroit meetings. Apart from Bill Rabe himself, perhaps the most interesting was a suave gentleman of the Old School named Russell McLaughlin. Erudite, urbane, learned to the nth degree, this author and former drama critic for the *Detroit News* and elsewhere took a kind interest in the young acolyte from Berkley. Enough so in fact to talk to me about Shakespeare, Christopher Marlowe, George Bernard Shaw, and of course, Sherlock Holmes.

In addition to those rather irregularly scheduled meetings of the Amateur Mendicants, there were a few luncheons as well. Some of those allowed me to drink in the entertaining and scholarly musings of Russell McLauchlin. For instance, I recall his telling me yarns about the early days of the "scion" societies as they were called, and how they'd seemingly sprung from the loins of their True Parent, the Sherlockian Church of Rome, in the form of the Baker Street Irregulars of New York City. That sage organization, as I would learn to appreciate was the Nirvana and Valhalla of Baker Street affairs. Vatican-like to the cause of keeping the memory of Sherlock Holmes green, the "BSI" was wrought out of Doylean pages in 1934 and through the unparalleled efforts of that great bookman, Christopher Morley. At the time I am "rediscovering" here however, I learned that the Irregulars were under the helm of Dr. Julian Wolff, "Commissionaire" of that auspicious organization. It wasn't much longer that I initiated a correspondence with Dr. Wolff, and of course, met him at the 1965 gathering. There I encountered a squat, rather bull-doggish gent with an impish smile and eyes that twinkled behind his wireless glasses. Even before meeting him that night, I knew that I valued making this man's acquaintance. Further, and toward that end, today my scrap-books bulge with (now rare) pamphlets, monographs and those wonderfully map-like Christmas cards sent and personally inscribed from the Captain of the Sherlockian ship himself.

Coming back now to Russ McLauchlin. Apart from his past-tense aura, capable of reaching from his own youth even further back to the Victorian and gaslit world of Sherlock Holmes, Mr. McLaughlin easily captured his memories and brought them to life. Just so in his slim memoir of a bygone era in Detroit, *Alfred Street*. One of its selections betrayed his youthful penchant for Conan Doyle's eccentric sleuth and perhaps his earliest famous portrayer.

"So we used to clamor for stories of Sherlock Holmes and my father, a great enthusiast, was always happy to comply, often relying on his own powers of invention for thrilling plots of an impromptu nature. He was careful to inform us that all his stories—even his excursions into fancy—had been collected and written down by a certain Dr. Watson, who enjoyed the incalculable advantage of being the great man's friend and room-mate.

But the second reason was perhaps more potent. Suddenly Sherlock Holmes came to life, not the 'real' Sherlock, we dimly understood, but an altogether satisfactory facsimile. For William Gillette came to town, as part of his famous first tour, and every young gentleman on Alfred Street demanded, with the utmost in passion, to be taken to see him, even if the family were in consequence obliged to temporize with the butcher."

If my grandchildren ever do chance to read this memoir, I hope they sense the magic experienced by their grandfather's own youthful incarnation. Further, in this account I have set out to describe a vanished world, and one which was rare for celebrating an even earlier time. And at the risk of sounding presumptuous, I must state that, as the saying goes, "their like will not be seen again," this fact is probably sadly true. It had much to do with the kind of men who decided to venerate the memory of Sir Arthur Conan Doyle's greatest, most immortal of creations. And for the sake of doing so they left a legacy, part fact, part fancy, sometimes scholarly, often ribald, and decidedly memorable. But inasmuch as memory tends to fade with time, the only means of recapturing the glow of a star which has long ago burned out, is to offer some form of picture. This then, attempts to do exactly that. And individuals like Russell McLauchlin and Bill Rabe created a template of sorts for many of us to aspire toward. Like Sherlock Holmes himself, I believe that in some crazy way, without them I would be rather a different sort of chap. And given that we are the sum of our meetings and experiences, who should be surprised?

And on a closing note: in 1984, more than two decades after making the acquaintance of perhaps the Amateur Mendicant Society's most venerable officer, I chanced to move into the very set of Detroit brownstones along the river which once had served as home for Russ McLauchlin. Self-sufficient on account of its underground garage, small grocery and cleaners, the Motor City's venerable Alden Park Towers appealed to me on many levels, not least of all my memory of having visited it in the company of Bill Rabe one well-remembered winter's night. Strangely, the sort of old-world magic I would eventually sense about New York had now been transposed to Detroit.

And there within Alden Park's citadel-like set of brownstones on Jefferson Avenue, we were welcomed by McLauchlin and his lovely wife. I enjoyed seeing their sizable and comfortable apartment. Something about it reminded me of that New York-ish atmosphere seen by my eyes so recently when I'd accompanied Rabe to the Irregulars fete.

But here's the odd, if not wonderful part of my story. Set the scene: many years later, I'm moving into bachelor digs at Alden Park. Given the year and point in time, sadly my friend and mentor is now no longer in residence here, or on any terrestrial plain. Therefore it seems all the stranger when I pay my first call to the below stairs market in the complex to make some form of purchase. When I am checking out, the owner-proprietor, who has been on-site for an age, bids me goodbye by saying, "see you later, Mr. McLauchlin." McLauchlin. McPherson. Highlanders both, I suppose. But having more in common than apparently met the eye. What do you think?

On looking back, I believe my brief friendship with Russell McLauchlin was a presagement for another genial and brilliant colleague named Ray Bradbury. Both of them were arch nostalgists. Each had a talent for not only remembering, but setting those bygone echoes down onto the printed page. Bradbury is well remembered for his sheath of classics, ranging from the forward-looking science fiction of *Martian Chronicles* and *Fahrenheit 451* to those lyrical evocations of childhood in *Dandelion Summer* and *The Halloween Tree*. And I, most fortunate of admirers, was blessed with more than a decade's worth of correspondence and telephone calls from Ray, who often enough would send greetings of "Mad Love" in his letters.

And I suppose as testament to a deep-seated mutual liking, it was not an unusual thing for my late-night calls from the Midwest to his earlier Los Angeles home on Cheviot Drive. Often within the autumnal season we both so enjoyed, I might call Ray and describe the Midwestern sky on a late October's night. And from his L.A. suburban lair the master would sigh and tell me tales of his youth. Most often those calls end with the valediction of "I love you" exchanged. That closeness, somehow related to but far apart from my own great affections for my late father, afforded me a warm and distant beacon in a sometimes dark and churning sea.

In fact, a bit of artistic depression had been my motive in first writing to Bradbury in 1996. I'd been feeling low and at a creative ebb. Therefore as a self-administered bit of therapy I decided to tell this great American writer how and why I had savored his work for so long. And to my great and stunned surprise, not long after I received his reply.

That epically first letter, dated September 25, 1996, began with the ground-moving comment from this suddenly unmet friend.

45

"Dear Mark McPherson:

Yours is one of the finest, warmest, most loving letters I have ever received. In line after line I find that we are indeed kindred spirits, with similar loves. I envy you your stage appearances as Conan Doyle. What absolute joy and fun. Holmes has played a huge part in my life beginning one summer night in 1930 when, left at home when my parents walked two blocks to listen to an outdoor band concert, I heard THE HOUND OF THE BASKERVILLES on radio, which terrified me so much I fled the house and ran through the dark to find my parents on the concert grounds and stay with them until the concert was over."

There was much more, and this was just the beginning of the beginning of a wonderful friendship. Ray regaled me with a host of other Sherlockian memories. And like Russ McLauchlin's conversations and works would, I found a true passport into the long ago by reading the words set down by these two aged but vibrant young boys. Both of those gents left their marks upon me, and I may be presumptuous to think that I might have somehow brushed the surface of their great creative souls. I think of that whenever I reach for my copy of *Alfred Street,* copyrighted in 1946, the year before my birth, or look to the wall to see the framed picture of dear Ray sitting in the George Pal Time Machine from the 1960 movie of that name. The mat on the picture is inscribed, *"TO MY SPECIAL SON"* and is lovingly signed by my adopted literary father.

By the time I had written to Ray Bradbury I'd already plowed a number of dramatic fields with an original, two-act play of my own devising and portrayal. This was "AN EVENING WITH SIR ARTHUR CONAN DOYLE," which will be described in the pages still ahead. However, for the present purpose, allow me to retreat in time temporarily, if only to set the scene.

Simply stated, for me the *entrée* to the worlds of Holmesiana was cast from the mold of the Amateur Mendicant Society. Moreover, given my chronological induction into the ranks of that resilient, scholastic, ribald, and decidedly male-only enclave, someone recently suggested that now, even at the staid age of seventy-two, I might well be among the eldest of the Sixties-era set of what has become a continuously dying breed.

For the uninitiated (who are unlikely to concern themselves with anything written here) it should be stated that the annual Baker Street Irregulars celebration is celebrated, like Christmas itself, along the lines of the Master's birth. Pundits have mused over the January 6th date, affirming that Holmes had a penchant for quoting "Twelfth Night" (January 6th) and further, was once known to forego foodstuffs on the 7th—presumably still suffering from a previous night's merriment. But what could have induced the Great Deducer to tipple? Most likely his birthday. In any event, that first week of the new year is usually associated with the fete. Accordingly, the Irregulars would gather in the Big Apple. There within safe confines there would be drinking, discussing, toasting, as well as the reading of stately (if not ribald) papers. Also, and "for the sake of the trust," Irregular Shillings would be conferred upon Sherlockians worthy of the cause. Early on, I believe Morley devised a crossword for prospective entrants, but soon it became a matter of what might be involved—what sort of noble or dubious distinction that might earn one the right to bear for his lifetime (if not thereafter) a Baker Street Irregulars Investiture.

Hearing those stories about the BSI from Messrs. Rabe and McLaughlin and a garrulous old lawyer type named Bob Harris, I found myself longing to be part of such an auspicious group. How little did I know or could I imagine, that before a short while I would see it all for myself.

Shock for Sherlockians
The Real Holmes Is Brought to Life in Death

SHERLOCK HOLMES OF BAKER STREET—A Life of the World's First consulting Detective. by William S. Baring-Gould; Clarkson N. Potter, Inc., $5.

By W. T. RABE

Sherlock Holmes is dead!

So is Dr. Watson.

To the thousands of exponents of things Sherlockian (organized into four-score societies in a dozen countries around the world) this will come as a shock. They maintain that Holmes is busy at beekeeping in Sussex at the advanced age of 108.

To millions of readers of the reports by Dr. Watson translated into virtually e v e r y printable language the world knows (Russian, Chinese, Japanese, Hindu, etc.) this report of the death of this historical pair will merely be saddening. Young generations of Americans, and many generations of other nations have had no reason to think of Holmes as other than a real person.

To the millions of Americans who remember the late Sir Arthur Conan Doyle the obituary and, in fact, the entire book "Sherlock Holmes of Baker Street—A Life of the World's First Consulting Detective," will be another confusing item in the continuing stream of banter and scholarly debate inspired by the Men of Baker Street.

The whole of the original Sherlock Holmes adventures is found in one rather hefty volume published years ago by Doubleday. The whole of scholarly writings about these writings would fill a seven-foot bookshelf. A mere directory of the men engaged in such ···gs and the associations

to which they belong ("The 1961 Sherlockian Who's Who and What's What") runs to 122 pages.

William S. Baring-Gould is the first author to assemble from the original writings, and the writings about the writings, a complete and exhaustive report on the life of Holmes, his parents and his

---

Mr. Rabe is a member of the Baker Street Irregulars, Old Soldiers of Baker Street, Sherlock Holmes Klubben in Denmark, and editor of "Sherlockian Who's Who and What's What."

---

grandparents. He has incorporated much new information of his own discovery.

Baring-Gould has held the Holmes-was-a-real-man pose to the bitter end. Sir Arthur is mentioned in one footnote, where he is described as Watson's literary agent. We progress through seven pages of bibliography before Sir Arthur is mentioned, and then for half a page only.

The reader need adhere to no cult or clan, however, to enjoy Baring-Gould's biography.

It is as good a yarn as Dr. John Watson ever wrote.

Like Watson's stories it has all the flavor, all the incidental information about Victorian life and personalities, and all of the sharpness of Holmes and the villainy of Prof. Moriarity t h a t have made the adventures of the consulting detective such fascinating reading, t h e a t e r, radio drama, cinema stories,

and television programing for millions of fans.

Baring - Gould fills many voids heretofore left blank in Holmes' life:

His first meeting with Karl Marx in the reading room of the British Museum;

His tour of the United States with an English Shakespearean stock company;

His liaison with Irene Adler and the birth of his son in New Jersey (the author reports that Rex Stout has never denied that this son is actually Nero Wolfe);

Holmes' capture of Jack the Ripper.

Sherlockian scholars m a y quarrel with Baring-Gould's explanation of the wandering wound of Dr. Watson (was it in the shoulder or the leg?) and his assignment of wives to the soldier-medical manbiographer (Miss Constance Adams, of San Francisco, was the first of three).

They will certainly dispute Baring-Gould's report that the great man of action simply died of old age on a park bench in Sussex.

The author's adventure began with a review penned by W.T. Rabe of *Sherlock Holmes of Baker Street*.

48

5
They Might Have Been Giants

"I went to a garden party" said one of Rick Nelson's final ballads. And so did I, one sunlit afternoon in the Summer of 1962. A royal garden gathering it was, or at least so it seemed. Not quite Buckingham Palace, but here I was once again at Bill Rabe's Ferndale home. This time winter had flown and others were present on Bill's sunlit patio. I arrived with my mother in tow, a fact which frankly mortified me. I suppose this had something to do with not being of proper age to have my own driver's license. Or that it seemed to constantly require some form of parental presence for me to appear in person. Regardless, after a time my mother diplomatically took her leave, returning home to await my call.

Present that summery day were the Rabe's, myself, and a few of Bill's special out-of-town guests. By name they were constituted of a rather hefty gentleman named John Bennett Shaw and his wife, Dorothy, and a thinner, rather serious version of Sherlock Holmes himself, named Peter Blau.

Now to most Sherlockians and certainly Irregulars worth their salt, such names as Shaw and Blau are etched into the annals of Baker Street. But to me they might have been giants, despite their seeming presentiments as mortal gentlemen. But on that afternoon I was somehow viscerally aware that these were also true Holmes scholars with valuable links to the past. Therefore I did my best to watch and listen (one of my inveterate pastimes), and when I could to join in on the conversation. And of course once again, as I'll doubtless remark throughout this account, no one could have persuaded that 15 year old fellow that both of Rabe's guests would one day assist and inspire him so mightily in adulthood.

But what I've described constitutes yet another piece in the growing puzzle. I suppose what meeting people like Shaw and Blau did do was to remind me of exactly how, and in what special way a childhood love of Sherlock Holmes could last literally a lifetime. Add to this these were the names which appeared on the by-lines within the *Baker Street Journal* and elsewhere. For these were the Sherlockian Royals. The Big Guns. The Keepers of the Treasure Trove. The Protectors of the Grail.

And on that particular afternoon in that quaint suburb, I was blessed to meet them, and they, dare I say it, in kind seemed inexplicably persuaded to take an interest in me. But why? Who can say with certainty? Or perhaps every grown aficionado finds himself reminded of his own youthful incarnation when something like that happens. That is, if they're fortunate enough to be in the right place and time.

So it was that my associations, courtesy of Rabe, the Mendicants and others broadened with my horizons. All of it seemed strangely evocative of another bygone time, as if I was experiencing a curious brand of *déjà vu.* And all of that chronologically for me some twenty-eight years earlier when a small group of appreciators came together and founded The Baker Street Irregulars.

Named for the rag-tag "arabs" or "street urchins" of the Doyle stories, the "BSI" did indeed reflect the very demographic once described by Sir Arthur himself: to wit, a pastime for *"the boy who is half a man, and the man who is half a boy."* (And in due course, for the so-called Gentle Sex as well.)

As time passed I grew into feeling something akin to a formal, but vaguely filial feeling for Bill Rabe. While old enough to be my father, he was not. Well traveled, mercurial, clever, and unharnessed by many of those rules which slow so many quick thinkers down, Bill was in fact quite the opposite of my beloved Dad. Which is hardly to say that my hardworking father, seemingly given to serving Mr. Ford's Dearborn, Michigan Rouge Stamping Plant for endless years, and mostly on what was designated as the "Afternoon Shift." In other words, a grueling, constant sense of responsibilities undertaken by a young man who first signed on as a welder before the war—who went off to the said conflict as a Marine—then returned and signed on for a foreman's program, with upwardly mobile opportunities thereafter.

I also had a mother who loved reading and introduced me to my first library. She and Dad encouraged my literary loves and nurtured the notion that one day their one-and-only might well be—what? A lawyer? An author? Perhaps both. Therefore and in aid of such hopeful opportunities, my folks gave me every chance, every break, every opportunity which an endless bank of love could allow. In other words, they unwittingly made straight my literary way by encouraging their only son to take a road less-travelled—that of the writer.

And strangely, as I now think of it, my parents gave their boy the paradoxical opportunity of being taken under the wing of another gentleman whose business it soon became to tutor their son in the lore of Sherlock Holmes.

And that was the way, after a period sufficient for George and Ann McPherson to trust Wilmer T. Rabe, that they acceded to his suggestion. This would ultimately involve nothing short of their son's first trip to the largest city in the world. And why? For the singular purpose of accompanying friend Bill to the 31st societal Birthday Party for Mr. Sherlock Holmes, courtesy of the Baker Street Irregulars.

Somewhere amid the stacks and files of my collection is a copy of *Esquire Magazine*, Sinatra is on the cover, but McPherson was tucked away inside. Yes, and clearly visible near the binding fold am I, looking young, pasty-faced, vested and club-tied. I am seated with a group of older gentlemen upon the occasion of Mr. Sherlock Holmes's Birthday Party. The date as I seek to recall it, was somewhere in the late Sixties. And there all around me are a cadre of others, a good many of whom were and are invested members of the Baker Street Irregulars Society.

Properly put, the official designation of those "invested" members signified the award of The Irregular Shilling for some deed or curious achievement or association, is "investitured." For that in fact is how the designation comes. Like a football player's number seldom if ever is re-worn, each BSI member received an appellation to do with the Holmes Canon. This they are known by, and as such they often feel disposed to include their appellative in correspondence, if not to simply write, "Joe Smedlap, B.A., M.A., Ph.D., BSI." It is, to say the least, as proud an honorific as any literary man might hope to bear.

But as I then found myself thinking, *The Irregulars!* To me the honor of belonging to such a group was something like being tapped by the Queen for a knighthood. And think what it signified, as —what? A king-sized bone for Rover? A huge wedge of cheese for Mr. Mouse? A trip to Carnaby Street for the keenest teenaged Beatles fan? You betcha. All that and more. And I was going to New York to see it all for myself! January of 1965 commenced a very auspicious year. And for me, there was no more perfect postscript to Christmas than visiting New York City. Given the time of year and the weather, my youthful eyes beheld

51

the night-lit metropolis as a kind of fairy tale landscape. It was otherworldly, and what better place than New York to loom large beneath a starry wintered sky? Magical is the only word to put to it then, and even now, while in memory's eye it returns.

My purpose in coming to story-booked Gotham was officially to be part of the Baker Street Irregulars gala. But there was also that "bit of business" which probably legitimized Bill Rabe's arrival. This of necessity involved making "informational' contact with a trio of individuals. And in each case there was I, trusty Watson, by the side of the tall man in the overcoat striding through the slush ahead.

The first of our extra-Irregular stops was Greenwich Village. There we were appointed to meet with a gentleman named Basil Davenport. At the time he seemed considerably older to me than his 64 years, but youth has its own partialized perspective. In any event, what I recall of that early evening was our host's apartment, which was loaded in library-like fashion with volumes. These had been culled and parsed and collected, and often enough, introduced by Mr. Davenport. As I would learn in hindsight, that thin and personable aesthete was well known by the honorific of "bookman" to the world of letters. In fact, his obituary would later commend him as having "carved his niche in the literary world." But as for that night in question in Old New York, I watched and listened as my friend and his contact spoke of whatever constituted their business. I meanwhile was much too busy taking in that Village apartment, which was filled with the voluminous tools of its owner's trade. Had he been a scientist it would have been his laboratory; a mechanic, his well-equipped garage. But in the case of Basil Davenport, collector and *littérateur*, his proper local world was something along the lines of the Great Library of Alexandria. Thinking of my own meager shelves back home on Wakefield, I conjured a notion of an unseen future day when I, too would possess my own tome-filled stacks of quaint and curious lore.

The second stop that weekend was to a musician and pianist named Ralph Votapek. Youngish, blond, and bound for a concert hall in Detroit in this New Year. But as I was duly informed by my companion and guide, this twenty-five year old artist had won the First Van Cliburn International Piano Competition two years earlier. So politely I sat by, interested, knowing my place as an adolescent onlooker. Truthfully, my only lasting impression of Mr. Votapek at the time was of the kind of gentle shyness he seemed to project, even to a lad who was his junior by only eight years. Ironically as well, little did I then know that the future would find this artist taking up a position in East Lansing at Michigan State University, ultimately my own *alma mater*.

The last of that trip's U. of D.-related commitments was to see someone I'd heard of, but was not yet fully aware of so as to be daunted by his accomplishments. This was Theodore H. White, still regarded as one of America's finest political journalists and historians. Recognized for his earlier reportage from China, he had become better known for his in-depth coverage of the 1960, 1964, 1968, 1972 and 1980 presidential elections

As an aside here, if not as a temporary leap ahead to the future, I find it interesting to take note of another of those curious dimensions of my youth. For as I have already mentioned, my avid interest in Sherlock Holmes had been preceded by a formative and dedicated attention to the medieval legends and stories about King Arthur. Certainly back then I had no inkling of what the future would reveal in accord with those old stories. Least of all, nor could I suspect that the day would come to find me more than an observer, but instead, a participant in the Arthurian Quest. But such has often enough been my lucky lot in this life of mine.

It may be pertinent here to give an illustration of how my youthful imaginings found it easy to move from Baker Street to Camelot. Doubtless this stands as another perhaps inexplicable example of how early seeds tend to blossom. Ergo, beginning in 1977 I found myself participating in a number of on-site activities in the United Kingdom's Somersetshire regions. For there, even as more than a decade's worth of press had reported, the actual historical-archaeological prototype of the fabled Camelot may have existed. Suddenly, and no longer compelled to restrict my childish attentions to a struggle to read Malory or an endless rehearsal of playings of the Richard Burton (and later Richard Harris) versions of the Lerner and Loewe "Camelot," I'd decided to get my hands dirty. And that I did. Over the course of the next decade and more I returned, again and again to Somerset's Glastonbury and the nearby Cadbury Hill, where rumor, wishful thinking, and some slight degree of spade-worked enthusiasm had suggested that "Here Lies King Arthur's Castle."

Today and in retrospect, the association of Cadbury Castle atop its eponymous Neolithic hillside may or may not warrant the faith of its former faithful. But if nothing else, that region has become charged with a kind of archetypal energy, as has the Glastonbury Abbey site itself, with its long-term boast of containing King Arthur's bones.

Like Holmes drinking deep of those Baskervillian Moors, I have climbed the terraced scapes of Cadbury Hill and addressed a Merlin-like hawk encircling me lonely at its crest. And I have stood before the *locus* of Arthur's Grave, first excavated by Benedictine monks in 1191. And I have been inspired by Somerset and its repute as the Summer Country of legendry. Aiding me in this self-appointed quest was my friend and mentor, Geoffrey Ashe. Author of numerous books about the "real" King Arthur, Geoffrey and I met in 1979. Intriguing as well, I recall, was our discussion over when and who Prince Charles would marry? I introduced the prospective, if not fictionalized theme of "what would happen if the Prince of Wales married a young thing who became his Guinevere to her Arthur? And further, what if Charles as the future Arthur of Britain (he bears the name in his sequence of royally christened appellations), should inevitably succumb to the curse of Camelot; i.e., find his plans for a kingdom foiled in part, by an unfaithful, if not treacherous wife? Or what, at the extreme, if the future king should himself become the engine of his court's own destruction?

Now those musings with my friend Ashe were two years before the royal wedding of Prince Charles and Lady Diana Spencer. But over time, even as I chanced to periodically remind Geoffrey, those prognostications about an archetypal "return" seemed to be coming true. And in a weirdly kind of concentric sense, I realize that at present, when the once-young prince and I are both senior citizens, the Old Story may still be unfolding.

But putting my "aside' aside, the point here is that from an early age I'd been smitten by the Arthurian Mythos. Moreover, at age 13 I had witnessed the advent and rule of America's own King Arthur, in the person of President John Fitzgerald Kennedy. I defy any person of my vintage to deny that something about our country seemed grander, bolder, and filled with possibilities with "JFK" at the helm. This notwithstanding his love of James Bond, his farrago at the Bay of Pigs, or his duels with Khrushchev at Vienna or in terms of the Cuban Missile Crisis. Ultimately and sadly, the legacy of Mr. Kennedy was snuffed out, much as Arthur himself, before he had a true chance to shine. Just as Arthurian Camelot was vaunted as a re-birth of wonder, if not a kind of golden age, so too were those brief "thousand days" of John Kennedy's administration barely enough to succor such an idea. And yet, and as many would hasten to regard it, "Camelot" in America did not truly arrive until the literal wake of November 22, 1963. And along with the rest of the world, at age 16, I watched the dark caisson bearing the body of our murdered leader to his version of Avalon.

But here's my actual point, at last. You see, the last of our visits in New York on that weekend in 1965 involved Bill Rabe's meeting with Theodore H. White. And Mr. White, as historians and Kennedy mavens will remember, was in fact the true architect of the idea of an American "Camelot." This, notwithstanding talk of how JFK's Peace Corps was his version of a Round Table retinue, or of how the young president had so handsomely and stylishly wooed the world. But it was only when Jack Kennedy was on his way to faery-clad Avalon, like Arthur long before him, that the true archetypal legend came to life. And it did so chronologically a week after her husband's death, when Jacqueline Kennedy summoned Theodore White to the Kennedy compound in Hyannis Port. And it was there that she specifically implored the author of *The Making of the President, 1960* to take on another task. For even as his earlier writing had produced some of the most influential work about the election and how Kennedy became our Chief Executive. Further, it had also won him the 1962 Pulitzer Prize for general nonfiction.

Now however, and doubtless on account of his loyal account of the late President's "brief shining moment," our former First Lady suggested to author White that he prepare an article for an upcoming issue of *Life Magazine.*

The premise of Theodore White's essay in *Life* would be explained as Jacqueline Kennedy's belief that her late husband's administration was very like that of the mythic Arthur and his much storied Camelot. Her idea was buttressed, no doubt by the contemporary and beloved Broadway musical of the sane name. Moreover, standing at the heart of her future-oriented concern was Jackie's focus upon the play's most sentimental closing lyric,

> *"Don't let it be forgot,*
> *that once there was a spot,*

for one brief shining moment
that was known as Camelot. "

This, as the President's widow advised, and/or instructed White, ought to be her late husband's living epitaph. *The archetype made real.*

So then on that wintry evening in my 18th year, I was in the presence of the man who, very like Sir Thomas Malory five centuries earlier, had made the idea of King Arthur and his many turreted kingdom, a mainstay of contemporary culture. But even stranger as it's occurred to me so many years later, isn't it remarkable that the authors of the classic novel *The Sword In The Stone* and the best-selling *The Making of the President 1960* were both named T.H. White? That, in the words of a fellow mystery buff, represents "high strangeness" indeed. Moreover, I'm still amazed that the coincidence of the "two Whites" in conjunction with the Arthurian Mythos has escaped either discovery or discussion elsewhere.

Personally, I remember Mr. White as a nice gentleman and something else. This amounted to my own most memorable detail of our meeting. It occurred on the heels of his conversation with Bill Rabe. Turning to me at one point, he paid me a compliment which I had, until that time, never been accorded.

"You're a very good listener" White said to me. "I've noticed that about you. And you know, that's a special sort of talent." And hearing this, coming from a Kennedy cohort and Pulitzer Prize winning author, I registered the idea. And I never forgot what it meant. Nor could I have, at the time, informed my complementor that one day I too would occupy myself with bringing a legend to life. But let that be another small entry in my contemplated-but-unwritten tome, *Had I But Known.*

The lion's share of memory of that New York weekend is spent on its essential purpose. I was to attend the birthday festivities of the annual Baker Street Irregulars meeting. It took place in a grand sort of dining room with ancillary chambers containing displays, books and other items. But inside, the part of that all-male throng which drew me like a lodestone, involved certain of the participants. And to me, foremost among that Irregular reunion was the legendary Rex Stout, creator of the equally be-legended sleuth, Nero Wolfe. I knew enough about him to recall that Wolfe was no razor-thin version of Holmes, but tended to a weightiness more resembling Sherlock's brother Mycroft. But such characteristics were, as I was later told, perhaps only genealogical. This, *vis a vis* a thesis either spawned or at least encouraged by Rex Stout, himself a devout admirer and follower of the sleuth of Baker Street.

The hypothesis which seemed to suggest a kind of "all in the family" premise was this: supposedly when Sherlock Holmes embarked upon his great post-Reichenbach hiatus, he did so in the company of the only woman who seemed to have stopped him in his tracks. This of course was 'the Woman,' Irene Adler of "A Scandal In Bohemia" infamy.

The Lobby — The Algonquin Hotel Lobby, circa '65

At any rate, the Stout Hypothesis had it that Holmes and Irene went off for a getaway to Montenegro. We know very little of how long that liaison lasted, but we were informed via certain supposedly reputable channels that the by-product of that Montenegrin fling was the birth of a child, a son. And supposedly, as Stout himself did avow, it was believed that the encoded tip-off of the Great Secret lay in the boychild's appellation: *Nero Wolfe*. And as philologists or crackpots tended to agree, that name bore the tell-tale "*er*" of "Sherlock" and the "*ol*" of "Holmes. Ergo, the name within the name. And further, the designation or royal ensign signifying the paternity of the world's greatest Victorian and Edwardian detective as conferred upon the modern day's most sizable of sleuths. Such at any rate is one of those curious, if not tongue-in-cheek legacies left by Wolfe's begetter; that, and of course that heresy which suggested that Watson was in fact a woman! Today I cannot help but wonder in this "trans-Jennered" day and age in which even coeducated Irregular meetings are *de rigeur,* whether Stout's suggestion that the good doctor was a woman might hold up?

But when I was introduced to Rex Stout I might just as well have been meeting one of the Mendicant gang, or one of Russell McLaughlin's vintage Sherlockian cronies. Which I do believe Mr. Stout was, at that. But to tell you the truth, perhaps the secret of my immediate and mutually pleasurable meeting with the great mystery author had nothing to do with Sherlock Holmes. Instead, it reflected what I'd brought to the Irregulars fete, in the form of my cumbersome black leather carrying case for my Polaroid Camera. Doubtless this memory will date many of us, but back in '65 this was a sort of state-of-the-art apparatus for not only taking pictures, but of seeing them only moments later.

And of course, there was the slippery slope associated with my then high-tech camera. Or should I say, the sticky slope necessarily involved with that primitive Polaroid's fledgling process. For you see, after shooting your picture, a button would eject the developing print. And after a suitable series of seconds, you peeled off the cover strip and *ces voilà!* But there was more to do even yet. For if indeed you were satisfied with your own Matthew Bradyesque accomplishment, you preserved your fresh photo, quite literally, by coating it with a handy-dandy roller tube in your carry-all.

And so it was that after asking for the privilege, I shot an impromptu portrait of Rex Stout. He in turn chuckled all the while, even as I pressed and shot, ejected and proudly displayed my handiwork to the great man. And honestly, perhaps even Brady himself could not have elicited a more receptive response from Lincoln than I did from Stout.

My portrait's subject examined the black and white rendering of himself, casually seeming to pose before a large cut-out, deer-stalkered representation of Holmes hanging behind the (appropriately named) head table.

I asked Mr. Stout if he liked the picture. He confessed that he did, and commended me on my prowess as a young photog. That wasn't his terminology of course, but it meant the same. And I couldn't help but to agree. So much, in fact, that after preserving it for posterity, I asked my subject if he would autograph his portrait? He consented with alacrity, as Dr. Watson might have put it. And I carried away that souvenir and kept it and treasured it.

Today, more than half a century later, I have the Rex Stout Portrait hanging upon a sagging bookshelf behind the chair that I now occupy, even as I key-board these words. It appears a shelf or so above another Polaroid. This one was taken in the bedroom of the Algonquin Hotel. Rabe and I were preparing to go downstairs and he was sitting on the edge of the bed. He's wearing a suit and tie and an overcoat. In his mouth he's clenching the remainder of a cigar. Whether he was posing or it simply reflected his mood at the time, the look on the man's face was, well, Rabe-esque. In fact, many years later I thought I ought to simply pay tribute to my old *confrere,* equating his scowling image to that of his like in "The Adventure of the Empty House." That's right, the old *shikari* himself, Colonel Sebastian Moran. And even now whenever I look at my impromptu portrait of Rabe, I feel it might well be entitled

"The Second Most Dangerous Man In London."

And while we're talking about the Algonquin Hotel. Without a doubt, I have met many remarkable persons in my life, and also may I say, through the "auspices of Mr. Sherlock Holmes." This is the story of one of them who touched me in a lasting way.

When I journeyed to New York with my friend Bill Rabe in the winter of 1965, not all of my urban adventures were involved with a wintry walkabout. Our base while there that weekend was that redoubtable hotel where such *literati* as Alexander Woolcott, Robert Benchley and Dorothy Parker had comprised members of the Algonquin's literary Round Table. These days however, the old place still wore a veneer of its former grandeur, but in a faded kind of way.

One of my favorite memories of the Algonquin that distant January had to do with its lobby. To me, that generous labyrinth of many islands consisting of trio-ed arrangements of wingbacks and armchairs, tables, and lamps seemed not only right for privacy, but assignations or covert meetings of all kinds. And it was one of those which involved an eighteen-year-old fellow and one eighty-seven years young Scotsman.

Even back then my young eye for trivia and recollection for minutiae was sharp. On that count then, one afternoon when Rabe and I were returned from some foray, I was left to my own devices. Having taken the small elevator down to the lobby, I wandered aimlessly into the greater room beyond the desk. I surveyed the handsome dark wood paneling and the regal design of the rich looking carpet beneath my feet. Finally I decided on one of the high-backed plush chairs near one of the squared lobby pillars. I sat there awhile indulging in whatever passed for my youthful sanctum musings. Probably just the notion of being so far from home, if not the reason for coming to Manhattan. *The 111ᵗʰ Birthday of Sherlock Holmes.* Rabe had told me this on the flight, and I had no reason to doubt him. After all, here in my company was the greatest expert on Mr. Holmes in my world. And then my musings were suddenly interrupted by a low voice. But not just any voice. This one was foreign. And not just English. But burled Scottish.

I looked over and saw a heap of an old fellow in dark suit and tie. But what was most imposing about him was his huge head, his nose a true beak, and his mane of snow white hair almost to his shoulders. And aware of this man mountain suddenly addressing me, I turned. And even as I did so I thought, *I know him.* But sadly in that moment, not his name, but the fact that I had seen this chap before, and on television. He was an actor, to be sure.

At any rate and to spare your suspense, the gentleman in question was indeed an actor named Finlay Currie, and had been so at that time for, by my later reckoning, sixty-seven years. Yet while I seemed to "know" him, I had yet to appreciate this man's body of work. But there was something decidedly magnetic about him, and suddenly I felt myself being drawn to his craggy smile and sparkling eyes.

"Ye're on yer own here?" he asked. I replied I was not quite exactly, but that I was in town with a friend. Also that we were in New York from Michigan for Sherlock Holmes' birthday.

That fact seemed to cheer the old Scot, but even more so when we traded names. And when I said "McPherson" he perked up in his seat like some sort of land mass shifting in its valley.

"Mac-Fair-Sohn" he said, nodding his head as he pronounced my surname in a kind of liltingly accented trisyllabic fashion. "Aye that's a fine name to be proud of, to be sure. And that makes us fellow clansmen as well."

Puzzled by the remark, I wondered how anyone would tie the clans of the Currie's and McPherson's together?

"Well it's fairly simple, lad. For you see we're both Highlanders. Your clan entered Scotland long, long ago and settled in the remote northlands. Eventually they begot what were called 'the Five Sons of Muirich,' from which the name 'MacMuirich,' or 'sons of Muirich' came to be. Another branch became the MacPhersons or 'sons of the parson.' Your name's a sort of word picture in Gaelic. In any event, my name of 'Currie' comes from 'MacMuirich' as well, which makes us cousins of a sort. So *'slainte mhath'*" he said, pronouncing that strange phrase *"shlan shee va"* as he raised a nearly empty glass from the table beside him. I smiled and nodded back in agreement to what sounded like the old man's toast. As I did so I decided to vacate the comfort of my armchair to trade it for the smaller wooden chair beside Mr. Currie's own.

"It's an old toast, that means 'to your good health.' You may need it some time or other," said my companion. "Say it with me again, "*Shlan shee va.*"

I repeated the words, which were Gaelic. And for those of you purists, and apart from my phonetic description here, the real thing is spelled *"Slainte Mhath,* expressed by my Scots expert to be pronounced *"slantchih va. "* Obscure to all but those in the know, I suppose the toast gained credence with the televised series depicting the books by Diana Gabaldon called The Outlander series.

That celebratory toast was a gift which Mr. Currie gave me that time in New York, in the Algonquin, and in that snug nook where two fellow clansmen sat together. But that's not quite the end of my anecdote. For as the future would prove out on too many occasions, sometimes it is only retroactively that you sense a kind of after-the-fact savoring or appreciation for something which came and went much earlier.

Little did I remember with much clarity upon our meeting back in '65 that five years earlier my new friend Currie had been in the Walt Disney film "Kidnapped" and I'd probably seen it. That no doubt had accounted for my remembering his face, if not for having seen him on the Big Screen in "Ben Hur" or "Francis of Assisi" or even earlier, in "Great Expectations," filmed the year before my birth, in which he'd played the ferocious convict, Magwich.

But "Kidnapped" was the real signifier for me as I now look back upon it. This also has much to do with my own family background, as charted by my Aunt Zelna Randall's son Lou in Australia. His forte has become the Randall-McPherson genealogy. And among a trove of other information, perhaps the most exciting to me involved my great-great-great-great-great-great grandfather, Daniel MacPherson. For you see, as my kinsman's intrepid research has ferreted out, Daniel was impressed, or as you might say, kidnapped from his home in Inverness, Scotland and brought by British press ship to the New World many many centuries ago. In fact, tradition has it that no less a scribe than Robert Louis Stevenson had heard about the lad's travails and recreated it in his classic, *Kidnapped.* There the story's protagonist, young David Balfour is the kidnappee, and he is eventually taken to meet a renegade Scottish chieftain who has taken refuge against his Sassenach oppressors. To achieve this he hides in a cave, and is kept for years through the help of his clansmen. And the name of that chieftain was Cluny MacPherson. A fascinating story, isn't it? But here's the hook:

in the 1960 Walt Disney version of "Kidnapped," the part of Cluny was played by—you guessed it—Finlay Currie! Coincidence? Or better yet, as an old clerical friend of mine used to put it, a "God-incidence?" I think so. And that may also account for the following curious fact: over a course of years and in connection with a project soon to be described, I often found myself passing through Inverness, Scotland. And always when I did so I couldn't shake a strange sense of familiarity. In other words, *I seemed to know that town.* But how? Only later, when my cousin provided the genealogical key did I suddenly comprehend. For believe it or not—and I do—my own distant kinsman had once lived in Inverness-shire, and from there he'd been stolen across the water from the Old Country, if only to one day establish our family line in the New World. Just so, I 'knew' that town, for in a sense, it had once served as my "home," albeit in a long-distance sense!

As my cursory exploration of that gentleman's credits in in *Wikipedia* reveals, Finlay Currie's reputation as a veteran of stage, screen and television is one seldom repeated. Of course in the case of this great actor there was a great deal to be impressed by. Over the years I've met not a few famous thespians, many of them of the British variety. Rathbone, Guinness, O'Toole, Harris and many others come to mind. Stars all indeed, but few of them with the talent or charm or durability equal to this old gent's simple staying power. Having by his own admission first taken to the stage in 1898 (Sherlock Holmes might have seen him!) this professional character actor had appeared in about sixty feature films by the time I'd the good fortune to meet, if not find myself briefly befriended by him. He had what they call "a very good run," both on stage and off. Finlay Currie passed away three years after our meeting, at age ninety.

I've replayed my VHS version of the Disney film which starred Peter Finch and even a walk-on from a youthful Peter O'Toole. But for me, it's Mr. Currie's movie, especially when David (James MacArthur) meets the exiled chieftain, who asks him to drink with him. So he, Davy and their colleague Alan Breck (Finch) raise their cups. Cluny toasts the restoration of the Scot's king, James Stuart, who is also exiled. But David balks. Breck explains that his young friend was "born a Whig." Nevertheless, they hoist their drams and silently drink. And whenever I play this bit I imagine Finlay Currie's "prequel" to our own salute, half a decade later, with myself filling in for David Balfour! *"Slainte mhath!"*

And on a final, further note: in preparing myself to address this memoir, I chose to re-visit any number of key Sherlockian sources. In this fashion I hoped to refresh not only a much challenged sense of memory, but also to see if certain of my eldritch emotions could be rekindled?

In particular and in preparation for discussing my momentous "meeting with Mr. Holmes," in the person of Jeremy Brett, I set to reviewing the complete set of Granada adventures. And for some reason, perhaps owing to this being more the "right" time to discover it, the other night I realized that I had yet to see the "Extras" portion of one of the discs. I took special note of the fact that included here was an interview with Sir Cedric Hardwicke's son Edward, who must be remembered as perhaps one of the gently greatest—if not the greatest of portrayers of Dr. John H. Watson. This is of course high and deserved praise, to be shared, curiously enough, with David Burke, who also appeared in a number of the early Brett series.

But the "extra" in question made me eager to hear "Watson talking about Watson." I also knew that my own memory of meeting Mr. Hardwicke in 1988, at the time I'd met his co-star and seen the two of them on stage in the Jeremy Paul drama, "The Secret of Sherlock Holmes." At the time I'd been struck by the low-keyed gentleness of this fine actor, whose own catalogue of screen performances was extensive. But more about that in a bit. For now, the matter of what I found, tucked away there in the Hardwicke interview.

When I saw and heard this, coming from Hardwicke's own memory of his late father, I confess to being initially staggered, and secondly, pleased in that way we are when we see Serendipity raising its handsome head to help us along.

The point worth mentioning here involved not Brett or Hardwicke, but the latter's famous father. This was made by his allusion to the curious fact that Sir Cedric had actually played the role of Holmes in a 1945 BBC half-hour radio broadcast of "The Adventure of the Speckled Band." But most noteworthy, to myself at least, was hearing Edward Hardwicke cite the fact that *it had been Finlay Currie who'd been his father's Watson*. Go figure. And that, my friends, I now include as a kind of additional "evidence in the case" suggesting that my earliest Holmesian forays seemed consistent, even when they seemed not to!

My meeting with Finlay Currie was a meaningful prelude to my first decidedly historic brush with the Baker Street Irregulars. However, little did I know that upon the brief occasion of our coming together at the Algonquin Hotel, a strange bit of serendipity had already been at work. This was neither evident at the time but involved yet another "McPhersonian," if not Sherlockian dimension involving my clan's "relationship" with Mr. Currie and his portrayal of my long-ago ancestor. This then via the significant fact that that robust old gent had also played the part of Dr. Watson, a tidbit which patiently waited half a century after our meeting to rise to my attention!

So then, file this portion of my early adventures within the folder marked SYNCHRONICITIES. And if you thumb through this you may also come across the memory of when in 1985 I took my wife to the MacPherson Clan Museum in Newtonmore, Scotland.

Among the fascinating relics depicted in the small museum, one thing struck me greatly. This was the broken fiddle which legend says had belonged to Jamie MacPherson, a dashing "free-booter" immortalized by Robbie Burns in his poem "MacPherson's Lament." There is also a musical rendition dubbed "MacPherson's Rant."

At any rate, the story went that as he was about to be hanged in 1700, brawn Jamie played a last jig on his fiddle. Then he smashed it over his knee and the emissaries of his arch-rival sent him to his glory. But also as the tale insists, within moments a rider entered the town's limits carrying a pardon for James MacPherson. You see, it seems his nemesis, one Duff of Braco knew the pardon was en route, so he advanced the shire's clock.

That then is the story of Jamie's fiddle and a story which I believe out-laws and out-rivals even that of Jamie Fraser in the *Outlander* saga.

So imagine then our wandering through the clan Museum, inspecting all sorts of ancestral memorabilia. And then of coming to one rather dusty showcase. In its corner are some old clippings and photos. They seem to depict yet another M(a)cPherson of America. But this one is oddly unique for two reasons; first off, he is an ardent Sherlock Holmes aficionado. And secondly: he has been undertaking a series of expeditions at Scotland's Loch Ness in quest of its storied beastie.

Yes, there I was in the show-case's cluttered corner. I had somehow managed to gain entrance to the repository of my ancestors. And where I hope, I remain to this day.

And now let us skip back and forth in time to discuss--The Irregulars. And of course, to that seminal meeting in '65. I recall that among that all-male crowd there were other new friends and a sea of faces, some of them famous. For instance, there was my chance to once again see Bennett Shaw and Peter Blau, as well as my opportunity of shaking hands with someone I'd also longed to meet. This was none other than William Stuart Baring-Gould, author of *Sherlock Holmes of Baker Street,* and as we all must still commendably recall, his two-volumed edition of *The Annotated Sherlock Holmes.*

To this day I equate the name of Baring-Gould with my most seminal of Sherlockian inquiries. Naturally he is to be held accountable for the world's first and best-remembered biography of Holmes. Then of course his annotated *magnum opus.*

Sherlock Holmes is once heard to observe that "art in the blood takes the strangest of forms." Was that then the reason behind Baring-Gould's prescience in producing two of the greatest works of the Irregular world to date? Or perhaps he was but reflecting a genetic disposition toward what amounts to some of the Western world's greatest literary folklore? I dare to call the Sherlock Holmes stories that. In their ways they might be perceived on a level of certain of Britain's most enduring and curious traditions, as were chronicled by the Rector of Lewtrenchard, Devonshire, the Reverend Sabine Baring Gould? His *Lives of the Saints* and immortal hymn "Onward Christian Soldiers" are well-remembered. In contrast however, the cleric's *Book of Were Wolves* is more obscure, save for savants of the unusual. And somewhere in between are Baring Gould's folkloric accounts of certain Devonshire superstitions. Therefore and with such a powerful artistic legacy to follow, is it strange that his descendant was able to articulate, discuss, and explain those works which both Conan Doyle and Doctor Watson presented to a vast readership?

But as I well knew, it was William Stuart Baring-Gould's Baker Street biography, or in truth a review of it, that had catalytically first led me to Bill Rabe's door After passing through it, I had made the acquaintance of his friends, who just happened to occupy rather rarified spaces in the gaslit world where dwelt those "two men of note" we came to admire. Ergo, and *quod erat demonstrandum,* it might be said that without W.S. Baring-Gould's excellent work, I might not have ventured so far.

There is also another enduring and bittersweet aside which I have debated including within this memoir. But it is somehow seminal not only to my youth and my love of Sherlock Holmes and even more. And it deals directly with Mr. Baring-Gould's groundbreaking biography of Sherlock Holmes, aptly entitled *Sherlock Holmes of Baker Street.*

Even now my memories still depend upon my personal copy of the book in question. Today it reposes in its space as part of an expansive library of Sherlockiana. Its well-deserved rest is also attested to by its well-thumbed and rather frayed sepia dust jacket. This in turn represents a thousand perusals throughout the corridors of both youth and adulthood. And even in this instant I recall myself peddling down the busyness of Woodward Avenue from my Berkley home, all for the sake of procuring the volume that had been reviewed in the *Royal Oak Daily Tribune.* Yes, that very copy which reflected the impending magic of its reviewer's praise. And that review and that tome had in unison spurred me on, and who knew then what a long charge into the future they would bring?

But Baring-Gould's *opus* also signified two other somewhat Proustian dimensions which blended rather sweetly, then bittersweetly, into one. These concern the fact that at that shimmering moment when all things Holmesian seemed breathed through silver, I worked at a bookish job. Quite literally that, in the form of my becoming a page (another apropos bit of terminology) at our community's Berkley Public Library. During perhaps the second year of my tenure there as an after-school and weekend employee, the library moved to re-built premises nearby. And among those newly-configured "stacks" I navigated, behind carts-full of volumes arranged in alphabetical and Dewey Decimal order, was a familiar friend of sorts. Recently ordered and now destined to occupy its place within a non-fictional, albeit literary section, I discovered the presence of Baring-Gould's *Sherlock Holmes of Baker Street!*

I cannot express what I felt upon seeing that numerical designation blazoned under plastic upon the spine of that book. For here and apart from these many aisles in my library devoted to FICTION, now this particular volume was going where it ought to be: to a section reserved for NON-FICTION, ergo actuality, history, and real life.

I do not know how it came to be that *Sherlock Holmes of Baker Street* was given its non-fictional classification. I remember feeling a strange sense of glad elation, pride, and an almost proprietorial aura of achievement. The truth however, was otherwise. Nevertheless, I often paid visits to the book like a friend, if only to see if it had proven popular or was appreciated by those initiates or aficionados of Sir Arthur Conan Doyle's master detective? And all of this in turn managed to birth another notion, which I gave full vent to over the course of one long ago summer

To put it plainly, I was smitten. Yes, in love the way only an adolescent boy can be, if and when he is stricken by what the troubadour poets used to call "sublime love for the inaccessible." In this case however, the young lady in question was accessible to a certain degree. In fact, I had seen her, and yearned to do so, from our mutual time from our Fourth Grade level, into junior high school, and thereafter, high school in our small suburb of Berkley, Michigan. But it was at a young and romantic mid-point of that time that I'd conceived of my idea. *Rather than risking defeat and my own subjective shyness as well, what if I approached my enamorada in words? Further, what if I informed her that I would leave her a missive at a specific place, at a specific time? Now all that remained was the where? and when? of it.*

My enfevered plans were expanded and soon executed. They began with a stamped note to my young lady to her home on Wiltshire Street. My brief missive instructed her to visit the local public library, now only perhaps twenty minutes from her front door. Once there, she was asked to find a particular volume bearing a specific Dewy Decimal Number. And the volume in question? You may have well guessed. It was William S. Baring-Gould's *Sherlock Holmes of Baker Street.* And did the plan work? Not "by 'alf" it did. In fact, over the course of that magical summer, my secret love and I exchanged missives. On my part it was always via a three by five card bearing lines of bad Byronic longing, and always signed "'Y.N.A.'" This , to my own romantic soul stood for "*Your Nameless Admirer.*"

There is of course a bittersweet postscript to my story. For after that vaguely poetical summer, the communiqués between "'Y.N.A.'" and his subject were terminated for good. But not before a thin sheaf of literary classics had been left and in turn, collected. Better yet, there were also those times when her correspondent found a token from the lady herself. He yet recalls having requested her image, and much as Edgar Allan Poe might have invoked his muse and earthly goddess, further asking for her image. So too did I. And I got it. A photograph. A tangible evidence of our mystical, albeit unreal relationship. And from that time on, my dear Watson, she became *the* Young Woman.

The postscript to this seemingly unrelated aside is two-fold. I did not write to the object of my affections again; or at least, not for many years. We lost track of one another about four years later, but not before I was unable to shed my rather heat-seeking attentions upon her. And then she moved away from Berkley to Plymouth, Michigan, as I'd heard. And we were not to cross paths again for another three years. And only then and rather unexpectedly on a cross-campus bus-ride at Michigan State University, *I saw her again.*

The long and short of the thing is this: now emboldened by my status as a university junior, I not only saluted the young lady, but asked her out. She kindly declined my overture. Some while later I tried again, but once more and true to form, to no success. Nor did I, I think, ever consider asking her, "do you know who I am?" And when she would shake that angelically blond head of hers to the negative, I would proclaim *"I am 'Y.N.A'"* But I never did. No, never, until the passage of six more years. By that time both of us had experienced life and loves and sadnesses which are not so atypical of the young. But for my part, I was depressingly aware of the fact that I had never let the image of that young woman vanish from my mind or heart. So much so that a dream finally propelled me into action. In it, I stood on a set of steps with the lady of my desires. And I said to her, "what will you do now?"

She replied, "well I suppose I'll get married and have children." That was all it took.

After giving the matter much thought, I resolved to find her again. I succeeded by tracing Barbara's (her name revealed at last) family to Plymouth. There a directory search found my target's parents. Daringly, I rang the number. When the mother answered, I asked after her daughter. I was duly informed that the object of my chronic affections was living there, at home, and was now a teacher of hearing impaired children. And it was at that point that I was asked who I was? Nervously, foolishly, I gave Mrs. H. a *nom de plume* of sorts. I seemed to hear her at the end of the line, her mental key-punching sifting through any names she might have recalled from her earlier stint as a member of the Berkley P.T.A. But obviously she had to draw a blank. For the name I'd given her had not belonged to Mark McPherson, save as a ruse.

The rest of the story engages rapidly. I arranged to speak to Mrs. H's daughter a few days hence, upon what happened to be Labor Day. And at the appointed hour I called, and suddenly found myself hearing *that voice*. The sound of her went with my cumulative memories reeling all the way back to that now ancient, end-of-term June day on the playing field at Berkley Elementary. For there the two of us had stood. In my hands I'd held a Brownie camera (an apt precursor to my later Polaroid). With this I snapped two photographs. The first was blurred through the agency by my own shaking hands. The second was better, and treasured for quite a time after. But now, incredibly that same little 4th grade damsel, as well as her post-collegiate incarnation, was at the end of the phone line.

At one point nearly an hour later and after playing a kind of hedging game, she finally asked me who I was? Finally, and tired of hiding behind three by five cards and the camouflage of about fifteen year's worth of time and place, I took off the mask. And as I did, the lady was directing her attention to the Berkley High School Class of 1965 Yearbook. There she found me. Yes, looking down upon my clean-cut, smiling visage, and doubtless trying to put it into context with that college guy whom she'd successfully repelled, not once, but twice.

So then, and perhaps sensing that it was perhaps also time to bring out the Big Guns, now I did so.

"Do you remember a long ago summer when you went to the library and looked in the pages of a certain book?" I asked the voice at the end of the line.

"The one about Sherlock Holmes" she stated at once. In my mind's eye I could see her nodding.

"That's right. The one where you found the cards from 'Y.N.A.'"

"Yes?"

"Well that's me" I confessed. "I am 'Y.N.A.'" *The Final Revelation. Zorro removes his mask. Clark Kent unbuttons his shirt.*

I cannot say for certain the how and why, but the consequence of that epic Labor Day telephone conversation translated at last into glorious reality. The following week I found myself parking before the colonial house on Beechcrest and then making the long trek up the front walk. Glancing up, I saw someone on the other side of the summer screen door. And in that moment I swear to goodness I was hoping it would all end there. *Maybe she'll weigh three hundred pounds. Maybe she'll be horrible. Or maybe she'll think I am.*

But my worst fears went unanswered. Instead and in their place I saw her standing there, as the Beatles once sang. And when I did my heart went up like a rocket. And all I found myself needing to do in that moment was to get by the dragon at the gate, in the form of Mrs. H, who by now had been apprised of my actual identity. Which is to say, not the made-up name I'd given her on the phone. Just so, the lady bore down on me with a glare that seemed to say, "you're the one who lied to me on the phone." Well it would be nice to say that that part of the story never mattered later on. But strangely, I think it did. However the part I remember best, as does the lady herself even now, was that we locked eyes like a missile seeking its target. And when we left that house and window-shopped our ways to the Mayflower, where we had dinner, it was all I could do not to burst out in song. No more mystery cards. No more shoot-downs. No more wishful dreams. Now we were together again for the first time. And I knew, even after returning to my bachelor digs, that I could never let her go ever again.

This part of the saga concludes with an interconnected beginning and end. I did get my fondest of wishes. The young lady and her former "nameless admirer" dated and courted and were even secretly engaged a while. You see, she didn't want her people to know about it "until everyone's getting along better." So we held fire a bit, although the reason was about as realistic as waiting for the ice to melt around THE TITANIC. But not so very much after, we eventually married. And over the course of nearly five years our joys were great, as were unfortunately our consequent sorrows. What began as a dream ended as something else when we parted and divorced.

To this day the recollection remains razor sharp of the day this writer was compelled to dismantle his customized version of Holmes' famous sitting room at 221B in the basement of his former home on Carriage Way Drive.

Seemingly a moment ago, or so it then felt, I had carefully and lovingly put every piece and artifact into its proper place. There were even Christmas eves when my wife and I would sit there, listening to an archaic recording of the Yuletide-based adventure of "The Blue Carbuncle." She would needlepoint and I, nearby in Holmes' chair, would puff away on my pipe.

But then and as memory still informs me, the music was suddenly stilled. And the metaphorical machinery seemed to grind in reverse and at warp speed. And when it did, no longer the beloved and sharing observer, now my about-to-be-former lady-wife stood by in silence, watching me literally tear down my dreams. Yet I also recall a hint that something may have informed her of the wrongness, the de-sanctifying nature of what was happening. This when she said, "why don't you leave it all here?" And for a moment hope soared. Was this the Hollywood moment, when tides were turned and all was forgiven? No, it was not. For it took me only seconds to realize what she was suggesting: *the room could remain, but I was to take my leave*. Even as I did.

But who can say how or why things happen? Better, no doubt is the present-day fact that eventually both my childhood sweetheart and I went our separate ways and married two other wonderful people. To this day we remain on friendly terms. But also to this day I suppose neither of us can or likely will ever forget what I fondly describe as our "Sherlockian summer." Or of how they came together, courtesy of a writer named Baring-Gould and his subject, Mr. Sherlock Holmes of Number 221B, Upper Baker Street. Unwittingly, both of those gents managed to conspire like Cyrano to become our romantic intermediaries. And all because of "that book about Sherlock Holmes." But Fate conspired against that admission so many years ago when I had the privilege of shaking the hand of William Stuart Baring-Gould.

So then, silently if not somewhat secretly, I thank the odd company of a reviewer, an author, and of course, a certain Victorian sleuth for doing their best to aid the cause of true love. But that, as you may well recall, does not always run smoothly. That it exists or existed at all is the miracle of the thing, I think. And because of that, Messrs. Rabe, Baring-Gould and Holmes were each present when certain of my many and fondest of dreams began to come true, however temporarily.

"The Second Most Dangerous Man in London?"
W.T. Rabe

mercy
college
of detroit

artists
series

AN EVENING WITH
BASIL RATHBONE

Sunday, February 9, 1964 ▪ 6:30 p.m. ▪ McAuley Auditorium

"A Rathbone 'Evening'"

The youthful author "meets The Beatles."

6
Basil and The Beatles

In his professional capacity as informational officer for the University of Detroit, Bill Rabe had a score of set duties. But he had others as well, and many of them of a self-created, driven, even creatively aggressive degree. To begin with, he knew the business of journalism, which he'd honed over the years, I believe, even from his experience during the Korean War. On that score as well, he was, as he would have admitted himself, a flack in the style of Mencken or O. Henry. Moreover, his press credentials also earned him the capacity of conceiving of, writing, or getting a news item published. This fact was bolstered often enough via my own personal experience, in Detroit or elsewhere, of seeing him walk into a city room and plant an item that would appear in print the next day. Or possibly of walking over to a telephone booth in a restaurant or bar and ringing up a contact across the country. And as a result? A story engendered. A rumor made real. Part prankster, part academic, many parts the ink-stained wretch, W.T. Rabe had a sort of fearless ability to use words to his advantage, or to the benefit of whatever master he served. Dauntless, sometimes ruthless, humorous, and as I came to see over the years, at times seemingly impervious to friendly overture and as vague as a block of ice, this man became the living template for my future self.

It may be that the only aspect of our earliest meeting I regretted involved the matter of timing. As I'd learned, Rabe had written an academic thesis on the art of Stanley Laurel and had actually met the surviving half of the immortal comedic duo of Laurel and Hardy. This subject fueled Bill's interest in the great comedic team, and one that was furthered by the book *Mr. Laurel and Mr. Hardy* by John McCabe—a Rabe longtime pal, a Shakespearean scholar, and a chap I greatly enjoyed meeting. But that would have been before both my time and my "prime" as Rabe's youthful helper. There was however that seeming moment later, just on the cusp of our first meeting, when Bill had spent some time with the poet Robert Frost, who had visited the U. of D. And then, finally, it was my time. This resulted in my meeting the likes of Edward Teller and Ralph Nader, and even a certain British actor named Basil Rathbone.

Not long ago I read a Sherlockian account which concerned the later extent of Mr. Rathbone's extreme dislike of "scion" societies, if not their members. In other words, he resented being hounded, if not professionally branded as an actor wearing a deerstalker cap, both literally and figuratively. So much so, in fact, that he succeeded in echoing a scene in perhaps the fourth or fifth of those wartime propaganda films in which he co-starred as Sherlock beside Nigel "Bunny" Bruce as his Dr. Watson. In that, and after two decidedly appropriate Victorian "period" films, it was decided to bring the detective and his chum into the Forties and the wartime effort. And on that note and in one of the later films, Holmes reaches for his double-billed, ear-flapped cap on the rack as Watson says "Holmes, you promised!" So instead, Sherlock/Basil reaches for that woolen Donegal hat he seemed to favor throughout most of the sleuth's efforts at winning the Second World War.

I read a report by one Irregular named Richard Lesh, member of the group dubbed the Maiwand Jezails, of how Basil Rathbone had visited Indiana and not only that, had actually appeared at the local Holmes gathering. So astonishing in fact was this report, if not Lesh's entertaining and hosting of the great actor in his home, that upon hearing it Bill Rabe had grabbed a plane and arrived to see it all for himself. And that no doubt had set a certain tone for Rathbone's appearance in Detroit for a stage performance at Detroit's Mercy College in February of 1964. When news of the great actor's appearance was announced there was great excitement. And as you might imagine, the remark that "Sherlock is coming to Detroit."

But a few months later in the autumn of February of '64, that legendary British boy band played their role again. This when they were to make their appearance on the Ed Sullivan Show. At the time, I don't suppose there was a more hyped televised event, notwithstanding the Kennedy-Nixon debates, or possibly those Sunday Disney nights when Davy Crockett was airing.
Yet there was a conflict concerning that night of nights. And quite unexpectedly, it materialized out of thin air with a telephone call from Bill Rabe.

I had learned both to thrill and to jump when Rabe called. Not perhaps so unlike the good Watson's reaction when his colleague appeared, if only to utter "the game is afoot!"

In this instance however, "Holmes" put the question squarely to his teenaged Watson.

"How would you like to meet Basil Rathbone?"

Well how does a religious zealot answer when someone offers the chance to meet God? That may sound irreverent, but the analogy is apt, at least to an appreciator of Mr. Sherlock Holmes or his famous impersonator on-screen. I mean, anyone worth his deerstalker cap who stood a chance of seeing or meeting the star of "The Adventures of Sherlock Holmes" or "The Hound of the Baskervilles" would have been crazy to forego the chance. And I wasn't crazy.

But I was ecstatic. Without a doubt the notion of seeing Mr. Rathbone at close range was tantamount to someone lending you a time machine and setting it for *"221B, BAKER STREET, VICTORIAN LONDON FEBRUARY 9, 1895."* Yes, I was about to see my hero at hopefully close range.

I accepted Bill's invitation without hesitating. By now I'd learned to trust in W.T. Rabe's abilities to get to the thick of things, like a passenger finding the best seat on the train. On that score then my expectations were quite naturally high, coming as they did on the heels of the magician's most recent feat, conjured the previous autumn. That time had been heralded by the question, "would you like to see the Beatles?" *Well, did Sherlock Holmes enjoy a pipeful of shag?*

And then of course there is the matter of that conflict I mentioned a moment ago. For you see, not only was the evening of February 9, 1964 to be associated with Basil Rathbone's special appearance in Detroit. Something else was also in the works, and it had to do with four of his British contemporaries. That's right. The Beatles making their own special appearance in New York. And as every card-carrying teenager knew, they were going to appear on the Ed Sullivan Show—*Sunday night—February 9.*

That's right, friends. I felt as if we were talking about two ships colliding in the night. For on February 9 and in living color in Detroit, as opposed to the black and white broadcast of Mr. Sullivan's show beamed in from New York, Basil Rathbone was going to take the stage at Mercy College. And I was going to be in his audience. Had I not had the opportunity, and were the very idea of "Sherlock Holmes" coming to the Motor City not a prospect, I would have been at home, glued before the old Motorola. *Yeah, yeah, yeah.*

Now as one grows older he learns rather rapidly the difficulty of being in two places at one time. That was my dilemma on that February night in question. How to see Basil Rathbone and still see or hear the Beatles? The answer to the question seemed obvious, but was also fraught with difficulties of a prospectively technical nature.

I was committed and eager and prepared to see Basil Rathbone in the flesh. But as for the Beatles? Who knew if that chance would ever come? For now, however I elected to witness their televised debut after-the-fact. I would tape record their appearance on the Sullivan show.

Younger readers may be compelled to understand that "back in the/my day," one could not DVR a televised performance. Nor, until another old-fashioned point in time could they make a videotaped copy of what had gone out "live." Ergo, and given the status of the stone age of media when we were younger, a tape recorder was akin to being state-of-the-art. And in my case, and very similar to my being fortunate enough to have taken a Polaroid to the Irregulars fete, I did possess a rather sizable Webcor tape recorder at home.

No tech wizard I, but in contrast my beloved mother's skills in elementary electronics were akin to her manning a NASA interstellar craft. But imagine my trying to explain to that good woman, again and again and again, that at the given moment on the Sullivan show, she must press this button and also the one marked RECORD. Successfully managed, this technical feat would complete the mission of acquiring a captured recording of John, Paul, George and Ringo in their momentous "live" performance. And if achieved, this would leave me free to accompany friend Rabe to the Mercy College performance of the Man Who Was Sherlock Holmes.

Everything about that evening did manage to work out rather well. As I discovered upon returning home, like Cinderella after the ball, Mom had followed my directions, and had even written them down. Just so, when Ed Sullivan said *And here they are—the Beatles,* she'd made the magical passes set down for her, and I got my Scotch Recording Tape of my musical heroes.

And as for my other, earlier hero? Suffice it to say I may have been just a tad disappointed that Mr. Rathbone made no mention whatsoever of Sherlock Holmes on the Mercy stage on that crowded Sunday night in early February. In point of fact his stage show focused upon the "great poets" and others. Interestingly too, and as I would discover years later, in his autobiographical memoir *In and Out of Character*, its author fondly alluded to his appearance in Detroit and at Mercy College. He also seemed to attribute his willingness to come to his fondness for a certain nun of his acquaintance. And like so many of us who have been inspired or cajoled by a good sister, so too did Rathbone agree to pay a call upon the Motor City on a chilly night in February of '64.

"An Evening With Basil Rathbone" was, as I say, notable for many reasons. First of all, its star offered a solo outing of performances culled from his apparent favorites of drama and poetry. Throughout, there was of course the man's own presence, unmistakable despite the passage of years. And while time had softly chiseled that brow and aquiline profile, there without doubt was the snappish papa in "Barretts of Wimpole Street," or the swashbuckling anti-hero of "Captain Blood" and "The Sea Hawk." There as well the snide Sheriff of Nottingham, and his later successor in the Roger Corman "Comedy of Terrors" and other Poeetical flicks.

But close your eyes and listen to that voice. It was that same which denigrated, cajoled, and summoned Nigel Bruce forth in that parade of wartime Holmes films. Yes, and the same Sherlock nevertheless who had earlier stalked the moors in "The Hound of the Baskervilles" and appeared in its prequel, "The Adventures of Sherlock Holmes" with George Zucco, Ida Lupino, and of course, Nigel Bruce. Aye, the very same figure in flesh and blood, now commanding a stage not many yards from where I'd sat entranced.

There was of course that other obvious element; chiefly the absence of any Sherlockian material in Rathbone's "Evening." Instead that time was populated by fascinating anecdotes and dramatic and recitations, all rendered by the man himself in those familiar vocal tones which millions had come to know and love.

After the theatrical performance there was a reception on the Mercy College campus. The meeting room was full and I followed Rabe through the crowds and to a reception line. When the time came, at last I got to shake the hand of Sherlock Holmes, and in moments manage to pronounce myself as awestruck. Yep, a satisfied customer. But there was little time for chat. This was a sort of command performance line for everyone to get their chance to touch a bit of old Hollywood. I wondered later if Mr. Rathbone regretted agreeing to follow his performance with a "meet and greet?" If so or not, by the time I moved along and looked back, I could see that he was tired. And I couldn't blame him. Nor could I know at the time of his supposedly rabid dislike for being appreciated as Holmes by fawning fans. The reason here had much to do with a lifetime's worth of work, yet being condemned to deliver the undoubtedly most famous of his scores of parts. Yes, forget the fact of his countless stage and screen appearances. Or even, as he had reminded his audience, that in playing the villain to Errol Flynn's heroic Captain Blood or Robin Hood, the fact remained that he, rather than Errol, was the far better swordsman.

"I could have dispatched him at any time" Rathbone had stated, which evoked an outburst of applause from his delighted listeners.

It also occurred to me in hindsight that Basil Rathbone's dislike for being "type-cast" in the public's mind was not so unlike Arthur Conan Doyle's dislike for his most logical, if not consuming of inventions. In that respect one could compare the actor's animosity for Holmes with the author's own. But unlike Rathbone, Sir Arthur got to kill that meddlesome sleuth off. Yes, pushed him off a Swiss precipice. And only later did he resurrect him, doubtless when the price of bringing Holmes back from the dead was right! And as a postscript here, so too did Basil Rathbone consent to appearing as Holmes later on, even to the point of burlesque. But after all, even famous actors need the paycheck, don't they?

But let us return to the conclusion of that evening at Mercy College.

There are times in one's life when something happens, or someone says something, or doesn't, which will later ring not only true, but appropriate. I had my own occasion for that on that evening. The reception for the star was winding down, while I, from my place across the room had kept my eagle eye fixed upon Basil Rathbone. For that reason, and after a short while, I noted that he appeared to have detached himself from the last of his adulators. Suddenly I saw him moving like a player edging down a field, unencumbered by his opponents and immediately free to make a run for freedom.

Now I found myself moving as well across the crowded room. My eyes were locked on my target as I did so, even to the point of watching the Great Man move to the coat-check and retrieve a rather large tweedy overcoat and his hat. It was *the hat.* Not the deerstalker, but the Irish Donegal, and seemingly the very same bit of headgear he had worn through the course of those dozen B-films designed for propaganda during the war. Perhaps it was his own hat. Or perhaps he had made it so over the course of time?

From a close distance and like a bloodhound trailing a target, I slowly closed in on my quarry. I watched as he approached the glass foyer doors, beyond which lay the snowy street and a chilly winter's night filled with steaming traffic. But as I drew even closer, I saw that Mr. Rathbone was now standing there, within the shell of the glass doors. *He's waiting for a taxi* I thought to myself. Or perhaps, and as might well have been likely, the evening's star was on the lookout for whatever transportation might get him back to his hotel?

In any event I felt my feet propelling me to that place now only yards away. And there, as if contained or feebly protected, or in essence, in full view of anyone coming up from behind, Basil Rathbone stood in statuesque form, looking like a 71-year old Sherlock Holmes attired in his soft tweed headgear, his hands stoved down into the deep pockets of his great coat.

My actions in the moments to follow seemed to have been choreographed. For now as I stepped forward I felt the cold brass handle of the glass door as I pulled it toward me. I recall that as I did so there appeared to be a kind of intake of air, as if a vacuum had been shattered, with the sound of that exhalation in the atmosphere. Now I was suddenly standing behind the tall figure who suddenly wheeled about.

In that instant one can only imagine the cinematic prospect of having followed Sherlock Holmes, only to have your quarry turn on you, his goshawk glare fierce, that beak of a nose scenting danger, his iron-firm jaw set. Or at least that was how it seemed in that frozen parade of seconds. What, if anything might that young pursuer have said?

"A long time from now and just as you played Sherlock Holmes, I'm going to portray his creator. And I will look like, sound like, and do everything I can to resemble Sir Arthur Conan Doyle."

But fortuitously I said nothing to the man standing in the vestibule.

Instead Rathbone looked at me with an expression which seemed a medley of frustration and anger and simple exhaustion. *Not another goddamned well-wisher. Not another gushing teen. Not...*

And then I finally spoke. When the words fell out of my mouth no one could have been more surprised than I myself. I heard a voice sounding much like my own saying *"Don't take the first cab, and don't take the second."* Thinking of it now I smile, because what I chose to say to my companion was an echo of something which Sherlock Holmes tells Dr. Watson. He's instructing him not "to take the first cab" on the street, lest it contain an enemy. And I more than suspected that Rathbone knew it too. And from the softened, momentary smile I received as I'd spoken it, he did

As if it were yesterday rather than half a century ago, that scene of a younger man and his older hero continues to be frozen for me in a kind of mental amber. And when I call upon it still it replays itself, like a clip from a beloved film.

In the moment it is as if we are both frozen in time and space. Rathbone's glare alters just a touch, like the snowman suddenly warmed. As he smiles that eagled gaze transforms and softens and the mouth which had once pronounced the solution to so many mysteries seems to open slightly but does not speak.

Now back away said a voice inside my head. *Back away and leave him in peace. And if you do, one day you will be glad you did. And you will remember this moment, and you will tell others what it felt like.*

Heeding my own advice, I took a step back and retreated through the glass door. And as if it had been timed or pre-arranged, I saw a car pull up to the curb and watched as the living embodiment of Mr. Sherlock Holmes approached it, opened its door, and climbed in. In a trice they were both gone. And I was left there in the lobby. Alone. But glad. And possessed of a memory that would last a lifetime and possibly longer.

Editorial note: *There is perhaps nothing so edifying to clarity of thought than starvation. Mr. Holmes knew this for certain, and even as he expounded at the conclusion of "The Dying Detective." To wit, this observation, written during the course of a "cleansing" phase, days away from a scheduled colonoscopy. And the case in point here? It has to do with the aforementioned passage concerning my youthful "moment" with Mr. Rathbone. Moreover, I wish now to address the context of my injunction to him not to take either "the first" or "second" cab.*

As I say, while in the throes of two day's absence of solid sustenance, I made a rather clear-headed deduction; to wit, my comment to Mr. Rathbone regarding cabs was astute, but where the deuce had it come from? Curious, I set to work on finding the quotation and its source within the Canon. Here however and drawing a blank, I set to seeking an answer on the computer, courtesy of my colleague Mr. Google. He however could not help overmuch. So then, re-phrasing my question three times, to wit: "Where in the Sherlock Holmes stories does the detective tell someone not to take 'the first cab?' I found a clue. This in the suggestion that the line was actually to be found in P.G. Wodehouse's novel Psmith, Journalist. There the protagonist allegedly says, "as Sherlock Holmes told Dr. Watson, 'do not take the first, or the second cab." However, closer in theory to my source, I wondered "where and when did Holmes say that?" Applying myself to the problem, I decided to go, as S.H. often does, to "good old Index," in the contemporary incarnation of my colleague Jon Lellenberg.

Keeper of the keys to many mysteries (for that was once his trade) Jon fired back to my e-mailed query, "it's not there. It's in the Gillette play."

And so it was. And after perusing through my 1946 edition of FAMOUS PLAYS OF CRIME AND DETECTION, I struck the gold I sought. This in William Gillette's adaptation, Act IV, Scene I, where the sleuth advises an allay, Parsons "My dear fellow—my dear fellow! In times like these you should tell your man never to take the first cab that comes on a call—nor yet the second—the third may be safe!"

86

Gillette! Well at least, I thought, the source was close enough to the Real Thing to matter. Better than, say, a pastiche, or even some jibe by Doyle's friends and parodists, Jerome or Bangs.

But this was not the end of the matter. For now, my food-starved cerebrations also compelled me to ask myself, "when by 1965 had my 18-year-old self seen or read William Gillette's "Sherlock Holmes?" Good question. Because to the best of my recollection, I did not see the play dramatized in person until 1979. Moreover, although I had some privy access to William Gillette, via my friend Rabe's LP collection, "Voices From Baker Street" (which actually included a rare snippet of Gillette speaking lines from his adapted work) the much-sought "cab" remark was not to be found there.

So then, compelled to ask myself, "did you really say this to Basil Rathbone?" or did you transpose the comment later, retroactively in memory? I have struggled with this, before coming to the resolution that indeed, I made the remark.

And here is the most meaningful post-script to my aforementioned query. Still feeling at sixes-and-nines about the "second cab" quotation, I put the question to the one man I ought to have vetted it with to begin. Here was my colleague and first publisher of this memoir, George Vanderburgh.

I presented George with my manuscript's conundrum and shortly after he simply smiled and said, casually enough, "The Final Problem."

Hearing this, I thought to myself, "wouldn't it be nice if it were that easy?" However later that afternoon and with access to my weathered copy of the Illustrated Sherlock Holmes, *I thumbed to the appropriate tale. Within moments I struck gold.*

"In the morning you will send for a hansom, desiring your man to take neither the first nor the second which may present itself." *So advises Holmes to his faithful friend as they prepare for the Continent. Curious as well, it's a fact that the corner of the page upon which the elusive admonition was printed had been turned down! But as to the "how?" of the thing, I cannot say, apart from thinking, "that young chap possessed a strangely keen memory for things. And thank God, I muse, he still does!*

But let us now move from "Basil" to "the Beatles," shall we?

As everyone had heard in the autumn of '64, the Beatles were making a cross-country tour of America and were to perform at Detroit's Olympia Stadium on September 6. And just as other members of my teenaged tribe at Berkley High School were well aware, anything resembling a chance to see the Fab Four in person was akin to Christmas, summer vacation and your Birthday rolled into one. So it was that I was probably as quick as Wiley Coyote in replying to my friend's question: *"Would you like to see the Beatles?"* Answer: *"I would love to see the Beatles."*

To make a very much longer story short, I accompanied Bill Rabe and a couple of crew members to the backstage area of Detroit's legendary hockey and performance venue, Olympia Stadium. And at a given point I did in fact see that incredible quartet at close range. But better than that. In point of fact, the table at which John, Paul, George and Ringo were to sit had been marked with placards. And in true Rabe-esque fashion, before each of those four seats there was a large paper cup and a pitcher of hot tea. Unsurprisingly, then, when the popular quartet of rock minstrels took their places, each of them savored their "cuppa," courtesy of W.T. Rabe.

Oh and there was of course the rest of the table's staging. For beside the guests of honor at table's end were Bill Rabe and myself. That fact was preserved a thousand times by shutters clicking away and tv cameras present, and by one gentleman employed by *The Detroit Free Press* named Tony Spina. A Pulitzer Prize winning photographer, Spina's pictures of the Kennedy Inaugural and a score of other historic images had garnered international attention. But on that late afternoon in early September, his subjects were about to be immortalized, and Messrs. Rabe and McPherson beside them (in the uncropped versions, at least).

That then was how I got to shake hands with the boys from Liverpool, if not to aim a portable tape recorder mike at my heroes. Rabe took a picture of my doing that from over the shoulders of one of the lads, and that picture boldly appeared in my high school newspaper, *The Berkley Spectator*, for which I was an editor. And that picture, along with the cover story's image, of John, Paul, John, George, Ringo, Bill and Mark, gave "proof of life" to the claim that I had indeed met the Beatles.

I recall other touches which were reminiscent of that backstage press conference. The first was that Rabe wisely collected each Beatle cup and labeled them appropriately. I heard a rumor (I think from him) that his kids eventually showed the Spina picture to their friends, and sold replicas of those tea-cups many times over! I also recall the scene of madness, after being privileged to watch the Beatles' concert, when we left the building, passing by crowds of outgoing girls who not long before had sat, jumped, screamed and cried on seeing their fondest dreams in the flesh. Upon asking us if we'd been near their idols, when one of us had foolishly nodded, some of the fans made a point of touching and caressing and slapping every bit of equipment on the dolly, if only to make contact with their untouchable heart-throbs.

I also distinctly recall, on seeing the musicians on stage from a "stage left" position nearby, that after Ringo hit his first drum-beat, the din of the crowd grew so shrill and high-pitched that all sound was reduced to a kind of high-pitched whine. It reminded me of photographs I'd seen of their other concerts, at which police had inserted bullets in their ears to plug out the high-decibel noise.

I'd say practically any American teenager alive at the time would probably agree with my excitement of seeing, hearing, and even getting to chat briefly with the Beatles. Oddly, that energy had not dissipated twenty-six years ago when I came across a newly-published volume entitled *Beatles '64: A Hard Day's Night In America*. As you might guess, this was a compendium of the quartet's concert schedule that year. Upon thumbing through it, I found the Olympia Stadium, Detroit citation, which included only a picture of Paul McCartney. Earlier however, and auspiciously perhaps on August 24, which was my birthday, the section on Los Angeles included a backstage close-up of the Beatles simply labeled "Detroit." In it were those famous lads with Bill Rabe at table's end. However and on the next page, another photo view from behind the boys, in which my companion and myself are quite visible in the shadows! Here then was an image I'd never seen that featured not only the Fab Four, but also the two fellows at the table's end: *Rabe and I.*

89

So go ahead and try imagining what it's like to view, for the first time in your life, a picture taken twenty-five years earlier of yourself and arguably the most famous rock and roll group in history. I believe the generationally correct reply here might well be "Far Out" or even further!

And that was how magic had seemingly happened, or happened to me in 1964 when I chanced to meet not only Basil Rathbone, but also a quartet of his younger countrymen, known as–The Beatles.

7
Appendix Lost, Heart-Throb Found

Among the trove of memories within this collection, as I now look back upon them from the futured vantage of 2021, a few loom gigantically and as incredibly special. No doubt one's chronological perspective has to figure in, even as I look down upon the exploits of that youth from Berkley back within the Summer of Love known as 1967.

Further, and also like so many who will populate these pages who were alive when my words were set down, their majority are now gone. But not so much "departed" as I see it, as more likely "simply needed elsewhere." But in common those blithe spirits have left in the rain-bowed slipstreams of their beings an incredible tapestry of words and images. And I, lucky sod that I am, got to share an instant of space with them.

And now, viewed from my much-weathered perspective, I can't help but to find myself thinking of the lady who was to play a key part in my initial journey to Great Britain. In strictly Sherlockian terms I suppose you could say that for me, she was "The Woman." For this, my friends, was the late Dame Diana Rigg, whose passing this last year, like that of Sir Sean Connery, marked a kind of indirect benchmark in the creative life of Yours Truly. Which is to re-state, rather like the truest embodiment of James Bond, the physical presentiment of "Mrs. Emma Peel" of Avengers fame and more, leaves me with a tug in the region of the heart. As did, seemingly a few moments ago, did the passing of Patrick Macnee, aka "John Steed," from the confining bonds of this mortal coil. He too was extremely kind when we met, and shared this once-younger American's passion for that seductively red-headed vixen whom he always called "Di."

But for myself? Diana Rigg will always be the same purple cat-suited and nubile 28-year-old lightly freckled beauty who once smiled and congratulated me upon being ingenious enough to figure out a way to meet her. (And all that had taken was my managing to be stricken with a sudden case of appendicitis!)

So then, after what I might dare to call "The Adventure of the Cab-Seeking Actor," I found myself excited over and over again at what had constituted my actualized "meeting with Sherlock Holmes." And like Moses come down from the mountain, the parade of days that followed were full of the memory of Basil Rathbone's performance, of his handshake, and of course of that final, most private of moments which we had shared.

In typical fashion as well, and very much akin to Bill Rabe's presentation to me of photos of myself with the Beatles many months earlier, now and true to form he had another bit of memorabilia for me. This, in the form of a glossy eight by ten print of a scene from "The Adventures of Sherlock Holmes." It was the iconic moment when Holmes stands with a youthful looking Watson before the headless statue, recently decapitated by the villainous J. Carrol Naishe's Argentinian *bolo.*

The photograph suddenly in my possession was notable as well for the fact that it was autographed by Basil Rathbone. But not merely once. No, for a piece of paper adhered to the bottom left of the picture, reading *Basil Rathbone,* and across the upper torso of the headless statue the inked semi-inscription read *Basil Rath.* Incredibly as well, the reverse side of the photograph also bore the actor's full signature. In other words, a thrice-autographed picture of Basil Rathbone as Sherlock Holmes! Quite the rarity. At the time I was full of wonder and gratitude to the individual who had managed to secure this bit of the True Cross for me. In fact, I still feel the rush of excitement which flushed over me when Bill Rabe bestowed his gift. In fact, and once again, as I am writing these words, I am able to swivel around and to see the picture in its silver frame. And to think to myself about my great good fortune all those years ago at being in the right place at the right time. And no doubt of my having been befriended by the right fellow. On such a basis then, it must be stated that rather obviously this memoir is at heart an *homage* to not only Sherlock Holmes, but also to those people and places who metaphorically managed to stamp my passport for "Baker Street." W. T. Rabe was certainly one of those. *So thanks, Bill.*

Throughout the days which followed my new baptism into the Gospel of Watson, I steeped myself in new ventures. I began to read omnivorously, to use the canonical term, and to collect. Before long my once vacant shelves were groaning. I also took an interest in the "writings about the writings." Doubtless Baring-Gould's master-work

92

had shown me the value of parlaying what needed to be an almost encyclopedic knowledge of the finer points within the sixty Doylean (Watsonian) titles. In this fashion I also subscribed not only to *The Baker Street Journal,* but also to its British counterpart, courtesy of The Sherlock Holmes Society of London. My correspondence began to branch out as well. And after daring to introduce myself to such as Dr. Julian Wolfe, the Irregulars Commissionaire (and chief sparking plug), and to follow up with Shaw, Blau, Harris, McLaughlin and others, I sent my *missives* further afield. Next thing I was receiving Christmas cards from the Marquis of Donegal, the titular head of the UK's major Holmesian scion.

Meanwhile, my "apprenticeship" to Bill Rabe took on many dimensions. More than simply accompanying, I hoped to be of value in a practical way. Perhaps I was to some slight extent, helping him as I did with updating his *1962 Who's Who and What's What.* He was even kind enough to not only give me a citation there, but to accord me a kind of co-editorial status with his *Commonplace Book*, an extensive press clipping compendium for all things Sherlockian.

Looked at in retrospect, I suppose I was preparing myself for something vaster, tho' I had no way of knowing it. Perhaps I gained an inkling after entering university in the autumn of 1965, and in turn busying myself with a host of other things beyond the ken of Baker Street.

But always the Anglophile in me responded to pertinent stimuli. Just so the notion of other stellar mystery figures, such as Sax Rohmer's Nayland Smith and Dorothy Sayers' Lord Peter Wimsey. There were others of course who constituted a retinue of what one author eventually dubbed "The Rivals of Sherlock Holmes." Research began to inform me of the growing number of Sherlockian imitators which fell fast and steadily with the success of Conan Doyle's nearly serialized "adventures" in *The Strand Magazine.*

I maintained contact with Bill Rabe, but now from a gradually escalating distance. Which is not to say a bad thing, exactly. Truth to tell, it is doubtless a reality that children grow older, and as they do become taken up with their expanding mind-sets, as well as their personal worlds. Nevertheless, Rabe's influence was contagious and felt by most within his range. That circle now included my parents as well, and for a very particular if not alarming reason in the summer of 1967.

That so-called Summer of Love in '67 was the occasion when I found myself on the brink of visiting Great Britain, the land of my dreams. The means for doing so involved my participation within a Michigan State University American Language Education Center (AMLEC) extension program. Reflecting my declared major at MSU in political science, the theory was that I would have the great chance of studying comparative political systems where the Mother of all Parliaments had been created. First however, my exotic future itinerary would commence with a couple of days in Paris. After that a boat crossing over the English Channel, and at Dover I would be ready to make my move landward.

But before I made my first Atlantic crossing, I was compelled to honor a promise to my parents. I needed to make some money, so it was agreed that I would spend several weeks doing exactly that. Boldly, foolishly, loyally, I'd announced to my father that I wanted to "hire on" at Ford Motor Company—but not as the boss's son. You see, at that point in my Dad's automotive career, he had risen from fledgling welder before the war to foreman and eventually, to his place as Assistant Plant Manager For Maintenance at the Ford Motor Dearborn Assembly Plant.

As I say, I wanted to earn my pay the hard way. And I did. I loaded fender sections on the Afternoon Shift, which was a grueling, dead-from-the-neck-up way to collect a check. In fact, I recall a gentleman telling me later that he'd met his son's reluctant jibe about not going to college with a tour of the Rouge Stamping Plant.

"I took him to the loudest, dirtiest part of the plant, and said to him, 'if this is what you want to spend your life doing instead of college, go ahead.' But after surveying that war-zone, my boy announced he'd had a change of heart." Obviously imagining yourself getting older in those Satanic mills was its own negative incentive, I thought.

But George R. McPherson's boy was now in the thick of it. Working shifts, taking breaks with the other inmates, and wondering if the summer was ever going to move ahead? I remember being told by one of my co-workers, an old Maltese fellow who was veteran of the plant, that there was a rumor going that I was "G. McPherson's son."

"Me? I said. "Don't be ridiculous." Suddenly I felt like a mixture of St. Peter denying and Sherlock Holmes trying to stay within the character of a disguise.

My comment was met by a nod of that grizzled Maltese head, and the response, "you're right, McPherson's kid is probably studying in Europe at some fancy school." *Close, but no cigar, sir, I mused.*

Looking back now, when I got to it on the event horizon, I don't remember approaching the grand trip abroad as Yankees of the 19th century or earlier might have. In other words, devoid of any idea of making the transatlantic trek and "conquering" England. No, a Norman king named William had already done that nine centuries earlier. Fortunately as well for me, I suppose, neither had I any predilection about my being the one conquered. Some things you aren't just meant to know. In that regard I would be taking my blows soon enough.

And then came the time of departure I recall experiencing a fatalistic sense that being this close to seeing the land of my dreams, something was going to intervene to prevent it. In fact, so worried did I become that I insisted to my mother on the way to Metropolitan Airport that she take some extra flight insurance on her only son. Yes, I had that level of a premonition, but a good deal of my unease involved not knowing exactly why.

And then came lift-off, the journey over the water, and next morning, my first bird's eye glimpse of a country other than my own.

France was not England, and our arrival at Orly Airport and thence into the city was a bit of a crush. Years of high school and college Spanish did little to assist me to understanding the officials, the signs, or the occasional rudeness of certain of those DeGaullist locals. Suffice it to say that the account of my Parisian sojourn will go untold here, rather like Sherlock Holmes' real hiatus, or Watson's account of the Giant Rat of Sumatra.

I will commence after the Dover crossing and a hurly-burly nautical voyage of a couple of hours which, like some discourteous Europeans also on board, left me a bit confused and unsettled. This, I thought at the time, was not the way to make my grand arrival to the land of King Arthur and Sherlock Holmes. Therefore I vowed to make good use of my time when the train carried me to Victoria Station and to that juncture of the trip which had been pre-arranged. I was curious about my lodgings, and as it turned out, rather rightfully so.

I was directed by AMLEC personnel to the coordinates of my local destination. This proved to be a suburb of London called Forest Hill. Superficially a rather ordinary, albeit British version of a suburban community, with streets full of late Victorian or Edwardian structures with small lawns and postage sized "gardens" behind, I was ready to blend in. Little did I suspect however that if I had any apprehensions about being a young stranger in a strange land, there was also an equal sense of resistance in the offing.

I was prepared to adjust to my new "digs" as the Brits say. This as I rapidly discovered on knocking upon that smallish green door, involved being hosted by a late-middle aged British couple. Quite honestly, I'm ashamed that my memory does not allow recall of their surname. So for convenience I'll call them the Browns. Our repartee began at once when Mr. Brown surveyed my companion (there were two of us as AMLEC 'guests') and me on his doorstep and remarked that we looked nothing at all as he had expected. When asked what that image might be, he replied by vividly describing a large cigar-smoking fellow in a Panama hat. Obviously Mr. B.'s exposure to my own countrymen were as limited as my own to his.

Sadly or not, we never had much chance to get to know the Browns. Don't know why, exactly. I didn't smoke big cigars then, and I remember being told that my twenty-year old, clean-cut, somewhat shy self brooked no obvious reasons to offend. There may have been something about my fellow-traveler's demeanor. He was, as I recall, a bit brusque, if not self-preoccupied. He'd said a couple of things to me which I let go by. Who knows what he might have managed in the name of reversing US/UK international relations? Nevertheless, it was not a love match for reasons mysterious as well as known. As for one of the latter, and at the risk of sounding rather coddled or rigid here, I'll give you one example from my perspective to judge upon. It had to do with my first English breakfast.

Now when I use the term "rigid" it might well have been reserved for Mrs. B.'s morning table. For there as I discovered from Day One, was something I hadn't planned on, and frankly, haven't seen since. Clue: it involved the toast rack. Answer: as my colleague and I discovered with quick astonishment, our hostess apparently thought it right to make the morning's toast the night before. Ergo, by the time one sat down to break his fast, what stood up in Ye Olde Toast Rack could have been used to re-roof the house. Not exactly a crime against Queen and Country, I suppose, but certainly something new.

As I say, and even as I remain to this day uncertain as to the reason, the Brown's young American guests were notified that they would be moving on. Gratefully for me it was to two other and separated destinations. I don't know where my rude friend went, nor did I care. But as for me, I was to trade the sameness of Forest Hill for the charms of Dulwich. As my guidebook also informed me, this bit of English greenery, toll-gate and all, was reputed to be "the last hamlet in Britain." But there was something else in the back of my mind which suggested a kind of serendipitous connection to Dulwich. But what?

My "transfer" to a larger house with a set of friendly, humorous and overall pleasanter owners, was tempered by the additional fact that their large dwelling was also populated by a set of other foreign students. I recall a Norwegian fellow and a German boy, and two girls. Of that couple, I was smitten somewhat dumb by the short-haired Aryan beauty I'll call Astrid. *Not bad. No, young master, not bad at all.*

And now it is time to talk about Lord Byron and I.

From the time I'd been at university and even earlier, one of my other great interests was the life and works of Lord Byron. Don't know why, exactly. Truth to tell, countless years earlier I'd seen a British film starring Dennis Price as the debauched poet in "The Trials of Lord Byron." After that, who knows? Perhaps this young limping lord's near tragic romantic sensibilities reminded me of my own? At any rate, one of my intentions upon arriving in Britain was to visit Newstead Abbey, Byron's ancestral home in Nottinghamshire, in what tourists are also told is "Robin Hood Country."

So even as I'd made my fantasy plan to visit Newstead, suddenly there I was in Dulwich, where, according to certain sources, the young

Scottish laird had attended something called Dr. Glennie's Academy. But as to what exactly, and where precisely the Academy had been? No one seemed to know. I vowed to put on my invisible deerstalker and find out. And now, there I was, probably about to walk the same lanes and avenues and forest-clad venues as my idol.

But as I settled down with my AMLEC classes, I used my generous free time to wile and wander. I marveled at the beauties of the hamlet, as well as the grounds of its old college and famous art gallery. The former had been established as an "alm" by the Elizabethan actor and Shakespearean contemporary, Edward Alleyn. Yes I rambled about, found many interesting things, and met some very nice people. But at the end of the day I always seemed to wind up at the local pub on the green, the Grove Tavern, nursing a half-pint (I was a novice tippler back then) as I conjured plans for my "Byronic Adventure."

Meeting my fantasies head on, I finally made the move on Newstead Abbey one morning. A pleasant train journey brought me to within a bow-shot of Sherwood Forest and Nottingham. There the town was dominated by an imposing and cavernous place, seemingly older than Robin or his medieval Sheriff. At its foot stood another pub. This one named "Ye Olde Trip To Jerusalem." It was a Crusader watering hole, according to local tradition. I therefore paid it the proper attention and then looked for a bus to carry me to the gates of Lord Byron's ancestral country home.

Newstead was where the Byrons had lived, died, and according to local experts, still haunted the forested and ruined prioried premises. It was also there that the young "mad, bad, and dangerous to know" George Byron spent a decadent chapter or two of his youth. Yes there at Newstead he cavorted, and indulged in those passions of a lifetime. For instance, chasing skirts, toasting out of a goblet made of a monk's excavated skull, and dashing off poetic thoughts, such as "let us have wine, women, mirth and laughter—sermons and soda water later." Or roaming through the dusky corridors of the ruined abbey, if only in search of the spectral and hooded ghosts said to manifest. Also cavorting with his Newfoundland hound, Boatswain. Sadly however, his canine friend died unexpectedly, and his lordly master had him buried with an appropriately poetic monument. Further, he announced to one and all that when his time came, George wanted to be bricked up with his loyal companion Boatswain. But "sadder things of sword and pen" and all that.

I suppose that among a short list of places, Newstead's Abbey site and ancient family manse was the one place, I felt prone to encounter my own Byronic haunting. As things turned out, I had my innings there, and elsewhere, and the story is, I presume to think, worth telling.

The day I first visited Newstead Abbey it was suitably bleak and threatened by intermittent rain-showers. On remembering it, I can't presently think of a better way of describing the place than "it looks like an archaic landscape in a black and white photo." But as you will see, there is perhaps an intuitive reason for that, too.

I remember feeling as if my short bus ride and arrival was a kind of homecoming. Remember, I was twenty at the time, more romantic than now, and if anything, I had chosen to summon up an impossible kinship with the late Lord Byron. Or was it improbable?

There were a few tourists and other doddlers present that early afternoon. One couple served my purpose when I requested that I be photographed sitting on the plinth of Boatswain's grave. Yes, even as I sat unaware of my own future share of to-be-lamented feline and canine friends.

Meanwhile I cajoled a passing stranger to snap a picture of myself, reposing on tomb's border, where doubtless the Newfoundland's sad master had also sat. Yes, and perhaps reciting the lines he'd specially composed in honor of his absent friend.

> *"...When all is done, upon the tomb is seen,*
> *Not what he was, but what he should have been:*
> *But the poor dog, in life the firmest friend,*
> *The first to welcome, foremost to defend*
> *Whose honest heart is still his master's own,*
> *Who labours, fights, lives, breathes for him alone..."*

Those lines in Byron's "Inscription On The Monument Of A Newfoundland Dog" speak the sort of volumes which countless dog lovers would recognize. In fact, as I originally penned these lines my own Boatswain, Bradbury, is barking at some sort of summer movement beyond the front porch's balusters. And coincidentally enough, this day as I annotate my manuscript, happens to be National Dog Appreciation Day. I swear it.

I knew the story and carried its memory with me there, to that octagonal, urn-capped tomb wherein lay the mortal remains of a faithful friend. Yes there, almost in reach of the ruined priory archway that connected to the house, and the room I would discover young George Gordon had chosen, if only for its strange provenance. You see, he believed in the old stories of Newstead's phantom monks, one of whom was supposed to have dwelt where, or near the place the poet chose for his own more temporary rest. And as for something more eternal, it's said that his Lordship had stated that after his own final breath, he wished to be interred with Boatswain. But that did not happen. Instead the Sixth hereditary lord expired in Greece at age 35. He was brought home to England, and refused repose where Westminster Abbey's poetic royals rest, he was buried not far from Newstead, in a country graveyard vault at Hucknall Torkard. But given that proximity, and if indeed spirits are allowed to roam far afield, like Marley's Ghost, who's to say that Boatswain and his owner do not prowl their ancestral grounds? I should like to think so, at any rate.

Newstead's great hall and corridors and other suitably Gothic interiors were suited to my mood that day. And upon entering Byron's bedroom with its four-poster and windows looking out toward the park and lake and also the shell of its bygone chapel, I did not seem to feel the owner's spectral presence. However I continued to take pictures during my visit. Coincidentally or not, the one shot in the bedroom did display an arced band of light when developed. Had I been wrong in thinking myself alone in that lordly chamber?

Before leaving the grounds I also chronicled my visit with exterior shots of Newstead's panoramic presence. The lake before it was an obsidian mirror, and the woods framing the manse and its grounds hovered like dark gauntlets holding the place within their timeless grip.

The next day, still full of my Byronic mood, I paid an impromptu visit to London's Portobello Road and its fabled antique market. Not quite the veteran flea marketer I would become, back then I merely went in search of treasure. During that first stay in Britain I would return to purchase a rather smelly coat which seemed redolent of Carnaby Street and also an unworking Swiss watch in its brass hunter case, the style of which allowed one to flip the lid and also to peel down the back to inspect the works. Last of all and toward a better, more usable purpose, I purchased a Malacca and ivory fitted sword-stick. This purchase thrilled me more than those others, for pin-pointed at the haft of the silver blade were two unmistakable initials: "*M M.*" I took that to be an omen, and given my Christian and surnames, who wouldn't? And as unbelievable as my story seems, as His Lordship himself once remarked, "tis strange, but true." Come by sometime and I'll show you my sword-stick.

And speaking of concealed cold steel, there's also a retroactive and Sherlockian post-script to this part of my account concerning how I found my lethal walking stick. Forty-three years later in the Robert Downey film "Sherlock Holmes," Dr. Watson's (Jude Law's) weapon of choice is a sword cane, which is about a 95% replication of my Portobello Road acquisition. Coincidence? Or what about my unremembered, and recently rediscovered recollection, upon seeing my walking stick in the 1985 Spielberg film "Young Sherlock Holmes?" There however, the hidden blade was wielded, not by Watson, but by Holmes' fencing master and the man who became at movie's end "Moriarty." And last but not least, that same sword-cane appeared in a later "Avengers" Jack the Ripper-themed episode. Entitled "Fog."

But if there was a strange blend serendipity following me that week, if not and a Byronic overtone of it to boot, consider dear reader, what the next day at Portobello presented. I can only account for it as simply as it occurred. You see, I was strolling down some lanes chock-a-block with boxes and crates and walking up to one on my right, slightly higher than the top of my head, unaccountably I raised my arm and reached over the edge. My fingers brailed the contents, which felt like a frame. Moving closer, I gripped its edge and withdrew the object.

My heart went like a war gong when I saw what I had retrieved. It was indeed a wooden mahogany picture frame, and behind its old glass my eyes registered a familiar sight: *it was Lord Byron's ancestral home, Newstead Abbey!* And even to my untrained eye, I could tell it was old. 19th century, at least.

Now feel free to compute the odds for or against what took place in those moments as I'd paused before that mountain of box-work. Or of my instinctual need to reach up and into one of those containers. Or of finding what I did—and what it was. Magic is the only word that came to my mind that day in 1967, and it remains the best description for that event even now.

But pause another moment. There is more to come.

The following day, two after I visited Nottinghamshire, I was strolling down what passed for Dulwich's main street, feeling aimless and indisposed to attend that afternoon's class in comparative British and German politics. So instead I'd set myself on one of those brief rambles which I'd come to enjoy, and particularly so at this early morning hour.

Shops were open and just opening as I aimed my way to a bookseller, unvisited until now. Walking into the shop, I took in the welcoming shelves, and a few moments later bid the proprietor, a rather pleasant faced elderly lady, a good morning. She responded in equal fashion and disappeared through a curtain to the back of the store. But as I was studying her inventory she reappeared perhaps five minutes later, and with a request.

"I wonder if I might impose upon you?" she asked.

"Of course" I smiled. "What would you like?"

"Well, it is the greatest imposition, but I was just putting a pot of tea on and realized that I was out of milk. There is a shop just down the lane, but I do not want to close up, or leave the place unattended, and…"

"I would be glad to stroll down for the milk" I replied.

"Are you absolutely certain it's not too much to ask?"

"Absolutely not" I answered, and before I could counter her gesture, the lady held out a pound note for me to use in making her purchase.

The long and short of things is this: I went down the lane, purchased a bottle of milk, returned with it, handed it over, and was in turn invited by the lady to join her for a cup of tea. I accepted. And it was then that those inaudible magical gears must have re-commenced their motion.

Being so early, and with her curtain pulled back, the proprietress and I were able to sit down at a table in her library-like back room, with a view to glimpsing any other prospective customer. We chatted amiably, she asked about "my situation" in being in Britain. I told her about the political science program and my studies, and of my excitement in visiting her country. She asked in turn what I liked about its literature. And without hesitation, I spoke that single and magical password: *Byron*. Then I went on to regale her with a description of my recent trip to Newstead, and even the more recent and rather uncanny business of my finding a print of the house and grounds at the antiques market only yesterday.

The proprietress listened to me with a strange smile flirting upon her lips. And some while after the lady got up, excused herself, and said "Wait here. I have something to show you."

When she returned she held out a rectangular cardboard box. From it she withdrew a tanned, seemingly cardboard covered volume, the spine of which appeared to be chipping away with time. Accepting it, I studied the label upon that spine, which read *Don Juan, Cantos VII, VIII, 9s.6d.*

"Do you like it?" she asked me. "It's part of the first edition of Byron's *Don Juan.*" I recall her pronouncing the Spanish name "Joo-an" the way British considerations of Cervante's *Don Quixote* often described that masterpiece as "Kwix-oat."

"It's wonderful" I whispered, carefully perusing its pages before handing it back. "A real treasure."

'It is, in a way, but not really to me" the lady continued. "I acquired it a bit ago, but I don't have your—associations for its author. What would you give for it?"

I answered with an explanation which no doubt sounded like an apology. Something to do with my being an impoverished American student. It was then that she made her businesswoman's overture.

"Would you give me five pounds for it?" she inquired.

Five pounds. Mental calculations made that $13.95 US currency.

"Of course I would" I retorted. "But surely this is worth much more."

"Quite honestly, I think you should have it" my companion answered. "Given your recent adventures, it would be a perfect way to conclude your visit, don't you think? So if we are agreed, it's five pounds."

I finished my tea, received my purchase in its box and a bag. I was also informed that "should you be interested in the provenance of this edition, you could take it to Foyles in town." Further, she indicated that there was a catalog description within the box which might add to my enjoyment of my first first edition.

I left the shop that morning on a cushion of air. Also, noting that I was still early for my class, I hopped on a bus into London proper, and set my course for Foyles, the great antiquarian book emporium.

While I passed the time during the brief bus-ride into town, I opened the bag and from the dusty box. Then I retrieved the page of catalogue documentation. I saw there that the volume in question described the "uncut set" of Lord Byron's classic. All of the 16 cantos were listed, and a small leaded mark was placed beside Cantos 6-8. But what I discovered next seemed to rivet me in my vibrating seat. For in penciled handwriting a notation had been made at the bottom of the single page from some firm called "Maggs Bros. Ltd. London." The penciled inscription said, "*Nov. 1937. High price due to scarcity of Cantos I & II, according to Hodgkins, to whom I showed my 6-8 in Oct. 1945.*"

1937. 1945. I considered those years. Apparently this edition containing Cantos 6-8, published by John Hunt in 1823, the year before Byron's death. *In other words, the present article had been in its owner's possession for 30 years!* Ergo, it had not, as the lady herself had informed me, been "acquired recently." And now once again I heard the phantom-like echo of her voice, "*given your recent adventures, it would be a perfect way to conclude your visit…*"

And yes, as I then thought and still do, *Dear madam, it certainly was.*

That brief and shining moment in London and its environs in the summer of 1967 in Swinging London went spinningly, if not and winningly for me. My classes weren't over-challenging, and probably so given the fact that they were only the means toward the end of getting me to Camelot and Baker Street and Dickens' house and Dr. Johnson's as well. Of seeing Westminster Abbey and Parliament and the National Gallery and the battlefield at Hastings and the British Museum, and then, what I suppose might well be called "My Set-back."

Even before trading Berkley, Michigan for London, England, my mother had presented me with a few volume's worth of worries. These included warnings that "you can't drink the water over there," "you can't drive over there," "you can't talk to strangers over there," and as for girls—well, I don't remember what she said exactly, but Mom always had a way of framing things in that department which encouraged her only son and heir to remember that "he who travels fastest travels alone." In other words, don't pick up any British hussies. And keep your traveler's checks safe in a money belt or something secure.

I also remember talking to Bill Rabe before going over. He had some suggestions about places to visit. More than that, it was a curt telephone version of "bon voyage" that sent me on my way.

After being in London and my pleasant little hamlet a week or two, I found myself wondering if I had not after all, violated one of my mother's vital tenets? This occurred to me when I was coming back from seeing a film in London one Friday evening. The picture was "Zulu," starring a very young Michael Caine. The plot being historically re-created involved an Alamo-like stand-off involving a handful of British soldiers and their fire-besieged garrison attacked by thousands of Zulu warriors at a place called Rorke's Drift. Their king and general, I seem to recall, was named Shaka.

I enjoyed the film, but not the ride home. For suddenly I was experiencing a weird sort of abdominal pain unlike any I'd ever known.

This immediately conjured my mother's voice like the Ghost of Hometown Past, Present and Future admonishing me with the chanted taunt, "you drank the water, didn't you?"

I suppose I'd violated most of my mother's strictures on the spot. Since arriving in London I sampled a good deal. Water or not, a pint of bitter, a touch of roast beef at Simpson's, or even a burger at the unfortunate

Wimpy's or better, a Big Mac at the newly opened British version of the Golden Arches in Piccadilly Circus.

But whatever the reason, on that night heading home the pain was definitely there. On my return to my digs I told my hosts about it, and they said if by the next day I didn't feel better, I could call a doctor they knew of. They gave me the number. And by the next day, now severely cramped, I used it. And then I took a taxi to his small "surgery" as they call them. And the gentleman examined me, and sent me home with, of all things, a box of suppositories! Now I'd never used one of those, been administered a suppository, and least of all, ever considered giving myself the treatment for any reason. But I did that too. *So much for new experiences.*

Now cut to the sight of me limping out of a bus the next day. And within that same hour to the doctor, advising me to telephone my friends or professors. Then to get myself to the hospital. *What?* The hospital. *And why? Because it seems your appendix is about to burst and it needs to be* removed.

The doctor's diagnosis hit me like a Louisville Slugger to the back of the head. *Appendix bursting? Removal? As in surgery? Too right, my friend.*

And here's what followed as concisely as we can state it. I took a cab to the hospital. I checked in. Was placed in the emergency room in a small chamber where I was strapped (notwithstanding my now rather sensitive right side) into a gurney. I remember signing some papers. Then another room. Prepped for surgery. Then wheeled into the operating theatre, and before going out like the proverbial light, I was aware of a pleasant face craning down as I was wheeled in. It belonged to an American studying medicine over there. Great. And then things went dark.

I suppose if I dreamed or astral-projected while under the effects of the anesthetic, it might have had to do with reaching the folks at home. For you see, despite trying to call my parents over the transatlantic line, all I'd heard was the phone ringing. Back in those days there were no answering machines for the likes of us, and certainly no one else to take the message at 2665 Wakefield. So I decided to call my instructors. These consisted of at least four faculty friends I'd known from my tenure at State, and where I'd actually worked in the Humanities Department office, part-time. But no joy, as the Brits say, there either. All I could do therefore was to inform my Dulwich landlord and his lady that I was about to go under the knife. Which I did.

By the next day or the evening before it, I came to find myself in a hospital ward. One of the nursing "sisters" informed me that as soon as they'd brought me in from surgery I'd tried to climb out of bed and onto my feet. That, no doubt, because I knew I didn't belong in a hospital in England and especially not so when no living soul of family or friendship knew where the hell I was.

But it got better. My hosts contacted my instructors. My instructors contacted my parents. And my dear, put-upon and helpless mother and father could think of only one thing to do: *Call W.T. Rabe.*

And calling Bill Rabe made sense. After all, he was the closest thing to Sherlock Holmes as far as my folks were concerned. Well as I later found out, Bill did some checking and assured them I was going to be fine. Not much more than that, but doubtless he knew, as I would discover, that my impromptu appendectomy was done free-of-charge, and courtesy of the United Kingdom's National Health Plan. Yes, God Bless socialism. But best of all, and as I regaled countless listeners for years afterward, I now had *"Made In Britain"* engraved over my newly won abdominal scar!

And then of course another odd twist, reflecting as it seemed to, my pre-operative choice of films. I told you that I'd gone to see the action film, "Zulu," right? Well imagine my mood two days later. Propped up in my bed sipping a straw-ful of orange squash, I suddenly took note of the headline on the newspaper being read by the chap just across the aisle. Boldly, its mile high headline proclaimed the words
"DETROIT BURNS."

Clamoring to the nurses and making a sudden request to see his copy of the news, moments later I was reading the dire news for myself. Yes, Detroit was burning. Racial hatred had reached its apex. And the Riots of 1967 would go down as an indelible mark upon the future history of the Motor City.

Inevitably as well, I recall, from my transatlantic outpost I seemed to keep hearing the familiar lyric to the popular song running through my mind. 'Hot times, summer in the city.' And I remember wondering, there and supine in a hospital bed, my mind racing, would this recent insurrection serve as the sparking point for a powder keg detonating across America? All I knew for certain was that throughout that long hot Summer of '67, my homeland was seemingly the opposite of Swinging London and "The Summer of Love."

It's a strange feeling when you are told your distant, familiar world is coming apart. Inevitably I couldn't quite forestall the worry over what sort of chaos I might find when I returned home? Fortunately for most of us, and particularly the suburban dwellers of Berkley, Michigan, the nationally reported riots did not come within range of our town. They did so in Detroit however. And there are some in our beleaguered city who even today continue to feel that Motown has never been quite the same ever since the flashpoint of '67.

My transatlantic adventures assumed a kind of Dickensian turn when the doctors informed me after a few days that I could be returned to Dulwich to recover, or sent to a rest-center, formerly a grand old British stately house, to recuperate. I chose the latter. And before you could say "Elementary, my dear Watson," I was transported into the Surrey countryside. And there indeed was the old house, staffed by a gaggle of young nurses waiting to meet me—for as it turned out I was the only patient within their age range! Good times. Lots of flirting and smiles, and even a short-sheeting of my bed once when I got a bit cocky. Wrong word, that. And then there was my only roommate, who pronounced early on that "this was no place for people like us." He was eighty, at least.

I enjoyed my time at the old manse in the country. All the more so when I'd learned that this was the very region where the so-called Surrey Puma had been sighted. That's right, a sort of feline version of the Baskerville Hound, which had been disparaged, rumored, but eventually photographed. And there I was, within a wood's worth of one of Great Britain's latest phantoms!

Upon eventually returning to my digs in Dulwich, I determined to make the best use of my time. The days of my stay were growing shorter, and I needed to tick off the other places on my list. Near the top of those was Stonehenge. And with that goal in mind, the game was once more afoot. I for my part was maybe a bit less fleeter on my feet. My side was pretty sore, and as I was duly informed, my incision had developed a mild infection. But none of that was enough to keep me from seeing the world's most famous set of standing stones.

Another train trip and a bus excursion and a short hike and I was there. The Salisbury Plain. And before me that Dance of Giants which legend insisted had been transported there by no less a one than Merlin, Camelot's arch-magician.

As at Newstead Abbey, I importuned a fellow tourist to snap my picture as I stood there, rail thin, in zip jacket, khaki jeans and desert boots, beneath the trilithon arch. I also scraped up four or five pieces of what had presumably come loose, from one of those megalithic pillars put into place by old Merlin. These I eventually preserved in a plastic box, along with the date of my securing them. The container is still on the table in my library. The small typewritten strip inside reads *"Fragments of Stonehenge-Salisbury Plain, Wiltshire, UK. Collected by M.M. 8/19/67."*

I was doing my best at this point in time like a wounded, albeit heatseeking missile aimed at my greatest of British fantasies. But I would be remiss not to regale you with one of the literally last miracles of that odd trip. It all had to do with a prediction I'd made in early June of that year. It had been uttered to my dispersing comrades in the House of Brutus in our dormitory at Michigan State University. I was often encouraged by my chums to "look her up" when I got to London. And the "her' in question was none other than the sexy British actress Diana Rigg, better known as "Emma Peel" in that popular dark adventure comedy known as "The Avengers." The boys all knew of my passion for Miss Rigg. Like myself, many of them reveled in each weekly installment of Britain's other most exciting export, in tandem with the "British invasion" in music, and even earlier, the exploits of Sean Connery, aka Agent 007.

However, something about the droll, somewhat eccentric series featuring Emma Peel and her Edwardian-attired colleague John Steed offered up an atmospherically and more darkly spy-crafted aura than James Bond and the Men from U.N.C.L.E. combined. Furthermore, who could resist Mrs. Peel in one of her skin-tight leather jump suits, tossing baddies around like the martial arts princess she was?

Therefore and given my obvious feelings, having grown used to the pictures of Diana/Emma on my college desk-top bulletin board, it made sense to announce to my fellow dorm rats that I would indeed "look her up" if I had the chance. But never in my wildest dreams did I suspect what would shortly occur. And all it took was a transatlantic flight and the removal of one twenty-year old appendix to achieve it.

I remember being somewhere I don't now recall exactly, and meeting a gentleman with whom I engaged in a bit of polite-but-idle conversation. This was a week or so after my being discharged to wander, the freshly-wrought and pink scar in my side already tingling with healing and the duress of the "patient" not being content to lay abed for the rest of his sojourn.

The gentleman had asked me point blank, "why are you over here?" Flippantly, I immediately replied. "Well officially I'm supposed to be studying. But truthfully I'm here to meet Mrs. Peel and to see Twiggy." I also told him about the strange case of my disappearing appendix, and of how I was now trying to make hay while the English sun shone over my time in the United Kingdom. (*Footnote: And unless the reader is unaware, the "Twiggy" in question was just about the hottest thing in haute couture modeling in '67. As svelte as her professional name, she reflected the Carnaby Street mood of Mary Quant and the Swinging London of fact and fiction. And then came the bombshell.*)

"Well as it happens, I work out at Boreham Wood where we shoot 'The Avengers' my new colleague said. "Would you like to come out to see your Mrs. Peel in action?"

My Mrs. Peel? In person? Black leather jump suit? John Steed in his bowler? I couldn't have imagined a better offer—not since a few years earlier, when Mr. Rabe had asked, "how'd you like to meet the Beatles?"

You betcha I'd like it.

Cut to the Wandering Boy now making use again of British Rail and the bus service. Next thing I'm in Elstree and at Boreham Wood where they kept the Avengers. The way had been paved for me, courtesy of my new contact. And before you could say Lotus Elan (Mrs. Peel's jazzy little sports car) there I was in a studio on the sidelines, even as the cameras were recording the final dramatic lines of none other than my Vision of Loveliness Personified: Diana Rigg. Pink cat-suit (I wasn't disappointed) and boots. Standing on the set before me. In the flesh.

Now what you ought to know, and as I quickly discovered, my nameless new friend had gone back to the Avengers set and regaled Ms. Rigg with the tale of a young American student, bent on coming all the way over just to meet her, who was suddenly struck down by appendicitis. Did that good boy not deserve a favour? Indeed, he did. Matter of fact, given the twinge in his side, he'd probably earned it! Diana Rigg wrapped her scene in an episode entitled "Murdersville" with the off-camera explication of "Epic!" And then she strode off-set. *And was now moving directly toward me.*

I could rely purely on imagination to try and conjure up how I felt that day, or how my fantasy-based enamorada looked. But there is evidence that survives for both of those. You see, photos were taken of Diana and I, with yours truly, looking rather post-operatively gaunt, but nevertheless ecstatic to gaze into those eyes and note the light dusting of freckles which the cameras and make-up techs often tend to conceal. Oh, and upon my leaving she'd presented me with a glossy 8x10, which she ins*cribed "For Mark-Congratulations on your ingenuity! Sincerely, Diana"* (Erroneously or not, that luscious lady seemed to suggest that I had auto-induced an exploding appendix as the means of meeting her!)

And then of course there is the place played by "Murdersville" within the extensive "Avengers" canon. To me, quite frankly the only ones worth bothering with are the "Rigg Era" episodes. Toward that end, I can still replay my video or DVD version of "Murdersville," and can yet savor that final, "epic" scene after which the lady walked over to me, gazed into my eyes the way she did Steed's, and captured a part of my heart forever.

Mrs. Peel (Diana Rigg) and the
post-operative author in the summer of '67.

Twenty years later, the author and
"Mrs. Peel" in London

In closing and as another post-script, I remember returning to town and Dulwich, filled with the experience of at least partially fulfilling my home ground prophecy: *"I'm going to meet Mrs. Peel and see Twiggy."* And that evening I traded adventures with my pleasant host, who had his own special encounter that day. It seemed he'd been in a stalled traffic queue, and looking over to the limousine beside him. There and smiling back from her backseat perch was none other than Sophia Loren! That had made his day. But for me, I suspected that courtesy of Ms. Rigg, she had made my year!

My days left in Britain were now dwindling to a precious few. One of my last hamlet-based explorations involved a visit to a local museum. And there I encountered that mysterious "something" about my newly acquired hamlet which had eluded me until now. Talk about serendipity. And when I discovered this bit of history, I seemed to hear a gong ringing. For there in the museum I was apprised of a basic historical fact; namely, that when the time had come for that academic establishment known as Dr. Glennie's Academy to pass, a public house came to stand on its site. But of greater interest to me, and on a par with certain of my other "coincidental" involvements lately, the source stated that the original pub had over time become the Grove Tavern. In other words, *the very site where often enough I had ended my searchings, mug in hand.* And that was enough to decide me on making the Grove one of the final stops of what had become a sentimental journey indeed. But this time, I vowed, I would raise a full pint to Lord Byron. For at this point I had felt as if we'd grown closer!

POSTSCRIPT: *Upon returning home I got my photographs developed. I was generally pleased with those as evidence to my parents and friends of the scope of my travels. However, what sent a tingle up my spine, unfelt since visiting Newstead, and then Portobello, and then the little bookshop in Dulwich, was the printed pictures showing Byron's bedroom and that long shot I'd taken of the house and the lake and the woods.*

Now I've told you about the warp of light, which I continue to describe as "Byron making himself known in his bedroom." But it was the other picture which seemed to manifest a kind of real supernatural energy. I saw the connection upon first examining my print, and then even went to the trouble of having that photo blown up to 8" x 10" detail. And it was obvious, not just to me, but to anyone who cared to look. You see, the perspective and angle and borders of the photograph I'd taken at Newstead exactly matched the view and the borders of the framed print I had purchased at Portobello Not nearly. Not almost. Exactly. Right down to the edge of the ancient clusters of arbors framing the house. No question. Not a bit of imagination or wishful thinking. The photograph and the print could have been overlaid. And as for the photograph? It might have been taken from countless angles, a hundred different ways. But not like this. For what I had captured that day seemed to be the visual echo of the old scene portrayed in the 19th century print.

P.P.S.: Here is a final anecdote which put the icing on the cake, in a way. It has to do with what I told my "Avengers" contact when he asked me why I'd come to Britain. Recall, I cavalierly said I was using my student status as a "cover,' when in actual fact I was "there to meet Mrs. Peel and to see Twiggy." And with that kind gentleman's help, at least the first portion of my unwitting prophecy had come true. And as the for the second? Well imagine if you will the final moments of my stomping the terra in Great Britain. I am walking rather dejectedly through Heathrow Airport to catch my flight home when I become aware of peering eyes. There are gaggles of people around me tittering and gawking. I cannot think why. Is it the odorous vintage flea-market double-breasted coat I've decided to wear, despite the heat, rather than jamming it into my already over-stuffed baggage? But no, it is something and someone else.

Just ahead of me and in line of sight to those folks on the periphery of the terminal's broad hall, a young short-haired, doe-eyed mini-skirted dolly girl is walking, in company with her companion, a garishly sheepskin jacketed bravo with puffed up hair and long sideburns. And suddenly, like the crowds all around, I recognize them both. I have seen them in photographs, both at home and over here. They are the world's skinniest and most famous of mannequins, Twiggy, and her dubiously named boyfriend/manager Nigel, who'd publicly re-christened himself Justin de Villeneuve. And they too are about to board a flight. But odds are, as I found myself musing, they won't be winging their way to metropolitan Detroit.

And so, dear reader, in that fashion was my Great British Adventure concluded. I may have departed the United Kingdom *sans* appendix, but otherwise full of a rich trove of memories. Most memorable as well, I had met Mrs. Peel and within moments of winging my way off that sceptered isle, had indeed "seen Twiggy." Prophecy Fulfilled. Just call me Nostradamus.

ATLANTIS : A search for a hidden place of beauty . . . in a warm clime, of course

THE QUEST of three local men for lost Atlantis is not as bizarre as it might seem without quiet reflection.

Ancient Egyptian priests are credited with passing on to the Greeks a legend of a mighty kingdom somewhere off the Straits of Gibraltar that once conquered most of the Mediterranean from a base where larks sang and only soft breezes blew.

That was Atlantis. For thousands of years the imaginations of dreamers have been haunted by visions of stately temples rising from the sea bottom, of statues of beautiful women and heroic men reposing far below storms, in silent, azure deeps, visited occasionally by respectful Nereid sea nymphs.

There are other mysteries. The Greek Isles of the Blest. The Welsh Avalon, where sorrowing and wounded King Arthur was transported after the destruction of the Round Table. The lost Breton city of Is. The Island of the Seven Cities. All Edenic places where tranquility abounded, sorrows were erased and wounds healed.

The new seekers of Atlantis are concentrating on Bimini, an island off the Florida coast where the climate, at least, matches the legend. If one is going to seek a paradise it ought to be in a place free of ice and fog. You may not find what you are looking for, but the looking is good.

The new explorers are also interested in discovering Ponce de Leon's Fountain of Youth. That's too heavy. Few people have the strength to cope with youth more than once.

But let us not scoff at those who seek Atlantises. Everybody has an Atlantis ... out there, somewhere.

The Atlantean Editorial View

116

8
The Platonic Ideal

To the best of my recollection, nowhere within the Sherlockian Canon is the subject of Atlantis ever mentioned. Nor among his extensive quotations (which in truth often belay what Watson originally took to be his paucity of philosophical knowledge) does the Master quote Plato. Had he done so, I sometimes wonder if the case of the world's most missing continent, as cited by that Greek sage, would have been of appeal to the Great Detective?? That the idea of such a thing may have intrigued him, I do not doubt. Nevertheless, the seeming absence of Atlantis may not be an indication that it was not to be considered. And why? Well here the reason may be as simple as this: (a) *either Dr. Watson deliberately did not mention Atlantis; or* (b) *there was a specific reason for this enigma's deletion from the Canonical record; or* (c) *Holmes' biographer simply forgot to add it to the roster of his friend's casework.* In each of these instances we may also fall back upon a somewhat Biblical explanation. Recall the ending of St. John's Gospel, wherein he says:

"there are also many other things which Jesus did, the which, if they should be written every one, I suppose that even the world itself could not contain the books that should be written."

And at the risk of seeming to draw a contrast between the Master from Nazareth and the Master of Baker Street, London, there is an analogy of sorts. For even as post-Watsonian scholarship has demonstrated, the "books about the books" have vastly outnumbered the four novels and fifty-six tales which comprise the Sherlockian Logos.

Is it then possible that given the extensive record of Sherlock Holmes's casework, recorded and not, that something the size of the lost Atlantean continent may have slipped through the cracks? Or perhaps, like the subject of vampires or the paranormal instances of Spiritualism indulged in by Holmes' Doylean alter ego, Professor Challenger, there is a kind of "undercover" recognition of "lost" Atlantis.

To begin with consider the source. Plato originally cited Atlantis in two of his Dialogues, *Timaeus* and *Critias* in the fifth century B.C. There the philosopher described it as "that sacred island lying beneath the sun." Thus was the legend and a conundrum born. Antique when it was supposedly repeated by the ancient Egyptians, Atlantean lore would be parsed many times. The Elizabethan age's Sir Francis Bacon even employed that phantom as the exemplar of his own notion of a perfect society.

In Plato's wake. generations of fantasists, theorists, scientists, archeologists and others have breathed new life into an eldritch idea. And in the phantasmagorical Sixties, Atlantis became part of the counter-cultural milieu when the Scottish troubadour Donovan made it an anthem. In his dulcet, Celtic voice he said

> *"The continent of Atlantis was an island which lay before the Great Flood in the area we now call the Atlantic Ocean. So great an area of land that from her western shores those beautiful sailors journeyed from the south and the north Americas with ease in their ships with painted sails.*
> *The great Egyptian age is but a remnant of the great Atlantean culture. The antediluvian kings colonized the world. All the gods who play in the mythological dramas and all the legends from all lands were from fair Atlantis.*
> > *Way down, below the ocean*
> > *Where I want to be,*
> > *She may be*
> > *Way down, below the ocean*
> > > *Hail, Atlantis!"*

But what of Atlantis in the Victorian era? And more specifically, if there was a covert or deliberately concealed act by Watson to avoid direct mention of the Platonic land-mass, where then was it found? Here the answer may be as close as the work of his fellow physician and colleague, Dr. Arthur Conan Doyle.

In 1927 Conan Doyle published *The Maracot Deep,* a "science fantasy" tale that involved a deep-sea oceanic team of explorers who encounter denizens of legendary Atlantis. The team's leader, Dr. Maracot, referred to as "a dry stick of a man," is possessed of certain aspects of Challenger, but is on the whole more amiable.

The key to the mystery at hand suggests that just as Edward Challenger launched an expedition to the "Lost World," so too did Maracot plumb the existence of Atlantis. Importantly as well, both men are converts to a realm of belief which exceeds that of logical materialism. In this regard, Challenger's gruff skepticism gives way in the face of evidence, as is demonstrated in *The Land of Mist*. And Maracot, respectively, is compelled to admit to "more things in heaven and earth" than may have been apportioned to his own, (or even Sherlock Holmes') unflappable philosophy. In point of fact, Challenger and Maracot are in direct opposition to Holmes, who kept his thoughts of the Unknown firmly in check.

It is known that Conan Doyle harbored a tremendous filial affection for Professor Edward Challenger, even going so far as to disguise himself as his fictive creation. But it is clear enough that Sir Arthur's beliefs evolved over time and were even open to such terrestrial enigmas as a remote jungle plateau where dinosaurs and pterodactyls freely existed. But soon enough those materially-based conjectures were appended by his even greater, otherworldly faith in Human Survival and voices from Beyond, if not fairies cavorting in a rural English wood.

It is I think Conan Doyle's mental explorations with *The Lost World* and *The Maracot Deep* which provides us with the likeliest link between Holmes, Watson, Doyle, and Plato. Both of those works suggest a man of hardened reason allowing himself to believe not only in what might have been, but in things which some might say never were.

And in a final overview of Sherlock Holmes, we may conjure with the notion that perhaps he did know of the Atlantean myth, if not the efforts of thinkers within his era to prove out its veracity. Not perhaps as zealous as Professor Challenger, it may be that there was a kinship between the simian academic and the cerebral detective. Nevertheless, the nature of that relationship is yet to be unraveled. Might they have been genetically related? Or might their only connection have existed via a nexus between them, *vis a vis* Watson's friend, Doyle?

Also lending toward a presumption of Holmes' Atlantean awareness is his own demonstrated antiquarian interests. We know for example that he was familiar with eldritch manuscripts, medieval motets, philological roots of extinct language, regal relics, ancient rituals, and even the background of at least one "ancient British barrow." Therefore it is not improbable to consider that a corner of the detective's out-of-the-way knowledge and other *outré* matters may have involved perhaps the most mysterious of all Platonic citations. Doubtless too he would have had a sense of mystical Camelot, as celebrated by Tennyson in Holmes' day, or golden El Dorado or the fabled Cockaigne. Of them all however, he may well have considered Atlantis one of the world's most enduring Golden Age mysteries. Nor would he have been unaware of Ignatius Donnelley's popular work *Atlantis, the Antediluvian World,* which was published shortly after Holmes took up residence on Baker Street. *Quod erat demonstrandum.*

As a post-script to this mini-essay on "Sherlock Holmes and Atlantis," there is another final and rather curious link which I feel necessary to include here. This is a rather singular fact which concerns my late friend, Dame Jean Conan Doyle. As cited by Andrew Lycett in his excellent *The Man who Created Sherlock Holmes: The Life and Times of Sir Arthur Conan Doyle,* Jean, or "Billy" as she called herself in her early teen years, actually lent her father a hand with the writing and research of *Maracot.* I find it intriguing to imagine that "the daughter of Sherlock Holmes" no doubt took great pleasure in making such a contribution. Here the reason may have had much to do with the chronological fact that in 1912, the year of Jean's birth, *The Lost World* was published. And what fun she must have had assisting her father in preparing for that next grand expedition!

Now then, to return to the nearly recent present....
I know for a fact that in February of 1981, the spirit of Sherlock Holmes traveled to the island of Bimini, some fifty miles east of Miami. Also that the purpose of that trip was founded in the idea of furthering the quest to find the ancient source of Atlantis. I know all this simply because I was there in my self-proclaimed capacity as the Project Director of ATLANTIS 1.

My decision to orchestrate a three-man team to explore sunken stone configurations off the Bimini shoreline was considered by many to be a grand and mysterious, if not madcap adventure. This fact is reflected by at least two news clippings preserved within my "Atlantis" file. The first is a staff report from *The Ypsilanti Press* entitled "Ypsilantian pays visit to what may be Atlantis."

Living as I then did about thirty-five miles from my Detroit workplace, Ypsilanti allowed me access to a quieter existence, if not to water. I'd found the advantage of that in my first forays to Loch Ness five years earlier. Back then I trained daily in an inflatable surplus raft, conditioning myself to believe that the sunny and shallower conditions on Ford Lake were suitable to prepare me for the darker, rougher and deeper night-blind fathoms of Loch Ness.

Now however, Atlantis was in my sights. And like the Scottish project, its context had been re-awakened by two newsworthy events. The first of these involved research done by a professor of Victorian literature (right provenance, at least!) named David Zink. His book *The Stones of Atlantis* involved the theory that the J-shaped configuration of stonework at Bimini could be some reminder of lost Atlantis. Coincidentally or not, that was the very spot where the famous "Sleeping Prophet" Edgar Cayce had predicted that *"Atlantis would rise"* back in 1933. The curious part of the story is that Cayce had also opined that Atlantis *"may* yet *be discovered under the slime of ages of sea water near Bimini in 1968 or '69."* So consider the deep strangeness of this: in 1968, through the agency of the shifting sea-floor or other geologic condition, fragments of stonework resembling walls, pillars, if not what came to be dubbed "The Bimini Road" seemed to materialize. *And Edgar Cayce's prophecy was made at least thirty-five years earlier.*

The only part of Professor Zink's thesis that seemed more difficult for me to buy was his extra-terrestrial context. This somewhat resembled Eric Von Däniken's *Chariots of the Gods,* which predicated a long ago otherworldly visitation to Terra Firma. In Zink's case, he suggested that "entities" from the Pleiades star cluster had come down and inspired the wonders of Atlantis. As if in support, Cayce had earlier said that the Atlanteans had possessed vast technological powers, such as airships and ancient vehicles. However the greatest was a crystal-based gizmo which provided not only power, but ultimately, caused the destruction of the soon-to-be-Lost Continent.

Now we return to ATLANTIS I. According to the *Ypsilanti News* report,

"As you read this, Ypsilantian Mark McPherson may be three fathoms down in the Atlantic Ocean searching for the lost civilization of Atlantis. The legendary continent discussed by Plato is the object of his quest.

McPherson, 33, and companions Richard Lightbody, 40, and Scott Sloan, 32, of Detroit are now investigating what they think might be fragments of the fabled Atlantean culture, rediscovered in 1968 near the island of Bimini, just off the coast of Miami.

Although none of the trio are scientists, McPherson has a familiarity with folklore and legends, parapsychology and sonar equipment for underwater scanning. Sloan is an architect and avid sailor. Lightbody is an accomplished diver."

Earlier I'd prepared a press release explaining the reason for our impending trip to the Caribbean. In that I spoke of the growing belief that history and myth quite often seemed to trade places. Moreover, that some mysteries once regarded as impossibilities were being investigated and better understood through technology and a synthesis of fact with the trappings of legend. In the release I also described Plato's description of Atlantis in his "dialogues" and carefully included the subsequent opinions of scholars, mythologists and scientists regarding the validity of an "Atlantean reality." Carefully as well I included Edgar Cayce's 1933 prophecy, as well as the circumstances which seemingly had validated it thirteen years ago. For that reason, I said, as project director of "ATLANTIS I" I had elected to explore the coastal regions of Bimini. Among other objectives my priority would be to map the positions of those enigmatic submarine stones, if only to further the case that they were the byproducts of man-made effort, as opposed to natural erosion, etc.

A press conference was scheduled at Detroit's Dossin Great Lakes Museum. It seemed a perfect place for news of a nautically-themed expedition to be debuted. And so, amid maps and charts and models of sea-going crafts which had plied the Great Lakes, it was announced that three intrepid adventurers were about to go looking for a legend.

"On February 27, Richard Lightbody, Scott Sloan and myself will travel to the island of Bimini, located in the Bahamas, about fifty miles east of Miami, Florida" I stated. "Our purpose will be to initiate a two-phased expedition to explore an underwater site off the Bimini coast, where it appears there are the remnants of a megalithic configuration of ancient, man-made blocks. There are several such arrangements fringing the Biminese coastline, the majority of which have been unexplored, and have been discovered over recent years through aerial reconnaissance and very recently, through the employment of underwater side-scan sonar. The most prominent of the stone alignments is one resembling a reversed "J" shape, measuring approximately 600 meters on its main axis and about 100 meters across. On an equally curious note, this arrangement seems to have been predicted by America's most famous "Sleeping Prophet," Edgar Cayce, who announced that 'Atlantis would rise' in 1968 or '69—a prediction he made in 1933."

There was a decent turnout of press for our conference, and quite frankly the scene that day reminded me of another I'd seen in the film "Raise The Titanic." But ironically, I thought, what we were going after was even bigger than that yet-to-be-found fabled White Star liner.

Publicly there was a flutter of discussion about our expedition. But no criticism, per se, save for one telephone call I'd received from a Motor City high school science teacher. He'd chosen to berate me for downplaying the best efforts of scientific research to discourage archaic and usually mythic beliefs. And he added, "how dare you say what you did about 'science sometimes being short-sighted.' What right do you have to say that? And what right do you have to put together this expedition of yours?"

I listened to my critic patiently for several minutes. Then I informed him that all that had been reported was the fact of our interest in one of the world's great legends. As for the story, that came as a response from interested media. But that this was an interest which we were ready to follow up with our own energies, if not private funds. And therefore, much as I appreciated the call, all I needed the caller to understand was one thing: "I really don't care what you think of what I'm about to do."

I thought I'd handled my critic carefully, but didn't expect his next comment.

"Then do you have room on your expedition for one more member?" my scientific friend asked. I laughed, said apologetically that we didn't, and thanked him for his interest.

Before we caught our flight to Miami *The Free Press* published an editorial comment on the idea of our plan. It was entitled *"ATLANTIS: A search for a hidden place of beauty...in a warm clime, of course."*

But by this time I'd been interviewed numerous times on radio, television and in print. Some of them even caught up with my earlier investigations and their peripheral association with Sherlock Holmes. So then, I supposed if we were going to receive a drubbing, there was no way to prevent it. However, when the editorial appeared in our major daily publication, I had quite the opposite feeling.

The *Detroit Free Press* editorial briefly defined Atlantis, its legend, and what it meant to many among a catalogue of other mythic hopes and dreams shared for countless centuries. And then it concluded with these words:

"But let us not scoff at those who seek Atlantises. Everybody has an Atlantis...out there, somewhere."

I liked those words back in 1981, and I like them now. For they represent a certain level of truth which has stayed with me over the decades. And that also signifies the need in some of us to undertake a quest, however great or small, and self-commissioned or not. How was it Sir Richard Burton had once put it? *"The Devil Drives!"* And indeed he does.

From the moment the Chalk's International Charter seaplane hovered low over the intensely blue waters of Bimini, it occurred to me that if not Atlantis, then the island below us could well have been Paradise at one time. Visible on the ground were clusters of beach dwellings lining the shore and dotting the central body of the island. Occasional groves of palms and emerald underbrush raced past the shadow of the descending pontoon plane. But paradoxically as well, even the Eden beneath our wings had its darker side. And even as we would soon enough confirm in our forays, it was not unusual to turn from viewing the perfect and pristine sea view only to discover portions of ivory beachfront containing derelict vehicles or appliances, and even smoking piles of garbage.

But as we banked lazily, down into the small harbor of Alice Town, the tapestry of Biminese life and activity began to reveal itself. But Bimini was also a paradox: a melding of Fantasy Island and Tobacco Road, both of them shining and smoldering against the slow-motion rhythm of Caribbean lifestyle. Those who come to the island usually do so for the deep-sea fishing, reputed to be the best in the world. Hemingway knew that full well, and even based much of his novel *Islands in the*

Stream there. And in that same connection, perhaps the most memorable image seen on our trip was a framed picture of "Hem," a tommy-gun in hand, back from shooting marlin!

But for us there were many questions to be answered: would we locate the stones rumored to exist in the shadow-fathomed waters? Did some relic of ancient man, perhaps even Atlantean man, await us in an odd configuration of sunken stone blocks, like a submarine Stonehenge?

I have written of our exploits in ATLANTIS I elsewhere, and I do not wish to entirely violate the Sherlockian tenets of this memoir. Suffice it to say that even as I'd realized finding myself at yet another roundly imagined mysterious destination, I couldn't help thinking about Mr. Holmes. That's to say, and stretching the imaginary umbilical a bit, what if he had left the dankness of London and traded it for the balmy Caribbean? We know of course that he had experienced other climes, ranging from Sigerson's mountainous environs, to his own desert-like explorations at Khartoum or elsewhere. But given the chance, might he have chosen to dive down, if only for a look at a sunken sphinx, say, in the harbor of old Alexandria? Might he have pushed his surprisingly agile constitution even to such limits? And finally, if confronted by the prospect of some vestige of Atlantis, as near as eighteen feet below the shimmering surface, would he have not have jumped overboard?

But truth to tell, I wasn't channeling the spirit of Holmes that day when I was the first one out of the rented Boston Whaler and into Bimini's mystery laden waters. But that moment had represented a baptism of sorts; for after a childhood filled with the dream of finding Atlantis, here was I at last, prepared to do it!

We'd reconnoitered the insular coastline and its variety of junkyard artifacts. Further out we were ready at last to explore the underwater site of the reputed megaliths. We moored somewhere near the last humped back of the Three Sisters, a trio of jutting coral formations angling toward the nearby peninsula of Paradise Point on the island's north end.

Hovering above the purported site of the great stones, we could make out only a dark relief of pillow shapes cast in hues of emerald and brown. Peering over the bulwark of our small vessel, we were still unable to get a true view of the phantoms which resided some three fathoms below our hull. The day was fine. Sunlight danced along the surface of the water, heightening the optical difficulty. It was plain that only by going down would we be able to view the megaliths clearly.

As soon as our group entered the water we were struck by a weird sort of elation—of suddenly becoming a modern and alien extension of the scene below us. Now only the sound of our relaxed breathing through our sky-directed snorkels intruded upon the cool, vacuum-like silence. We glided over the green darkness, occasionally releasing pressure from the buoyancy compression vests we wore, which better allowed us to paddle-fin our ways lower, down to the seat of those cyclopean blocks.

And it did appear that the alignments on the shallow ocean bottom might be truly ancient. The great slabs could hardly be mere freaks of nature, as some had suggested. The look of hand-hewn stonework was obvious to us, particularly when we viewed portions of the rock from near the surface. Compared to the tide-eroded beach-rock formations found above and within meters of the shore, the megalithic slabs before us were symmetrical, many fitting cleanly together, some at right angles, still others stacked like cyclopean pillars. Then a weird panoramic effect seemed to materialize though the murk, and the stones loomed stark against the grassy sea floor, alien remnants of man's long-ago touch.

As we swam through that hazy terrain I remembered a photograph in Zink's book. This had been taken by a scientist who'd literally come face-to-whatever to a tall, coral encrusted column. But most unusual about it was what appeared to be some form of gear-work, or mechanical features upon the ancient upright. Impossible? Supposedly so. And yet there was that relic dubbed the "Antikythera Mechanism" retrieved many years from the Mediterranean depths. This proved to be what appeared to be a clockwork device with gears and fly-wheels, etc. The only problem here: *the "device" was thousands of years old.*

But as for the stone column and attendant gear-work seen down here, and even photographed, there was no explanation. Worse yet, when its discoverer had gone back to find it, it was gone. And as an eerie postscript, when the picture of the column was developed, what seemed to be a kind of glow was visible, as if emanating from that enigmatic object.

126

But as we probed those depths, our only company those static stones and occasional fleets of small, darting fish-life, we were confronted by the Unknown. For what, ultimately, were those stones meant to be? Were they portions of a wall, or a public building, or even an ancient residence? And were we now voluntarily trespassing upon the sunken shadows of a place once teeming with life in some ancient and now forgotten epoch? If so, were their ghosts keeping tryst down there, watching us?

Suffice it to say that first day began the drill of a week's worth of exploration. We photographed the J-shaped stone arrangement of the "road,' and I was able to put legs to my thesis that the remnant of the island-like shape of Bimini bore an incredible, albeit reverse-imaged outline of Thera, or Santorini in the Mediterranean. That island had long ranked as an excellent candidate for ruined Atlantis, its mass decimated by a volcanic eruption which had caused tremendous effects further afield.

But now and looking back on our adventure, I cannot begin to describe that first sensation of being "first in" before my team. And of my initial sensation of seeing a vast and emerald-hued mossy chessboard beneath us. And strangest of all, I'd thought, we three were about to be the pieces moving across that impossibly geometric field!

I also recall what I still remind my chums was a humorous interlude. But for them at the time, not so frivolous.

It was the evening of our initial day's adventure and we were sharing a meal at a small, pirate-like restaurant in Alice Town. Both Dick and Scott were eager to run the next morning, while I was content to pour over my notes on the terrace of our suite in the wonderfully named Bimini Big Game and Fishing Club Hotel. But as I say, my companions in work and friendship were both marathon-caliber runners. Now they were as eager to test the slight pathways and rugged streets of our island as I was to get back into the water. And it was one particular dimension of those gorgeously shimmering depths which provided the present footnote.

I remember mid-way through dinner that the subject of The Shark came up. It was one of them, Sloan or Lightbody, it doesn't matter now, who'd had a glance at my copy of *The Stones of Atlantis.* There Professor Zink had described the local customs and people and even the flora and fauna of the shore and its watery extension. And it was in the latter category that Zink had described the long-time presence of a twenty-foot-long shark which the natives had christened "Harbor Master." And also the fact, as my cohorts had now learned, that where we had been plumbing the depths in quest of a mystery, Harbor Master's domain also lay.

"Why the hell didn't you say something about the shark?" Scott asked. I sensed genuine concern on my friend's face. Meanwhile, Lightbody, laconic as ever merely took another pull on his Red Cap and grinned. I suppose one of life's great pleasures is reading a look of sheer panic on your pal's face. But only and ideally after the fact, once you're out of danger, and comfortable in a place where they serve cold beer.

"Well, he sort of came with the package" I informed my ATLANTIS I team-member. And he did. Which makes me wonder now, forty years later, whether the much older Harbor Master is still down there, possibly waiting for our return?

At any rate, and in greatly compacted form, such was the routine and the odd rhythm of our Atlantis Adventure. There were a few false starts and stops, such as very late one afternoon when our Whaler quit off the remote end of the island. Neither Dick nor I claimed to be real sailors. That was Scott's department, and bolstered by the fact that this young bachelor had a handsome sailboat back home, upon which we three had already voyaged. But today when the small outboard quit in foreign waters, Scott Sloan studied it, even as our trio found ourselves feeling like marooned buccaneers. On one side of our view, the Caribbean rolled out to the edge of the Bermuda Triangle. And on the other more populous side, the island waited in silence. Moreover, the part which was within wading distance of our stalled vessel looked entirely uninhabited.

Meanwhile Commander Sloan toyed with this and that and finally withdrew the pull-chord and with a deft slice of his pocket knife, severed it!

"What the hell did you do that for?" one of us asked.

Our curly headed companion looked back, his attractive features gone sheepish as he replied, "I don't really know."

The upshot of this new twist found us rowing toward shore, then jumping out, like Captain Kidd's crew looking for a place to bury the booty. But we had no treasure, other than a bit of gear and the oars, and a now entirely bereft boat with a dead engine. Marooned indeed we were.

But if that wasn't enough, once we got to the beach and began walking into the interior along a road distinctly hewn between the jungle roughage, we passed some signs. Each of these in turn gave a warning: PRIVATE PROPERTY. NO TRESPASSING. TRESPASSERS WILL BE PROSECUTED. THIS MEANS YOU. IF YOU GO ANY FURTHER WE CAN'T BE HELD RESPONSIBLE FOR YOUR SAFETY. Well, maybe that last one is a fabrication, but it carries the same general tone. For quite clearly we were now in a "restricted" sector of the island, which as we learned a bit further on, belonged to a company called Rockwell. But for ourselves on that late afternoon, those placards might well have echoed Dante's fabled admonition of
"Abandon hope, all ye who enter here."

Eventually and as The Three Amigos walked down the road with the sun sinking as low as our hopes, we heard the unmistakable sound of an approaching motor. *Rescue had arrived.*

Looking ahead down that perspective of road we witnessed the advent of a gleaming black vehicle, its windows dark as night. We stood there waiting for it, like Darby O'Gill seeing the otherworldly hearse in his path. And in moments the vaguely military-cum-black ops vehicle drew up to us as its driver's side window was electronically lowered halfway down. Inside the driver proved to be a dark fellow in a black, snap-brimmed hat and even darker wraparound sunglasses. His message seemed to deliberately echo the posted warnings.

"This is private property" the phantom said. Nothing more.

It was then that one of us, or two, or all of us, did our best to explain. *We were diving and our engine conked out. Without any other recourse, we came ashore and left the rental boat tied up to a tree-trunk. And so we decided to walk back to our hotel. But we wouldn't mind a lift.*

There was no nod of understanding, or even as we might have hoped for, a sudden and genial offer to give us a ride back to the Big Game and Fishing Club Hotel. Just an added reminder that we were technically in a state of trespass. Also the great and good kindness of saying that if we continued on we would probably find the road into town. *Probably.* Then without further word, warning, or hail and farewell, the Man In Black tore off down the road.

Well that episode is still fresh in my mind, even as it's fixed within the memory of my two friends. Living close by as we do, Dick and I like to speak of it often, and we take turns with a bit of long-distanced chiding of Scott about the "Adventure of the Cut Cord." Inevitably and whenever we do, Mr. Sloan, who is presently in Florida enjoying retirement, demurs and begins talking about how he had "interceded with the guy in the black car" for the sake of our communal safety. I don't recall that, exactly, nor does Mr. Lightbody. But we do agree on one thing: that adventure marked the start of our referring to our good friend Scott as "Scuttles." I'd christened him that by the evening of that disastrous day. It was probably over dinner and after a few drinks, which is the best time, I find, to talk about ship-wrecks, lost continents, and sometimes even the sharks that call them home.

And as for those three Don Quixotes from Detroit? Well they found their windmill (and their dragon), tilted at them, and came home. Scott and Dick returned to their familiar routines as did I, but with an exception. For I alone was the one seemingly bent on mysterious doings. In fact, by now something in my makeup could not neglect or ignore the Unusual in many of its forms. I think it has something to do with believing that our world is not necessarily all that it seems. In that regard I recall a statement made by that most curious of supernatural curates, Montague Summers. Speaking of what the author Catherine Crowe had once dubbed "the night side of nature," he stated:

"But the skeptics are happier in their singleness and their simplicity, happy that they do not, will not, realize the monstrous things that lie only just beneath the surface of our cracking civilization."

I suppose I agreed with Summers back then, as I do even now. And on just such account by 1981 I'd already found myself in a host of far-flung places where high strangeness was more the rule than the exception.

I wrote an account of our ATLANTIS I Expedition for *The Detroit News Sunday Magazine* upon our return home. Serendipitously, I found a copy of that under separate cover while perusing my files for this memoir. Strangely too, and sounding as if the words were not my own, I confess to feeling an old thrill of excitement when I re-read the first paragraph of the story entitled "Looking For Atlantis."

"...Somewhere beyond the garage-smoking shores of Bimini, older by far than the modern myths of Hemingway the God and his Islands In The Stream, something silent waited; something sleeping with its ancient memory sealed in the core of huge, sunken blocks of stone."

And they're still there, those old stones. Who knows but that the future may see the return of the intrepid trio flying their invisible banner of ATLANTIS II? But until then the enigma will survive in the shape of those hazy formations which suggest another time, and perhaps as well, a breed of people unlike any known to our own recent past or present.

At the metaphorical end of the day, I suppose we three had been offered the gentlest of lessons, spelled out by that newspaper editorial even before we'd set out.

"... let us not scoff at those who seek Atlantises" the editorial said. "Everybody has an Atlantis ... out there, somewhere."

Nice words, those. And indeed, I think we all do.

"ACD" on the case

Sherlockian deductions to try to unloc

Ypsilanti man relies on the cerebral to solve the Scottish mystery

By DWIGHT ANGELL
Free Press Special Writer

Poor Nessiteras rhomboteryx. What he's had to go through. He must think it's some kind of plot.

Each year scientists and laymen spend time and money probing the waters for him, using expensive and sophisticated cameras, echo devices and hydrophones, sonar and recorded beeper sounds, sexual allurements, sound simulations of distressed fish, boats and divers. And just the human eye. But this prehistoric creature—whose scientific name translates as "Ness marvel with a diamond-shaped fin"—commonly known as the Loch Ness monster, has defied all modern technology.

However, Tuesday 31-year-old Mark McPherson from Ypsilanti will leave for Scotland to try his hand. His approach, which lies somewhere between the pure scientific method and the eccentrics and exotics, is based on Sherlockian deduction, or as Holmes defined it: "From a drop of water a logician could infer the possibility of an Atlantic or a Niagara without having seen or heard of one or the other."

Mark McPherson in his re-creation of the famous sitting room of 221 B Baker Street . . . right down to the cap and pistol.

McPherson, who admittedly is as obsessed with the legend of the Loch Ness creature (this will be his third trip to Scotland) as he is with the Sherlock Holmes adventures (he quotes freely from the 56 stories and four novels), has, in this instance, combined the two obsessions.

Monday through Friday, McPherson is the director of information services for Wayne County Community College. He lives with his wife in a modest new house near Ypsilanti. He's clean-cut, bright and articulate, especially about his two predilections: the Sherlock Holmes/Dr. Watson stories and the study of paranormal phenomena.

And Nessie, as he is affectionately named, presently tops the list of the latter.

SINCE McPHERSON doesn't have the time or money for expensive equipment needed for exploring the foggy wa-

ters of Loch Ness, he relies on the cerebral. So what better person in the world to emulate than that greatest mystery-solver and detective, Sherlock Holmes! Besides, like Holmes, he has little scientific instrumentation and is depending on the power of deductive reasoning.

His first two trips to Scotland, in '76 and '77, didn't realize one photograph or sighting of the creature. But the trips were not wasted.

"The last two years haven't been a failure because, as Holmes would say, 'It is a capital mistake to theorize without evidence. And the first duty of an investigator is to collect that evidence and to theorize once he has it.' "

But perhaps more importantly, it was also on the first two trips that McPherson saw the possibility of the Loch Ness mystery being Sherlockian in nature.

"When I reread the 'Adventure of the Lion's Mane' and that the character that Holmes had avenged was a McPherson (Fitzroy McPherson) who had died at the hands of this sea creature, everything sort of jelled. And I began thinking how would Holmes have dealt with the magnitude of Nessie."

Well, the answer to that is quite elementary. Holmes would have sat in his chair near the fireplace in his residence at 221 B Baker Street and contemplated the

The Man from Daedalos — "On the Case"

Irene Rucinski and Sol Lewis (top of photo) head seance to try to reach Arthur Conan Doyle.

NEWS PHOTO / DON BATTEN

'Sir Arthur, is that you?'
Medium gets message for Holmes buffs

By ARTHUR W. O'SHEA
News Staff Writer

Everybody's coming to Detroit this political summer.

Jimmy Carter today. Walter Mondale last night. The Republicans next week.

And Arthur Conan Doyle at around tea time yesterday afternoon.

Not — of course — in the flesh as the living, breathing creator of Sherlock Holmes, the master detective, but as the spirit of Sir Arthur, long dead.

At least that's what the spiritualist medium said. She helped a group of Holmes fans try to reach the great Victorian mystery writer in a seance on the 50th anniversary of his death.

noted for trying once to raise the ghost of the late escape artist Harry Houdini in the room Houdini died in at old Grace Hospital. (Houdini didn't show.)

The "spirit" voice spoke through Mrs. Rucinski as McPherson was asking some questions.

"Do the numbers 221 have any significance for you?" McPherson asked, figuring this would be a snap for Sir Arthur since Holmes' address was 221 B Baker Street.

"Not any high significance," was Sir Arthur's offhand reply.

"Anything more?" McPherson asked.

"It has some significance to me," the distinguished author allowed.

"Only that it meant something to three people."

THE CONVERSATION meandered on like that — of interest mainly to the enthused few who join such organizations as the Baker Street Irregulars to keep alive the memory of the world's greatest detective.

Lewis called upon the spirit to predict the future. The "spirit" did that somewhat reluctantly:

Ronald Reagan will be elected president this year and Howard Baker will be his vice-president.

The seance ended. McPherson was asked if he would wager some money on the spirit's prediction.

"Sir Arthur?"…
"Another Long Distance Call" via séance

Vera Caspary, creator of "Mark McPherson"
and the author

9
The Business of "Detectivism"

Chronological Time Bar: The Present

At the time this was written I was reading both a new and an older book about Sherlock Holmes. The first is entitled *The Fifth Heart* and is authored by Dan Simmons. I recall enjoying two of his earlier novels, *The Terror,* dealing with a land-locked arctic crew marooned in ice and taunted by a primordial creature. The other was *Drood,* which concerned Charles Dickens as an author haunted by much more than the prospect of a trio of Yuletide specters. In contrast, *The Fifth Heart* shows us the Master Sleuth of Baker Street in a new and peculiar light. For this is Holmes harboring doubts over whether he is indeed real, or merely a fictional character? The plot is appropriately thickened in that the sleuth, in the guise of Sigerson the Norwegian explorer, is accompanied by the patrician American author Henry James. As the most recent of Watsonian companions, James is an amalgam of his own self-doubts and depressions. In essence then, these two make quite a pair.

But there is another reason for my recommending Simmons' novel. This has to do with my awareness of the depths of this man's Sherlockian research. The tell-tales of this are obvious to anyone steeped in the incunabula of Baker Street. Moreover, and having ingested an awareness of the standard background of Holmes, *vis a vis* Watson's "literary agent," Dr. Doyle, as well as other extra-Conanical (or canonical) sources such as Baring Gould's seminal *Sherlock Holmes of Baker Street,* the novelist takes his own considered liberties. To wit, much of what the reader has come to accept of Sherlock Holmes' family and background is said to be bogus. Moreover, Holmes' motives and training to become a criminal avenger are other than we believed.

But I feel that what Dan Simmons has offered us best with *The Fifth Heart* is an intriguing proposal: *what if the world's greatest consulting detective doubted his own image? His own reality?* Moreover, and banking on earlier treatments such as Billy Wilder's "Private Life," here again is Holmes lamenting over the scope of talents attributed to him by his chronicler, John H. Watson, M.D. Likewise the image in a kind of reverse sense was taken up by the Michael Caine/ Ben Kingsley film "Without A Clue." There "Holmes" is a hired actor portraying the fictional creation of his real-life begetter, Dr. Watson. And once again here is the matter of either mistaking or trying to force square pegs into round holes.

In the Official Version According to Doyle, we encounter Sherlock Holmes' observation that "there is nothing worse than a doctor gone wrong" (my paraphrase). And tucked away within the innermost sagas of Drs. Conan Doyle and Watson we must become aware of an obvious truth: that neither of these professional gentlemen were overtly successful in their fields of endeavor. Paradoxically, each ultimately garnered both profit and a public profile by presenting the world with their personalized renditions of Mr. Sherlock Holmes.

All of which relates in a way, I think, to the present memoir. For if nothing else, *An Irregular Life* presumes to be a kind of self-analysis of one man's voluntary absorption of a time and place, if not of an eccentric fictional proto-hero who may or may not be worth emulating in real life.

For myself, and these words cannot be assumed to reflect anyone else, the influence of Sherlock Holmes upon one boy-child and man's respective existence must be considered strong. Moreover and perhaps in testament of this, what you are now reading intends to reflect the degree(s) to which the "canon" of sixty fictional stories concerning an imaginary 19th and 20th century figure has tempered the actual existence of another in the 20th and 21st.

I am wondering whether it is truly even possible to be objective about one's own inner, or exterior self? Or about his willful and deliberate eccentricities? Or even worse, the reasoning or motivations for that individual's abidingly perceived and subjective yearning to carry fiction into the realm of fact?

But how to illustrate this notion? Perhaps we might take a leaf from another pending project of mine in which the "actual" prototype for the fictive "Bruce Wayne" chooses to expand upon the un-real "super" heroes of his day? He does so knowing that Super Man and Zorro and Doc Savage and The Shadow were all illusory, pulp-published and contemporary inventions designed to reflect a hero-worshipping society. But what if such a super-hero could become real? Ergo, he surveys the field and sets out to invade reality with the elements of fantasy. And the result of that endeavor? The Bat Man is born.

Here however and by extrapolating upon the appellation of "Sherlockian," I suppose I have deliberately carried my leanings toward Holmes of Baker Street to realms usually unvisited by my peers. Toward that end, for instance, I have not only admired key dramatic impersonators of Sherlock Holmes—I have met many of them. Moreover, I have not only thrilled over the considered prototypes for "Baskerville Hall," but upon invitation I have physically and geographically sought, as well as found it. And while others like to cavil or debate in clubby after-dinner fashion where on Baker Street Holmes and Watson kept their digs, I chose to research then affix the first plaque at London's shrine-like site. Further, in keeping with the mood of the Holmes stories, I elected to interest myself in the matter of "Who Was Jack the Ripper?" And building upon that quest even into its modern context, I consulted with a member of London's Metropolitan Police Force with regard to the "copy-cat" aspect of the 20th century's "Yorkshire Ripper."

To encapsule what the foregoing list of perhaps dubious achievements might suggest, each within its "Sherlockian" framework has consisted of a personal endeavor at problem solving. Carrying the notion even further, such undertakings have mirrored in their way an exercise in inquiry once applied to Dr. Conan Doyle's successful writings, *vis a vis,* of bringing "detectivism." into public focus. Such then has been the business at hand. In short, I determined to bring my skills and interests into the self-created arena of the mytho-historical investigator.

Lastly, and perhaps most significant as a minor footnote of my Holmesian "activism," while many have been content to admire Sir Arthur Conan Doyle and read his works and many biographies, I for one chose to "become" him, dramatically. And to do so, as will be described in pages yet to come, I would enlist the interest and help of Conan Doyle's only surviving child to assist me in bringing her late father back to life, if only dramatically. And in consequence of that incredible association, I was able, like Sir Arthur himself, to answer the query, "Is there life after death?" But in this case, it was by resurrecting the spirit of Holmes' creator on numerous stages around the world.

138

Perhaps you get my point here, which is not, by the way to blow a trumpet or demand special notice. Merely to state what to myself and those who availed my talents and interests were aware. Moreover, it is also to create a vehicle for reflecting the "how?" and "why?" of my Sherlockian penchants and the somewhat expansive perimeters which engulfed them. Furthermore, to provide an *aide de memoir* for many of the fascinating people and places encountered along my way.

Toward the latter end, I cannot express sufficient surprise at suddenly considering those "penchants" in their aggregate form. Moreover, to feel at first overwhelmed, and then overcome by a sense of great gratitude for the providential and often difficult circumstances which have allowed me to carry my credential as an investitured Baker Street Irregular into so many unusual quarters. The fact that I have not brandished it or used it to gain entry must speak for itself, I believe.

In reading these words, I am still struck by yet another effect of having admired the world's greatest logical detective to the point of emulation. Which is not to say that I, or any other aficionado was ever capable of "becoming" a real-life Sherlock. No, but perhaps instead by choosing to interest myself in mysterious or arcane events, and investigating them, but not from the snug comfort of an armchair.

And even as I would find myself employed as a college publicist, as had I seen my friend Bill Rabe do, my interests could not be wholly contained or hidden from public view. In due time, and after shedding my academic skin for another in 1986, I became, both in thought and practice, the creator of a discipline I deemed largely my own. But alike Sherlock Holmes, who laid claim to a kind of monopoly for employing his reasoning skills, I must defer to the master. Like him however, I became early on that in order to dominate a herd, it is oft-times necessary to leave it.

But "a discipline largely my own" sounds rather vainglorious, does it not? And within its context, I suppose it resembles the claim of someone named Sherlock Holmes, who once explained his livelihood as unique.

"I suppose that I am the only one in the world" he said. "London of course has lots of official detectives and plenty of private ones. When these fellows are at fault they come to me, and I manage to put them on the right track. They lay all of the evidence before me, and I am generally able, with the help of my knowledge of the history of crime, to set them straight."

And that is Sherlock Holmes's famous explication of himself as the world's first Consulting Detective. But was he that in truth? Or was this merely his ego-based self-estimation, based upon his own awareness that his services were much in demand? After all, there were many other sleuths in Old London, and a police force to boot. Perhaps he was not as alone in his field as he proclaimed?

Then of course there is the realistic prospect of what the authorities actually thought of Holmes as a rogue agent from the start? For doubtless he, very like the Bat Man in decades to come, was considered yet another potentially dangerous amateur element on the fringe, be it of criminal or lunatic persuasion.

It is perhaps a confusing reality apparent to its author that the present memoir does, like Mr. Wells' *Time Machine,* have a penchant for moving chronologically back and forth. In that regard. I have taken the liberty here to cite my own efforts at a kind of individualized investigation. No more than that. For instance, and as will be shortly seen, such efforts may well have commenced in 1969, when I was enlisted to track down the historical prototype of the literary "Baskerville Hall." Here it has struck me that such a "casual" enlistment resembles in a fashion the manner by which Sherlock Holmes became persuaded of his trade after assisting to resolve the death of his friend Trevor's father in "The Gloria Scott."

My interest in more formally (and publicly) scrutinizing certain mysteries followed in earnest over the course of many years since 1976, when I managed the first of nine privately funded expeditions to Loch Ness, in quest of its most famous monster. In 1978 and again in 1980, taking a leaf out of Conan Doyle's psychical notebook, I coordinated two attempts to reach out to the Great Beyond. The first of these was the historically "Last Attempt To Reach Harry Houdini From His Death Room in Detroit's Harper Grace Hospital." For this I brought two "sensitives" to our impromptu séance table. And their goal? To place a "long distance call" to Conan Doyle, British Ghost-booster Harry Price, and the Great Houdini himself. The outcomes of that event, scheduled half a century after Houdini's passing, were interesting, if not problematic. Or better yet, mystifying.

But first a few words concerning what Sir Arthur himself once described as "the psychic matter." In my own instance, as will be described in this memoir, my youthful self sought to challenge those specters who liked to interfere with his sleep. Moreover, so keen did I become to learn more about the Unknown that I suppose one might say I came "full circle" *vis a vis* my arcane interests.

Undoubtedly my fledgling Catholic upbringing (peripheral at best as it was) had left me with a palpable awareness of a mystical otherness which waited to be found. Moreover, my childhood exposures to death, in the shape of my uncle's passing quick on the heels of my grandfathers, had left me stunned, if not petrified. Factor in here as well a grim fascination with the Dracula figures of Lugosi and in my own day, Christopher Lee, and you had a recipe for more nightmares.

Over time however, my interest in whether there was something beyond this mortal coil of existence took many shapes. At this time I also learned of the ghost-busting career of Harry Houdini, whose fervor to disprove psychic mediums may have in reality been fueled by his desperate need to believe that his dear and deceased mother had somehow survived the bonds of death. In other words, she and legions of departed others may have graduated to a kind of eternal Summer Land. There then, and free from the woes of what Shakespeare called "this mortal coil," a blissful eternity awaited the worthy.

And like Houdini I suppose I sought solace in the idea that an "after" followed our "here," and better yet, that an entire world without boundaries existed. Years later I found an ample description of this notion in the lyric of Laurie Anderson, who sang, *"Paradise is exactly like where you are, right now—just much, much better."*

Of course there have always been religious and secular renditions of what Heaven or Paradise is like. Will it be purely individualized, or somehow a vast communal complex where robes are worn, harps are played, and streets of gold pavement lay beneath our heavenly feet? For many, including Mark Twain, such a tableau might better signal a veritable "hell of a heaven." Therefore for the likes of him, he said, while Heaven might be preferable for its climate, the Place Down

Under (and I don't mean Australia here) was more fetching for "the company."

As I approached adulthood I also found myself fascinated with the paradox of how a British author named Doyle had not only created the world's greatest logical detective, but himself personally believed in an extra-terrestrial after-life where you could savor the amplified pleasures of one's formal life, complete with seeing those we loved and liked while on earth.

There on the Other Side as Sir Arthur described it, time and woes and worry and sickness would be bereft of their temporal monopolies. But not so love and friendship and perhaps the best of one's spiritual orientations, which were all possibly mere earthbound previews of eternally coming attractions. Just so, the begetter of Sherlock Holmes believed without reservation in an Edenic place complete with eighteen holes of golf and a stiff whiskey thereafter!

Despite certain scriptural maledictions associated with communing with the dead, I grew increasingly interested in the subject of spirit communication. Here too I became intrigued by the talents of Spiritualistic mediums, and early on, with the astonishing reputation of the Scottish psychic performer, Daniel Dunglas Home.

Taking such separated, yet related interests aboard, my own opinions were formed. Moreover, and like Conan Doyle himself, I struggled to reconcile a spiritually-tempered material world with that "other venue," which was the consummation devoutly to be dreamt of by Christians and others.

This then is the preface to the Houdini Séance, which was seated within the "death room" in the old wing of Detroit's Grace Hospital. And it is there that the world's great escapologist had passed away on October 31, 1926 at age 52. And now, fifty-two years later on October 31, 1978, I was prepared to oversee the last séance from the aforesaid site, which was about to be demolished.

It was quite a scene. Assembled within the old hospital room were myself and about eight others. The party included reporters as well as two psychic mediums, or "sensitives." Meanwhile outside in the corridor, an oddly relevant, as well as unclinical assemblage had gathered. I was later told that a hospital researcher had pressed a stethoscope against the closed door of our impromptu séance room!

But once we began, only one of our pair of mediums felt able to proceed. That left her companion, who pronounced herself willing to begin. What I stated would be required of her was to "place a call" to Doyle, Price, and Houdini. As what is called a "control" in the psychic field, I had not informed the sensitives of our intention before the session.

Cutting to the chase, my rare medium did claim to reach all three gentlemen from the bounds of the Great Beyond. Doyle said that we would need to "read between the lines," which I suppose was an apt thing for an author to say. As for Price, he began to rattle on about an expedition he'd intended to make at Loch Ness to find its famous monster. And as for Houdini himself? He said he'd been working on a feat of bi-location when he'd died, and was going to be reincarnated in a younger member of his family. And as for that day's business? *Mishegoss,* scoffed the mage, which is the Yiddish word for "ridiculous."

But what frankly impressed, then bothered me a bit were two things. First of all, I had just returned from London where I'd had the great privilege of working with the private "Harry Price Collection" at London University's Senate House. I'd developed a nice rapport with the collection's curator, Alan Wesencraft, and been left alone to pour through Price's library of magical books and his extensive scrapbooks, photos, and artifacts. Among the latter I found a box-full of old "palming coins," used by a bygone magician named T. Nelson Downs. These had been gathered by Harry Price, who since his childhood had himself been an amateur conjuror.

At the end of my stay at Senate House I'd risked making a request of Mr. Wesencraft. Might it be possible for me to purchase one of the Downs coins, given that there were a good many of them in the collection? Here the old gentleman looked at me sympathetically through his thick spectacles and said, "I'm so sorry, but that would not be possible."

Imagine then my surprise two weeks later and upon returning home to receive a note from Alan Wesencraft. In it he thanked me for being so cooperative and hoped I'd enjoyed my time at Senate House. Moreover, as a token of our work together, he was enclosing something.

That "something" proved to be the T. Nelson Downs palming coin, used by its namesake for his on-stage tricks of manipulation. I was both honored and touched, and in tribute, fixed the silver coin to my watch chain.

Well anyway, while I'd been working with the Price manuscripts I'd stumbled upon something I'd previously not known about that intrepid ghost-booster and author of *The Most Haunted House In England.* Apart from his psychical research activities, I discovered that H.P. had taken an interest in the Loch Ness Monster, and in concert with Commander Rupert Gould, had planned an excursion to the lake to "hunt" the famous beastie.

That then sets the scene for my surprise when the medium, upon "reaching" Harry Price," began offering me comments from that discarnate gentleman concerning my own forays to Loch Ness. And I thought on hearing this, *she may have done her research and read an old clipping about my trips to the loch, or my interests in Sherlock Holmes. But how in this world or the next could she know about the Price connection to Loch Ness? Unless of course, she had read my unconscious mind?*

And the next bit of inexplicable business came about when I asked Irene, the medium, to do a bit of psychometry. For those who don't know, this is the art-form of "reading" residual vibrations from an object. Ergo, as the thesis has it, some object or even place may harbor powerfully "charged" emanations reflecting its past. Moreover as well, that the person capable of "tuning into" those vibrations as if receiving a radio signal, might decipher or describe them to some degree.

For my "target object" I gave the sensitive my hunter-case watch and chain. Upon it were two relics, in the form of a petrified shark's tooth given me by my mother and the silver Downs coin sent me by Mr. Wesencraft. She took the watch, gold linked chain and its two attached objects and began to gently knead them, as if to feel their energy.

"The watch and chain are not old" she said (which could have been merely a sharp observation). "But this coin (the Downs coin) has a feeling to it." She closed her eyes tightly and continued to rub the relic like Aladdin plying his lamp.

"This coin" said Irene, "belonged to one of the ones we have spoken to today." *Not bad. Do go on.*

"That's correct" I replied, suddenly deciding on a diversion. "This is a valued part of my private collection concerning magic. It is called a palming coin, and it once belonged to Harry Houdini." *There's a lie good enough to be true!*

The psychic reader looked at me now with a frown, her gray eyes opened, and then began to shake her graying head. *Why are you shaking your head?*

"No, it was not Houdini's" she replied. "It belonged to the other one." *You're good, madam. Or at least fairly clever. Or are you merely playing the game called Process of Elimination?*

I laughed as if I'd been found out. "Yes" I agreed. "Frankly, I was laying a trap for you. Because in truth this coin comes from my Sherlock Holmes Collection. It was once owned by Sir Arthur Conan Doyle himself." *Back at you. Touché!*

And then things turned peculiar.

"No" Irene said, shaking her head again and holding tightly to the coin on my watch-chain. "No, this coin belonged to the other one. Mr. Price." *What?* "And I'm getting something else from it. Something about a person who had this coin. An older man. Gave the coin to you. And something else, about his eyes. Trouble with his eyes." *The sound of warning signals growing loud as cathedral bells.*

I sat back and just looked at the rather slumped and hefty woman seated across the table. For what she'd just told me was tantamount not merely to privy information, but concerned a recent vignette out of my own recent past. For you see, upon bidding farewell to Alan Wesencraft we'd chatted about the days ahead. With some trepidation, he informed me he was about to undergo an ocular procedure to have two cataracts removed. He'd been worried about that. I in turn had assured him that I was certain that given the advancements these days, that all would be well. But how had she known, first that the coin had come from this "older man" who'd given me the Downs coin, and then about his eyes?

Madam, are you in fact reading my mind? I asked myself. For truth to tell, with so many other considerations, I had not even been thinking about those things at our session. So then, could the medium have somehow probed into my psyche that deeply? And if not, was it possible that it hadn't been Irene Rucinski, but Harry Price himself talking to me, about not only the coin from his collection, but also about "Nessie," a subject we'd both shared?

Here then was my first participatory capacity in an attempt intended to reach into the Hereafter. Our efforts were chronicled in a *Detroit News* article dated Wednesday, November 1, 1978 entitled "HOUDINI 'SPEAKS' AT SÉANCE: HE'S RETURNING FROM GRAVE." It recited comments allegedly made by Price, Houdini and Doyle.

On that same All Hallow's Tuesday in Detroit, in faraway Marshall, Michigan, Robert Lund, head of the town's Magical Museum made his own try at a "long-distance" call. I don't recall if Bob made use of anyone's psychic talents, but he said he'd hoped that if contacted, Harry Houdini's spirit would move a bagel around on one of the large milk cans he used as a trick.

The Houdini Death Room Adventure stands on its own as an exercise in the Unknown, Curious as well is the fact that I have encountered a number of books and documentaries concerning the King of Cuffs, but none of them has alluded to our experiment. A few years ago we sought to enshrine that episode in a Comcast broadcast entitled "The Houdini File." More distantly, there may exist certain of those newspaper morgues or clipping files which referenced the psychical endeavor to bridge the gap from Detroit's Grace Hospital to the Hereafter. Adding to those is this memoir. For like the proverbial "tree in the forest," we did "make a noise" with our séance, whether or not anyone chooses to believe it!

My experiences with mediums have been extremely rare. Not too much longer, and coincidentally, given the Lund Experiment, I coordinated an effort in the old National House Inn, at Marshall. There, in premises which had previously been those of a buggy works and a brothel, the sensitive performed, but did so with a sharp and slightly antagonistic

146

edge. I can't say why, exactly, but she and I didn't mix well. So much so, in fact, by the séance session's end, the sensitive turned to me with what she said were two important bits of information. The first of these involved a warning to me of sorts: I should be very careful in the near future, lest I suffer breaking my arm. Hearing this, I didn't know whether this was a warning, or a powerful suggestion? *Nevertheless I took her advice, and never broke it, by the by.*

But the second, post-scripted note from Beyond had a more problematic chill to it. This, when the medium counseled me to take another sort of care in future, in the event that I "took on more than I could handle" within the psychic realm. But behind that warning was something else: for as she calmly explained, the reason I needed to tread carefully was largely because *I myself had mediumistic abilities.* But to proceed. Having dabbled at the séance table, as had Arthur Conan Doyle, I gained nothing short of a great respect for the powers of the mind, as well as the possibility that "there are more things in heaven and earth…" You know the drill. Nor can I deny that in years still to come there were times when I'd realized I had indeed "took on more than I could." As you will see, this was demonstrated at Loch Ness in Scotland in ample fashion.

So accept if you will that the foregoing is but a bit of the line of country I'd enjoyed in my investigative work. And throughout it all I harbored an innate sense that this was something I was meant to do. Moreover, I'm tempted to say that I "was born to be a detective." If so, that would be close enough to the truth. But this is not a boast as much as a statement of odd fact. For you see, a year or so before my nativity, my parents-to-be watched a 1944 film starring Dana Andrews and Gene Tierney. The movie was entitled "Laura" and became quite popular, as did its haunting theme song, written by David Raksin and sung by Sinatra and many others.

At any rate, the young police detective in the film (Andrews) is named Mark McPherson. And seeing and hearing this part of the movie, my prospective folks said to one another, "if we have a son, that would be a great name!" And two years later when I decided to arrive, I was christened Mark Fredrick McPherson. And over the course of years to come, I would often hear the story about "Laura" and "how you got your name."

Now cut to the far-off future. It is 1982 and I am in New York at the Baker Street Irregulars Dinner and seated next to Otto Penzler, begetter of Gotham's legendary "Mysterious Bookshop" and its ancillary publication arm, The Mysterious Press. At any rate, the subject of my name came up and Otto told me he'd included an excerpt from Vera Caspary (author of the novel *Laura)* in a compendium of "mystery authors talking about their detectives."

"She told me she never wrote another Mark McPherson story because she couldn't think of one" my friend said. And then, and sharing my enchantment, my companion said, "you know, you ought to give her a call. She's living here in the city, over on Fifth Avenue. I'll give you her number. Tell her I said to call."

And that was that. Next day I rang Mrs. Caspary and told her who I was. At first I sensed she thought someone was pulling her leg. Imagine Conan Doyle unexpectedly having someone ring up saying he was Sherlock Holmes! But when I mentioned having dinner with Penzler last night and his suggestion that I call, to my amazement the lady suddenly invited me to her place!

I met Vera Caspary and was entertained by her in her charming Fifth Avenue apartment. She also confessed during our discussion to not having believed me until the last moment. She was also a bit impressed to learn that the chap bearing her character's name had done a bit of investigating himself. Add to that the fact that he was presently in Manhattan to celebrate Sherlock Holmes' birthday!

We parted on good terms, but not before Vera Caspary gave me a parting gift. This in the form of a recently published edition of *Laura* in French. And she inscribed the volume,

"TO MARK McPHERSON , WHOM I CAN'T QUITE BELIEVE IN."

Now let's travel a year later (t*ime seems such a relative commodity here*). I had the pleasure again of calling and then paying a call upon Mrs. Caspary once again at that very magical juncture of January when the BSI likes to celebrate the Master's Nativity. This time we had tea and I managed to have a picture taken of Vera and I on her sofa. A week later I sent her two prints of that photo and asked her to sign one. Which she did. And this time, I felt that I may have surmounted my literary "creator's" earlier disbelief. For the photograph which was posted back to me was inscribed

"TO MY FAVORITE DETECTIVE."

So there you go. I told you I was born for this business of detecting, didn't I?

Pressing on.

So it was that like Poe's "bi-partite man," I moved through the course of the years sustaining my living in a professional fashion, but departing from it whenever possible to pursue more unusual routes. A ghost hunt here. A visit to the Sphinx. A conference in Paris concerning the Shroud of Turin. A diving expedition to find Lost Atlantis. You know the drill. And like my ghost-hunting hero Harry Price in the Forties, I too often was interviewed or wrote up my exploits. Moreover, and as became obvious even before taking leave of my 'normal' pursuits, I realized that there might well be a price attached to leaving the herd, if only to wander solitarily through many a shadowy path.

In due time as well I began to see what I "did for a living" (as financially precarious as such an occupation might be) in comparatively unique terms. But this too was often enough a double-edged sword. After all, who would want to eke out an existence on the basis of chasing mysteries and phantoms? Truthfully, my only templates at the time were two in number. The first of those was Holmes of Baker Street. And the second was another fictive persona I'd encountered around 1982. Academic by nature, he was a renegade and danger-seeker. His *modus operandi* appeared to involve getting out, "into the field" where he got his hands dirty, if not bloody. And after pursuing his unusual, sacred, or supernatural quarry, he would return to society or the classroom, where cleaned up and nattily attired, he would regale his audience with his adventures. And that man's name was Indiana Jones.

Undoubtably Professor Jones' approach to truth-seeking was to reflect what Joseph Campbell once defined in *The Hero With A Thousand Faces*. In that brilliant treatise, Professor Campbell made the case for the true "hero." But not necessarily as the white hat-wearing savior of the day, who always won, or always got the girl. Instead, Campbell was careful to explain that the true Hero of the classical kind was one who went down into the shadows, risked everything, if only to earn the chance to return to the light and once again share the world of his fellows.

Years later I came to understand Joseph Campbell's point. Now and again I would try to share it with audiences, even taking the risk of stating, "You know, I too am a hero." And just before they were ready to sigh or as was more likely, turn upon the speaker, I would give them Campbell's definition. And when I did I realized that I had fulfilled a good deal of the archetypal "heroic" formula. For had I not left the herd, and willingly? And had I not been considered a voluntary "outsider?"

This notion was brought home to me on what was I think, the second occasion of my hying off for Loch Ness to go monster hunting. It was early evening and I was putting my bag into the trunk before moving ahead to the airport. As I did so, my next-door neighbor was loading up as well, but with sporting equipment. He was on his way to the local playing field, where his duties as a member of the local Dad's Club would consume the rest of the night.

You know, I couldn't help wonder at that moment if I had harbored a wish to be heading for the ball-park, rather than a transatlantic flight which would eventually see me in a boat, on dark water, beneath which a dinosaurian specie was rumored to exist? Or to be imaginatively fair, might my neighbor, being aware of my own odd penchants, have wished for a more glamourous destination for himself other than the local diamond? We may never know.

But such was the image I had honed, but not merely by being interviewed on radio, television, or in newspapers across the land. In realistic terms, I had chosen to cut myself from the legion of my fellows. And because of that I attracted the attention of strangers and frequently repelled the interest of former friends and lovers. Such then was the price. And what must Sherlock Holmes have felt during his own darkest nights of the soul? What about those times when he was accompanied by nothing other than his desire to heroically penetrate the darkness, if only to rise up into the light with a found or likely solution? Those must have been hard days indeed, and I cannot doubt that Sherlock Holmes would never have forgotten them. For as he states to his colleague, Reginald Musgrave in "The Musgrave Ritual," *"Yes," Holmes answered, "I have taken to living by my wits."*

And dear Sherlock must have known, as did I, what a perilous sea to sail that could be.

But I excelled. I created an "investigative agency" dubbed DAEDALOS, which was a bit of word-play for the Greek name of Daedalus, the Crafty Maker of the Cretan Labyrinth. Accordingly as well, I employed the emblem of the ancient *"labrys"* or maze upon my materials. At its core, that concentric tracery reflected the Cretan story of the Minotaur and its mythic opponent, Jason. But the *labrys* also bore the archaic signature of the double-bladed axe associated with the archaeological site of the Labyrinth. Representative of the waxing and waning of the moon, the *labrys* was also the timeless signet of the Great Goddess. And then of course there was the presence of something of a considerably more modern provenance. This, in the paraphrased shape of T.S. Eliot's poetic lines to the effect that when we reach the maze-like end-point of our quests, we may also discover its beginning. But more than that; by daring to peer between the bricks, what one finds in the mortar is often perplexing.

> *"Between the idea and the reality,*
> *Between the motion and the act*
> *Falls the Shadow."*

And there have been a great many shadows in my path, to be certain. And some of them weird enough, in Robert Graves' ancient sense of the word, to be portentous. So much so that the seeker himself might well be stopped in his tracks. I'd known times like those as well. Yes, moments when reason and logic and every daylit aspect tends to drown in the darkness. Particularly when you are in some remote place where something odd or mysterious or even impossible is supposed to have happened. Moreover, when it comes down to you and to that witness to the incredible who is aware that the world will doubt them. And on such account, usually the only ones who were ready to believe them were fellow witnesses. This, I found to be true for those who claimed a close encounter with ghosts, Bigfoot, UFOs, or even the Loch Ness Monster.

Understandably then, in "this line" such things as go bump or whatever in the night or day-time are not for everyone. In fact, the population of those who take them seriously enough to leave hearth and home to seek them is rather small. And why then do they persist? Perhaps they seek enlightenment. Or maybe they are merely trying to replace one set of nightmares with another?

And so I became "the Man From DAEDALOS." In most cases the rarity of my work served its point well. But there was of course that one interviewer who inadvertently pronounced the name of my agency for "field work and investigation" "Dead-Loss." *And given the leanness of some of those days, I could hardly blame him.*

But as far as the press and public? Well what self-respecting reporter does not want to interview someone who is serious enough to launch a diving expedition to Bimini for the purpose of discovering Plato's fabled Atlantis? Or of preparing for a deep-water dive into the 975-foot depths of Scotland's Loch Ness, in search of a monster? Or of actually producing, coordinating, and co-starring in an actual literary "Trial Of William Shakespeare" to address the fabled authorship question of "Who Really Wrote Hamlet?" There were other adventures as well, such as a succession of later visits to Great Britain's Somersetshire, where archaeological attempts were being made to find the historical, Dark Age beginnings of Camelot. I was there as well, spade in hand.

Yes, just as I would find myself in Paris to join experts and lay investigators gathered together to ask whether the Carbon 14 "de-bunking" of the Shroud of Turin as a 14th century forgery in 1988 was authentic? Season such inquiries into a fair share of ghost hunting in at least three countries, and follow that up with a chain of lectures and documentary films, such as "An Egyptian Odyssey," wherein I prowled the desert and even met privately with Anwar Sadat.

Now again, none of this is a vaunt or boast intended as a bid for attention. Please understand me. It is instead now being offered up as evidence of a sort that "the past is prologue." When I chanced to remember that line, quite honestly I did not remember if indeed it was of a Shakespearean origin? But indeed it turned out to be so. Appropriately as well, "the past is prologue" comes out of "The Tempest," Act 2, Scene 1. And possibly reflecting what we've been opining all along, the Bard's tale of Prospero and Caliban is also a tale redolent with fate and fortune, prophecy and magic.

So ask yourself even as I have inquired of myself, whether the Past has indeed served as the unwitting Prologue for what was to come as I came "of age?" So it would seem, for good or ill. To wit as well, certain of what I ingested in heady literary terms in childhood did find its way down the road to adulthood. But not for the sake of making me famous or rich or an Indiana Jones-styled American Idol. Instead of that, seemingly the reward would come purely from what one has learned. And that in aggregate form may result in much, or very little. It all seems a bit random. And why?

Well memory plus age does not always equal accuracy. Contrarily as well, those conditions may combine to conjure a perfect storm in which recollections may give way to any number of factors. That too, I suppose, relates to the second of the "Sherlockian" novels so recently read. This, in contrast to Simmons' 2015 publication of *The Fifth Heart,* is *A Slight Trick of the Mind* by Mitch Cullin, which came out in 2006. But the echo of that has become crystal clear with the current debut of the film "Mr. Holmes," starring Sir Ian McKellan as the 93-year-old sleuth limping through his recollections of a seminal, albeit unknown case never recorded by Dr. Watson.

My point here plays to the notion that the idea of Sherlock Holmes questioning his fictional and literary alter ego, or feeling free at last, in his ninth decade of life, to shun the publicized misperceptions of his true self, have a bearing on this memoir.

And taking the matter further, the hypothesis I am struggling with does not require that the memoirologist be great of any social note. It has to do instead with the idea of how we see ourselves, in contrast to how others see, or have been encouraged to see us?

Ultimately I suppose the resolve of those two fictional versions of an unreal character is very like that espoused by the great author, adventurer and eroticist Sir Richard Francis Burton. He wrote, and I read and memorized his words very early on, his admonition to

> *"Do what thy manhood bids thee do,*
> *from none but self expect applause.*
> *He noblest lives and noblest dies*
> *who makes and keeps his self-made laws. "*

Burton knew the costs of the game. But he played it and lived and I suppose died by those "self-made laws." He tried the poison and tested the limits. He ignored the warnings and ventured into terrains where angels, if not demons, feared to tread. Then he passed away a rogue. Never entered into the race strictly to be loved or admired, he ran it as hard as he could, as if on a track by himself. And for that, to me, he was of the cut of those who have been in their ways larger-than-life and tending to consume most of the oxygen in the room. To this day, our sense of Richard Burton is exceeded only by his ever-growing legend.

But aren't we all a bit like Burton? I wonder. Or possibly, and to our own credit or shame, might we not have wished we could be?

The author's first view of Brook Manor —
a.k.a. "Baskerville Hall" (1969)

10
Britannia, Redux

Still trying to follow the chronological rabbit down its hiding-hole:

In 1969 the second occasion of my hiatus to Great Britain bore its own indelible Holmesian stamp. That term, by the way, represents a British aficionado of Baker Street, as does its transatlantic American counterpart, of "Sherlockian."

I may honestly say that apart from or even despite my sojourn two years earlier, this time my attennæ for matters literary, and in particular, those of a Baker Street bent felt more keenly honed. And now at twenty-two I felt better inclined to address such issues. Curiously enough, the consequence of returning to the United Kingdom allowed me to experience a new feeling of comfort. Exotic yes, and exciting to be certain, the London of 1969 was still emblematic of its earlier traditional imagery. But now its streets offered the hybrid aspect of gentlemen in bowlers and brollies in company with those other counter-cultural, Sgt. Pepperish Carnaby Street figures which the magazines liked to represent as the tenants of "Swinging London."

In other words, that legendary city was hip and staid and historic and seemingly scented with patchouli or cannabis amid the heavy, pulsing beat of those British Invaders. To me, who had conquered America, only two years after my virgin voyage, London was like an ever-rolling documentary of cool, most of it set to the popular lyric "England swings like a pendulum, do…" Yes, and once again I was a part of it, but this time a little less staid, and a whole lot more keen on exploration. No longer beset by the feeling of being a stranger on a strange planet, now I actually felt at home. Nor was I afraid to get my hands dirty, metaphorically speaking. And with that thought, and occasionally thinking of my abdominal souvenir, courtesy of the British Health System, I entered and prepared to conquer.

I still smile on remembering my earlier arrival in '67. I was such a stick. I even remember something in my head at the time telling me that a certain degree of formality would be appropriate. Perhaps the image of the immaculately Pierre Cardin-tailored Avenger, John Steed, had played to my mood. For just such a reason, upon arriving there I did not eschew a three-piece suit and even an umbrella, brought with me across the sea. Naively, I made my way over, and once there was only once unwittingly apprised of how I came across. That was within my first week of my ill-fated tenancy in Forest Hill. Walking down the street toward a bus stop, I overheard two little boys as I passed. One of them said "there goes a proper Charley." At the time I took it for my seeming rather natty. It didn't take much longer to understand that the "Charley" epithet might well have been represented by the British pejorative "poofter." Suffice it to say that not all young men in waistcoats with bumbershoots were taken for John Steed-like sartorial spies!

Two years later however had made a difference in everything, including myself. Now as well, as I reminded myself, it was truly the time to explore London's Sherlockian/Holmesian associations. And apart from those, I resolved to make excellent use of my time in terms of my Anglophile's love of English literature, history, and of course, those wonderful old pre-and-post-war films. In the latter category and unexpectedly as always, I got my wish in spades.

Set the stage of the first part of my new and excellent adventures. Some of this related to my lodgings in a sort of youth hostel seated along the Cromwell Road near Gloucester Road Station. The place seemed more like a vacated London mansion, which it doubtless had been. Now however the place was run by some clerical sisters and provided rooms and breakfast for a number of travelers or international students. Such then was the basis for our American Language Education Centre group to be staying there.

One morning I was chatting with one of the younger sisters. We found ourselves discussing such topics as Peter Sellers, Winston Churchill, and Sherlock Holmes. Perhaps given the movie associations here, my companion was excited to inform me that the great British actor Alec Guinness sometimes came by the hostel to say hello. This connection came on account of that gentleman's own devout Catholicism. Now truthfully, I don't know why the star of "The Lavender Hill Mob," "The Detective," and "Our Man In Havana" chanced to drop into the hostel I was briefly calling home. I'm uncertain of whether there was even a chapel there. Perhaps however there was a priest or two, or some association with one of the nuns? In any event, I was told that Sir Alec did occasionally show one of his many faces, and should the great man visit while I was there, my informant would let me know. *Excellent.*

With your permission, I will put a "hold" on the rest of the story as it eventually concerns not only Alec Guinness but another film star of his acquaintance. For now and instead, it is time to speak again of Sherlock Holmes. He after all is a kind of constant Greek Chorus for this memoir, and without him my point should not be made. Therefore let us begin at the beginning, with what might be called in Watsonian terms, "The Case of the Baskerville Quest." And that, my friends, was initiated through the good courtesy of the redoubtable Sherlock Holmes Society of London.

For a few years at this time I had become an avid reader of *The Sherlock Holmes Journal.* I would thrill at finding its brown subscriber's envelope and its stamp from the Royal Post. And within those covers was an assemblage of Holmesian scholarship, the gist of which was published by the Sherlock Holmes Society of London, under the Honorary Editorship of the Marquis of Donegall. However from a more practical, probably day-to-day basis, the Society's President as Sir Paul H. Gore-Booth, G.C.M.G., K.C.V.O. A tick below Sir Paul was Philip Dalton, the SHS Chairman.

Now then and as I have discovered countless times to date, one of the problems of reaching back and writing a memoir such as this is keeping the past "intact." Which is to say, finding yourself a quarter century later and asking yourself, *"when did that happen? How could I not remember it more clearly?" "I mean, I was there, wasn't I?"*

But "time, tides, and buttered eggs wait for no man" observed John Masefield. Which is to suggest that the years and a legion of details, great and small, have a tendency to get in your recollective way. Therefore and not entirely as an excuse, I must admit in this specific regard that while I do not recall the "who" or "how" of the thing. nevertheless, I was duly informed that I was being invited to meet a few members of the Sherlock Holmes Society in a matter of days. Pondering the matter, I had drawn a blank. Perhaps a letter announcing my impending arrival had been sent before my going over? Or possibly the writer had been informed of my arrival by one of my own Sherlockian cohorts? Whatever the case, what remains on firmer ground is the fact that I was indeed to meet a few members of that August organization at the equally August Charing Cross Hotel near the Strand. Therefore eager, if not a bit nervous, I showed up at the duly arranged place at the appointed hour.

Now as every one of you must know, there are times when "real life" is more amusing, dramatic, even fantastic than anything seen on a printed page or a cinema screen. Just so did I find my first meeting with Britain's delegation of pre-eminent Holmesians.

I arrived at the Charing Cross Hotel, nicely dressed and uncertain of what precisely to expect. I was told I would meet a person named Philip Dalton, who would be my contact for the evening. Something about that term seemed vaguely Graham Green-ish, Fleming-esque, LeCarre-like, or, as was the case back in 1969, Deighton-istic. But back then I suppose I laced many of my real-life endeavors with images of detectives, spies and clandestine capers of derring-do.

I was informed I would be "met" within, or near the hotel's somewhat stately lobby. Obviously wanting to make a good impression, I arrived a tad early and settled into a corner wingback with a weather eye on the lobby.

Sitting there I eventually felt disheartened. From my vantage, there appeared to be no one looking like a British Holmesian. Constantly checking my watch, at somewhere around a near half-hour I nervously confessed myself ready to leave. But at that very moment I took note of the two couples seated nearby. Nothing odd about them, save for the fact that one of them uttered the suddenly overheard surname "McPherson." Antennae up and paying closer attention, I saw what appeared to be an expression on the speaker's face which bordered on irritation. And I asked myself, *now what are the odds that...?*

I decided to take the plunge. Getting to my feet, I walked over to the couples, only to sense in that moment that the group was not two, or four, but perhaps more like six or more persons.

"Excuse me" I intruded, directing my remark to a nice looking Englishwoman, "but are you waiting for someone named Mark McPherson?"

The lady looked up at me in surprise. Then the pleasant faced middle aged gentleman by her side half-rose and said, "indeed we are. But he appears not to have arrived." To which I smiled, felt a bit sheepish, and admitted my "secret" identity.

"I'm afraid he has" I confessed. "I'm Mark McPherson."

"And I'm Philip Dalton" the stranger said, extending his hand. "And these are members of our Society. We're actually expecting a few more, but we were worried that our guest of honor had failed to show up." *Guest of honor? What happened to a few drinks among a couple of members?*

Well the eventual and collective response of that evening as I recall it, was one of mixed amusement, non-plussedness, and the general notion that the Holmes Society's British members now had a Yankee renegade in their midst. And at twenty-two, a young one to boot. In any event, I was informed that the group, representing an entourage of the SHS, had all arrived to meet me, and to offer me dinner as well. I professed myself duly honored, and apologized for the social gaff of my sitting there like the famous wax effigy of Sherlock Holmes. Nevertheless, I also I found myself musing *"but don't you think you might have revealed yourselves?* And then it occurred to me that to my own credit, perhaps I did not seem so much like the Yank in the Panama Hat and cigar, or the Proper Charley of two years earlier? Still and all, I suppose we could have arranged for someone to wear a pink carnation or some revelatory, tell-tale emblem. It occurred to me as well that had this tryst been the other way 'round, and involved an American assignation, probably at least half the group would have sported deerstalker caps. Fortunately, that didn't happen here.

Later and upon replaying the events of that fascinating evening, it occurred to me that had Dr. Watson set it down, he might have entitled it "The Curious Incident Of The People Who Sat Mute In The Nighttime." Not quite as telling as what the "dog in the nighttime" did not do within the "Adventure of Silver Blaze" perhaps, but it stands out as memorable nonetheless.

And as for my first and only get-together with the Sherlock Holmes Society of London, to this day only two things stand out as memory trolls backward. The first was my immediate liking for their Chairman, Philip "Pip" Dalton. And the second was the acquaintance suddenly forged with an older, somewhat garrulous gent named Charles O.

Merriman. His capacity as it turned out was as the Society's Honorary Treasurer. But more obvious that night was his penchant for researching certain topics of Holmesian interest. And as I would find, one of his favorites involved the quest for the actual prototype of "Baskerville Hall."

In curious fashion as well, at the end of my summer hiatus in Britain (and its related adventure) I returned home to find the Summer, 1969 issue of the SHERLOCK HOLMES JOURNAL. To my own pleasure and surprise, on Page 48 I came across "Random Baskerville Jottings" by Charles O. Merriman. And there, like an echo of our own lengthy, albeit abbreviated dinner chat, was my new British colleague's bit of armchair fieldwork.

Now with all due respect to Mr. Merriman, I say "armchair" fieldwork, given his own opening explanations beside me at dinner. After toasts and a bit of diagonal chit-chat the table 'round, I found myself conversing with my elderly companion. He informed me that he had long been an aficionado of Conan Doyle's *Hound of the Baskervilles,* and had taken a special interest in that literary classic's historical counterpart.

I recall our discussion of the many sources for *The Hound,* and even the role of Conan Doyle's friend Bertram Fletcher Robinson. For it was the latter who had supposedly suggested the theme of ghostly hounds to the author during the course of a golfing vacation. That conversation would ultimately blossom into Sir Arthur's notion for "a real creeper" of a tale. But more importantly, the year at this juncture was 1903, and a decade after he had willfully murdered Sherlock Holmes at Reichenbach Falls. But whether it was the public's constant din about bringing their favorite detective back, or whether the theme of a spectral hound was too good to waste on a non-entity, he took a rather clever course. Ergo, after his new novel was written, it was presented as a "posthumous memoir" of Mr. Sherlock Holmes. Thus the master sleuth was able to make a past-tense reappearance, to the joy of both publisher and reading public alike. And with publication of *The Hound of the Baskervilles,* the answer to one of those burning Doylean questions was now available: *Was there Life After Death? Obviously there was, if the price was right.* And let us not cavil over the fact: Arthur Conan Doyle knew he had a cash cow in Holmes. So why not milk it?

But as Merriman was quick to inform me, the matter of where the "true" Baskerville Hall was seated was still a bit of a mystery. For instance, some had suggested Fletcher Robinson's home, Park Hill in Dartmoor, where he also kept his coachman, Harry *Baskerville*. Others had preferred nearby Haytree House, or the Welsh Border region Claro Court, which bore a connection to the Baskerville family. Then too there was Lew Tranchard Manor, home to the great Dartmoor folklorist, the Reverend Sabine Baring-Gould, also ancestor to the modern-day author of *Sherlock Holmes of Baker Street*. And nearly last of all among the presumptive candidates was Hergest Court near Claro Court. This was the lowering country seat of the Vaughan family, which had an association with a supernatural hound. Moreover, the Vaughans and Baskervilles had intermarried. And a further clue here: Fletcher Robinson had all but admitted that his specific notion of a specific hound had been drawn from a Welsh pamphlet on folklore. I say "specific," inasmuch as the British Isles are redolent with tales of "black" or "phantom" hounds. Among these was a calf-sized, saucer-eyed beast called "Old Shuck," a name derived from the Anglo-Saxon term for "demon."

In any event, Mr. Merriman explained, if originally of Welsh origin, the Legend of the Hound had seemingly been transported to Devonshire and Dartmoor. And it was there that Conan Doyle had first heard of the theme in earnest from his friend Robinson. There as well did he meet Harry Baskerville, who, as the theory goes, was eventually transmuted into "Sir Henry Baskerville" in the eponymous novel.

"But there is another connection in Dartmoor that needs exploring" Merriman mused, even as he reached for the carafe and topped off my wine glass. Accepting it, I sipped as the Society's Treasurer told me about one of the Holmes canon's most undiscovered treasures: Baskerville Hall.

He took a bit of time to describe what he called The Case For Cabell Manor. Seated in Buckfastleigh, in Dartmoor, the home of Sir Richard Cabell, who died (supposedly) in 1672, had much about it to recommend it as the seat of the Baskervilles. And if not their ancestral seat, then surely a place rich with a frightful provenance as the birth-site of the fabled Hound.

From what I could gather, not unlike Sir Hugo Baskerville in the tale, Sir Richard Cabell was regarded as a bad lad. But more than that; for unlike the novel's 18th century devilish protagonist, Sir Richard was demonical in his own right. So much so that his vampiric reputation had succeeded him, even to the point of his interment in a ground-level penthouse, or pagoda-shaped tomb at Buckfastleigh Parish Church. There to this day there are rituals which remain to ward off Cabell's lingering spirit. Moreover, and in Dracula-esque fashion, Sir Richard's tomb had been of solid rock, a "table top" grave with a protective slab above it, a building around it, and barred windows to keep strangers out, or perhaps, I mused, to keep its dastardly strange inhabitant "in?" And let's not forget the post-script here: upon the lord of the Manor of Brook's demise, it is said that the specters of black hounds flared and seethed over the moorlands!

I listened with fascination as the grandfatherly chap on my right concluded his remarks. He did so by also informing me that his present belief was that Brook Manor, home to Sir Richard in life, bore every insignia of being "Baskerville Hall."

"Amazing" I said, resisting to add "Holmes" to my comment. "Your research is very exciting." The older man thanked me and paused before resuming.

"It is that" he continued. "But there is one rather slight but insurmountable obstacle in furthering my cause." "And what would that be?" I inquired.

"Well for starters, we need a bit more reconnaissance for the house. Better photographs than what little we have of Brook Manor. And secondly, well the fact is, the present owner is no aficionado of Sherlock Holmes."

"As in 'trespassers will be shot'" I observed with a laugh.

"Something toward that end" said Charles Merriman with a grim, steely smile. "Sadly, I am too old to go tromping about the Moors."

I registered his comment, feeling in that instant rather sad for the old fellow. And it was then that the scene seemed to shift. And it was initiated once again by the diminishing of the now less than half full carafe of wine before us. As he was about to continue, my host reached for it, and once again did his best to replenish my glass. And as this was achieved, he continued.

"But you know, Mark, you are a younger man. You could get in there and get the goods. Could you not?" The glass which was poised within a few inches of my lips now seemed frozen in time. *Me?* "I don't know" I replied. "I suppose I could. I would love the chance to see a bit of Dartmoor."

I do not recall what Charles O. Merriman's response to me was in those moments. I don't seem to remember him saying, "well then, Bob's your uncle," or something to that effect. All I do recollect was the feeling of suddenly finding myself within a drama within a drama. And without expecting it, now I was standing there before the unseen camera.

Suffice it then to cut to the chase, which began early the next day. It commenced with my making a pilgrimage to one of those spots in the City which Dr. Watson had lightly veiled in *The Hound of the Baskervilles* as "Stamford's." This was none other than the very real Stanford's Geological Establishment on Longacre Street near Charing Cross. As in Holmes' own day, the Stanford establishment continued to deal in cartographic materials, and more peculiarly, it remained the sole London agent for the sale of Ordnance Survey maps.

To my great pleasure, I found the place standing and perhaps little changed from the day and *locus* of the Victorian era. And now I, like Mr. Holmes, was there to procure a "one inch to one mile" ordnance of Dartmoor.

I was now resolved to embark on my great adventure within a day or so. Armed with the peculiar warrant of a masterful Holmesian, suddenly I'd become his secret agent of sorts for the mission ahead. And secret was perhaps the appropriate term. For given what old Merriman had said of the popularity of Holmes aficionados (and in this case a Yankee Sherlockian), I wasn't expecting a warm welcome.

When I got back to my digs I began to study the accordion folds of the ordnance map and in particular, the part of it in a radius around Buckfastleigh. And like Holmes and Watson before me, I anticipated a rail journey, which would conduct me from Paddington to Exeter and then on to Newton Abbot. From that market town it would be necessary to debark and make the rest of the way via a bus, and from thence, on foot. Which is exactly the route I took two days later.

I recall a couple of things about that trip before I set out to take it. One of those was my comment to some friends, whom I thought it wise to inform of my movements. First of all, as I'd detected, the area in question was more than remote. In fact, between mires and moors, portions of the landscape had been designated for their "Archeological," "Beauty Spots," "Ecclesiastical," "Stately Homes,' "Water Features" or other aspects of interest. In my case however, how to explain those color-coded designations which all but rang out, *"you don't want to venture here, mate."* Some of those were even strategically earmarked as past or present RAF shelling sites.

To the latter point, *vis a vis* my entering the periphery of the British military's shooting gallery of sorts, I read something interesting not long ago. This had to do with the notion that supposedly the use of munitions within remote rural niches of Britain had at times actually stimulated the local environment. To wit, the belief that upon "military land," wildlife still thrived, and that despite the imminent threat of detonations, the absence of humans generated certain country areas as natural reserves. An extreme example of this was Cumbria's Warcop, where the shell shattering of the ground had resulted in increased badger sets, deep down beyond the explosive points of impact.

Further study of my Stanford's map revealed a set of multi-hued keys for height of terrain, etc. But most noticeable to me were the plentifully specified red-labelled areas were punctuated by the word "DANGER." All of which would have made my mother's day, I mused. And a good thing Mrs. McPherson had no inkling of what her baby boy was getting into this time. And hadn't she warned me about drinking the water, eating the food, or breathing the foggy air only two years earlier? I could scoff at that in retrospect, but I still carried and would forever more my well-healed appendectomy scar. Often I imagined it invisibly emblazoned with the words MADE IN BRITAIN, and once in a great while I'd still feel a twinge, reminding me. But at any rate, as I consoled myself, I don't suppose Mrs. Holmes or her husband were ever properly prepared for what their errant son had in mind for himself.

So picture me at Paddington Station. No cuddly bears in site, however. Instead only one American Grail seeker in ball cap, khaki zip jacket and jeans and boots. A knap-sack and a rolled up piece of plastic, which in theory was going to shield me from the damp ground, should I resort to camping in the wild. But that prospect, truth to tell, was not overmuch on my mind. I suppose what was instead was the idea of training and bussing and walking into the interior. After that I would find Merriman's Brook Manor, shoot some pictures, and re-trace my steps. As easy as that. But what was that old chestnut which said, *"Want to make God laugh? Just tell him your plans."*

There was also another little glitch I'd discovered as I waited to board my train. This to the effect that in the Department of the Exchequer, I had no more currency than might allow me to get to my destination. And as for the idea of getting back? No joy there, as my British friends might say. And all I knew for certain was that I was about to take on a lunar mission with only enough gas to get me to the surface. That, by the way, is a somewhat apt and timely simile, for a couple of weeks earlier, NASA had landed the first men on the Moon. I recall actually being patted on the back, as if I'd had something to do with it. But I hadn't. Those brave astronauts had made history on their own. Yes, just as I was now trying to do within the field of Sherlockian Research. But this did not alter the fact that someone (myself) had been rash in his planning. Just enough in the way of pounds sterling to buy me a one-way ticket to Newton Abbot. And a few quid to pay for what I was pre-informed would be necessary for bus-fare. After that, I was on the hoof, quite literally.

Now, as to the details of my rail journey into the depths of Dartmoor, suffice it to say, as I followed the approximately same route by rail that both Holmes and Watson had in *The Hound,* or another adventure, I felt not just the rhythm of the tracks, but also the sound of the game being proverbially afoot.

Alone with my thoughts now in the comparatively modern British Rail compartment, I imagined myself instead in that earlier version of the dynamic duo visualized by Sidney Paget for *The Strand.* Most Sherlockians have seen this illustration, in which Watson listens closely as Holmes leans toward him and ticks off his points on his open hand. Both of them are bound for Dartmoor, as was I, but their goal was "King's Pyland" in "The Adventure of Silver Blaze."

But looking at my reflection in the window I might have been disappointed. For nor was I togged out in my ear-flapped cap or hooded, maxi-lengthened travel coat. Instead I was dressed for a rough expedition, and I probably under-dressed even for that.

And then of course there was the landscape, and what one old poetry professor of mine liked to call the idea of "poetic fallacy." This, when Nature seemed to reflect, or empathize the mortal condition. Well if that was so, then my condition at this time was adrenalin-charged and ready for whatever might come. So I'll merely suggest what I saw beyond my compartment's view. For the most this constituted a dulled panorama of those ever-graying skies racing over and at times cloud-shadowed landscape when the sun tried feebly to make its stand. And what I saw, I mused, did in fact mate with my mood. For nearly everything about those chiaroscuro hues of my outer world had taken on the burnished aura of the Unknown.

And now, finding myself on the brink of one of Sherlock Holmes' greatest adventures, here I was at summer's end, also aware that the rustic world around me seemed suddenly cloaked with the dank fetid heaviness of autumn. This then was the Doylean portal I had deliberately chosen to enter. Just so as well, here was the actualization of my plan for moving deeper into the vales of those storied moorlands.

I'd gauged my schedule to reach Brook Manor by later that afternoon. As the map's ordnance key indicated, the measured distance between my destination and the terminus of Newton Abbot was about ten miles. These I planned to cover by bus, or at worst, by hitching a ride if possible. After that, I thought, it would be the work of my twenty-two year old legs for getting me safely there and back.

After reaching the station at Newton Abbot about half-past one, I scouted about and found the small bus station. Given the hour, I did my best not to give in and devour the roast beef sandwiches I'd purchased at the little shop at Gloucester Road Station. I was going to need sustenance for the day and night ahead, I told myself. And after that? Who knew?

The small bus, or coach, contained only a few passengers. In fact, I believe I was among the last to ride it to my partial destination, which terminated at cross-road. Nor do I recall if I consciously compared that moment of disembarking with the one in *Dracula,* where Jonathon Harker is left at the Borgo Pass in the darkness before he makes his midnight connection to reach the Count's castle?

I do seem to recall asking the driver if I was headed "the right way," as I unfurled my ordnance map with its grease penciled markings at Black Tor and Cross Furzes, where my destination lay. I think he nodded and gestured ahead on the road, even to where the foliage seemed to assume the shape of an elemental tunnel. And I wouldn't have been surprised if he'd looked upward, to where the roiling skies of Dartmoor were giving a very fair preview of rain. And then back at his lone American passenger, whom he was about to surrender to the elements.

But there I was as the bus rambled away. Sherlock Holmes in khaki jacket, baseball cap, with a shouldered knapsack containing a few sandwiches, a water-flask, a battered "torch" or flashlight, my camera, a small box of cigars, a copy of *The History of Buddhism,* a paperback of *The Hound of the Baskervilles,* and of course, my all-purpose plastic tarp. But would that be sizable enough to double as a tented roof, if the situation demanded it? The answer seemed predictable, as was the inference: this was no way to plan a rough expedition into those realms once described by Conan Doyle himself, in a note to his mother. Dartmoor was, he wrote, "a great place, very sad and wild." Perhaps, I thought, when this is over I'll write my own letter home and say the same. Or would I? Thinking of this I'd studied a number of passages in my paperback of *The Hound of the Baskervilles* to help pass the time on my journey. I found an extra-chilled modicum of cold comfort there, especially when I re-read Sir Hugo Baskerville's own warning to his offspring, to

"...forbear from crossing the moor in those dark hours when the powers of evil are exalted."

"We had left the fertile country behind and beneath us" said Dr. Watson in his own bit of travel narrative *"We looked back on it now, the slanting rays of a low sun turning the streams to threads of old and glowing on the red earth new turned by the plough and the broad tangle of the woodlands. The road in front of us grew bleaker and wilder over huge russet and olive slopes sprinkled with giant boulders. Now and then we passed a moorland cottage, walled and roofed with stone, with no creeper to break its harsh outline. Suddenly we looked down into a*

168

cup-like depression, patched with stunted oaks and firs which had been twisted and bent by the fury of years of storm."

And with that view quite literally in mind, I proceeded to hike for almost two hours. My Stanford's ordnance map served its purpose, and it occurred to me in rather after-the-fact fashion that it might have been prudent to have brought along a compass. On that note, suddenly all I could imagine was my father's face, and a shake of his woodsman's head. On one side of the coin, no doubt he would have been doubtless proud to know that his only son—that same heir of his loins who had never displayed the slightest interest in joining him to shoot or gut a deer—was now somewhere in Britain's Back of Beyond. And on the other side of the family coin? Probably a saner version of my mother's panic, had she an inkling of what her darling boy had now willingly entered into.

And then to no spectacular surprise, I heard the toll of the thunder. As I trudged on it seemed to grow louder, like that old business in Irving's *Rip Van Winkle* when he described Henry Hudson's men playing their ghostly game of ninepins.

There was no trace of rain for perhaps another half hour, at which time I suspected I was getting closer. But closer to what, exactly? Ideally the answer here was meant to be: Brook Manor. But all around me everything seemed to conspire to say *"You're not wanted here. Turn back."*

From somewhere in memory's depths, I heard the old injunction: *"Abandon Hope All Ye Who Enter Here."*

But then, and as if spoken by in the familiar tone of an invisible companion, I heard still another platitude: *"In for a penny, in for a pound."* Sound advice I thought for this perpetually only child who had read and liked the title of Christopher Morley's book *The Man Who Made Friends With Himself.* As a result, I'd taken that idea literally to heart some time back. And because of it, I'd always felt myself to be in good company. Now however I began to feel a little guilty over having dragged him here, to the Back of Beyond.

But nor could I refrain from reminding myself of another rather obvious truth; in the Pennies and Pound Department, I was already in a deficit condition. And here, walking through this darkening wilderness, I was "in" all right, but without the prospective financial resources to get the hell out of Dodge, if not Dartmoor.

I decided to take a breather. Leaning against a large rock, I withdrew my canteen, took a swig or two of water, and extracted my well-thumbed copy of *The Hound.* And there in that moment I flipped to the point in Doctor Watson's account when Baskerville Hall first comes into view.

"The avenue opened into a broad expanse of turf, and the house lay before us. In the fading light I could see that the center was a heavy block of building from which a porch projected. The whole front was draped in ivy, with a patch clipped bare here and there where a window or a coat-of-arms broke through the dark veil. From this center block rose the twin towers, ancient, crenellated, and pierced with many loopholes. To right and left the turrets were more modern wings of black granite. A dull light shone through heavy mullioned windows, and from the high chimneys which rose from the steep, high-angled roof there sprang a single black column of smoke."

Compelled onward by that passage and after. checking the map again, I continued my march

A quarter of an hour later and when I gained my first, real glimpse of Brook Manor, it was with an odd mixture of feelings. Suddenly I felt a medley of crazy thoughts. Some of those even involved my own fellow countryman, who only days before had braved worse conditions to land on an even more desolate terrain than this. They'd done that hoping for, but with no ironclad guarantee of even returning home. And for me? I too had gone into unknown territory with an objective in mind. And for all intents and purposes, looking down into the valley ahead, I'd reached it. *Houston, The Eagle Has Landed*

To begin with, the place was smaller than the one described in the novel. It looked old enough, to be certain, but still the house itself lay in its small valley setting like an oil painting daubed in emerald hues. And within that frame, as if in a tableau from some Hammer Horror film, the entire place seemed off-putting. But not entirely in a bad way. Instead, I might say that everything in that strange, tea-time-less hour suggested a sense of what used to be called *faery*, as in weirdly

170

enchanted. And that seemed to begin with the archaic dwelling ahead, where one could easily imagine some white bearded magus bent upon his strange workings.

From my own safer higher prospect where I looked down upon the allegedly vampiric Sir Richard Cabell's old manse, I shivered. Everything about this place, I thought, felt unreal. And out there at the end of a long lane which wove its way below me, only to lace through the emerald treescapes, my destination now awaited in the shape of that 17th century old pile.

Above me now and splashed across the foreground and distance, the skies had taken a turn for the worse. Tides of gray and darkening clouds were swirling like a martialing and billowed armada. And then as if for the first time, I heard the thunder's full effect, like cannon-fire. And behind it I knew, the torrent was about to break loose.

Decided that it was high time to make base-camp, I back-tracked along the forested rise. Eventually I found a hillock with a kind of concavity to it. Not exactly one of those stone and prehistoric huts seen by Watson or even still marked on the ordnance, I thought it might do. Quickly and even as I felt the slow tattoo of raindrops increasing, I began to canvas the area for fallen boughs or branches. Would that I could have mined out a further depression in that rugged hillside, but there was not enough time. Therefore instead I managed to scout out some sizable tree limbs and tall lengths of logs which would add a lean-to dimension to my impromptu hut. Over these I draped the plastic sheet, and then more branches, doing my best to tuck the sheet into the interstices of my cabin-less-but-log structure. And just as the downpour began to torrent down for real, I edged my way into my darkened sanctuary.

As to how long exactly the deluge lasted, I can't say for certain. Here the reason has more to do with the fact that it stopped and started endless times. By the time there appeared to be a lull of sorts it was already dark. And there I sat like Mr. Badger huddled in his cave, but without his amenities as described in Kenneth Graham's *The Wind In The Willows*.

I took consolation in my lonely placement, as Holmes himself must in his solitary vigil on the moors. And like him, I smoked. But in my case it was a special indulgence of those days, or at least, that summer. This took the form of nicely packeted small cigars from Switzerland. These, like my favorite beef sandwiches, were available from the station shop at Gloucester Road.

Oddly, the first draft of this memoir did not include the allusion to my youthful fling as a cigar aficionado. What rang a gong of sorts, however, was a bad fragment of a larger poem I'd written (probably for some girl) about that time. The only fragment which lingers is the line, *"cigars in the night, o'er the blackest of moor-land."* (I warned you).

And that criminal exercise in verse did in turn spark a dendron which allowed me to be reminded of that other *vital* addition to my "supplies." Those wonderful small cigars! I still miss them.

Eventually and after a short and flash-lit perusal of my Buddhist chronicle, I decided to spare my batteries by switching off the torch. Which left me there feeling the dank and the chill, and hearing the seeping sound of the rain coming down through the nest of oaks and yews which hovered over me. Yes quite alone, many, many miles from civilization, albeit within probably a quarter of an hour away from the nearest house. But with regard to whose house, if not whose woods these were, I realized my limitations. The echo of what Merriman had told me had preserved a set of barriers which stood between myself and what some would call the common, if not old-fashioned courtesy of offering a stranger shelter for the night.

Yet contrarily, and given what amounted to an intrusive foreigner's deliberate trespass upon this very ground, who in their right mind should have expected the aforesaid "courtesy?" Would I, in a comparable situation? Probably not. Which left the alternative. I began to think of a shotgun blast in the night, or the loosing of imaginary dogs. And then of course, there was the archetypal matter of the Canine In Question—or in other words, the Hound From Hell. In the safety of the rail carriage I'd devoured its description. But now, here, those words haunted me in an entirely different way.

"Plucking at his throat, there stood a foul thing, a great, black beast, shaped like a hound, yet larger than any hound that ever mortal eye had rested upon. And even as they looked the thing tore the throat out of Hugo Baskerville...as it turned its blazing eyes and dripping jaws upon them..."

To stave off my own fear, I decided on distraction. And like a greedy beggar I put paid to the sandwiches and nearly drained the small plastic canteen I'd found in a shop along Cromwell Road. Suddenly my rash action reminded me of one of those films in which provisions are low and need to be shared. And there was always someone who wanted more than their allotment. But now that chap was myself. And I only had him to blame.

It was not all that late when I began to will myself to sleep. With nothing else to do and unable to get out for a sodden, nocturnal ramble (which would have been foolish, anyway) there was nowhere else to be. So with that apparent and grim knowledge, I kept reminding myself that if I could just sleep away the night I might wake up to a rainless, sunlit world. And after that I could get on with the lunar mission. But the business of willing one's self to slumber is never easy, even in a comfy bed and a pleasant room in your own Home Sweet Home. Stand that against the prospect of being cold, thirsty and damp, and trying to keep from blaming yourself for agreeing to a mad-cap idea. I even resorted to conjuring up a vision of old Merriman, cozy before his electric fire and the telly, sipping his cuppa or something stronger. If so, did he feel the slightest psychic twinge, telegraphed across the moors and back to civilization, transmitted by the sap he'd cajoled into risking life and limb, and all for the chance of getting him a lousy photograph? On reflection however, even that seemed doubtful. So instead I hunkered down, doing my best to put myself under, if only to sleep away those dread hours when those elemental evils were said to be afoot.

Eventually I managed to doze off. Sporadically I'd come to and then drift away again. This was the way it was, until all hell broke loose. The first harbinger of this was the sudden feeling of a blast of cold wet spray as if blown onto my face. The second was a blaze of white when what appeared to be lightning actually struck something within fifty feet or so from my refuge. That on its own was enough to stun me. Never in my twenty-two years had I seen lightning make contact with *terra firma,* and certainly never within shouting distance of where I crouched. And on the heels of the strike there was the unavoidable sense of a slurping drip of something heavier than rain, as if some night creature were taking a dump on my makeshift hovel. I grappled for the flash-light, and switching it on revealed the torrent pouring down on

173

me, with gobbets of mud or silt seeping from above, through what, not that longer ago, had been a thick plastic canopy supported by relics of what had once been the local woodland.

There was nothing for it but to make an escape. This I did, aiming the torch into the wall of the night, which was as black as the ocean, and just as wet. Standing there like a dumb figure, I reached down for the sodden tarp, which I managed to wrap around my shoulders. And after that it was *Port Arms and Quick March.*

From my earlier recon by dusk, I knew where the ground gave way to the path which ran like a brown ribbon toward Brook Manor. Using the beam of the flashlight to trace it ahead of me in the pounding rain, I tried to be calm as I followed it, like Jack's trail in the Beanstalk tale. And as I seemed to Braille my way along, my head was suddenly full of a thousand Saturday Matinee images. But not of Jack's Giant. No, undoubtedly something more like those string of Christopher Lee epics which had managed to keep me awake on countless occasions. Yes, Hammer Horror indeed. And there I was, in a shilling shocker of my own devising. And worse yet, the only place in the locality where I could beg for sanctuary just happened to be an old house which used to belong to a supposed vampire! *Fangs for the memories.* Good times, indeed.

As I attempted to follow the trail I became aware of the blessed presence of a light just ahead. Thank God they're still awake down there, I told myself. With that thought in mind I urged my way through the downpour, and a few moments later, halted in my sodden tracks. Aiming my torch at a stand of trees I'd used as guideposts earlier, something fell on me like a ton of bricks. For the glimmer I'd been following had not emanated from Brook Manor. Rather, I was willfully moving toward some other phantom beacon. But what? Swamp gas? Will of the Wisp? St. Elmo's Fire? And weren't there strange luminous emanations which Harker saw along the road, en route to Castle Dracula?

Deep breaths. Get your bearings. Take it literally one step at a time. And proceed with caution.

Now I seemed to hear that chorus of admonitions as if from my inner counselor—everything in fact with the possible exception of *Please Wash Your Hands Before Exiting.*

And finally I did get my bearings. Not long after I stood once again upon the rise looking down upon the House That Was Supposed To Be Baskerville Hall. And I thought to myself that here and now and given the reality of what that place was, it could well have been associated with a ghostly hound, or a pack of them, for that matter. And best of all, and true to my earlier suspicion, there was indeed a light shining in an upper casement of the old manse. Which meant someone was still awake. As to whether or not they were prepared to greet a stranger trying to come in from the storm, well that was something else. But it was worth a try. And so I headed down that long and winding road, and in fifteen minutes or so, I was standing before the main entrance of Sir Richard Cabell's ill-fabled residence. Trying not to think too much of its back-story, I approached the broad front door and looked up as I did so. But then, as if on cue, and in sync with the driving rain, I watched as the light in the window overhead was extinguished!

Suddenly the old house was now also dark as pitch. And there was I, sodden in my plastic cape, the beam in my feeble torch ebbing down. And I found myself suddenly thinking, "What would Sherlock Holmes Have Done?"

Now there was simply no way I was about to walk up to the front door and signal my arrival. Young, more naïve than now, if not soaked through and mud-spattered, I still had enough sense to consider an alternate plan. Therefore I chose to make a retreat and follow the periphery of the old dark house to its rear precincts and out-buildings. And there to no surprise, I saw what resembled a garden house-cum-stable. Giving a burglar's glance back at the old pile behind me, I approached the garden house door and tried its old latched handle. No luck. Stiff, either through time, or rust, or very likely, an unseen lock, it resisted the best attempts of the American Raffles on its rainy threshold.

Well as they used to say, when circumstances press hard, *"youth replies, 'I can.'"*

Funny, isn't it, how certain lines of poetry or prose stay stuck in your head? I guess it all depended on what they meant, or would mean for you in future. For example, only months ago I'd enrolled in a class in Milton and was informed the first day that we'd need to commit about 325 lines of the poet to memory—just to take the final. Well I'd managed that, and the day after my exam all that were left were about two or three lines. Which just goes to prove out Sherlock Holmes' comment about jettisoning bits of information from his brain-attic if they had no utility.

But as I knew, I had a retentive ability for trivia that resembled flypaper, and stuck there, to quote the future words of Robert Stephens in "The Private Life Of Sherlock Holmes" "stuck there is a staggering amount of data, mostly useless."

Yet I'd always made a bit of room for Shakespeare, and Holmes, and as I've said, even that dashing explorer Dick Burton and his axiom "do what thy manhood bids thee do." I'd long admired Sir Richard for his scholarship and feats of derring-do. Once asked why he had done what he had on occasion, that swashbuckler wrote;
"Starting in a hollowed log of wood—some thousand miles up a river, with an infinitesimal prospect of returning! I ask myself "Why?" and the only echo is "damned fool! the Devil drives."

I suppose it might have been the Devil driving me into that primordial landscape, or even daring me to brave the elements, if only for a glance of something unseen by many others. Regardless of that, what remained clear to my twenty-two-year-old sense of survival were two words, telegraphed to my brain: *Find shelter.*

In the finest traditions of Hornung's Gentleman Cracksman or even Sherlock Holmes in the "Adventure of Charles Augustus Milverton," wearing a mask and equipped with his yeggman's (burglar's) tools, now I applied my meager pocket jack-knife to the old handle. With a fiddle and a bit of rotating business such as I'd once seen David Niven employ in a "Raffles" film. Just so, I eventually heard the tell-tale "snick.*" And with that the latch was undone!* And in only moments I was inside a musty, largely vacant room with what resembled a kind of bench against its wall. I heard the ongoing tattoo of rain upon the old roof. And I knew I was a bit drier for its shelter Also, for these moments, at least, hopefully safe from the hell-hound's flaming jaws.

176

There are all sorts of beds, ranging from the most luxurious to the makeshift. I have known my share of types, both rough and royal over time, but given my circumstances that night, the chance of slumber on that garden hut bench was not at all bad.

I awoke to milky daylight coming through a small upper window. A bit stiff, I raised myself to a vertical position, stretched, and studied my now revealed surroundings for the first time.

The room must have been used as a storeroom at one time, for there were shelves on the walls containing an assortment of bottles and cans. There may have been a garden implement or not, I do not recall. There was however a treasury of empty bottles of formerly spirited vintage in an Everest-like heap in the shed's furthest corner. A pity indeed that I hadn't managed to pick the lock to the wine cellar! Nevertheless I was grateful for the snug, if not spare harbor I'd found last night during the storm.

Cautious as the interloper I was, I peered through the crack of the partially opened door. I inhaled the first tang of the early morning after air. It was damp, and my ears registered the drip-drip sound of water leaving some ancient eaves.

I made an inventory of my rough camping gear and checked inside the flap of my knap-sack. From its depths I withdrew the camera in its case. This I strung around my neck as I re-snapped the canvas flap. Readied now for my mission, and like an interplanetary invader taking the same "one step for mankind" which my fellow countrymen had done upon the Moon's surface this very month. Stealthily, I ventured forth.

It was a suitably half-misted but muggy morning. My watch informed me that it was only a bit after six o'clock. Quick calculation told me I'd crashed in my burgled accommodations for probably about four or more hours. *And now what?*

Mentally I recalled the circumstances which had brought me this far. First the dinner, and meeting Charles Merriman, then hearing his narrative concerning finding Brook Manor. And also of course his remark and dubious compliment to me, of "but you're a younger man." *Ergo: you can go out there and risk being shot by trespassing upon some landed gentleman's private property.* Which meant as well that I, as a comparable stripling, might follow the general's orders and embark upon a mission. But at least the Society's Honorary Treasurer had refrained from the classic wartime line, "God how I wish I were going with you." But you know, he might well have wished for that very thing. For at the time, nearly half a century ago, I had no way of knowing what age could do to prevent you from trying something your Younger Self might have pulled off. But now, and well the cusp of 70, when knees do creak and back does ache, I can appreciate the sense of employing one's younger designate for the sake of entering the Vales of Danger.

In any event, I reviewed my purpose in (a) getting here, and (b) acquiring a better photographic survey of the terrain, and of course, the house. These were the only and best ways of establishing what might pass for "proof" in the Sherlockian/Holmesian world. And that was predicated upon the highest degree of probability. And upon such reasons did the law and the prophets now hang. I had ventured this far, I had braved the night and the elements, and now what was left was to record my adventure. For what after all would have been the value of the trip taken by Armstrong, Aldrin and Collins, had they not arranged for their landing to be replicated, photographically?

Stealthily, I walked the perimeter of Brook Manor. The old stones of the house were lichenous and suitably Gothically atmospheric. Indeed, one could imagine Dr. Watson putting up here, or the astonished mood of Sir Henry Baskerville, the new heir, upon learning that this storied and be-legended pile was now his?

I thought of those things as I took a few pictures. But it was only upon rounding a corner and approaching a tall casement window that I was stopped in my tracks by what I saw inside.

There are images which may well be with me until my end. Yes, taken and deliberately preserved, as with my now long-ago Polaroid Camera. That is, of course, if memory lasts and God gives me the benefit of recalling what I've chanced to see in my time. If not, then these words must take its place.

But I tell you, among that catalogue of images, near and far, beautiful and staggering, miraculous and daunting, this one will remain in relatively simpler contrast.

As I stood there in what amounted to the flowerless bed before the window, I felt as if I were observing a scene from one of my childhood's fairy tales. For there and beyond the wavy glass pane only feet away from where my voyeur's gaze beheld him, crouched a small creature. Now I say "creature," but there was a man, but one of seemingly elfin, almost Rumpelstiltskin stature. Moreover, his look resembled something out of Grimm's collection, for he was small and wore a kind of embroidered pill-box cap. From beneath its edges two large ears and feathery wisps of white hair protruded. And nearly in half profile, I saw that this fey figure was clean-shaven, but wore a pair of old-fashioned wire-rimmed spectacles perched upon a sharp nose. And there he knelt beyond the window on the floor before the fire.

I cannot now say if the little fellow was stoking the nascent flames of his hearth, or perhaps reciting a chant before a small cauldron? Or whether he was in fact preparing a pot of gruel or soup upon the hob? And last of all, and as was probably more likely, the gentleman in question was simply stoking his morning fire into warmth?

I can only compare my reaction in that moment to the scene described earlier on in this memoir concerning my "private moment" with Basil Rathbone four years earlier. That, and of how I had parted from the great actor with a voice in my head whispering to me alone, *"Now take a step back and leave him be. Do this, and I promise you will have this scene embedded upon your memory for the rest of your life."* And paying heed to that voice again now, that is exactly what I did.

I took pictures as I retraced my way away from Brook Manor and then, quickly as I could, up the cypress-flanked path to the place on the rise where I'd stood, both upon my arrival, and again, earlier this morning when the sky seemed to have come crashing down.

It required a bit of a hike to reach the place on the road beyond the wood from which I'd taken leave of the bus. I harbored the hope that some early morning transport would come along. Eventually, nearly an hour later, one did. I managed to hitch a ride from a passing lorry into town. And once I reached the bustle of Newton Abbot I established my bearings, which chiefly regarded the location of the rail station.

But then like a reminding canker, the recollection of my present dilemma made itself apparent. *How was I going to take the train back to London if I didn't have a pound to my name?*

But to that young traveler's credit, he remained calm and set his mind to the problem. And then, like a windfall or a blessing, he heard his mother's voice.

"Always keep your traveler's checks with your passport, or somewhere safe" she had counseled me once again before The Second Great Sojourn. And its addendum: "and *if you can, stash a check somewhere else, just in case your passport or luggage or other checks are stolen.*" Well, I now thought, thank God I'd listened to her.

I remember the elation I felt when I sat down upon a streetside bench and withdrew my wallet. Re-examining my distinctly empty billfold, I flipped the plastic windows over and came to one containing a photograph and my M.S.U. Student Identification Card. Tweezing the envelope's edges into a bow, I reached in and unfolded what I'd found. *Ces voilà!* It was one tightly folded Thomas Cook Traveler's Check for the denomination of Fifty Dollars, U.S. Currency! In that precious moment of discovery I silently thanked God, then heard myself say, as if she might hear it, *And thanks to you, too, Mom, for about the thousandth time for your help*

I took a deep breath and looked around, smiling Then glancing at my wristwatch I saw that it was now nearly nine o'clock. That might well mean time for a bank to open. And with this thought in mind I ambled down Newton Abbot's quaint main street and eventually came upon that oasis-like sign. It said BARCLAY'S BANK. And further cheering, I saw that the bank's posted business hours were about to commence at 9:00 AM.

The rest of my tale is rather simple and uncomplicated, but with a suitably dramatic conclusion. For after cashing my check into pounds sterling, I walked down to where I'd been informed I would find the station. There I confirmed the departure schedule for a train headed to London, and fortunately enough, in barely an hour's time. Just then from somewhere near I heard two sounds. The first was a voice echoing through the station, informing travelers of their tracks. And the other was my stomach growling. That was a signal indeed, and one I chose to honor within minutes, having spied the welcome sight of a small café adjacent to the Rail Station's entrance.

I ambled across to the café. It was empty, save for its proprietor at work behind the counter. He gave me the up and down, and then, as if confirmed I was no threat to the general peace, asked me what I'd like? As he did so however, I found myself drifting into his head, just as I chanced to get a glimpse of myself in a small wall mirror. And there looking back at me was something between a coal miner and an accident victim. The stranger peering back was tired looking, a streak of something brown on his cheek, and his jacket and pants soiled and looking as if he'd been involved in a mud-rolling contest. What must this fellow think? I asked myself. And what would I think in his place?

I withdrew from the knap-sack's straps and placed it along with its rolled up piece of filthy plastic and put them on the floor. Then I took a low stool before the café countertop. I ordered tea. And then toast and some "bangers." The man behind the counter nodded and before long, reappeared with a steaming mug which he placed before me.

"Bad night" he said. There was a lilt in his voice which I took to be a bit of the local Devonshire dialect.

"It was" I answered. "You should have been out on the moors."

He looked at me as if establishing the fact that not only was I a Yank, but around the bend as well. Or perhaps the first of those repeated the other?

"You were on the moors?" he inquired.

"I slept out there" I heard myself say. But I didn't explain. *Not a word about phantom hounds, legendary manor houses, their possibly vampiric owners, or collapsing lean-to's. No, nothing at all of interest.*

And then came the café man's riposte, which seemed, even at that time, to be the perfect way to conclude my adventure as written. I watched as my companion took a long swipe at the countertop before him with his rag and then leaned a bit forward a bit, as if he were about to share a confidence.

"Bad place—the moors" he said. Hearing his words, and recording them for posterity, I took a swig of my tea and merely nodded back.

And that concludes my foray into those elemental and much haunted woodlands of Devonshire Also the fulfillment of my informal "commission" to take the case of an elderly English gentleman who had done his best to map a modern myth.

And as for Brook Hall being the actual, be-all, end-all "Baskerville Hall?" It would be over-bold, if not presumptuous to insist so. I believe no one would agree to that more than Sir Arthur himself. So let's simply say that like those persons frequently cited as the solitary "basis for Sherlock Holmes," or even, the "best performer as our favorite detective," you have to draw a line, if not a breath, somewhere. Only then and if you've done your research you might choose to make your own educated appraisal.

And as for this Irregular business of establishing the "reality" of "realistic fictions" it's rather like the matter of catching lightning in a bottle. It's fun, and also possible, perhaps, but hardly enough to produce the real thing once-and-forever. I wonder if you'll agree?

King Arthur (Richard Harris)
and the author at Tower House

Camelot Redux: The author and Richard Harris
two decades after their meeting.

11
A Toper at King Arthur's Court

Here is an episode which is memorable, but in part for the wrong reasons. Nevertheless, I have chosen to set it down at my own peril. Chalk it up to "youthful exuberance," if you will. That being so, it remains a part of my personal history. And that, as you are about to see, once brought me to the suburban stronghold of a king.

On rare occasions there is the strangest nexus between things, which I long ago learned to accept. One of them occurred in the Summer of 1969 and it began in London when I met a pretty young woman at a party. She informed me rather casually that she worked in some kind of press capacity, and was at present attached to the production of "Cromwell," which starred Richard Harris in the title role. But here comes that odd connection: then co-starring with the former King Arthur of the 1967 film "Camelot" was Alec Guinness. And as I learned to my further surprise, so too was the fine English character actor Douglas Wilmer, whom I remembered playing Nayland Smith to Christopher Lee's Fu Manchu, and even earlier in a televised Sherlock Holmes series. The odd-ball post-script to that, unfortunately, would be Wilmer's cameo burlesque as Holmes in Gene Wilder's "Sherlock Holmes' Smarter Younger Brother."

I told my partying friend the story about the nun who'd told me that Alec Guinness sometimes dropped by the Cromwell Road hostel. So far, I lamented, I had not spied the latter over my morning corn-flakes. She laughed, and then made me an offer I could not refuse. "Would you like to see them shooting 'Cromwell'" she asked. "Maybe you'd have a better chance at meeting your hero that way?" And I considered the serendipity of the thing: *Guinness on Cromwell Road, vs. Guinness in "Cromwell."*

I said that indeed I would like to watch the movie being made. And yes, I thought to myself, *to see not just one hero, but two.* For even as I knew at that time, I'd harbored a chronic and somewhat inexplicable interest in Richard Harris. Quite naturally there was his key role in "Camelot," and for other films as well. "The Man Called Horse" was a favorite, as was his later "Juggernaut." And then of course all of that was now buttressed by the musical phase of the actor's career. That had seemed to commence and end in big-time terms with "MacArthur Park." I remembered playing the heck out of that LP and studying the piratical visage of Harris on the album cover.

In a related fashion as well, I still preserved a set of tabloid clippings from my British trip in '67. Two years earlier those had painted an even stranger, more boisterous picture of Richard Harris, and in part the story had involved the actor interviewing himself! Moreover, the serialized tabloid fodder had involved a wild romp in which Harris had taken a group of pals on a 'round the world junket to celebrate his recent divorce. Billed in print as "My Honeymoon Without A Bride," the lurid stories began by describing how the now-divorced actor had offered his now ex-wife Elizabeth the chance to join him to "consummate their divorce." Unsurprisingly, the lady refused. Which left King Arthur with no one to party with other than his bodyguard and a pack of chums and a beautiful girl they picked up along the way.

Which brings me to the strange case of how I did in fact meet not only Alec Guinness, but also his younger fellow-player and the much advertised star of "Cromwell," Richard Harris.

My new contact gave me her working telephone number and asked me to call her the following week to see what could be done. I pronounced myself very happy indeed to do so.

Now, how exactly did everything proceed? And at the risk of slowing things down, first a bit of back-storied information. To begin with, I was once again back in London in conjunction with a Michigan State University American Language Education Center program, just as two years earlier. This time however I was there as an advisor. Also, my Humanities Department friends were over again, so I didn't lack for companions. Although—there was a certain young lady (we'll call her Sandy) who was on that trip. Her presence managed to make the prospect of a junket in London somewhat difficult. For you see, not only had I courted, loved, and "won" the heart of the young lady during the last two years of my undergraduate studies at East Lansing, but had gone even further. Actually, youthfully, foolishly, rashly, etc. we had even discussed the idea of marriage. But in my senior year and on the brink of graduating, the young lady, who was two years my junior, had a change of mind. Somewhat shattered, I did my best to register her youthful (and doubtless wise) change of mind, if not heart. Suffice it promised to be a difficult summer. But fortunately for me, also present on that trip was Sandy's older sister, Jeannie. I suppose I'd always been attracted to her sis, but now for the most part I probably made best use of her as a sounding board. We laughed, we talked. She commiserated. I even took her on a day trip to Newstead Abbey. Maybe I was thinking that somehow my old friend Byron would have an answer. But he didn't.

To quell my pangs of heart and to keep busy, I'd agreed to join a group of our Michigan State Humanities gang for a rather curious and clandestine event. This, as I discovered, was the culmination of a secret plan long in the making, involving the London wedding of a member of the MSU Humanities faculty and one of his students of about my age. Their undercover liaison had gone on for a while stateside, and both had thought this particular London summer to be the perfect means of their becoming man and wife.

So there it was. We were informed that upon the upcoming Friday, "Professor Smith" and his secretly betrothed "Susie" (those are not their names) would be tying the knot in a British Registry office downtown. A few of us grudgingly went to witness the civic nuptials, and after that we were to gather at the rented house of one of the other faculty members (this one already married—and not to one of his students).

Suffice it to say that the afternoon's civic event, followed by a luncheon and drinks at the Prof's house were enough to provoke any number of emotions. The long day's culmination into an aimless evening. My thoughts about a colleague's decision to elope. My musings about my own ill-fated debacle of a romance. Yes, all of that by around four p.m. when I detached myself at last from those pretending to be merry-makers and found myself wandering aimlessly toward the Cromwell Road. What a sad prospect, eh?

For there was I. Young. Untethered. And thanks to the recent party, "three sheets in the wind," or bladdered as the Brits might say, and in any event suddenly footloose in London on a late Friday afternoon. Poor me. But I'm doubtful any of you will feel much pity. Nor should you.

And that was when the Big Idea came to me. Serendipitously, a mental claxon went off just as I passed one of Britain's most archetypal of icons, the red and windowed telephone kiosk. And somehow, inexplicably as well, that scarlet call box served to remind me that tucked away in my wallet, I had a specific phone number.

Now retreat in time just a bit. Regarding that publicist who had offered me the chance to watch "Cromwell" being filmed, earlier in the week I'd been asked by her to ring her at work. Unfortunately or not, when I did exactly that someone shunted me off to another number to reach my party. And then when I finally succeeded in connecting with my prospective contact, she informed me that she "couldn't talk just now."

"Look, I'm at Richard's house right now" she said, and hastily informed me that she was also in the midst of some PR work concerning the star's role as the Puritan savior of England. "You'll have to call me (she gave me still another number) on Monday. We'll get it sorted then." I said I would. And that was that. *Or was it?*

Which brings us back to the lonely Friday afternoon in question. Feeling rather exhilarated already, and now recognizing what I did in fact possess in my back pocket, created an even more exuberant notion: *For I had Richard Harris' private home telephone number in my wallet.*

I walked over to the call box and fiddled in my wallet. *Voila!* the number as originally copied down. Then another bit of deep-sea diving for change. British coinage was if nothing else, enough to make you feel as if you were carrying a pocket-ful of doubloons. Stranger yet, and as I'd been aware of in my earlier time over, just the kind of unused change you might put on the dresser at night, or in your piggy bank, had an unusual historical dimension to it which U.S. varieties didn't.

As I'd discovered in '67, just the English Penny with Britannia on its face, might have been coined as early as the 1860's or earlier. And still in circulation. To wit, by the time I'd returned home, my collection had included those large round brown British pennies bearing images attesting to Queen Victoria's youth, her middle age, and her seniority. These, as well as other past-tense denominations were still in circulation and still being pressed into call boxes such as my own. And that might be why "there'll always be an England." But I digress.

I inserted the necessary coinage into the phone's maw and heard the tell-tale pips, then the machine clanking as it digested my money. And suddenly at the other end my ears registered a rather high-pitched, almost falsetto sound.

"Yes? Who is this calling?" the voice demanded.

I took a deep breath and took a leap toward my explanation. But due to the fact of my buoyant, albeit only now slightly less than inebriated condition, I started to ramble.

I began saying that I "was calling for Mr. Harris." Then a bit of my story about Alec Guinness at the hostel and then the publicist offering to get me onto the movie set. I suppose it was about at that juncture that I realized that despite my estimations, I was not as sober as a judge, no less a first-year paralegal.

"But let me understand" said the rather sensitive-sounding voice at the other end. "Do you, or do you not know Richard Harris?"

I was on the line in more ways than one. Not precisely, I explained, as much as the fact that I was about to. This, as well as the fact that I was due to meet him on the set of "Cromwell."

"To reiterate, you do not know Mr. Harris, or have not met him. But you planned on doing so. And somehow this has something to do with Alec Guinness? Did he tell you to call?"

I responded by saying that I was rather pressed, but had been given this number and told to call. And for that reason, even now, I was seeking to speak to Mr. Harris.

Fuddled at least, the voice at the other end paused before seeming to rise a few decibels.

"Now, what did you say your name was? Mark McPherson. All right. Hold the line."

Seconds passed as I felt the foolishness of my attempt. I thought of just hanging up, but somehow common sense never got that far. I waited a minute or so and then heard a breathless sound at the other end of the line.

"All right. I took your message in. And when I said a Mark McPherson was on the phone, he said "Who the f*** is she?" So I took it from that you are not acquainted."

"You're not understanding me" I persisted. "I never said I knew him. I said I was supposed to meet him, but things have been busy, and…"

"Now you listen to me" the little voice continued. "I'm new here, and it will be my job if you cause me trouble. But rather than listen to this crazy conversation any further, I will give you the address, but only if you agree not to ring again."

I nodded to myself in the call box. It may or may not have occurred to me that I was about to be brushed off. But would the rather fey voice talking to me have actually given me Richard Harris' home address? I decided to take the chance.

"Fine" I agreed. "Go ahead with the address." Then reaching into my jacket pocket I took down the coordinates. It was a Knightsbridge address. Tower House, on Melbury Road. And with that the line went dead. I hung up, pushed open the call box door and reeled out into the early London evening. Success? Failure? Who knew? But as one of my new colleagues might have put it, it had bloody well been worth a try.

After a bit more rambling I found my way to the nearest underground station. After a bit of subterranean cartological guesswork, I mapped out the means of arriving at what was (presumably) Richard Harris' door.

The system for "the tube" from my earlier visit still served. It meant visually taking note of where you were and where you wanted to go. Then it was just a matter of judging which train line would connect where to bring you closest to your destination. Ergo, something like *"Blue Jubilee south to Green Bank, south to Brown Bakerloo, east to Red Strand."* Now that's an unreal route and improperly color-coded, but you get the picture, given those ever-present underground maps presently found at topside and "down below" amid the vast labyrinth of London's railed Underworld.

190

Well I could lie and say it all went smoothly from there. *Absolutely spiffing. Champion. Wizard. Top drawer.* But nothing like that in reality. You see, and chagrined as I am in even writing this, many decades later, I was in no fit condition to go anywhere fast on the Underground or elsewhere. And because of that, and thanks to an excess of bottled ale back at Humanities House, I might just as well have emerged from a collegiate fraternity kegger at Homecoming, although I was not quite, as they say, wasted. But I was running on fumes. And no one to blame but myself. Oh, and of course that voice so easily summoned in my brain which recited,

"Man, being reasonable, must get drunk. The best of life is intoxication."

That damned Lord Byron again. And I supposed even now he was looking down (or up) at me and chortling at my condition.

Nevertheless, and in spite of my decidedly deplorable condition, I made it across London. And after two false starts, I emerged into the pleasant evening air of Old London Town an hour and a quarter later, fully prepared to follow up my directions.

Knightsbridge. The neighborhood I now found myself visually exploring was one of those old vestiges of London in its heyday. Yes, a time when so many of its now re-polished mansions had gleamed with their initial veneers. But today in that shadow of tradition and former Empire, I was standing at the core of so much seasoned elegance.

I suppose it was just about then that I came to my senses, quite literally. You know the feeling: suddenly you realize you are charging head-first into danger, just as the young sub-altern Winston Churchill once felt upon leading his stallion into a herd of devilish dervishes. And now, just so myself. As if spurring my imaginary steed onward, I was standing there with the crumpled piece of paper containing my hastily copied information of what—maybe an hour ago? clutched in my fist.

In other words, my primitive and somewhat inebriated version of personal Land Sat pressed into action, suddenly I was looking up at a tall wrought iron gate and a bronze plaque which corresponded with my directions. It read TOWER HOUSE.

Now in order to protect the less than innocent if not the privacy of the object of my imminent intrusion, I will not describe in more precise geographical terms the whereabouts of the place in question. Allow me only to say that the gate and the short drive and the Victorian seeming mansion beyond them were not entirely out of keeping with a celebrated star of the British stage and screen.

I pressed on. Through the gate and along the walk. Then up the flight of stone steps to the portico-ed porch and the sizable doorway. There was a knocker of some kind on it, and without thinking, I used it. Then I waited. But within perhaps about 4.5 seconds, something rather unexpected happened. It was quite remarkable really. For like a sense of *Satori* or a blast of mystical enlightenment, suddenly my mind was washed over with a cold and clear breeze. And it was as if through the agency of those fleeting but ebbing seconds, I suddenly found myself becoming completely and quite stunningly sober.

And now for "the rest of the story," which radio's pioneering broadcaster Paul Harvey used to say, continued to be filled with a series of incredible events. Incredible, to me, as I'd unwittingly managed to put myself within a *milieu* quite foreign to any I'd known to date. And it began with my uninvited presence on that summer's night in 1969 before the great doorway of "Tower House."

So I'll describe it as it happened. I'd knocked on the door and a moment later two things happened. The first of these was that I had the sudden epiphany of feeling entirely sober. And secondly, the door before me was opened by a tall, not unattractive, but decidedly burly fellow. Stranger yet, I knew him on sight and from memory. My curious ability to recall random and meaningless data now culled both his name and purpose from a set of British tabloid clippings I'd kept for the past two years. Those had to do with Richard Harris' madcap "Honeymoon" *sans* bride. And among his entourage and depicted in one of the story's photos, stood the man now standing in the doorway before me. This was Reg Locke, Harris's bodyguard, driver, and general factotum.

I heard myself bidding the imposing figure a good evening, and called him by name. In return, he looked at me the way one of Sherlock Holmes' subjects would have on being rendered information of a privy nature by a perfect stranger.

"What do you want?" the bodyguard asked.

In the moments that followed I did my best to re-cap the story about Alec Guinness, my meeting with the press associate, her promise of my visiting the set of "Cromwell," and last of all, my frustration of being about to return to America without meeting the man of the hour.

Well truthfully, I expected to be given the gate, quite literally, by Harris' enforcer. But instead he simply bore down on me and said "wait here." The door was re-closed, offering me yet another opportunity of scampering. And in that most lucid of moments, I found myself harking back a week or so ago, and to my standing on another threshold, but in Devonshire, amid the crash of thunder and lightning. And had I not considered ringing Ye Olde Bell (if there'd been one) or knocking on the front door of Brook Manor, if only to seek shelter? And even then the full realization of what I was about had filled me with dread. Just as now.

It really was only a matter of minutes when the door re-opened and Reg Locke looked down on me standing there. Looking back, I did my utmost to come across as something other than I was. "You'd better be on the level" was all he said. And with that he beckoned me on and I followed him over the threshold and into the foyer of Tower House.

What I recall of what transpired thereafter is a medley of what I knew at the time, and what came back to me slightly after, the way patients undergoing hypnotic regression re-capture aspects of their past. In particular here is the matter of what I said when the next words fell out of my mouth.

We walked down a hallway flanked by colored leaded glass windows, each of which seemed to feature female figures of ill repute throughout history. Was this an intentional feature reflecting the old house's newest, famously womanizing inhabitant, I wondered?

The corridor ended at a larger, open space, dominated directly ahead by a king-sized fireplace which sported two incredible features. The first of these was the long medieval broadsword which was angled against the unlit hearth. *Excalibur,* I thought.

And then there was the second feature, which reflected the rather familiar looking figure reclining on the floor, his elbows upon the hearth's ledge. And I thought *Here Lies King Arthur*. It was none other than Richard Harris.

Now as I've said, it took a while thereafter for me to remember exactly what I said as I walked into that room, aware as I did so of others also present. There were what appeared to be eight or ten persons, men and women, all of them also reclining, divan style, around an appropriately round, low table filled with an assortment of food and drink. They were all stilled at the arrival of yet another guest to King Arthur's Court, and this one obviously an outsider. As if fellow actors awaiting my line, they were all mute, as was the red-haired fellow in the sweater and tee-shirt who was the obvious founder of the feast.

"I apologize for being so late" I heard myself say, as if some ventriloquist from another room were controlling my vocal chords. 'I wasn't sure that by the time I found this place that you'd still be awake." *Stupid. Nonsensical. How must it have sounded coming out of my American mouth?*

"Well" said Richard Harris appraising the sight of me, "you're here now and it's quiet enough to be a wake. So sit down and have something to eat."

Looking directly at my host, I nodded and walked over to the circular table and its inhabitants. And as I did so the conversational din picked up, someone shifted to allow me to slide down and join them. And that was how it went. I also recall the fellow sitting next to me, his hair fashionably long and a silk cravat knotted around his neck say, after hearing my explanation, "I don't bloody believe it. I tried for months to get into this house, and you just walk up to the door and ring the bell? Amazing."

Yes, it was amazing. And no more so to anyone during the course of that long evening than to I myself. And just as equally amused was Richard Harris himself. During that time we managed to speak, one on one, and I told him the saga of my prospective meeting with Guinness on the Cromwell Road, and then of the press girl, and the film set, etc. He just looked at me and shook his head, remarking something like "bloody incredible." But more amazing still, he invited me to accompany him to the film studio the following day.

"You can see us shoot and I'll introduce you to Alec." And I accepted the invitation in a jiffy. And some hours later as the party seemed to be breaking up, it was suddenly time for me to take my leave as well. However as I made my solitary way back down the hall I noted that no one else was following me. Instead, it seemed as if my fellow guests were pairing up and charging out and up stairways and down corridors together. But not I.

I left Tower House and passing through its now shadowy gates, headed back to my temporary digs across town And lest you think the coincidence was lost upon me, it wasn't. For as I told myself, I was now making my way home to the Cromwell Road, but only with the intention of returning here tomorrow morning. For then I had an invitation from none other than "Oliver Cromwell" himself to join him as he was in the process of making a movie.

The next morning dawned brightly as once again I found myself walking up the broad porch steps of *Tower House*. I'd found myself thinking last night that the plaque on the gate ought to have read CAMELOT. For like the sword and the man who'd wielded it in the film of the same name, the name would have been just right.

As I was picking up the morning paper the front door opened. It was Harris.

"What happened to you last night?" he asked.

"I went back to my place on Cromwell Road" I replied, handing him the paper.

The internationally famous actor looked at me, puzzled. "Didn't you like Anne?" he asked.

Now before going much further, a word or three of explanation. "Anne," the lady in question was a gorgeous young Frenchwoman named Anne Kristen. She, like Reg Locke, had been among the *dramatis personae* of Harris' 1967 post-divorce road show. And I even recalled that somewhere, France I believe, he invited her to accompany him, and offered to further her hopes of becoming a model. Well yes, we know how that sounds. But even in his own self-interview, the "Camelot" star asked himself, "is she merely intended to fill the empty spot in your bed?" To which he answered his own question with the retort, "No, and there has never been an empty spot in my bed."

From what I had heard from the young lady herself, Richard had indeed wangled some modeling assignments for Anne Kristen at *Harper's Bazaar* and *Vogue*. She was that good-looking, even out of the model gear and make-up. But I also received the impression that the rest of the time she led a somewhat lonely existence, waiting for the master to return to Tower House.

"Yes, I liked her very much" I answered, remembering his introduction of his attractive young friend last evening.

"Well then, why didn't you stay?"

The question stunned me for a moment. And then I began to feel embarrassed and not quite the swinging Londoner, or American, for that matter.

"I guess it was because she was—well—your protégé" said I. Yes, I actually used that word. And when I did, Harris shook his head and smiled.

"Hell, I'd have given you my wife if I still had her" he stated, even as he reached over and gave me a playful cuff on the cheek. The gesture was accompanied by that Limerick-lilted laugh I'd become accustomed to hearing in the days ahead. So it was that I followed Harris into the large limo-styled vehicle parked in the driveway of Tower House. Climbing in, I saw that Reg Locke was already in place. He had served in the capacity of chauffeur for R.H. ever since his boss supposedly ran into a double-decker bus.

So there I was, suddenly en route to our destination, which proved to be Shepperton Studios in—unsurprisingly, Shepperton, Surrey, just outside of London. And there perched beside me sat the bonified star of a host of well-known films, including "Cromwell," which was now in-the-making. And as for myself I? Well I'd been asked to tag along, but not without purpose. You see, Harris asked me to read out the racing results to Reg up there in the front seat. And so I did. My companion opened the paper I'd handed him on the porch, then folded it over to a portion of the Sporting Page. And I proceeded to read out the winners in such and such a race at wherever.

The rest of the story of how I met "King Arthur" and became, for howsoever a brief time, a member of his court, can be told in a limited, but interesting fashion. The story began, or continued upon our arrival at the Shepperton Studios. I walked in with Richard Harris, who had a word or a jibe for nearly everyone, and as I couldn't help but notice, seemingly an intermittent flirtatious overture for nearly every woman he passed.

But it was only when we entered the dressing and makeup area that my heart took a jump. This, when suddenly standing before us was the living presentiment of His Majesty King Charles I of England who had been historically deposed by Oliver Cromwell. Yes, there the monarch stood, but looking beneath the long curls, large black hat and moustache and chin whiskers, like Alec Guinness.

"Alec, I want you to meet this young rascal" said Harris, lightly punching my shoulder. "He wanted to meet you, so he banged on my door last night, and as a result, here he is. Can you believe it?"

I stepped forward to take the offer of the proffered royal hand. And as I did a montage of films starring the man before me began to reel through my mind. *Our Man In Havana. The Lady Killers. Kind Hearts and Coronets. The Man In The White Suit* and many, many others. I burbled something about this being a great honor, and Sir Alec replied that he was very pleased to meet me. We may have shared a few other inanities, but that was pretty much it. And so we moved on, but before Harris was about to be transformed into the eponymous Cromwell, another recognizable figure appeared before me.

I don't know whether it's as they say, cricket or not to justify this memoir's Sherlockian overtone by including this rather sizable section on "Cromwell" and Richard Harris, but here's the hook which I offer in order to make the connection. For standing before me outside the makeup room, was none other than Douglas Wilmer, whose job that day was to embody Thomas Fairfax, a warrior who would sit in judgment of his king. But also lurking behind that cavalierish demeanor were the Rathbonian features and gallant presence that had abetted any number of great actors in a score of greater films. But as I stood there in the Shepperton studio annex, the only ones that sprang to mind was "El Cid" with one of America's favorites, Charlton Heston. And of course, as I mentioned earlier, the Fu Manchu films, in which Wilmer's Nayland Smith bore a number of what might be aptly called "Holmesian" traits. There were of course the dozen or so Sherlock Holmes televised features. But to be fair and honest, I'd only seen pictures of Wilmer as Holmes, for the television program had not reached America, and in 1969 the day had yet to arrive when digital versatile disks (DVD's) even existed before allowing their owners to capture classic televised performances going back to the media's Stone Age.

Timidly, no doubt, I said hello to Douglas Wilmer, who may well have overheard my boisterous companion giving Alec Guinness my back-story. But here's the most curious part of the thing. Twenty-odd years later I chanced to correspond with Mr. Wilmer about Sherlock Holmes, and he in turn offered to meet with me at his home near Woodstock. I accepted that invitation and spent a wonderful long afternoon chatting with the man who even then was busy recording the works of Drs. Watson and Doyle. He told and showed me how he managed to lay down his recorded readings right there in his comfortable flat. And we chatted of many things, including our unusual first meeting on the set of "Cromwell." He was actually charming enough to probably fib and say "you know, I do believe I remember you. But it was quite a long time ago." And yes I agreed, indeed it was.

We spoke as well of our common love, in the form of the Holmes Canon. Also of the physical business of bringing the master sleuth to life, even as he had. In this regard he had much to share, *vis a vis* other portrayals, ranging from Basil Rathbone to Jeremy Brett. He also shared anecdotes of working with the likes of Charlton Heston, whom he liked, and Richard Harris, whom he didn't like much at all.

But to finish off the account of my mad-cap meeting with King Arthur, or his alter ego Richard Harris, a couple of observations. At the end of that summer in 1969 I managed to spend the better part of a week coming from and going to "Tower House," if not getting to know its occupants. One of those chanced to be the attractive and doe-like Anne Kristen, with whom I formed a kind of—what shall we call it?—a rapport, however brief. There were others as well in passing, like the actors Michael Jayston and Marty Feldman, the famous lyricist, Leslie Bricusse, or the irascible screenwriter, Wolf Mankowitz.

And then of course there was "himself." I thanked him for his tolerance and left saying I'd hoped we'd meet again. And indeed we did. I would see Richard a couple of times over the years, with the last time being in 1981 when he showed up at Detroit's Fisher Theater for a reboot of "Camelot."

It was with a certain sense of sadness that I left "King Arthur's Court" and aimed myself homeward. On our final evening together Harris was feeling under the weather. That had managed to scotch earlier plans to make a group visit to London's Talk of the Town night-spot. At that time Richard's friend Sammy Davis Junior was appearing.

It's a curious thing to put things into perspective at times. I mean, once I did get home a month or so later I saw that Richard Harris was going to be on the Tonight Show. So I stayed up and watched it. Johnny Carson and Harris got along well, but I was surprised when the popular host asked the star of stage and screen a certain question.

"I understand you were in, what do you call it over in London? A punch-up?"

Harris smiled contritely and then gathered speed. 'Well you see, John, it was like this…" He then proceeded to describe how he and a few friends had gone to the Talk of the Town to see Sammy Davis. Trouble loomed large when RH overheard a remark made by a man seated nearby.

"He used a rather bad and unfortunate term to describe Sammy" he explained. But when the Tonight Show's staffers did their best to bleep the explicative, eyes as sharp as mine managed to glean it out. Let's simply say it was insulting on both an ethnic and racial level.

"I asked the man to repeat what he said, and he repeated it" Harris explained. "So, I just took a punch at him and he hit back, and before you know it his crowd and my crowd were getting into it."

Hearing this anecdote, I suddenly realized that but for an incipient cold on Richard Harris' part, I might have been in his "crowd" that night, and in the melee, for the sake of defending the honor of Mr. Sammy Davis, Junior!

So that's the story. A photo was snapped of Richard Harris and I on that last evening at Tower House. I'm spiffed out in a three-piece suit, leaning in on a marble, decidedly royal-looking throne upon which "King Arthur" sits, looking either unwell or more than a bit under the influence. *Sans* dragon helm or shining armor, my companion is slouched in tee-shirt and sweater. In essence, more the Earl of Limerick than the liege lord of Camelot.

As is certainly the case of all of us, I observed Richard Harris over the course of the years. Yes, even as he became a figure of fun on the guest divans on the Carson or Letterman shows. And as he morphed—or evolved—from the young Arthur into the elder magical statesman Dumbledore, in the early Harry Potter films.

And then he was gone. The king was dead.

Long Live The King!

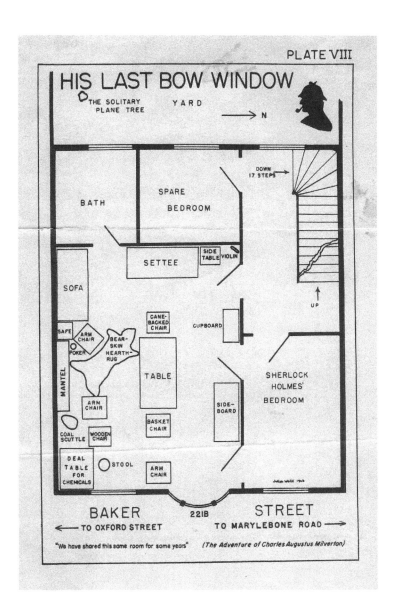

221B "The Room Without A View" —
a glimpse à la Julian Wolff

"221B"— The historic 1951 Abbey National Version

"221B"— The Grosse Ile Incarnation

12

The Room Without A View

At the close of my second trip to London in 1969 I paid another sentimental call upon Baker Street. Two years earlier and a bit dewier eyed I'd made the pilgrimage for the first time, with all the attendant excitement of a faithful reader who finally arrives at what might be termed, quite literally, "the scene of the crime." And with that arrival no doubt my formative Sherlockian interests had also been baptized by my ability to stand at last upon the tangible incarnation of that fabled stretch of pavement.

But even today, seemingly a light year later, I find myself aware of the curious lodestone that remains Number 221B, Baker Street. But to do so is to necessarily embark upon a journey steeped in fact and marinated by fancy. *Id est,* as they say, for to seek out the material abode of an immaterial figure requires a truly open mind and perhaps something more.

To begin with, and while there was such an avenue even prior to Mr. Holmes' tenancy, the facts of the case attest to a certain grim truth: *there never was a "221B" during the heyday of the world's most famous consulting detective.*

Baker Street's chronicle began at the end of the 18th century. Its name echoed Sir Edward Baker, the illustrious friend of Edward Berkeley Portman, the prominent developer and speculator, whose own appellation is reflected by the neighborhood's other eponymous square.

It was through Edward Baker's planning that his namesake street was laid out and became one of London's most desirable sectors. However its sea-change from fashionable *locus* to a middle-class residential and commercial quarter only came seven decades later upon the construction of the Baker Street Station. Within the next twenty years the area would reflect the ambience invoked by the gist of Drs. Watson and Doyle's immortal descriptions of it. For it is there and in what most scholars now accept as the year 1881 that his friend and "Boswell" commenced his sharing the urban residence of Mr. Sherlock Holmes.

Much has been written about whether or not Dr. J. H. Watson did in truth seek to conceal their Baker Street digs by concealing its actual address? That would of course provide an answer, if not an alternative to the endless opining over the location of perhaps the most important address in popular world literature. Here too does the premise that Holmes' Boswell disguised their address seem more than reasonable on balance. Moreover, if we are to presume that Watson's Victorian counterpart to the modern era's blogs was *The Strand Magazine,* it's easy enough to understand. And why? Well simply on account of the fact that the career of London's best-known detective was being revealed in serial fashion. Here the very idea of a "real-life" practitioner being described in what many might assume were fictional terms carried with it certain conditions. One of those was the ability of a reader who might be a prospective client, admirer, or worse, an enemy of Sherlock Holmes to know where to find him.

A question to consider is if indeed Watson camouflaged Holmes' address, how difficult might it have been to find its actual counterpart? Obviously Scotland Yard knew where to track him down, as did Professor Moriarty. But on a limited, yet regular basis, so too did those prospective clients wishing to avail themselves of Holmes' help. As an addendum here, and as viewers of the McKellen film "Mr. Holmes" depicts, Holmes comments to his client that he has found his undisguised address, as lightly veiled by Dr. Watson.

Therefore it makes inordinate sense to presume that Watson's masking of his colleague's actual address was more of a creative, rather than security-minded device. Such license may have also been in keeping with the chronicler's practice of concealing the actual identities of Holmes' visitors and clients, if only, as the rubric has it, "to protect the innocent," if not others as well.

But before we leave this aspect of the subject at hand, I find one of the most intriguing elements in the Sherlock Holmes stories to be the means by which the public grew to know their man. Here we also find the strange balance of Holmes' denigrations of Watson's treatments contrasted to his sure knowledge that but for the efforts of his friend and biographer, London would not have so boldly echoed his name.

There is I think, a bit of a paradox here, but one which only signals Holmes' own sense of human vanity, if not astuteness. For very like Jesus of Nazareth before him, he knew there was no better way of getting your message out than to seemingly encourage a sense of secrecy about it. Moreover, he was aware that the best means of professing his skills would be through the agency of his confidants or disciples. Ergo, and as the best display of all, the Gospel According To Dr. John H. Watson weathered all, including the regular bout of Holmes' own dismay at the artful depiction of his work.

"Honestly, I cannot congratulate you upon it. Detection is, or ought to be, an exact science, and should be treated in the same cold and unemotional manner. You have attempted to tinge it with romanticism, which produces much the same effect as if you worked a love-story or an elopement into the fifth proposition of Euclid."

So says Holmes in *The Sign of Four*. But surely he is venting a bit of spleen at his colleague's work, all the while knowing that without such "romanticism," his clinical undertakings would have found a relatively fallow field. However, and given the broader vista of *The Strand's* readership, the strata by which the Holmesian "gospel" might be mined was there. Moreover, to presume that its central character was of such stuff as to eschew recognition would be false.

Clearly Holmes loves the game not only for its own sake, but for how it challenges him and affirms what he believes to be his own unique status as the world's first consulting detective. Here then is an ego, and one geared to saying "look at me" like a magician who demands the attention of his audience. And here we have what I think is an important key: *audience to Sherlock Holmes is a necessity*. All of his hermetic preparations and even his intermittent and private eccentricities are in aid of his return to the hunt. And for the sake of that, in no way or time does he shy away from being noticed. In fact and under certain carefully controlled circumstances, he is adept at stage managing his observer's attention, and quite often with a dramatic flourish which marks the *denouement*.

But to return to the notion of Watson's possibly deliberate practice of veiling places, persons, and titles. To begin with, he may have in some wise "encoded" the stories with alternate identities. Therefore, and well aware that there never was a numeric "221" Baker Street in 1881, he may have diverted the reader's attention from the truth. And why? Once again, we cannot say with ultimate certainty. No more, say, than did Conan Doyle himself when he claimed not to have been on Baker Street, when it is a fact that he had been photographed in a studio there. But to what end the ruse?

Baker Street of Holmes', Watson's and Doyle's day was much physically shorter than today, and existed within the reach of Portman Square and the corner of Paddington Street to the east, and Crawford Street to the West. To the north, "Baker Street" continued as York Place. As for its southerly sector, its structures were numbered consecutively, from Numbers 1-42 on the east, and Numbers 44-85 upon the west.

But it is the fabled "221 'B', for the French "*bis,* or second floor" which was offered to a public which itself might be well aware of the deception. For any reader, the latest copy of the *Strand* in his fist, could have established the non-address with little difficulty. And they might also have followed down Watson's clue-like descriptions, as were laid down in "The Empty House," even to the point of tracking the *locus* of "Camden House," which stood across from Mrs. Hudson's property.

Still the great game of Sherlockian Pursuit continues to this day, even as it was conducted in less organized terms nearly eight decades ago to establish the True North of the Doylean mythos. Details great and small have been scrutinized, and seekers have oftentimes been emboldened by the notion that certain strange serendipity is there to assure them that fact, rather than fiction is at the end of their quest.

Ergo calculations regarding sunlight and shade, opposing structures, the presence or absence of street lights, backyard trees, or the proximity to the rail terminus have all played their parts in the hunt for the true *locus* of "221B." Investigators of many ilk have made sterling cases, all of them bolstered, paradoxically, by the reality that such an address could not have been found in Holmes' moment of time.

A prime example here might be Number 111 Baker Street, which fell prey to the war-time Blitz. Not only physically, atmospherically, and numerically evocative of Number 221, 111 also wore the serendipitous quality of standing across from a building still blazoned "Camden House," as was duly noted by Dr. Gray Chandler Briggs in a bygone day. Regrettably however, and much in the vein of establishing the coordinates of Atlantis upon modern-day charts, all we are left with are clues. Curiously too, and despite the absence of Holmes himself, or his chronicler, what we are bequeathed is an enduring exercise in surmise. And in its wake? The rich panorama of the stories themselves await us, as does a trove of related scholarly efforts marked by text and a few grainy, if not ghostly photographs.

Perhaps the most visible updating of the quest for the Sherlockian headquarters came through the auspices of The Abbey National Building Society in London.

Since 1932 the society's headquarters which encompassed Numbers 215-229.Baker Street afforded a special service to the faithful. For to their lasting credit, Abbey National went so far as employing a number of part-time agents serving in the capacity of "Secretary To Mr. Sherlock Holmes." They in turn would answer an unending flow of letters directed to Baker Street, much in the more generic fashion of postal services accommodating seasonal letters to Santa Claus. Moreover, by lending credence to the existence, if not modern-day "retirement of Mr. Holmes to tend his bees in Sussex," Abbey National added to the mythos.

However since its renovation, relocation, and subsequent transition to the present day, the Holmesian focus of the myth-made-real has been shifted to Number 219, where the Sherlock Holmes Museum now thrives. It is seated at a midpoint not far from Baker Street Station, Madam Tussauds, and an imposing nine-foot bronze statue of the Great Detective is fitted out with deerstalker cap, pipe, and Inverness cape.

As for the Holmes Museum, that like the bestowal of a literary provenance for, say, Dickens' Bleak House or Miss Haversham's domain becomes a newly-wrought custom burnished by time.

Today London pilgrims find a converted structure unofficially which is self-designated as "221B." It now includes a gift-shop, tea-room and upon its second level, the Sitting Room, Holmes' bedroom, as well as upper exhibition space. For visitors this has become the Mecca of Baker Street. On one hand, through its many efforts toward authenticity, it does morph a certain sense of verisimilitude unlike many others. On the other however, this *faux* historical-cum-literary site has engendered a sort of touristy and circuslike atmosphere which cannot help but conflict with the specialness of the geographical terrain in which it exists.

If only by virtue of its predominance today, a staggering number of visitors arrive daily and depart from the Holmes Museum with the sense (if not a slew of souvenirs) attesting that here indeed was that very spot where the world's greatest detective and his colleague shared a dwelling. Who then is to say them nay? Sir Arthur Conan Doyle is a long-distance call away, and even the considered Holmesian authorities give the place little shrift, save as an evocative oddity.

In thinking about the Sherlock Holmes Museum on Baker Street today, I cannot dismiss it entirely, if only for the sake of its metaphorical value. Alike William Shakespeare's Birthplace in Stratford-On-Avon, the spurious underpinning of its claims have become overwhelmed by the desire of its public, who "want to believe." Ergo, why should a little thing like veracity manage to poison the waters? And in the case of Sherlock Holmes, unlike that mythically-historicized phantom called Shakespeare, the case is doubly problematic. This is warranted by the Sherlockians own valedictory boast for the "digs" of Holmes and his biographer: to wit, that "here resided two men of note who never lived, and so can never die." The proposition is rather neat; rather like the fact that Somerset House, that national archive for births and deaths, find no indication of Sherlock's demise. Ergo, he has become immortal.

From the purist's point of view, it is relatively easy to find the prospect of the 21st century's Sherlock Holmes Museum to resonate with its own special sense of paradox. In reality however, it does indeed serve a fragment of the metaphorical, almost iconic *raison d'etre* of reminding us of Conan Doyle's greatest creation.

And not unlike other re-creations of "221B," whether it be the Sherlock Holmes Pub on London's Northumberland Avenue, the Château Lucens, the Swiss chateau where Adrian Conan Doyle re-seated that reliquary domain, or, even my own garaged annex, where the Sitting Room has been faithfully constructed.

In other words, the shrine to Sherlock Holmes is in essence invisible, while its altar has been made tangible as an elaborate museum, a room, or even a shoe-box-sized miniature. All of them count as reminders as our wishful belief in the ghostly gaslit world of a bygone era, where "it is always 1895."

But there is always a degree of innate magic in (re)visting Baker Street. Not unlike those venerable sites in Jerusalem, where hordes of pilgrims seek to make "contact" with the past, I find a comparable scenario at work today on Baker Street. Harking again to the more "sacred" aspect of, say, the legendary *Cenaculum,* or Upper Room where tourists are told the Last Supper was held, today's Sitting Room and its attached infrastructure afford the visitant a focus for their fantasies—a touchstone of sorts. And like Jerusalem's plurality of Jesus-related tomb sites, it falls upon the believer to make their choice. For myself, and speaking as but one man, I cannot help but rue how the changing times have offered up chaff for wheat. Or perhaps I am merely uttering the complaints of someone who once knew something for its earlier, less cluttered, and seemingly purer form?

There is a parable and an analogy of sorts available here to make my point. Take for example my own recollections, commenced in 1976, when I first visited the region of Scotland's monster-haunted Loch Ness. My purpose in being there was essentially curiosity. I mean, after all, here was perhaps arguably was one of the world's greatest paranormal, if not zoological mysteries. So then, setting my invisible deerstalker toward Scotland, I privately funded my own expedition, and obtained credentials from *The Detroit News* to fly over and investigate the case.

Over the course of approximately nine times to visit the land of my father's ancestors, it became my habit to base myself in the nearby village of Drumnadrochit. Nearly four decades ago, that "place beyond the bridge" wore a sort of Brigadoonish demeanor. Monster-hunter or not, you could walk down those quiet streets and even out of village precincts toward the nearby Temple Pier without bother. And by "bother" I mean to suggest any form of commercialized tourist hype. Back in the day I recall one small 'Monster-Burger" stand during the summers. And yes, there were even small placards near trash barrels which implored "LOOK FOR NESSIE, BUT DON'T BE MESSY." That was basically all. Of course you could find small versions of the "beastie" in some shops, as well as the inevitable postcards, which featured everything from contemporary pictures of the Great Glen, to one depicting an underwater phantom "captured" by a scientist's underwater camera. But here's my point: there were no sensationalized, money-glomming enterprises back in 1976. That took a bit of time.

Ruefully, the last time I visited Drumnadrochit a decade ago, its quiet streets were busier. The once vacant hills, their crests shrouded with morning mists, were now punctuated by modern and expensive summer or full-time houses. Both in the village and on the fringe, the Religion of Nessie had been inflated into large scale dimensions. To wit, where there used to be only the rather evocative Victorian "Drum Hotel," today it has an attached motor lodge, and a Monster Center, complete with a "full-sized recreation" of the legendary creature in a pool on the grounds. And further afield, in the famous loch, I was sadly informed by one of the locals that even the waterway itself had become "polluted." 'But not just by trash, said my informant, "but by people."

The latter remark reminded me of a reply I rather casually uttered a couple of years earlier to a journalist. Unable to get to the loch to investigate those perennial reports of whether or not "Nessie" existed, he asked me, as a veteran Nessie questor, *"Bottom line: are there monsters at Loch Ness or not?" T*o which I answered him in no uncertain terms. *"Absolutely" I replied. "But most of them are on shore."*

Monsters, be they phantom hounds or not, and detectives or even Napoleonic villains notwithstanding, these days Baker Street is much changed from Holmes' day, or my own. Apart from the Museum there is also a Sherlock Holmes Memorabilia Company at Number 230. And once pilgrims also found themselves lured to the aptly named Sherlock Holmes Hotel at 108 Baker Street, complete with its Dr. Watson's Bar.

Catering to the mavens and merely curious, the Memorabilia emporium struck me as nice in its way, and was delivered from being purely profitable for its purpose by what it also contains. This, like a holy relic, in the form of the very mantel before which Sherlock Holmes cogitated throughout the Granada series. Doubtless it may still feel the seeking and finding aura of the late and much-lamented Jeremy Brett.

It is rather astonishing how the subject of Sherlock Holmes has remained not only enduring, but worthy of being re-cobbled into what is metaphorically New Millennial wine within a 19th century wineskin. In recent years we have seen at least two attempts to modernize Holmes, cleverly (as in the case of the cleverly mounted PBS "Sherlock" and even painfully (to me) with "Elementary," which adds transforming Dr. Watson into an Asian woman.

But when such things happen I revert to what I consistently recommend as therapy: *retreat into the past.* Get your dictionary-sized copy of *The Complete Sherlock Holmes* and lose yourself. Or perhaps even indulge yourself in so many of those now classic Holmes films, ranging from Barrymore and Rathbone to Neville, Plummer, Cushing, Wilmer, Lee and even Roger Moore—right up to the brink of laughing uncomfortably at Robert Downey assaying Holmes as a short, slovenly and unshaven reprobate who drinks formaldehyde as a stimulant. *Basta! Enough!*

As perhaps a valedictory comment on the past, present, or future physical location of "221B," all that matters is what the observer believes in his heart to be true. After that one might feel free to embrace the Churchillian License, which I think applies just as well to Sherlock Holmes as to King Arthur; namely, *"it's all true, or it ought to be; and more and better besides."*

Now then, and to leave the physical and external notion of the Holmesian Baker Street, if only to consider what I deem to be its equally fascinating counterpart: the interior of 221B itself.

Apart from all other considerations, I tend to take a kind of average of every physical or mental image of that room among rooms. For it is sacred space. Moreover, it has come to serve a purpose unlike the lion's share of literary backdrops for the world's most famous figures, be they real or no. For only in the Sitting Room at 221B does time suspend itself. And with Holmes and his faithful friend, we imagine ourselves also sitting back and conjuring over the pungent scents of shag tobacco beside an embering sea-coal fire. And upon those hallowed walls the gaslit dances, and beyond those dappled panes the fog curls like cat's tails around the nearby lamp-posts. It is a finely wrought world, and a consummation we dare to devoutly dream of inhabiting.

I suppose my chronic fascination with the physical premises of Holmes' lodgings began quite early on. It came at that ancient, formative, fairy moment when I first laid eyes upon a photograph of the Holmes Sitting Room. This was reproduced upon the back book jacket of *The Complete Sherlock Holmes* published by Doubleday. Its source was the 1951 Festival of Britain Exhibition of Great Britain recreating Sherlock Holmes' professional "office" chamber within the

Abbey National Building Society premises. That to a great extent fixed a kind of visual template for offering a "real" glimpse of the Baker Street shrine. I even recall seeing a bit of rare footage which not only described the display as a "museum," but included the dubious factoid that Conan Doyle's *Valley of Fear* was the initial Holmes adventure.

My first glimpse of the photographic record of 221B was somewhat akin to viewing the Shroud of Turin. Initially, commonsense tells you that it cannot be: yet some sort of magical, inner sense says, *Yes, it is just as it ought to be.*

Another view of the Sitting Room was made real for me upon my first trip to Great Britain. This involved my first visit to the Sherlock Holmes Public House and Restaurant on Northumberland Street, Westminster. Presently seated where once the Northumberland Arms, a hotel mentioned in *The Hound of the Baskervilles,* stood, the pub stands not far from Old Scotland Yard and a Turkish bath once patronized by Dr. Watson. Storied ground, indeed.

In its way the Sherlock Holmes Public House existed as London's first ongoing collection of museum-like memorabilia. Alike many of the city's themed watering holes, this one goes a step, if not seventeen steps, further. But one needs to ascend to the second floor for its revelation. For there visitors discover an authentic, if not somewhat confined and tatty rendition of "221B." But let me retreat. "Tatty" sounds pejorative. As if to suggest that in the wake of so many glamorized presentiments of Holmes sweet home, this ten by twelve foot echo might seem less real. To the contrary, actually; for had one visited the "true cross" itself, they would likely have been unimpressed. After all, what Watson's chronicles depicts is simply a moderately well-tended domicile of two bachelor gentlemen. Imagine then something vaguely resembling a better-behaved rendition of an adult frat house.

But when I first studied that upper display of the Holmes Pub, a pint of bitter in my fist, I was impressed. And two decades later when I returned to that eccentric bit of space, if not with many intermittent visits in between, I remained captivated by that first nascent image brought to life. I recall as well sharing dinner with a friend before that small *tableau* behind the glass. I eventually learned that the hostelry's collection had been culled in part from the earlier '51 Exhibition; I felt that I was viewing The Real Thing. Much of this, I think, reflects what Mario Praz, who has been called the "historian of the home" once defined as *Stimmung*, or "mood" in German parlance.

Add to this as well that the atmosphere impressed upon Holmes' sitting room is one mostly re-echoed and parsed by those who are its temporary, rather than permanent visitors. Their views, apart from Watson's own, have traditionally adorned Mrs. Hudson's street-facing chamber with a sense of *terra cognita* in the fashion of a well-appointed doll house with its recognizable interior features. For it was the actual embodiment of that grainy photo I'd spied back in 1962 for W.T. Rabe's suburban review of William S. Baring-Gould's masterful *Sherlock Holmes of Baker Street.*

Over the years I would encounter various pictorial versions of the Sitting Room, including that of the Château Lucens in Switzerland, owned by Conan Doyle's son, Adrian. Nowhere, perhaps, has such painstaking fidelity been achieved, even to the actual Holmesian vintage of those *objets d'art* which filled the room. As I recall, the chamber's recreator even went to the extreme of simulating fog beyond the window panes!

There were other emulations as well, and those in turn undoubtedly served as the set-prototypes for such filmed presentations as the Ronald Howard televised "Adventures of Sherlock Holmes," or the British films "A Study In Terror" with John Neville or "The Hound of the Baskervilles" featuring Peter Cushing as the master sleuth. Later on we would see those hallowed premises again, as with the purposefully claustrophobic room in "The Seven Per Cent Solution," or the rather grander Baker Street incarnations in "The Private Life of Sherlock Holmes" or "Murder By Decree."

And then of course still to come was that iconically recognizable recreation of the Granada Studios-Jeremy Brett productions of the "Adventures," "Memoirs," and "Casebook of Sherlock Holmes." With the latter and as an army of fellow Holmesians would agree, seeing Brett and his Watsons, David Burke and Edward Hardwicke evoked nothing so fine as the original Sidney Paget illustrations.

As Jeremy Brett himself once informed me, he had often gone to great lengths to simulate the artist's depictions of Holmes, whether those poses were meant to be registered or not. What mattered, the actor explained, was that *he* knew the authenticity of the matter. I found that element to be true myself, as when I was tutored by Arthur Conan Doyle's daughter in such matters as "how did he stand?" or "how did he address an audience?" or even "how did he hold his pipe?" And countless audiences in for my "Evening With Sir Arthur Conan Doyle," it became irrelevant as to whether my observers took these things for verities: I knew them as such. And knowing it, I walked out onto that stage with loins metaphorically girded! And the parable here? Perhaps to state that some things in their reality are merely the byproducts of either habit or happenstance.

Now then, perhaps another "Sherlockian Side-bar." This one has to do with my own time spent in those sacred Baker Street quarters. Upon my youthful and gradual exposures to the "clubbable" aspects of the Baker Street Irregulars and their national and internationally-based peers, my knowledge expanded, as did my bookshelves and over time, my correspondence.

One exciting and unsuspected by-product of my youthful overtures in writing to Lord Donegal in London or Julian Wolff in New York were a number of kind responses in various graphical forms. For example, there were Dr. Wolff's wonderful Christmas cards which often took a cartographic form. These might colorfully indicate Holmes' European or even British meanderings, and to this day remain highly collectible artifacts. So too perhaps the lay-out of 221B, also via the good doctor. Unwittingly, I may have made an impression upon the BSI's kindly Commissionaire, for over many years he gifted me with a good deal of treasure. Today a perusal of my stuffed scrapbooks finds the likes of such rarities as *The Practical Handbook of Heraldry, A Visitation of Conanical Arms, A Ramble In Bohemia, A Case of Scotch, Still Waters, An Irregular Chronology of Baker Street,* as well as *A Second Supplement To An Irregular Guide To Sherlock Holmes by Jay Finley Christ, Gleanings By Gaslight,* and much more. Today such bibliographic items are beyond collectible to the right person. And I fell into that category in my own naively youthful fashion.

But among my trove of collectible cards was that one outstanding and vintage Julian Wolff item entitled "Mr. Sherlock Holmes (9)." In triptych fashion, this three-sectioned, in-color panorama was sub-titled "Operation House Moving From Baker Street to Château de Lucens,

214

Switzerland" Unfolded, it revealed the wall-by-wall details of the Sitting Room as recreated by Adrian Conan Doyle. And there beneath the photograph was the catalogued list of every Sherlockian detail, from "General Gordon's picture" to "John H. Watson's Brandy Flask" In all there were by my count ninety-two items revealed there in pictorial fashion. All of which serves as another evidential means of materializing those random objects which have become iconized within the Sacred Writings.

Harking back as I've been doing a good deal of late for this project, I try to recall the first time I managed to physically create my own version of the Baker Street premises. I think this may have been around age thirteen when I did my best to convert a shoe-box into the 221B Sitting Room. But as a rather worn manila file folder reveals, over subsequent years my efforts at "inhabiting" that sacred chamber took a variety of shapes. There was, for instance, a shadowy room of one bachelor apartment given to a makeshift mantle, a basket chair, armchair, and assorted Sherlockian details. This was duly followed by a marital apartment corner, followed by a full basement space carefully outfitted to include even a couple of subterranean windows artificially illumined to give the effect of reality.

I recall a curious means of gauging the fidelity of that aforesaid and fine chamber by two equally curious incidents. The first of these involved my once casually balling up a bit of paper and tossing it into the "fire," which was electric. Secondly, and evoking my transformational mind-set, the day I heard a commotion from outside and walked over to the curtained window, which was in truth the basement wall done up to resemble a casement!

I loved that basement-level rendition of Baker Street. I read down there, I smoked there, was interviewed there, and often cogitated there. On one occasion I recall being lost in my own irregular thoughts and eyes closed, fingers steepled, became aware of an odd, audible sensation. My ears and brain told me what it seemed to be, and given that, I continued savoring the sound, like a dreamer choosing not to awaken. *For what I had heard and was hearing, was the weight of someone sitting in the vacant basket chair on the other side of the fireplace. I repeat, as if some unseen occupant had arrived in this room, where I'd presumed myself entirely alone.*

I waited in those moments before hearing it again. And it came. A subtle shifting and weight creating a clear suggestion of someone's weight upon that wickered seat. Who might it be? Holmes? Watson? Moriarty? Or some other spectral visitant?

As a sidebar here, for years I have considered that strangely audible phenomenon within my former and below stairs replica of "221B." What accounted for it? How might it be possible? Considering the matter a good deal, it finally came to me that rather like Christopher Reeve's character in "Somewhere In Time," perhaps the key to time-travel, even in the literary sense, was "setting the scene." Replicate the atmosphere and then relax into it, and who knows but that you might be able to "go back." Did I do that? For now at least, the jury remains out on the matter.

But coming back to that moment, as I'd sat there, eyes closed, meditating. For when at last I re-opened my eyes there was, of course, no one there. The phantom had either flown, or being a phantom and invisible, might still be there. It reminded me of the tale I'd heard about the Sherlock Holmes Pub on London's Northumberland Avenue. Its upper Sitting Room corner in place since the early Fifties, a story was told how the cleaning lady had chanced to glance up, if only to see a robed man seated in Sherlock Holmes' armchair behind the protective glass. Blinking, she looked back if only to see an empty piece of Victorian furniture. The Ghost of Holmes? Who can say? But I for one would like to believe it.

As Is write this I nearly omitted something which may also explain how the past, albeit fictional, might be summoned to life. This involves a token, or relic of Baker Street which I've treasured over the years. It consists of an actual brick taken from the original structure where the Abbey National Building Society's headquarters stood when I arrived to "place the plaque." Emblazoned, unsurprisingly, "221B," this hefty artifact was given to me by the Secretary To Sherlock Holmes himself, and managed to add happy weight to my checked luggage back in '78. Since then this "bit of the True Cross" has occupied a favored position on my bookshelves, and most recently, within the latest re-conjured incarnation of my own version of Holmes' Sitting Room. And there it reposes even now, perhaps as a conductor that emanates the distant sounds of foot and transport along the once gaslit expanses of Upper Baker Street.

Moreover too, for all I know or hope to believe, that bit of manufactured former stone and mortar survives today as a conductor— of not only a literary golden age, but of the inspirational mindset of a yesterday which took root in this writer quite a long while ago. And who knows whether like a Wellsian time machine of its own, this object does not allow Holmes, Watson, Mrs. Hudson, or a score of others to speak to me from the Past?

And speaking of my own recent yesterdays, my version of "221B" circa 1979 felt its own tectonic shift. For here were two forms of parting, with the first involving the end of my marriage and the second my wrenched self-eviction from the aforesaid subterranean Sherlockian reconstruction I'd created in Ypsilanti, Michigan. But like a specter, that setting or a portion of it would duly follow me to Detroit and the riverfront brownstone where I was next to reside. However even then I was unaware that like a cosmic notion seeking its own sense of fruition, the "Holmes Room" would continue to evolve. First in literally miniaturized fashion, and ultimately upon a life-sized scale within the ancillary shell of an eighty-year-old stable-cum-garage in Grosse Ile, Michigan.

The prospect of the chamber I now share with the great detective and whatever other ghosts may choose to seek refuge in the compound behind our "Gray Gables" began in stages. This is doubtless on account of the metaphor involving my ability to re-build not only my life, but also a haven for my longest term of fantasies. These originally came to pass as a reflection of a new day, a new marriage, and our tenancy of a then-136 year old Carpenter Gothic brick manse facing the Ontarian shores of Amherstburg. Locally known as "Gray Gables" for its owner, Major Horace Gray, this would become my own sanctum sanctorum, if not the sparking point of many written words. Moreover, the old house would become the rehearsal hall of sorts for a repertory of dramatic ghosts. Just so, over time did Conan Doyle, Winston Churchill, Bernard Shaw, Wyatt Earp, C.S. Lewis, Theodore Roosevelt and Mark Twain all tread those centuried floors, stairs, porches and verdant back yard before embarking for a host of theatrical venues.

As I would initially discover, behind its aptly gabled riverfront façade stood a second story bedroom just right for Mr. Holmes. Accordingly then, my new Mrs. Hudson and I converted the guest bedroom into

"221B," in fine fashion. Flocked wall-paper, "V.R." pocked into the wall, the hearth, the chairs, the pictures, maps, bearskin, etc. And perhaps best of all, *a flight of seventeen steps led from the ground-floor to the Master's Chamber.* Amazing, Holmes! As a post-script as well, consider my sense of "rightness" here upon recalling that the most prominent of two chaps named McPherson in the Canon is Fitzroy McPherson of "The Lion's Mane." More curious yet is the name of his academic place of employ: *"The Gables."* Coincidence, do you think?

But here too a confession. Eventually my fervent Sherlockian spirit became, shall we say, contained by another and related project, soon to be described. In short here, this involved my dramatic foray as Sir Arthur Conan Doyle in 1987. Working with Dame Jean Conan Doyle, meeting Jeremy Brett and a score of others, it was as "ACD" that my sentiments now seemed to dwell, rather than with Holmes. On that account, and owing to my also working on a new literary project involving Edgar Allan Poe, I made a decision. This was also tempered by the generous number of Poe-etical books and artifacts I'd acquired to date. And so the decision was made.

It has seemed right and even proper in retrospect that "221B" would give way to Mr. Poe, just as any true Sherlockian must cede the honor of the Master's inception to the author of "The Raven." For as Conan Doyle himself admitted, without Poe's master of ratiocination, the "Poe-etic" Chevalier Dupin, there would likely not have been the reasoner of Baker Street in his present form.

Thus did those seventeen steps also eventually lead the visitor up to the bedroom door marked with a small plaque which reads *"POE 1849."* For you see, 1849 not only signified the year of Edgar's passing, but also the one in which our home, "Gray Gables" was built. On such a basis then it seemed right and fitting to me to celebrate my friend "Eddie," and the chap my literary father Ray Bradbury used to call "my Papa."

And as for Sherlock Holmes and the iconic Sitting Room? Here I suppose there was a psychological dimension playing its part. For ever since taking up the task of "becoming" Holmes' and Watson's true begetter, the Sherlockian Canon had assumed a sort of a diminished and vestigial shape. As if in accordance, my physical upstairs re-creation was downsized to a foot-long bit of shelf space constituting a meticulous replica in miniature!

In other words, my Doylean role and awareness of the author had become an extension of the larger whole, in much the way that my late friend Dame Jean Conan Doyle once described a photo of myself posing beside the great Holmes re-creator, Jeremy Brett. I'd remarked that in the picture I seemed broader, even my cranial size exceeding that of 'Sherlock Holmes.'

"Oh, but Mark" insisted Jean over the transatlantic line, "the photograph shows things as they were meant to be. My father was always so much bigger than Sherlock Holmes!"

I suppose everything is a matter of perspective, isn't it? I also remember that my first inclination was to reduce "221B" to a miniature-sized foot or so of space on a library shelf. That in turn reminded of an old Spanish tradition which speaks of the Devil's ability to lift up rooftops, if only to peer down at the mortals within. And here it would be remiss not to mention a comment of Holmes himself in "A Case Of Identity." There he remarks,

"If we could fly out of that window hand in hand, hover over this great city, gently remove the roofs, and peep in at the queer things which are going on, the strange coincidences, the plannings, the cross-purposes, the wonderful chain of events, working through generations, and leading to the most outre' results, it would make all fiction with its conventionalities and foreseen conclusions most stale and unprofitable."

There was an aspect of that "roof lifting" I suppose in the idea of reducing "221B" to a Lilliputian scale. Having done so, I, like God, Gulliver, or the Devil himself have arranged each little artifact in accordance with its well-known blue-print. So much too, perhaps, for the seasoned adage about the Devil being "in the details." And I suppose he often is.

In accordance with my musings, I eventually chose to go beyond the friendly, weathered walls of our home, if only to skip across to our many-bayed garage, which was once upon a time a former stable and thereafter an early 20th century workshop for Henry Lane, an engineer and occupant of "the Gables" long before us. Also as I would learn, the cob-webbed annex of two other room represented the echo of Mr. Lane's year-round care-taker.

And as for the garage-cum-Holmesian shrine? Well in due time what was conceived was finalized into two adjoining chambers. The first of these upon entering from the woods-facing easterly portion of our property now resembles a Victorian gentleman's book-lined flat. For some odd reason I decided to christen this "Sir Richard's Room," on account of the Orientalia, carvings, Egyptian statuary, swords and firearms all suited to a rogue such as Richard Francis Burton.

The Burton Room in turns leads into the Sitting Room proper. The observer crosses the threshold into a bi-windowed chamber featuring the familiar fireplace to the left fronted by a bearskin, deal top table with chemical apparatus, the bust of Holmes, Watson's desk, assorted maps and pictures, the fabled "V.R." pocked into the walls, and of course bookcases lined with the necessary commonplace, scrapbooks, and assorted other rare volumes. In short, here then is Sherlock's Idea Lab, even as it is so well-described by Dr. Watson's memoirs.

Unsurprisingly perhaps, I do not over-frequent my transplanted rendition of "221B." In fact, the deer which constantly pass through our rear wood see more of Mr. Holmes' door than I. I know this if only for the sake of taking note from our kitchen window whenever the action-sensor on the light behind the garage goes off.

Initially I took the spectral illuminations to signify a possible intruder to my forest sanctum. Ultimately however it became, as I say, a matter of my deer friends. Yet of a more puzzling aspect is the how? and why? of the Sitting Room's lights occasionally being turned on. For this bit of mystery I might rationalize by saying that perhaps old Sherlock is working late? But much more likely, I believe, is that Henry Lane's caretaker is sending me a message. I only hope it involves his pleasure in now sharing his digs with the world's most famous detective!

At any rate, the aim of all this rambling is to state that apart from the curious element of its geographical or chronological situation, the look and feel of Mr. Holmes fabled Sitting Room is a sort of fixed point. And apart from a bit of contention over "bay" or "bow" windows, the rest of that *mise en scene* is carefully set down within the "Conanical" Doylean scripture channeled by Dr. Watson.

"I have my eye on a suite in Baker Street which would suit me down to the ground" Holmes tells his friend Stamford's colleague, himself recently returned from the military in Afghanistan. And here it all begins. The two agree to share digs and in short order they move their belongings into their new Baker Street address. From the description we are offered, one might intuit that Watson's own contributions were more spare than those of his colleague. This no doubt was owing to the fact that Sherlock Holmes was known to have resided (perhaps until that momentous meeting at St. Bartholomew's Hospital) on Montague Street, close by the British Museum. We have little to go on for those earlier times when, presumably, the young researcher may have honed his deductive skills and conceived of his unique occupation.

It is tempting as well to consider what Holmes' own bachelor surroundings were like on Montague Street? Was he a lodger? Or was he occupying rooms provided by a relative, as Michael Harrison has opined in his excellent *In The Footsteps Of Sherlock Holmes*?

Regardless of the "how?" and "why?" it may serve us to believe that the Holmes who sought and found a base for his detective's operations was not so much changed as before. Which is to suggest, doubtless he was a rather solitary, if not strange young man of eccentric habits. Tempered by an omnivorous taste for curious chronicles, and well rehearsed in those disciplines which would serve him, cerebrally and physically for his calling, his surroundings probably mirrored something of his "mental landscape." And what does that suggest?

It is likely that the young and pre-Watsonian Sherlock Holmes would have inhabited a self-made environment full of those items which challenged and intrigued him. Thus the prospect of a library of books, maps, guides and charts is likely. Here might have been the nascent point of Holmes' encyclopedic scrap-book collection.

Add to these things a museum-like array of what might seem to the casual observer artifacts suggestive of matters quaint and curious. Likewise some degree of chemical apparatus, given that this field of study seems to have preoccupied him. There may well have been weaponry of a ballistic or hard-edged kind. Pistols, knives, foils, even sabers. But were there bullet holes in the walls? Not impossible. And what else? Perhaps a collection of clothing as might suit someone with an actor's penchant for costume or disguise? And if indeed, as Baring Gould and others have imagined, the youthful Sherlock ever acted on the stage, such tools of the histrionic trade might well have been present as well on Montague Street. Stretching our imaginations as well here, and given the subject of "Mr. Sherlock Holmes On The Uses of Disguise," one can only wonder who and what seemingly made regular usage of his residence's back door?

One hopes that what Watson described as "No. 221B, Baker Street" presented an upward move for Holmes as well as his new colleague in the making. Apparent here is that their new lodgings were central enough and convenient to such services as British Rail, the post office, and certainly a full range of commercial enterprises. All of that within easy range of those older and newer structures that were typical of those edifices which lined the Baker Street of the late 19th century.

We know for example, and find reinforcement through the bulk of the sixty Holmes stories, that the premises Holmes and Watson shared encompassed "a couple of comfortable bedrooms and a single large airy sitting-room." We have this on Watson's personal authority from *A Study In Scarlet* onward. Moreover, the subsequent detailing of these premises is sufficient enough to construct a computer-assisted landscape of it, which has to date been done many times.

From the beginning however, we also have the related evidence of the original illustrations which accompanied the Watsonian chronicles, principally in *The Strand Magazine*. There and presented by the able Sidney Paget, who inadvertently took the original assignment from his good-looking artist-brother Walter, we see not only several repeated features within the sitting room which mirror the storied descriptions.

Further, the case may be made that in re-creating such details, Paget as illustrator painted, quite literally, what he knew. This statement may well be interpreted, I think, on two levels. The first of these involves the *Strand* depictions, in which Holmes is borderline handsome and does in fact echo the features of Sidney's sibling artist. Here perhaps is what might be termed a case of "relativity" in the initial presentation of Holmes, just as Conan Doyle's father Charles portrayed the detective wearing his own chin-whiskers. In like manner, and just as the author's sleuth is initially presented wearing Sidney Paget's favored headgear, the deerstalker cap becomes Holmes' most recognizable "brand." Such a tradition continued even to the juncture of the American actor William Gillette's desire to portray Conan Doyle's detective on stage. And for that the dramatic fixture of wearing the fore-and-aft cap, *à la* Paget was deeply seated "in person." Here as well came yet another of the Holmes props, within the context of the curved stem pipe, which was later caricatured for effect by making it a Meerschaum. In truth however, it was Gillette's belief that the curved, rather than straighter stem pipe, allowed for an easier delivery of spoken lines.

Secondarily and pertaining to Sidney Paget's ongoing and contemporary presentations in the *Strand's* pages, there is that element of repetition within the illustrations. Moreover, in accordance with a number of not ungenerous descriptions by Watson in the tales, Paget creates an attendant physical dimension. And in that regard these proportions were in turn reflected by a sense of constancy, *vis a vis* the furnishings and their arrangement within the stories. This may be explained by two possibilities; namely that (a) Paget painted "what he knew," applying his own personal tastes or fixtures, *à la* the deerstalker, or (b) perhaps it may be assumed the artist possessed a privy knowledge of his subject? If so, then how?

Is it not conceivable that someone, either author Watson or his editor-agent Doyle, arranged for such a visit by the artist to what he was about to present? Indeed, were such the case we might well rely upon the authenticity of the Paget depictions, being as might be, a mirror of the real thing. And taking the matter further, what if it were the "wrong" brother who showed up at the premises? Might that then have explained why it was Sidney, rather than Walter, who took up the *Strand's* commissions?

So then must our reliance or interpretation of the geography and components of Sherlockian/Holmesian Baker Street have a tendency toward mirroring not just their creator, but their redactors as well. And yet and as has been stated here, at the core of the local cosmos we come to know and love the Sitting Room of "221B" as well as our own domiciles. But why so, especially if the genesis of such a layout was the byproduct of a random, if not casual use by its proprietors?

I have often considered the amusing fact that had Holmes been more orderly, or more "modern," we should likely not associate him with his cluttered bohemian dwelling. Or at least, it would be a far different place. Moreover, we may assume, given his fellow lodger's own comments over the years, that Dr. Watson was tolerant, but in no wise as unconventional as his friend and colleague.

As a somewhat related aside, I recall one of my wife's comments to me over the years. These concerned our now 172-year-old home "Gray Gables," and that portion of it which has reflected her husband's many curious pursuits. For instance, how many wives will tolerate their front parlor resembling a museum chamber dedicated to Napoleon Bonaparte, complete with the Emperor's death-mask? Or who among them might calmly smile when a stranger comments upon the cluttered library beyond the front parlor, where walls of medieval weaponry, cases with pottery shards, or even a standing Egyptian mummy is a day-to-day fixture?

"You know, all you need to do is to become famous" Dori once remarked. "That way this house could just be turned into a museum."

Along such lines, it occurs to me that if Mr. Holmes ever had a wife of his own, who conceivably might have tolerated the cramped confines of his bachelor establishment, what may she have said? No doubt something like, *"this place stinks of chemicals and tobacco,"* or *"don't even begin to think about shooting that gun indoors! You'll ruin the wallpaper! I don't care whose initials those are!"* In other words, *there's a limit to bringing your craziness into this place.* Or to quote a good friend's lady wife just across our lot: *I can't live like this!*

But when Holmes resided in Mrs. Hudson's rooms, both with and without his Watson, there was no one, not even the landlady herself, who could curtail his "craziness." All things being relative, such was merely considered his method, and doubtless best endured by those within his purview.

Then of course there's a final point to be made. This concerns the specific arrangement of furniture and other "artifacts" known to exist in the second floor sitting room of Number "221." For without a doubt, the cigars in the coal scuttle, the jack-knifed correspondence on the mantle, the initials of Victoria Regina pocked into the wall, truth to tell, it was all purely random. Which is not to say that Sherlock Holmes ever gave a thought to everything in those rooms having a "proper" place. Further, when pictures were hung or decorations both quaint and curious arrayed, they were done more upon whim than plan. Paradoxically however, today we see the "plan" of Baker Street as being as detailed as a blueprint. In other words, every jot and tittle described, not unlike the Old Testament's Mosaic specifications for the Ark of the Covenant. Comparably secular in contrast, nevertheless it is here that the canonical Gospel of Watson usually begins and ends.

And here then is the major warrant for our knowledge of those accommodations shared by the detective and his colleague. Moreover, and artistically related to Watson's stories as they appeared in *The Strand Magazine*, there are as we have stated, Paget's fundamental illustrations. I say "fundamental," in the sense that these most contemporary renderings of Holmes' digs are the first and most distinctive of a generous series of depictions of the Baker Street rooms which include the sitting room, as well as the bedrooms of its primary occupants.

But there is a problem with Paget's illustrations, and one which has afforded some of us a bit of bother. This has to do with the artist's continuing sequence of reliable images. It also amounts to the fact that perspective notwithstanding, the Sitting Room of Number 221B does tend to pictorially alter itself over time. In other words, and apart from such portable elements as chairs or tables, it is the seemingly immovable features of the streetside windows, mantel and hearth, or even the primary staircase or adjacent bedroom door itself which often gives us pause. Ergo, and limiting our focus chiefly to Paget, rather than Gilbert, Tittle, or even Steele, the initial renderings of Baker Street appear to offer a continuing frame of reference, save for when that frame is distorted.

Some of the physical features of the Sitting Room may be addressed in terms of alterations to the premises achieved over time. For example, the matter of the "two broad windows" fronting Baker Street is taken up by Paul McPharlin in his excellent 1947 article "221B Baker Street: Certain Physical Features" within Volume 2, Number 2 of *The Baker Street Journal*. Therein the author explained the prospect of how, among other details, the initial street-facing windows of Holmes' flat are alluded to in "The Mazarin Stone" and elsewhere as a "bow window." Moreover, the dynamics of "Mazarin Stone" complement the McPharlin premise: that prior to Holmes' tenancy, the occupant(s) may have altered the façade windows which adjoined the room next to the sitting room to accommodate a bay window, erroneously cited by Watson as a "bow window." In this fashion a conservatory of sorts is created which enables Holmes to exit his bedroom and to change places with the Tavernier waxwork of himself. As the *Journal* article also graphically describes, Sam Merton's comment of "too many curtains" must allude not only to the fenestral draperies, but also to the conservatory alcove itself, which is also shaded.

But windows notwithstanding, how to explain the variety of positions for the famous hearth? How also to define the means by which the entrance doorway morphs into different positions?

For consistency in reckoning out the topography of Baker Street's most famous sitting room, one cannot help but to take an average of the Paget illustrations in view of the stories themselves. For unlike Dr. Watson's prospective veiling of names or dates, how likely is it that he would forget or dissemble, *vis à vis* the arrangement of his shared living quarters?

Therefore, when Dr. Thorneycroft Huxtable pours through the sitting room doorway and collapses onto the hearth's bearskin, we may presume a sort of proximity of one to another. The fact that Paget's illustrations buttress this is in favor of an authenticity, I think. And yet what such a combined assessment of pictures and story may call for is a readjustment to that which has come to be the accepted layout of this room. This fact may be gleaned from the likelihood that Sidney Paget drew "what he knew" or remembered of chairs, divans, bookcases, mantel-pieces, *etc*. On this level as well, it is to my mind acceptable that we treat the SP presentation of the Baker Street digs to be one of an authentic nature, if only as a bit of the "True Cross," or like an ancillary relic kept in the presence of the Holy Grail.

And yet the perennial questions remain: was the mantel on the north or south side of the room? Did Holmes sit to the left or right of the poker? Was the window of the usual, or of the "bayed" or "bowed" kind? How much then does any of it matter? Not at all. Or perhaps a good deal. And on that account we may in turn ask ourselves, *is such "authenticity" a concomitant of the stories themselves and what they suggest?* As a response to this, another McPherson Parable.

For a goodly long while Western buffs liked to allude to William Bonney, aka Billy the Kid as "The Left-Handed Gun," primarily due to the photograph of him posing in a studio. However, after a seeming age someone finally took note of the arrangement of the button holes and buttons on Billy's vest. Such scrutiny was sufficient to render a verdict that *the negative was printed in the reverse.* And with pronouncement, it was *adios* to the legendary image of the sinister-sided Forty-five on the Kid's hip. But to what effect was its elimination detrimental?

So then, whether through casual action or even error, an object within a domestic landscape may find itself placed here or there. Which is not to say that these placements are mandated or irrevocable. Only to state that they may be chiefly the result of some random, or momentary act. And then of course there is the alternative of utility or common sense.

Often enough we tend to forget that if an armchair was placed by a bearskin rug by the fireplace at Baker Street, its design was likely convenience as well as *la mode du jour* or the vogue (however eccentric) of the hour. Perusal of the pages of *The Strand Magazine* will evidence a general Victorian plan of design which may direct that which was "fashionable" on a number of social levels. However we must remember that in the instance of Holmes and Watson, two bachelors who thrived on *outré* adventure, if not a lifestyle many might dub unorthodox, it is questionable as to whether they were in any way 19th century *fashionistos?* They were instead, both in literal and figurative terms, much like Edgar Allan Poe's earlier ratiocinator Dupin and his own friend and narrator. Both of them lived for the nocturnal world of Paris, even to the extent of camouflaging the brighter trappings of day. Undeniably, and as Conan Doyle himself came close to admitting, those gentlemen were quite obviously working models for Holmes and Watson some four decades later. Which is also to say that eccentric individuals in the present day and age may echo Holmes or Dupin for their tastes. If so, they will do so by choice or emulation, but without any deliberate intention of seeming "normal." That is an enormously relative term for anyone, beginning with myself.

So let us extend the premise by going back to my wife's comment about "all you need to do is to become famous." Let us say, for argument's sake, that I do achieve some eminence. Moreover, that I am described in literary or media terms in terms of my attire, my associations, and my life-style. Good so far? Alright, then let's precede by my shifting from the computer to consider my cluttered desk. What do I see?

Upon the desk there are a trio of antique magnifying lenses. Beside them is a Grecian-styled plaster box containing pens, a pair of spectacles, and a small tool-box containing six small screw-drivers. And to the right of the desk is an antiqued lamp with a green glassed, bowl-shaped shade.

Okay. So this is my point: given the great unlikelihood that I should somehow become immortalized over time, to the point at which someone wished to re-present my life or my circumstances, would it be strange if they did not describe my working premises? And if so, might they not have described my desk, with its layers of artifacts, source materials, and tools? And should someone recreate, for reasons presently not discernable, the "look" of those chambers, might they not attribute intent, or motive, or some secret purpose to the way those spaces were filled? Perhaps so, despite the fact that what presently encompasses my blotter relates to what I am writing here. Also, the incunabula and memorabilia (two good Sherlockian terms!) which adorn my work-space are to a great extent only the random arrangements or even careless by-products of a lazy man. Which is not therefore to suggest that this is some form of diluted, Platonically idealized version. That, or the peculiar inference that *this is the one, true plan of how my desk should look.*

For such reasons then it has occurred to me that what is more often "re-created" of the Holmes Sitting Room is but a freeze-framed image of a place in a given time. It might not represent its permanent or captured visage, but merely a temporal arrangement which might have been altered or completely re-structured over the years.

And what happens if indeed we remove Holmes from Baker Street? For one thing, to do so might be to re-site Robin from Sherwood, Arthur from Camelot, or Alice from her Wonderland, if not to shatter the looking glass in which we've come to see her face. Secondly, we would be interfering with that milieu which Holmes himself has structured, wittingly or not. For obviously we all know what "home" feels like. As did Sherlock Holmes, most assuredly, who was glad to re-enter his little cocoon after the years of his post-Reichenbach hiatus. Moreover, we learn that pains were taken by both Mycroft Holmes and Mrs. Hudson to keep those sacred chambers in their orderly disorder, even after the effects of a fire. But why do so? To make a shrine? As a tribute? Or as we come to find, as the unchanged and fixed point by which Holmes himself may function. For without those eccentric spaces, in effect a Rorschach Test or a litmus for his mind and persona, both the man and the detective would have been different.

And it is for those reasons, perhaps, that we have come to revere, if not to become fixated upon creating that insular, interior world of Baker Street as carefully as we may. It is the Western world's Victorian *omphalos,* and the center of its own gas-lit world. And more important, I believe, than what the sitting room looks out upon is what its windows allow us to see inside. There is something perhaps to the notion of that room; namely, what it signifies is indeed a "room without a view." It is the room itself which is most evocative. For that reason we cherish it. We dream of it. We re-build it lovingly and dream of inhabiting it. For perhaps we too are awaiting the Second Coming and the return of the world's once and future problem solver from the Avalon where he continues to dwell.

The subject of "221B" will always remain somewhat sacred to me. To this day I feel a kind of umbilical connection to that room first encountered in my first wondrous reading about it. And thereafter, from the canonical stories to eventually standing upon the actual street where as Vincent Starrett said, "it is always 1895." Yes, and in my case alone, imagining that beloved from shoe-box to stable.

This is all said, of course, without my own awareness of Conan Doyle's (or Watson's) comments on the matter of décor or purposeful arrangement of items on Baker Street. Most likely they, or even Holmes himself might well have stated that a chair is positioned here or there, a desk or work-bench seated where the lighting is good, or even bullet holes shot into a wall may simply reflect wherever the shooter may have sat.

In other words, then, in reality the arrangement(s) within the sacred Sitting Room may reflect some simply practicable or random degree, and less of any secret, or iron-clad intention. Or, to quote another analytical investigator of the day named Sigmund Freud, "sometimes a cigar is just a cigar." Therefore, no deep-seated or indelible meaning need be attached. To do otherwise is perhaps only to add unnecessary icing to an already elaborately decorated cake!

Time Capsule Entry: It is presently the first day of June, 2021. The last year or so has been plagued by the pandemic which even now continues to threaten quotidian existence. Now however and for the moment, localized, state and national vaccinations have afforded hope where only a sense of barrenness has dwelt. And not unlike the Black Death which threatened and decimated much of Elizabethan London, today too my friends in the capital are confronted by the specter which had literally "locked down" the metropolis. But now, with hope eternally springing forth, the masses are beginning to congregate again, even as they (or none of us for that fact) have heard the "all clear" call. But that is what London did, I suspect, five centuries ago, and does now, even as we, even in Michigan, aspire to know Life As We Knew It.

And here at "Gray Gables" the past continues to waltz within the confines of our walls. In my library there is always a sense of unseen motion that ceases only upon my arrival. And out back, where the stable-cum-garage sits, in those two back chambers the essence of 1895 has been summoned, like an oracle that mirrors Conan Doyle's and my own sense of an eccentric detective who inhabits those digs.

And like the library's stilled silence in winter, as if filtered by the frozen landscape beyond its windows, there exists a conjuration of the Longago—and even, dare I suggest it, a not-so-distant-age which is evoked by one adept author's artistic accomplishment.

For that reason then, I suppose that the shades of Holmes and Watson, if not the Forerunner-Begetter, Edgar Allan Poe, do yet come and go here, like spirits in flight. At this stage of my tenancy of the old house and grounds, I would be surprised only by their absence. For I've come to share these eccentric spaces with a retinue of friendly strangers. And one day, I suspect, some future tenant of "the Gables" may gain a glimpse of one, or perhaps two tall gray strangers who come and go unannounced, Yes, as if as if they know every corner, from basement to attic, from forest to river's shore. And that may well be the discarnate shade of myself, in company of the forerunner and builder of "Gray Gables," Major Horace Gray.

The first plaque honoring "221"
Christopher Bazlington, Sherlock's Secretary,
(The Abbey National Building Society),
Geraldine Moriarty, and the author

13
A Plaque On All Your Houses

As I gauge it, the present memoir has progressed a decade or so thus far. Which is not to suggest that there is a formula for such things. Other biographical treatises might weigh in more modestly yet, with their subjects worthy of even greater extrapolation. Contrast here for theory's sake, the biographical legion of those "lives of William Shakespeare," all of which are, to say the least, "extrapolated" if not predicated upon a paragraph or less concerning Mr. William Shakespeare of Stratford on Avon. Or take, for example the multivarious profiles of Napoleon or Alexander, then weigh them against the quartet of foundational *vitae*, upon which Christianity chooses to assay the existence of Jesus of Nazareth. And then if you will, consider that other modern and "sacred canon" of four novels and fifty-six short stories which remain to tell us of Mr. Sherlock Holmes and his life and times. Given its scope, if not the materials derived from such gospel-like accountings, one cannot help but agree that such a body of work and its derivative materials is impressive indeed as a lasting monument.

Having chosen to undertake *An Irregular Life,* I am continually reminded that the business of chronicling one's own possibly dubious achievements is a curious exercise indeed. I suppose that the sheer act of compiling a memoir runs at odds with the notion that (a) most of us never endeavor to tell our own stories or (b) believe that in some fashion certain others will be there to guard what amounts to our individualized trusts. But what if neither of those options is feasible? Is it enough to simply say *"que será, será"* and allow the past to drift away? Or worse, find whatever amounts to your legacy left in the hands of those ill-quipped to tell it.

I have been persuaded that at least one multi-faceted dimension of my own past may be of some use to literary historians of an Irregular ilk. With this said, I will continue by following the chronological thread of those persons and circumstances which have influenced me in the matter of Sherlock Holmes. As is probably obvious, such an umbilical connection to the "truth" here is nevertheless, in the words of Conan Doyle himself, a "tangled skein." And if anything, it has become my conviction that it is with the objective of the skein's untangling that I have chosen this means of accounting for myself.

I have said much to this point about W.T. Rabe as an influence in my young life. Were he still living to take me to task for much of this, he would be 100 years of age. That's slightly older than the aged protagonist of the Ian McKellen film "Mr. Holmes," which has garnered a mixed bag of critical appreciations.

I make the contrast between Messrs. Rabe and Holmes if only because to me, the former gentleman was singularly responsible for sparking so many of my Sherlockian sensitivities. Moreover and as future pages will illustrate, our friendship and my evolution would ultimately take a curious turn. And in a strangely paradoxical fashion, I believe that "turn" was shaped by how much and how well I had learned by my friend's example.

But what cannot change, and what may remain memorable to me in whatever annals exist to chronicle Sherlockian lore is its membership. In other words, its acolytes and its priests, its devotees as well as its critics. In short, what amounts to a decidedly singular set of irregular personages, past and present, who revere Mr. Sherlock Holmes in their own ways. And Bill Rabe was certainly one of those.

A man of many passions, perhaps there is no more specific précis of W.T. Rabe's odd achievements than those officially defined by himself in that portion of his groundbreaking *Sherlockian Who's Who & What's What* of 1962. There and within the aptly named section of this guide entitled "The Followers," Rabe's listing says:

"RABE, Wilmer T. (1921-) 2271 Pinecrest, Ferndale, Mich.; academic publicist, U. of Detroit; AMS (archivist); Old SOB 's (founder and chief med. O.): SHK/D; MR: BSI (Col. Warburton's madness). Specialty: the military H. and production of original H'ian newsreels; "Baker Street Kino," a sound motion picture which includes several items, among them "From Baker Street to Reichenbach" report filmed along the scene of the route: Cards at 221B, a reprinting of cards found on Mrs. Hudson's silver salver; editor, S'ian WW/WW, 1961, Detroit; several minor items for the BSJ. Dedicated plaque at "Englisherhof, Meiringen, Switzerland, 1952, in name of Old SOB's; editor, "Voices from Baker Street," an LP record of S'ians and S'iana; three tv and four radio scripts on S.H. and Irregularity."

Of course much came in the wake of that long ago citation. Many will recall Rabe's single-handed effort to "Stamp Out The Beatles at the University of Detroit," which in turn begot drummer Ringo Starr's reply, *"We're going to stamp out the University of Detroit."* Great stuff, that. Or what about and upon his northerly egress from Detroit to Lake Superior College, when Bill kindled the Unicorn Hunters, or that other curious-but-appreciated movement to strike certain words from the English lexicon? That too was vintage Rabe. Such were the innovative and stylistic sorts of things I had observed at close range, and inevitably, was influenced by in my own later incarnation as (1) an avid Sherlockian; (2) an academic publicist; (3) a creator of a S'ian "scion" society; (4) creator and subject of a number of Sherlockian interviews and broadcasts; (4) erector of a plaque commemorating Holmes and Watson on Baker Street; and (5) playwright and performer in "An Evening With Sir Arthur Conan Doyle."

The aforesaid shopping list is not a boast. It is simply an accounting of such of my activities which I believe were integrally fused to my early relationship with W.T. Rabe. For dare I not say it, without that serious, humorous, orthodox, unorthodox, gregarious and often off-putting gentleman, I may well have chosen to remain in my armchair, if only to watch others such as he with a sense of amusement and admiration.

Often I look back and see my relationship with W.T.R. as one of a student-to-guru kind. For that reason, throughout my teen years and early adulthood, I suppose I was the unconfessed "Grasshopper" to my bearded mentor's "Master." And on that account, I as his willing disciple and accomplice went many places and sometimes with a mission of sorts which bore little proximity to either common sense or serious purpose.

Take for example one of my sequential trips to London. Since my seminal and appendix-losing adventures in 1967, my taste for Holmes's home-based city continued to lure me on. Such was the case years later, when I made a detour from my own self-commissioned errands to run one for my colleague back home. And the nature of that? Nothing short of serving as an emissary of sorts for Rabe in reflection of something he had done in the British capital twenty years earlier.

My quest was to take me to the London headquarters of the Burberry Company. You know the one, with their corporate ensign being that popular red, white and tan plaid in linings and all sorts of other dimension for trench-coats, rain-ware, hats, umbrellas, etc. Well in any event, prior to my going over, Bill Rabe pulled me aside and asked, *"how'd you like to wear a bit of history?"*

Now over the years I'd learned to take much of what my serious looking friend with not a grain, but a ton of salt.

"History?" I said. "Sure." And that's when he gave me the background, as well as my instructions, which involved visiting the Burberry London central locus and making a request.

"Twenty years or more ago I took my favorite trench-coat in for some repairs" he explained. "But for one reason or another I never claimed it. For that reason, I see no reason why you can't go by, get it, and wear it around town. All you need to do is just go into the store on Regent Street and explain the matter. Knowing Burberry's, and given the manner by which they pride themselves on quality, customer service, and tradition, they've no doubt got the coat in their storage vault."

Well, some would have merely shaken a head and just gone on about their business. But back then and given our shared history, I had no reason to doubt Rabe's purpose or this Quixote-like mission. So I said yes, I would do what he'd asked. And I did.

The morning I showed up at Burberry's staid location on Regent Street it required more than a bit of explaining. Imagine, say, going to London's finest tobacconist and saying, "I believe you're holding a pipe for Mr. Sherlock Holmes?" (Which also reminds me of a related story, which I'll share in a bit). At any rate, there I was, a young American with a serious purpose. And that, as I explained, had to do with another of my fellow countrymen who had prized their by-product sufficiently to put its safety into their hands some two decades ago.

I recall the look in the clerk's eyes as I told him, straightforwardly, why I wanted his assistance. But then, as efficiently as if I had asked about an item brought in only the week before, he proceeded to check the Burberry records. Now mind you, this was nearly half a century ago, and records for such things were not yet computerized, especially within a firm established in 1856.

Envision then, as I then did, some combination of an elaborate turn-of-the-century "difference engine" capable of sifting through a multitude of customer records. And somewhere within that mazework, I both imagined and hoped, was Rabe's Trench-Coat. And even now as I re-conjure it to memory, it seems to have assumed its own grand aura.

To my amazement and after only a minor bit of searching, the helpful employee achieved his "aha!" moment, without saying as much. Reverting perhaps to what in 1978 may have echoed the old strains of "there will always be an England," the gentleman copied out a code number or some such thing and promised to return shortly.

When the man from Burberry made his reappearance, he carried with him treasure. This in the form of an opaquely plastic bagged object clinging to an unseen hanger. Beckoning me toward an area beyond the counter near a fitting room, he hung the object up and then relieved it of its shroud-like covering. And when he did so, I beheld the object of my Grail Quest. But rather than a shining relic, this one was, shall we say, somewhat understated.

The garment or item depending upon its hanger resembled a gaudy mess of soiled khaki. Discernable upon it were a collar, shoulders, and a weathered field of material featuring a few front buttons and what resembled a belt of the same material. But what now stood before me was not in any way, shape or form a wearable item. This fact was underscored when the assistant did his best to remove the ersatz garment from its hanger and to offer it for me to try on.

I got as far as inserting an arm into the vintage khaki-ed sleeve when it fell apart. That is to say, not my arm, but the material which once had been so firmly affixed to the shoulder. It didn't help that when I got the other arm in and took the slightest of breaths, I heard what resembled the rending of the Temple Veil. In other words, everything was coming undone. Moreover, as I sought to cinch the coat's belt, which the clerk carefully, if not cautiously attempted to insert into the crumbling coat's loops, it broke away as well.

And there I stood, looking at my reflection in the tri-fold mirror beside the changing room. Glancing at myself, and then the rather dour expression reflected of my stately observer, I began by just shaking my head to no one in particular. And it was at that point, I believe, that I began to laugh. Now truthfully, I do not recall whether that one among a small coterie of Burberry's finest employees joined me in the act. No, for that would have been *infra dig.* But I know had he been compelled to share his thoughts, they might have centered upon such as "those crazy Americans." But surely, I thought, he had to accord me some degree of empathy here? After all, how could I have known that Mr. Wilmer T. Rabe's Bogart-styled trench-coat, checked in for revitalization within the era of the Korean War, would now bear a resemblance to the Shroud of Turin or something older, but in less a better condition?

The short of the thing is, I returned that bit of weathered haberdashery to Burberry and Co., to continue its tenancy within their vaults. Obviously, claiming no legal responsibility for the continued safekeeping of the garment still bearing their faded label, I could not be compelled to pay its ransom. Nor did I wish to. In fact, I lived in fear lest the employee suddenly presented me with some parchment account of the conditions attendant upon *"One overcoat-fees of storage to date."* I'd also begun to feel like someone sent over to barter for a prisoner of war, only to find when he gets there that he's claiming a corpse. Or maybe that's too extreme a comparison? But whether it was or not, it was plain that I would not be wearing out Bill's trench-coat (for that feat had been achieved decades earlier). He on his own had already done that. For from the general look of it, it had seen its day, if not been dragged through any number of trenches.

So it turned out that I would not after all find myself soaking up the possibly damp or dank atmosphere of Old London Town in late autumn while wearing the sartorial relic in question. As an ensign of someone else's past, it now resembled nothing so much as a tattered remnant of its former self. And in vestigial fashion, it now existed as simply a token of another vanished time. But not one worn like rusted or dented armor by this particular young knight.

So after thanking that helpful associate I left Regent Street's exclusive emporium. As I did so I imagined that Rabe's relic was either being returned to the vaults or possibly consigned to some subterranean pyre, where sacrifices to lost causes were sometimes made. Had it been part of a baseball game, I harbored little doubt that this would have been that trench coat's third strike. And like a very old dog being taken out for his last walkabout, part of me rued the fact that the coat never made its way to the pavement. But perhaps, ideally, it knew its owner and his ensign had been thinking of it. Yes, and one of us no doubt in its former, storied condition, when like its wearer it was prime for adventure.

Long after-the-fact, it occurred to me that had my trip to Burberry's occurred only three years later, I might well have envisioned Bill's waterproof's fate to be otherwise. Recall the ending of "Raiders of the Lost Ark," or even the last Indiana Jones epic, "The Crystal Skull"? In both of those the sacred Ark is deposited in a vast terminal or warehouse, if only to join thousands of other objects, both quaint and curious. It took very little imagination to envision my friend's apparel as part of that trove. Which also set me to imagining, by the way: *what if Sherlock Holmes had left Messrs. Burberry & Co. a cloak for repair, and had never remembered to claim it? Might it have become venerable, as was Dr. Watson's tin dispatch box-full of Holmesian cases at Cox & Co. Bank, Charing Cross? Food for thought.*

But as a postscript to "The Adventure of the Burberry Relic," I'll share a final musing, which I've entertained for a while. For as I remembered that when he'd originally informed me of it, Bill Rabe had said, "Go to Burberry's and get the coat and wear it around London." But he'd never said, "pay the storage and bring it home." No, for perhaps that trickster had known all along that the true state of his trench-coat was beyond ransom. And that, I suppose, renders it priceless, in one sense, at least!

But still the question remained, and remains to this day: was this madcap mission devised by my colleague a leg-pull, or entirely on the level? Or as with those Zen *koans,* or problematic exercises, was it merely a test? If so, had I passed or failed? Or perhaps I make more of the thing than existed. Very possibly by sending me off on this snipe hunt, Rabe was indeed pulling my leg at long-distance, and even at the risk of detonating his garment's already tenuous seams? If nothing else, like Watson sent on a seemingly senseless task, it is the fact that he went which may have gratified the sender.

And while we're speaking about any of those Rabe-esque pranks and productions, one shouldn't short-sell his ability to make history. For that is what he did in Sherlockian terms as long ago as 1951. This when Bill and his lovely wife Mary Ann, his beloved alphabetizer, proofer and copyreader, were both in Switzerland for a singular purpose. And that was nothing less than to continue or engender one of the finest of Sherlockian traditions, which was to officially commemorate a place and its Holmes-related purpose. In this instance it was to appear at the Swiss *Englisherhof* (known in 1962 as the Rossli) and to install an Old Solders of Baker Street plaque reading:

TO THIS VALLEY IN MAY, 1891, CAME DR. W. AND S.H. AND HERE HE BESTED THE INFAMOUS PROF. MORIARTY IN MORTAL COMBAT; THOUGH HE WAS THOUGHT TO HAVE PERISHED, HE ESCAPED AND RETURNED TO LONDON IN 1894. HE HAS SINCE RETIRED TO SUSSEX AND BEEKEEPING —OLD SOLDIERS OF BAKER STREET, NOV. 1952

Now as I've said, what the Rabe's did both engendered and affirmed a tradition which has yet to fade away in Irregular circles. Some have dubbed this pursuit "plaquiana," i.e., the business of putting up plaques to commemorate some special event. To wit, and at the Criterion Bar in Picadilly Circus, London, the Baritsu Society presented a marker in January of 1953. It read:

THIS PLAQUE COMMEMORATES THE HISTORIC MEETING AT THE ORIGINAL LONG BAR AT THIS HOTEL ON JANUARY 1ST, 1881 OF DR. STAMFORD, AND DR. J.H.W. WHICH LED TO THE INTRODUCTION OF DR. W. TO MR. S.H.

Ruefully, another somewhat perverted tradition reflects the fact that the Baritsu Society plaque was illicitly removed on Derby Day, 1956.

But also and reflecting what my other mentor Russell McLauchlin once threatened (paraphrasing, if not mangling "A plague upon 'o your houses" (Scene III, Act 1 of "Romeo and Juliet, "by uttering *"a plaque upon all your houses."* Old Russ, that clever scribbler, must have more than suspected the tenacious need of some Sherlockians to literally "mark their territory." *Shades of Kilroy Was Here.*

In such fashion was another marker affixed in Hampstead, Great Britain, at the Coach and Horses located in Heath Street. For it was there that Holmes and Watson passed on their way to burgle Mr. Charles Milverton's Appledore Towers.

Or consider the 1957 Norwegian Explorers bronze tablet at the fabled Reichenbach Falls. It reads:

ACROSS THIS 'DREADFUL CAULDRON' OCCURRED THE CULMINATING EVENT IN THE CAREER OF S.H., THE WORLD'S GREATEST DETECTIVE, HERE ON MAY 4, 1891 HE VANQUISHED PROF. MORIARTY, THE NAPOLEON OF CRIME.

In a related Reichenbach tribute, also in 1957 the Explorers also installed a bronze star upon an easterly rock-wall above the broiling precipice.

Also in a memorable and well-deserved location did my own Amateur Mendicants Society erect a plaque in St. Bartholomew's Hospital (Barts) in 1953. Its text reminds that:

AT THS PLACE NEW YEAR'S DAY, 1881 WERE SPOKEN THESE DEATHLESS WORDS 'YOU HAVE BEEN IN AFGHANISTAN I PERCEIVE' BY MR. S.H. IN GREETING TO J.W., M.D. AT THEIR FIRST MEETING.
THE BAKER STREET IRREGULARS—1953 BY THE AMATEUR MENDICANTS AT THE CAUCUS CLUB.

As an aside: when I visited "Barts" many years ago, I saw the BSI/AMS plaque, tucked away in a nondescript little room. I was further apprised that the old books on the shelves, some of which were to be binned, were of the "proper time of Sherlock Holmes." As was the famous lab bench stool, which pilgrims were sometimes shown. As the official accounting has it, not only was the cracked leather seat of bygone vintage, but it possessed the provenance of having been used at St. Bartholomew's by the young Mr. Sherlock Holmes. His initials were supposed carved on the underside, and those I saw as well. But dare I sit upon that relic? Did one leap upon the King's Throne in Westminster's Abbey? Did they pass through the barrier and take Dickens's chair on Doughty Street? Which is to ask, given the chance, do you sit on the True Cross? You betcha.

And as for the St. Bart's lab-seat's veracity? That tends to be relegated to the visitor and his own power of belief. But for me? I for one chose to believe it. And moreover, as Sir Winston Churchill said about King Arthur, that "it is all true, or it ought to be; and more and better besides."

Therefore and on the subject of paying honor due to any number of prospectively auspicious Sherlockian locations, I had my own thought in 1978. This reflected what I deemed to be a longstanding oversight by those who have set out to keep the memory of the Master green. In effect, the burning question of *"why was there no plaque on Baker Street?"*

Now some of the foregoing dilemma constituting what I took to be a true *faux pas* doubtless had to do with what realtors recognize as their primary factor of value: "Location, location, location." And over the years, and given the complications of a little detail such as there never having been a numerical "221 Baker Street," perhaps the matter simply slipped through the cracks? But as I also recognized and had known well, as had a corps of my colleagues, since 1951 Baker Street had vaunted such a street address and upon a site constituted within the block encompassed by the Abbey National Building Society. Ergo: it was time for a plaque upon their house, if not Holmes' own.

I'd carefully explored the idea of presenting a plaque in London at the one and very site where Sherlock Holmes continued to receive mail. Moreover, and as I was kindly informed by the then-appointed "Secretary to Mr. Holmes" Christopher Bazlington, the idea of a marker was in fact a fairly good one. So we persisted in our dialogue. And not long after and in the autumn of 1978, my good and Watson-like friend George Misakian and I ventured to London, plaque in hands.

Not bearing the signal distinction at that time of being an invested member of the Baker Street Irregulars, I knew I could not officially represent them. But we held a purpose in common. This, despite even the fact that back in 1962 W.T. Rabe had accorded me the distinction in his *Sherlockian Who's Who & What's What* "Followers" section description as a "BSI neophyte."

Well, I'm not certain of the shelf life of one's "neophyte" status, but at thirty-one I'd hoped to somehow make my mark through a host of worthy deeds. These had perhaps begun with my mission on behalf of the Sherlock Holmes Society of London back in '69 to forward the candidacy of Brook Manor in Devonshire as the "real" Baskerville Hall. I'd thought it would take something rather big to exceed that stunt for excitement, but now I believed I'd found one at last. *Finally: a plaque (the first) to commemorate Number 221B, Baker Street in London!*

On that basis then, and before setting out for Great Britain I'd contacted Dr. Julian Wolff, the eminent Commissionaire of the Baker Street Irregulars. Apprised of my purpose, and peripherally aware of my existence with the Mendicants over so many years, he gave his blessing. Excelsior!

Now as it had happened, in March of 1976 I had created yet another scion society for our Motor City This was the Napoleons of Crime of Detroit, and it has been distinguished by having among its honorary membership the likes of John Bennett Shaw, Bill Rabe, Philip Jose Farmer and even the author of the wonderful *Moriarty* and its sequel, John Gardner. Moreover, and apart from a generous group of attendees at Schweizer's Restaurant near the city's waterfront, the Napoleons celebrated its one-and-only meeting with a surprise guest, in the person of actor Alan Sues. A veteran of the weekly "Laugh In" television program, now Mr. Sues was appearing as Professor Moriarty with Leonard Nimoy as Holmes in the Royal Shakespeare Production of "Sherlock Holmes" at the Fisher Theater. Here too his nefarious credibility would soon be enhanced by standing villainously fast against Robert Stephens on Broadway in Gillette's play. Already baptized by Billy Wilder's idealized "Private Life of Sherlock Holmes," I'm informed that Stephens drew a nearly standing ovation the moment he appeared on stage. To his credit and attesting to his remarkable ability, the actor simply stood there, poised, basking in his audience's appreciation. Such then is the means by which the great detective has long captivated his observers.

To my own great pleasure, Sues as "the Professor" appeared before his curtain time, and in full villainous gear. To wit, photos were taken of Moriarty beside a large statue of Napoleon Bonaparte, and a plaque was unveiled that night. It had to do with the choice of Schweizer's for our historic assemblage of the Napoleons.

The back-story I'd created for Schweizer's, one of the city's oldest eateries, was that in March of 1914, Sherlock Holmes met Professor

James Moriarty there, on the brink of the Great War. Sadly, no truce could be announced, leaving the conflagrations to come five months later as an inevitability.

So it was that the Napoleons of Crime of Detroit had become a scion and "validated" by its purpose, plaque, and actions. Thus did we bring to London's Abbey National another marker, emblazoned with Frederick Dorr Steele's legendary profile study of Holmes, and which read:

UPON THIS SITE MR. SHERLOCK HOLMES, CONSULTING DETECTIVE SHARED RESIDENCE WITH DR. JOHN H. WATSON AT '221B' BAKER STREET. THE BAKER STREET IRREGULARS. 1978 BY THE NAPOLEONS OF CRIME OF DETROIT.

The Abbey National people were truly gracious. Chris Bazlington apologized for the fact that "Mr. Holmes was away and otherwise detained." But we were given a very warm welcome from the now retired detective's official Secretary, as well as from John Silcox, whose Abbey National title was that of "Secretarial Assistant." After the ceremonies and upon our return home, I received an appreciative letter from John, which read in part, "*I enclose various photographs of the plaque, Chris, Geraldine and yourself and hope you will find a home for some of them. The plaque itself is still in the main showcase in the entrance hall to the banking hall and should it be moved to a more permanent showplace then I will certainly let you know. Let me take this opportunity to thank you and your fellow members of the Napoleons of Crime of Detroit for your kind gesture. I only hope that the Society reciprocates in some way in the future.*"

A couple of points: firstly, on the occasion of our "presentation," Abbey National was in the throes of renovation. It was suggested that upon their work's completion, that this historic marker would be given a more permanent place of honor. And secondly, and tellingly, I think, the reference to "Geraldine" in John's letter. For she was the attractive cashier drafted for posing with Bazlington, myself, and the plaque. She'd been drafted into joining us from her post in the Banking Hall. Well so much for mission accomplished; or so at least, I thought. But as I would learn thereafter, a year or so after its presentation, the first plaque commemorating Sherlock Holmes and Dr. Watson on Baker

Street was stolen. Yes, purloined. Scarpered. Scrappled. Scrobbled. Nicked. And the culprit(s)? Their identities remained a mystery, until my friend Catherine Cooke at the Marylebone Library assembled the disparate pieces of evidence in the case. For it seems that in the wake of the plaque "doing a bunk," Abbey National did in fact hear from the thieves. Supposedly they offered the plaque back, and I'm uncertain of whether or not for a ransom. But worst of all, they and our historic marker were never heard from again. But there was, to my mind at least, another damning clue to consider. This harked back to "Geraldine," that attractive damsel who'd posed with Christopher Bazlington and I for the archival record of the day's ceremony. To me then, and from this day forth, all of the law and the prophets pointed to the singular matter of not the young lady's Christian appellation, but her surname: Geraldine *Moriarty.* That's right. Moriarty. And even as the company's in-house ABBEY NATIONAL NEWS wrote, "Having a descendant of Sherlock's great enemy actually working on the site of his home creates much amusement to many visitors to Baker Street."

Well all I could say, even as I stated to my able and methodical friend Ms. Cooke was, "it might be amusing, but it explains a good deal, don't you think?" Employing a Moriarty descendant in a bank? And worse, allowing her to inveigle her way into the 221B ceremony? What an insidious means of infiltrating an historic moment—*Moriarty in drag*! Or at least, something fairly close to that king villain's presence on that noteworthy October day.

The post-script to "The Case Of The Baker Street Plaque" found many, including Jeremy Brett himself, believing that the late-model oval-sized plaque which he himself had dedicated at Abbey National was the "first." It most decidedly was not. Or even that visitors to the Sherlock Holmes Museum presuming its "221B Baker Street" marker is both official and authentic. It is not.

Suffice it to say that while the "evidence in the case" remains, even as the "plaque in the (show) case" (where they put our 1978 plaque during Abbey renovations) went missing, the truth is available to those who seek it. And for the record, the plaque we negotiated and eventually presented on the approximate "Upper Baker Street" location, is indubitably the real "tree that fell in the forest." The fact that someone or anyone registered its "sound of its falling" or not did not detract from the truth. Our effort of forty-three years ago is now a matter of history, if not real mystery. Nowhere in any past or recent compendium is our event cited. True, nonetheless, this stands as one of those little enigmas tucked away in the past, waiting to be found. And as Brett/Holmes once commented, "isn't it delicious?"

Well, so much for the subject of plaques which occupies one small Sherlockian corner. But before leaving it, there is one parting story that I believe belongs here. It has to do with that brass and wooden marker which the Napoleons of Crime presented to Bob Schweizer in Detroit in that long ago March of 1976.

For quite a good while I used to enjoy going into Schweizer's for lunch, particularly if my guest or companion was even remotely interested in the notion that Sherlock Holmes may once have visited the not-quite-then Motor City.

On that score then, and keeping up with "playing the game," most often I'd be conducted to the table "near the plaque" on the wall. I remember once even asking the waitress, who happened to be uninitiated in my madness, "Say, is what that plaque says true? That Sherlock Holmes was in this very restaurant in 1914?"

I remember the lady waiting to take our order looking down at me, then at the plaque itself before responding to my query.

"Well, if it says so on a plaque on the wall, it must have happened, didn't it?"

So much for the authenticity of any number of "plaques on all your houses." And finally in closing this *post-post scriptum.* A year or so later I was with an associate for dinner at Schweizer's. And yes, we were seated near the Holmes-Moriarty Marker. But that wasn't dominating our conversation or even the object of our attention. (That honor, I believe, took the form of the eatery's incredible *bratwurst!*) Nevertheless, toward the end of the meal our waitress approached our table and apologized for interrupting. In her hand she had a silver dish, and upon it was a rather venerable looking pipe which seemed to have been well smoked.

"Beg pardon, sir, for intruding. Are you Mr. McPherson? Well Mr. Schweizer said to tell you that 'Mr. Holmes was in earlier and he left this. And could you get it back to him?" He thought you might be able to do that."

I looked at my guest, and then at the old pipe on the tray.

I nodded to the waitress, "I'd be glad to get it back to its proper owner," Yes, and even as I found myself silently musing, *how wonderful that the old magic lasts.*

And today? Well Schweizer's Restaurant is now long gone and has been replaced by some aspect of Detroit's riverfront renewal. Sadly, the plaque too has vanished as well. Perhaps to that Valhalla where plaques and other examples of rarified signage are consigned for posterity? Or is it sitting or hanging beside the Abbey National rendition?

But so much for plaques leading us eventually back to Holmes, Watson, and their London abode. I'm sure there are also others elsewhere, nicely lit and deeply etched. But of what sort, you ask? Well how about "CAMELOT: TWO MILES," or perhaps "ATLANTIS, FIFTY LEAGUES DOWN"? I suppose I came close enough to installing both of those over the years. Fortunately however, I did succeed in creating, for one brief, shining moment, a marker which directed attention to the quarters of S. HOLMES, CONSULTING DETECTIVE.

And just so is the route to a certain house on Baker Street findable still.

To: J. H. W. Addendum # II to My Original Communique

My Dear Watson:

I have continued to review McPherson's "irregular" Memoir and must confess to some slight amusement at the author's rather gross presumptions. While obviously those of what some would dub an "aficionado," these rather compacted recollections and attendant observations are evidence of both the writer's apparent sincerity, if not his mania for inhabiting a world which—as I must affirm—has largely to do with your own well-publicized work.

That the author elected, however unwittingly and at an early age to somehow emulate my methods is nevertheless in its way complimentary. Moreover, through some medley of circumstance if not desire, Mark McPherson has endeavored to look into many quaint and curious corners, which seems to be a fact. However and at the risk of my saying so, I believe that like your friend Doyle, his energies have been spent in a zealous pursuit of many phantoms, both real and not. Moreover, given that a lion's (or a Hound's) share of those are of what he willfully defines as a "Sherlockian" (cheek!) nature, he appears the chronic victim of the classic idée fixe—in other words, he has willingly decided to dwell, like Dunsany's railway traveler, in a world of his own compulsive devising. Given the amount of time this process has required of him, one tends to question whether the distinctions between what is "real" and what M.M. only imagines to be true actually exists?

With this said, it would be churlish of me to damn "Irregular Life" at this juncture. However, and truth be told, among the nearly eighty years of accolades which members of your cumulative audience have paid me, I cannot admit to relishing any individual's memories of myself or my endeavors. Save for your own, of course. However even there the license to dissect "my methodology or my person" has most often bordered on gross presumption, or worse

Nevertheless, none know better than I that any investigator's queries cannot help but to taint the matter before him. With that said, and having already read of spectral hounds, the placement of old houses and their furnishings, as well as actors, odd associations and memorial markers, one can only trust that more substance will follow.

On that hope, then, my own critical verdict must continue to hang in the balance.

Holmes

"Nessisteras Rhombopteryx"
The image that launched the quest

Elementary, my dear Nessie...

Sherlock Holmes buff McPherson is after you!

By ART BENTLEY

LOOK out, Nessie. Sherlock Holmes is after you. Nessie is known otherwise as the Loch Ness Monster. And Sherlock is known otherwise as Mark McPherson of Ypsilanti, MI., who spends every vacation focusing the deductive powers of his mythical hero on the mysterious Scottish lake.

"The deductive method Sherlock Holmes uses in all of his stories may be the best thing anybody has ever taken with them to the loch," McPherson, 31, an unabashed Sherlockian, said.

He may be right, too, because McPherson, a college publicity director, has seen something which, if it wasn't Nessie, was more than enough to puzzle Holmes's sidekick, the perennially perplexed Dr. Watson.

A couple of years ago, McPherson was observing Loch Ness through binoculars from a high promontory, when he saw a flock of swans disperse rapidly from the vicinity of what appeared to be a tiny dark island with a single big stump extending several feet above it.

He watched for several minutes. Finally, seeing nothing untoward, he gave up and started downhill. But misgivings assailed him, and he hustled back up for another look.

The "island" was gone, of course.

McPherson believes that Nessie is actually two monsters, one a serpent and the other a long-neck creature, both of which are prehistoric reptilian relics.

Holmes himself would have been proud of McPherson for the theory which he hopes will eventually put him in the right place on the loch at the right time so he can photograph the creature.

Several years ago, in an area called Lochend, sonar readings revealed the presence of stones in concentric circles on the bottom of the lake. McPherson likens the arrangement to Stonehenge. He suggests a relationship between the stones and the creatures. He thinks the stones may be the remnants of so-called magnetic "power centers," laid by the priests of an ancient people, and may hold a mysterious attraction for Nessie and her pals.

Evidence

McPherson contemplates such theories in the most cerebral setting imaginable — a re-creation of Holmes's famous sitting room at 221 B Baker Street, into which the basement of his house was recently transformed. It's authentic right down to details that would fool even Mrs. Hudson, Holmes' landlady.

"The last three years haven't been a failure," McPherson says, "because, as Holmes would say, 'It is a capital mistake to theorize without evidence. And the first duty of an investigator is to collect that evidence and then to theorize.'"

MARK MCPHERSON stands in Sherlock Holmes' sitting room, which is not at 221 B Baker Street but in the basement of his home.

From Moriarty to the Monster:
The author in his subterranean sitting-room–1977.

13
Nessiteras Rhombopteryx

I commenced this memoir by mentioning a request by my grandchildren to "tell them about the Loch Ness Monster." Their innocent query had much to do with whatever may have piqued their childish imaginations. A cartoon, perhaps, or a commercial, or any of a score of our first, youthful exposure to the dragons of yore.

Whatever the case, their mother informed Isabella and Christian that once upon a time, in fact further back than when she herself was a little girl, their grandsire had gone a-looking for "Nessie." And by sharing such news, I suppose Kristen managed to cast a strangely bright light upon the man she'd grown up knowing. And now perhaps, it might be her own offspring's turn to know him, and just possibly, to share in his slew of bygone adventures?

But you can't blame children of any age for being fascinated with Scotland's greatest bit of mythic history. After all, "Nessie" has been gentled into the almost bovine and most Disneyfied of fabulous beasts. Which is to say, that like its earlier cryptic kin the dragon, or our own more modern day "Abominable Snowman" or "Bigfoot," the creature of the Ness has become archetypally immortalized within the annals of monsterdom.

But speaking only for myself the memory of that most chronic of my many mysterious crusadings looms even yet in brilliant mental hues. Misty mountains. Fog-shrouded, night-blind waters. The tang of a fine whiskey. And the scent of Mystery, which has never left these nostrils. Or perhaps to put it a better way: this tale of Loch Ness—this theme—this context, which both energized and once nearly killed me, stands as perhaps the most curious, most engaging, and undoubtedly the most prolific quest of my life. And uncoincidentally as well as while we're at it, that long-term fascination may in its way be blamed on Sherlock Holmes.

What might be described as my Sherlockian Connection as well as my fixation upon a certain lake in Scotland was sparked back in 1970. This by the way was before I ever thought to trade my three-piece suit and briefcase for a monster-hunter's gear. And it began with a film called

"The Private Life of Sherlock Holmes" directed by the great Billy Wilder of "Some Like It Hot" fame. He and his writing partner I.A.L. Diamond wanted to create their cinematic homage to Conan Doyle's great detective, and this they did. But not without suffering the expense of seeing your dream literally pared to pieces.

You see, back in the day Wilder entertained the notion of creating a masterful canvas which would inform his audience of Sherlock Holmes' youth, his early cases, and most importantly, his seeming animadversion toward women. To achieve this he produced a film of some three hours length, nearly half of which was summarily cut by Wilder's producer's without his participation. Which led in turn to "The Private Life" enjoying neither great box office or critical praise. However over time the film in question has indeed been celebrated as perhaps the greatest cinematic effort of the 1970's. And notwithstanding its un-Canonical premise, it remains a perfect reflection of what Sir Arthur aspired to convey in the sixty Holmes stories.

One last cinematic footnote as well: given the excised portions of "The Private Life of Sherlock Holmes," the film's elusive totality has become somewhat legendary. And without the capacity until recently to completely re-construct Wilder's opus (with stills and story boards) there is yet to be a re-release of this epic in its originally intended form. And like that great Lon Chaney horror classic, "London After Midnight," an entire series of rumors and tales have enshrouded the film's legend.

I suppose that a certain part of the Holmes-Loch Ness fascinations actually hark back to what some might call a bit of "racial memory." This, by way of my family's paternally ancestral connections to Scotland. In that regard I was not required to become an "Outlander" aficionado to feel the trill of the pipes. For with those other and foregoing interests I was able to perceive a vast and heather-misted landscape full of beauties, wonders, and a lion's (or dragon's) share of tapestried darkness. And even now it seems, finely stitched into its warp and weft is the still visible specter of myself—as I was—as I was becoming—and oddly, as I am now. And still, like cosmic triggers firing off a cannonade of memories, the conjoined images of Sherlock Holmes and The Loch Ness Monster manage to spark these neurons and dendrons for what they suggest: *The Great Seeker and the Greatest of Mysteries Sought.*

So then, prepare if you will to encounter what I might term my true baptism into mystery, in the form of that *Optimum Monstrum,* or "first among monsters" worthy of being pursued by the master sleuth of Baker Street.

But having written the foregoing words, another thought now intrudes; i.e., that no doubt in Sherlockian or "canonical" verbiage, perhaps the most-voted-for candidate for the title might be the legendary Baskerville Hound. Well as it chanced and as you'll learn, rather uncoincidentally I would direct certain energies toward that end as well.

But as for "Nessie?" Like the Hell Hound of Dartmoor in the Doylean saga, his eponymous beast is steeped in a background of mystery and myth. Many of "her" critics also point out that like the Baskervillian anomaly, its essence was more to be found within certain very human devisings for the sake of gulling, confusing, or frightening the general populace. Ergo, the case for a supernatural influence is often threatened. Or at least it was when Sherlock Holmes quelled the problem with a revolver's bullets.

But in the chronic case of the Loch Ness Monster, some fifteen centuries-worth of witnessed and documented accounts have stood for its reality. Moreover, and unlike the Hound, the loch's reputed denizen(s) have been detected, traced, and even recorded through the agencies of science.

As I think back upon it, even today one true-ism seems to apply. Many years ago I was asked by a journalist, based upon my knowledge and personals experience, "Is there a monster at Loch Ness?"

My reply to that eager scribe was decisive and to the point.

"Yes" I answered, "there are definitely monsters at Loch Ness. But most of them are on shore."

But we all seem to cherish the long-distance accounts of fey or fabulous creatures, don't we? And is this not the key to at least three of the

Sherlock Holmes stories; a la "The Hound," "The Lion's Mane" and allusion to at least two other of Dr. Watson's "unrecorded tales;" i.e., the Giant Rat of Sumatra and Isadora Persano's mysterious worm. I suppose we could also allude to Roylott's agilely-trained swamp adder while we're talking night-shudders.

Other unknown and beastial dimensions loom large within the Holmesian Catalogue of Monsterology. Think only of the lethal little Tonga of Andaman Island infamy, or even Professor Presbury's Mr. Hyde-like alter ego in "The Creeping Man." Or shades of a Hammer Horror Dracula feature, lest we forget "The Sussex Vampire?"

Individual all in their strangeness, such seemingly otherworldly aberrations are to be found within the Sacred Canon. In ironic fashion as well, while eschewed as impossible by Sherlock Holmes, such things were not beyond the other-worldly view of his Begetter. One has only to consider Arthur Conan Doyle's penchant for the manner by which spectral and Spiritual intrusions tend to occur in our cosmos.

Quite honestly, prior to 1975, I'd given little shrift to the subject of monsters. However, soon enough I was rather like the early Ahab in pursuit of his white whale. And the monstrous creature now at hand? It was not only legendary, but bolstered as well by what the Latin definition of the term *monstrum* suggests as being somehow "wonderful' or even "portentous." And as I've already said, my fascination with fifteen centuries of tradition had much to do with something seated within the grain of my own Celtic homeland.

Moreover, even as the 1970 Billy Wilder film purported a horrifying encounter with the Ness's legendary beastie, it was something of an Holmesian object lesson. To wit, and in keeping with canonical tradition, it was demonstrated there that the "creature" was a man-created submersible. In other words and very like the Hound From Hell, that which was monstrous, if not supernatural proved in effect to be the by-product of thwarted mortal devising.

Nevertheless, it was the idea of the film in question which for me lent the prospective quest its heady flavor. Therefore and like an unearthly baying beast said to roam the moorlands, so too was the idea of a modern-day dinosaur unquestionably worthy of becoming one of Mr. Sherlock Holmes' greatest challenges. I mean, the very notion of pitting the Victorian super-sleuth against a seemingly primordial grotesquerie had much to offer. No doubt this them would later animate the adventures of Conan Doyle's Professor Challenger and his Indiana Jones-ish *The Lost World.*

Notwithstanding its decidedly un-canonical premise (although submersibles are alluded to within the canonical "Bruce Partington Plans," "His Last Bow" and the Doylean novelette *Danger)*, "The Private Life of Sherlock Holmes" was shown in America and abroad, but hardly to resounding effect.

For a legion of Sherlock Holmes aficionados, "The Private Life of Sherlock Holmes" still presents a sort of concentric mystery. For as has been admitted since its release in its edited form, the cinematic aspect of the Sherlockian "dog in the nighttime" principle is based not upon what viewers saw, but what they did not and in all probability never would see.

Originally Wilder's would-be epic contained two separate stories, as well as a flashback to the university days of Sherlock Holmes. These in the main constituted filmed but edited sections which fell to the axe of the studio decision-makers. As a consequence, sequences such as Holmes' inquiries concerning a corpse found in an upside-down room, or Dr. Watson's descendant receiving the detective's "tin dispatch box" are now non-existent and "presumed missing."

When Billy Wilder's film was previewed by Anthony Howlett, reviewing it for *The Sherlock Holmes Journal* in 1969, it was touted as "the much heralded, most expensive Holmes film ever, in colour and Panavision." He went on to predict that "The Private Life" might well become "*the* film concerning the great detective." But when those words were penned the movie was just entering an early phase of production. On the hopeful basis of its completion and release, a further hope was expressed that "this might perhaps be the film which will rival Fox's 'The Hound of the Baskervilles' (Rathbone version) of thirty years ago."

Interestingly, somewhat in the same vein as those great expectations expressed for "The Private Life," four years earlier and upon the release of the Sir Nigel Production (Adrian Conan Doyle's company) "A Study In Terror" it was similarly touted by Anthony Howlett. Like the Wilder concept of Sherlock Holmes *vs.* The Loch Ness Monster, "Study" also took the extra-canonical liberty of pitting the great detective against Jack the Ripper. In any event, upon its completion "A Study In Terror" garnered high praise indeed.

"What a surprise it is to welcome a really good Sherlock Holmes film" said *The Sherlock Holmes Journal's* review of "A Study In Terror" in 1965. Their phrase was bestowed upon John Neville as Holmes and Donald Houston as Dr. Watson. Once again exuding enthusiasm, the SHS's Anthony Howlett concluded his appraisal with the confession that "I expected the worst and was quite wrong. In my opinion, this is the best Sherlock Holmes film which has been made since Rathbone's "Hound of the Baskervilles" in 1939."

Anticipating the trend toward the Sherlockian pastiche which became so popular for so long, the introduction of an enigma, villainy, or even a villain unfound in the Holmes stories was expounded in Billy Wilder's 1970 film. Moreover, by virtue of its archetypal element of the legendary creature of Scotland's most famous loch, the prospect of "Nessie" loomed large, both literally and figuratively, as Sherlock Holmes's greatest adversary. Nevertheless, critical reception of Maestro Wilder's intended masterpiece was only mildly enthusiastic. Its deductive protagonist was alternatively reviled as effete or praised as "rather daring." Much of this had to do with the studied performance of Robert Stephens, a classical actor and the former associate director of Britain's National Theater. Playing the part of Holmes with panache and a droll, if not effetely satirical slant, his incarnation was unique in that it presented the great detective as a man trapped within his own myth. In the latter regard, "Private Life" excels in its suggestion that Sherlock Holmes may have been condemned by Watson's written accounts to become a luridly romantic version of himself. He further decries his friend's tendencies to romanticize his abilities in *The Strand Magazine.* To wit:

"...You have taken my simple exercises in logic and embellished them, embroidered them...you've described me as six foot four where I am barely six foot one. You've saddled me with this improbable costume which the public now expects me to wear.... You've made me out to be a violin virtuoso...the fact is I could barely hold my own in the pit orchestra of a second-rate music hall. "

In other words, and like the 2015 Dan Simmons novel *The Fifth Heart* or even the cinematic "Mr. Holmes," the famous sleuth is found painfully aware that he lives a kind of dual existence in which the "real" borders that other zone of his fictive self. And by encountering the detective's dilemma we may in turn be compelled to ask ourselves how anyone might survive under such a burden?

Nevertheless, film critics saw "The Private Life of Sherlock Holmes" in a variety of lights. "Not a perfect mix, perhaps, but a fond and entertaining one" wrote Vincent Canby in New York. However another British reviewer, Kim Newman, described "Private Life" as "the best Sherlock Holmes movie ever made," and "sorely underrated in the Wilder Canon." In contrast, America's Roger Ebert gave this muted epic "two and a half stars out of four." It was, he wrote, "disappointingly lacking in bite and sophistication." Such criticisms not withstanding, Mark Gatiss, co-creator of the wildly popular PBS "Sherlock" admitted that "The Private Life of Sherlock Holmes" served as a key source of his inspiration in bringing the detective back with a twist.

I first saw "The Private Life" in a theater in 1970, and then six years later when I actually rented a 16mm version and watched it a second time. To date I have viewed it on countless occasions on television, on tape, and recently on DVD. Still my feelings for this work remain warmer than ever. But this no doubt has more to do with my retrospective associations for the film, and of remembering what a catalyst it had been in shaping my own desire to hie myself over the sea in quest of my deeply distant roots. But not merely to sample its distilled "waters," but instead to float upon them at Loch Ness, even as I went in quest of its fabled monster. Nor had I any doubt that my old friend Finlay Currie would have had his own opinions on "yon beastie." Even now I could visualize his raising a dram to "Nessie!"

Only days ago I came upon an old scrap-booked clipping from some nameless tabloid. And there in generous space stood I, aged thirty-two. I was nattily posed in my then-subterranean version of "221B," briar pipe in hand, looking as if I were Holmes himself confronting another of those ink-stained wretches.

The story in question was headlined "ELEMENTARY, MY DEAR NESSIE," and in true tabloid fashion it included a grainy image of

Nessie, and a bracketed warning "SHERLOCK HOLMES BUFF McPHERSON IS AFTER YOU!"

And so it proceeded: *"Look out, Nessie. Sherlock Holmes is after you. Nessie is known otherwise as the Loch Ness Monster. And Sherlock is known otherwise as Mark McPherson of Ypsilanti, MI, who spends every vacation focusing the deductive powers of his mythical hero on the mysterious Scottish lake."*

The lurid coverage also described my passionate monster hunting and concluded, appropriately, with a rationalization which was in its way also a bit of what Mr. Poe's detective Dupin called "ratiocination" It then concluded with my being confronted with having failed more than once, to return home without the prize of the ultimate discovery.

"The last three years haven't been a failure," McPherson says, "because, as Holmes would say, 'it is a capital mistake to theorize without evidence.' And the first duty of an investigator is to collect that evidence and then to theorize."

Yes, I actually said that. But more importantly, here was an illustration of what in fact was a synthesizing of two of my most chronic interests: "Sherlock" and "Nessie." But how, I sometimes ask myself, did it really begin? When for instance did I become a monster hunter, and why?

The truth of the matter is that for one intrepid fellow from Berkley, Michigan, "The Private Life of Sherlock Holmes" may have jumpstarted certain urges which would find their eventual venting. To begin with, and most obviously, the Wilder-Diamond script for "Private Life" had seated Holmes' greatest challenge in Inverness-shire, Scotland. And it was there, five years later, that I avidly devoured *New York Times* accounts of how a Boston patent attorney named Robert Rines had created an organization called The Academy of Applied Science.

Moreover, the Academy's latest quest was quite literally "loched in" at the famous Scottish lake, where more than rumors of its fifteen centuries old "beastie" had turned real. Add to this reports suggesting that scientific equipment consisting of sonar and underwater photography had succeeded in "capturing" what eye-witnesses for at least forty years had claimed to exist. As for what that might be, candidates for a "mistaken" monster ranged from decaying logs, roe deer swimming and random wake patterns, to one of the most ludicrous, if not *apropos* Sherlockian explanations. This theory was founded upon the fact that while "The Private Life of Sherlock Holmes" was being filmed on location, the wire-framed property replica of the forged-iron Victorian submersible shaped like "Nessie" sank to the bottom. As a result, this option was added to the many accounting for the presence of a "monster" at Loch Ness; namely, that the movie property had managed to rise and float to the surface, then descend again! (**Authorial Note:** such theories about an iron-clad Nessie did in fact "surface" after sonar-trackers appeared to finally locate a carcass for *Nessiteras Rhombopteryx* on the loch's peaty floor. However, closer technological definition revealed this to be a remnant quite Sherlockian in nature: for what those electronic pulses had discovered was the untethered movie "monster" of the 1970 Wilder film.)

Upon my initial viewing "The Private Life," all I knew was that the notion of sending Sherlock Holmes on a snipe-hunt for the world's most famous monster was good stuff. Here perhaps was the proper measure for Holmes to out-do his scientific contemporary, Professor Edward Challenger and his dinosaurian conflicts in *The Lost World*. Moreover, for scope and general locale, placing the sleuth upon the surface of the Grand Canyon-deep Loch Ness carried with it more possible thrills than, say, chasing a baying, fiery-eyed giant canine across the misty moorlands. But a long-necked, hump-backed specie, still alive despite its supposed extinction 20 million years ago? Who in their right mind could deny that as one of the world's great adventures?

I suppose—no, I know, that there are certain books and music and even films which germinate within us over time. And for myself, "The Private Life of Sherlock Holmes" was and remains one of those. For it seemed to ignite a pilot-light of adventure in me, if not re-kindle a sense of adventure which I'd felt back in '67 in Dartmoor and again in '69 on Baker Street. And better yet, suddenly the thought of venturing off to the isles again, and to the home of my ancestral blood-line, was a hands-down terrific idea. If not a perfect means of escaping one's everyday reality.

So it was, after tracking the efforts of my fellow countrymen pursuing "Nessie" in Scotland, I decided to join them. I recall after reading one of the many press reports, turning to my wife and saying, "someone ought to fit up an expedition and go to Loch Ness and help them find the monster." She looked up from her needlepoint and smiled rather sweetly, as if to herself.

"You're right, they should" she said. And hearing those words register within my brain, I began to give the matter some Sherlockian thought.

Now cut to approximately two weeks later. After returning home from my job as a college publicist (shades of Bill Rabe), I set down my brief-case and made my announcement.

"Well, I've done it" I said. And in response, while not unaccustomed to her husband's many activities, my lady wife stood before me, arms folded, wearing another of her sweet smiles and asked, "done what?"

"I've created my expedition to Loch Ness" I said. "I've actually raised funds to go to Scotland and go in search of the creature." And then I explained how I'd come to this point. In the main this had amounted to creating a prospectus for what I was calling "Operation Long-Neck" and a number of prospective donor "targets" I'd set down to approach. Among those one had immediately paid off, in the form of two editors named Lubeck and Lutz at *The Detroit News*.

After gaining an *entrée* into those sacred editorial precincts I'd proceeded with my nearly-rehearsed Nessie-hunting pitch. And with the sort of impassioned furor I used to employ with the Executive Cabinet to gain additional advertising funding for the Fall Semester at Wayne County Community College, now I affirmed how and why it was important for *News* readers to be kept abreast of "the world's greatest monster hunt."

When I got to the end of my presentation, Lubeck slowly nodded and replied, rather rhetorically, "I like it." But not so his compeer. For Lutz, as I intuited, was the nay-sayer of the team, and the one seemingly engaged in his role of playing Good Editor-Bad Editor. Add to that, he seemed somehow as dour as his name. Moreover, he'd suffered through my impassioned proposal, even as I'd sought to explain the value of one bold Detroiter flying to Britain, training to Scotland, and then getting into a small boat and floating like a cork on the surface of a 745-foot-deep lake.

"I just don't see it" Lutz finally said, rendering his unsurprising verdict. Hearing those five deadly words, I thought that he might as well have put on the judicial black cap as he made his dire pronouncement. For you see, no doubt he knew, and they knew, and I knew they knew, that I needed both of these editorial forces to get what I needed. So I tried another tack.

"Consider in years past, when the Virgin Mary supposedly made her apparitional appearances before faithful multitudes in France or Spain" I said. "Did *The Detroit News* have a reporter there? And what about those reports in Medjugore, Yugoslavia in more recent times, suggesting that the Blessed Lady was going to come down again?"

Forlornly Lutz looked at the clock on the wall. No doubt my time was, as they say, "up." Then his focus seemed to be fixed upon his cluttered desk blotter. As he leaned forward, I thought he was either going to belch or suddenly invite me to vacate the premises. But instead of that he said something else entirely. Something in turn which was rather surprising.

"Well guess what?" he said. "We did send a reporter over there some years back. But the Holy Mother didn't come down." The way he was putting it, I mused, it sounded as if we were talking about a UFO, which in a way I suppose we were.

I heard the seconds on my life-meter ticking away. And then without thinking I just dived in again

"But what if she did come down tomorrow?" I asked Lutz, "and what if when she made that appearance you didn't have a reporter there?"

Lubeck and Lutz looked at one another. Both were probably thinking about lunch, the weekend ahead, or simply what their work-place would be like without yours truly sitting in it?

Lutz began to fiddle with the small pile of *New York Times* news-clippings I'd pared, pasted up, and inserted in a nice manila folder as evidence for my case. Then the dreaded Magistrate gave Lubeck the slightest of tell-tale shrugs. And then it was his partner's turn to speak.

"All right, Mark. You can go" the friendly editor said. "Now, how much did you say this was going to cost us?"

And that pretty much was the way it went. *The Detroit News* bankrolled me for a return flight to London and a few dollars more for what I'd envisioned as "provisions." In the latter regard I knew I'd need some additional support if I was to flesh out an additional shopping list that included some books, maps, some underwater gear, and a kind of elaborate Raytheon fish-finder which could detect the presence of something larger than an oversized salmon beneath one's boat.

Now what I haven't told you involved achieving a kind of "license" to go Monster Hunting. You don't get those at the nearby hardware or sporting goods emporium. Rather, you needed to go to the source. And for that, I followed up a few leads involving Dr. Rines, of *The New York Times* reports, and his Academy of Applied Science. Both before and after officially launching my efforts, I phoned, corresponded with, and eventually flew to Boston to meet my contact and his friends in person. Along the way as well I became conversant in such things as side-scan sonar technology and the chemistry of freshwater bodies, or even, and importantly, what the fossil records showed that might suggest any form of "dinosaurian relict survival." Speaking of which, the most recent event back then had been the British naturalist Peter Scott's zoological designation for our beastie: *Nessiteras Rhombopteryx,* or "Creature of the Ness With the Diamond Shaped Fin."

Ultimately there was a greater underlying question at hand: was the notion of finding a supposedly vanished specie of dinosaurian-era creature crazy? Perhaps it was not. For after all and even as I'd read, in 1938 a specimen of the Mesozoic Coelacanth, presumed extinct for tens of millions of years, was pulled up, recently alive, out of African waters, and then again not too much after that. And since '38, other similarly "vanished" specimens of fauna had made return appearances.

It was upon such studies a branch of scientific pursuit had been created, and was now enjoying a new vogue. It was called Cryptozoology: the study of "hidden" or perhaps even "phantom" animals. That then was my new objective. I would embark upon becoming the best damned amateur cryptozoologist I could be, *vis a vis* Loch Ness. And as I became aware, so too were other investigators pressing ahead with their own subjects. Apart from "Nessie," those in the main were now involving the matter of whether a surviving Neanderthal specie might exist in the Himalayas or even our own forest-clad and mountainous northwest wilderness? And the hunt itself had bred a kind of private fraternity of monster-seekers, most of whom spoke the same cryptic language. *Yeti, Sasquatch, Alma.* And of course, now *Nessiteras Rhombopteryx.*

When I met Robert Rines and his Academy of Applied Science crew I was fortunate enough to convince them that I was in some way worthy of joining their Round Table. But not as a scientist. Then as what? Not a hunter in the usual sense. But rather, as a kind of investigative journalist, willing to put his neck on the line, if not the surface of a bottomless lake.

Given my newspapering credentials, I remembered Conan Doyle's Edward Malone, the young free-lancer who'd joined Professor Challenger's team in *The Lost World.* But that fellow had gone out on a risk-your-neck mission in order to win his lady fair. A silly enough reason to put yourself at risk, I mused, even as Malone himself discovered at the end of his exploit. But he had been looking for something. And much in the cut of other fictional heroes of his day, often the igniting spark had to do with the risk involved. You know the drill: "if they capture you, you're on your own." And that in due part had impelled Malone to land upon a strange South American plateau which time had seemingly forgotten.

Meanwhile my own motives, whatever they truly were, had now sufficed to fly me across the ocean, if only to put me in possible harm's way. There were not a few times, both before, during and after that I did examine my own reasons for breaking out of my rather normal shell. And I suppose on the whole it did have something to do with romance, but not for the sake of wooing one woman or another. I already felt secure in that realm. But no doubt it was for the simplest, most obvious reason of all: *we all want to make our mark.* And how better to do that than to leave your workaday world and trade it for mystery, myth, and adventure?

And that was most likely my primary motivation in making that first sojourn to the land of my ancestors. In doing so, and looking back now at the young fellow who took up his cudgel, I say once again that I am proud of him. In other words, he didn't disappoint me. And like that Christopher Morley-esque man "who made friends with himself," I never quite felt alone. Moreover, it was simply unlike any sensation I'd ever experienced before. And I suppose you might say it was the "beginning of the beginning" for my investigative interests.

But Romance notwithstanding and as I've already suggested, the business of monster-hunting is funded, quite literally, like most others. And in order to meet those essential overheads, I made a plan for fundraising. In the overall sense here however, my efforts proved of precious little success monetarily. Paradoxically, perhaps, such a level of austerity actually earned me a citation in a curious publication entitled *Michillaneous,* a compendium of unusual people and feats within our native Michigan.

Methodically, I started out by mapping a number of prospective "targets" for underpinning my Scottish expedition. To begin with, I recall visiting an elderly gent named Charley Helin, who, like Detroit's local television adventurer George Pierrot, used to travel the world, seeking out exotic places and things. I'd grown up watching with my folks as these guys would go hither and yon, and I suppose seeing them do it kindled a sense of youthful adventure. But now and rather suddenly, I was about to undertake my own.

I recall George Pierrot saying to me that my plans were both "admirable and exciting." He paid me the further compliment of telling me that I reminded him of himself in his youth. And then the sound of the boom falling, making a sound that rhymed with "but I can't give you any money."

Detroiter Charley Helin to my mind was a likely potential source, given his time in the waters of the world. When I visited him in his high-rise office I took note of a museum's worth of photos and mounted trophies of his piscatorial conquests. Yes, fish of many shapes and sizes. But no monsters among them, at least none that I could see.

Mr. Helin heard me out, and his facial features were much more relaxed than those I'd witnessed in my Good Editor-Bad Editor session at *The Detroit News* a few days earlier. Instead the Big Fisherman sat there and digested my spiel, which went back to St. Columba in 565 A.D., the Age of King Arthur, and how this holy man had repelled the "beastie" at Loch Ness. Then I moved forward to the 19th century, and then into the 20th, when early reports featured witness accounts of a long-necked, hump-backed creature sounding or descending into the peaty depths of the Ness. My crescendo of sorts led to filmed footage shot in the 1960's by a chap named Dinsdale, and then of the latter's affiliation with Rines and his Academy of Applied Science. I rounded the corner here with the latest reports of sonar profiles of "something large" in the loch, as well as grainy underwater footage of a huge fin, eight to ten feet across, passing by the sonar-camera unit. According to the Jet Propulsion Laboratory at Pasadena, what their computerized process in analysis suggested was nothing of a kind of creature known to reside in Loch Ness.

My pitch finally completed, now I waited. And there in that silent office far above the muted traffic on the Grand Boulevard, I sat amid the evidences of a lifetime spent in search of adventure. And then the adventurer himself replied.

"It's a fascinating story you tell" he said. "However, I'm afraid I can't help you. Personally, I don't believe there's a monster in that lake. Maybe a big sturgeon, or more likely a log bobbing up from the bottom. But nothing like a dinosaur, if you get my meaning?"

Yes I said, as I rose from my leather chair and extended a hand to my interlocutor. I got his meaning, loud and clear.

"Well" I concluded, "I won't waste any more of your time. Thanks very much for seeing me. It was a pleasure meeting you."

"Not at all" said Charley Helin, standing behind his massive desk. And just as I was halfway through the door, I heard his strident voice once again. *The Parthian Shot, I mused: what's it going to be?*

"But say," I heard the worldly fishing expert call out. I half turned in the doorway.

"If you do see something, you let me know, will ya?"

I smiled back and couldn't resist a bit of bravado. Was I rude to fire back? Or just cocky? Maybe a little of both.

"I don't suppose we'll ever meet again" I replied. "For after all, you've just told me for certain that there's nothing there." And then I took my leave.

In postscript I offer this last recollection. Near the top of my list of prospective donors was one quite prosperous attorney with whom I'd had a nodding acquaintance for a few years. When we finally sat down in his gorgeous Fisher Building office he listened to me intently. And when I reached the end of my delivery he leaned forward and said "fascinating." And then asked a question. "How much are you looking to raise for your expedition?"

Well hearing my legalistic colleague sounding so interested at this juncture, I madly made a few financial calculations. *Don't be greedy* said my own inner counselor.

"About five hundred" I replied, as casually as I might have put my cards upon the table. And I watched my companion.

The man smiled and stretched in his expensive desk chair. And then I heard his words, which I will never forget.

"Wow. That's not very much" he said. "I was expecting you to ask for a great deal more. Five thousand, maybe." Hearing this, I felt relieved. Perhaps the better part of valor was, after all, in making a reasonable request. *Thank you, good sir. Now if you will just make out your check to...*

"But I'm not going to give you the money" my companion announced. 'And I'm going to tell you why."

I shifted in my seat, strangely un-disappointed. And actually eager to hear his reason.

"Mark, I've got a good many causes that I choose to support. But none of them are monster causes. Do you get my drift?" I did. I said so. And that was that. Fair enough. Worse yet, I actually understood his point. Crippled children. Dread diseases. Poverty. Illiteracy. But goosenecked monsters that didn't realize they were extinct? I'd probably have turned me down myself. *But nothing ventured...*

There was however a surprising twist to my efforts and even the magic trick of informing my wife that she was now married to a genuine Monster Hunter. To begin with, sooner or later the local press got wind of an unusual story, and mine was certainly that. Before long I was fielding calls at my office asking for interviews, but not regarding my college of employment. Instead, many of those little "CALLED WHILE YOU WERE AWAY" pink stickers read, *"Want to talk to you about going after Nessie."*

Next thing I knew I was giving the odd lecture or two on the subject of "The Mysteries of Loch Ness." Then there was the CKLW radio interview across the bridge in Windsor, Ontario. Bob Bauer the program's late-night host was a genial fellow, and in short order we hit it off like old chums. And in the wake of what seemed to be a hundred other pre-expeditionary media chats, it was one of Bob's questions I still remember best. He looked at me in the cramped confines of his studio booth and asked me, "What frightens you?"

I heard the question and took nary a moment to reply.

"A great deal" I heard myself answer. "But none of it obvious."

There were more radio and newspaper and even a few wire-service pick-ups describing my intended voyage. A local television studio sent their newest female reporter out to film me at my daily training. For you see, in '76 we lived in a nice little lakefront apartment. And in order to anticipate the time I'd shortly be spending on some very deep water, I'd elected to go out in a raft upon Ypsilanti's Ford Lake. And on one of those days, the attractive young future anchor got into the inflatable with me as I rowed us out into the shallows. We actually did an interview that way, and it got a good deal of play. And on many such occasions, the fact that apart from my other interests I was a Sherlock Holmes "fan," brought the elements of a good mystery story into focus.

That then set the scene for preparing me to go in search of perhaps one of Scotland's best tourist-trade assets. I suppose you might well have said the same of Holmes, *vis a vis* London's endless stream of visitors? But now I was about to combine them both.

St. George "The Dragon Slayer."

15
St. George, The Dragon, & The Beast

The year 1976 signaled my first of numerous forays to Loch Ness. It is however safe to say that with each of what constituted eight arrivals, my departures were fueled by the desire to return. Here it became a consequence of my chronic love affair with the sometimes dour, often gorgeous tapestry of mist-shrouded hills. And always there was the brooding sense of something deeply-seated and elemental lurking unseen. And what more perfect monster lair than a one hundred and twenty-six fathom deep, peat-stained glacial crevice. And there within Scotland's Great Glen is a vortex—perhaps many of them—leading, according to some, to the past and present. Yes, all of it capable of evoking that very quickening one only feels by being part of it all. That, and of course by considering whatever your reasons might be for wanting to share that primordial landscape with its notorious "water horse."

But when I first I embarked upon my new side-line as a Monster Hunter I'd realized there was little enough to guide the prospective seeker on his quest. I mean, it's not as if there's a play-book for "How To Find The Holy Grail" or a manual for "Picking The Loch." No, not unless you believed the principles of hunting for big game, or big game fishing, or whaling was in any way commensurate. But it's not.

I suppose in hindsight such seekers might have better spent their time perusing two literary classics instead, in the form of *Don Quixote* and *Moby Dick.* Which is mainly to say, if you're planning on tilting at one of the world's most legendary windmills, it's important to know how. Likewise, if you believe in the phantom presence of something which has existed, at least in the mind's eye, you need to get your bearings. And that aspect may be complicated by how you expect to encounter something which may be in essence, intangible. That by the way is one way the Scots tend to view their "bogle," or "horny beastie," as a sort of now-you-see-it-now-you-don't proposition. Which only becomes more abstract if indeed a seemingly zoological enigma may be gauged to be a ghostly, or even inter-time-dimensional phenomenon.

So harking back to the "getting your bearings" department, perhaps the only rule to follow is whatever works. Simply stated, within the chronicled realm of Loch Ness's most famous denizen, the number of trustworthy Quixote's or Ahabs is small by compare. For that reason then, no one has offered a better game-plan than Indiana Jones. Once asked if he had a plan, he replied, *"No, I'm makin' this up as I go along."*

But on a more serious level, this is much to do with the reason one decides to hunt his designated prey. Factor in as well the mind-set required to beard a prospective beast, be it of real or even quasi-historical provenance. And that, my friends, presents its own sort of tangled skein. For starters there is the question of motive: *why does anyone attempt to stalk any living creature?* Here the usual answers have much to do with the "sport' involved. The stalking, the pursuit, the chase, the confrontation, followed by the "dispatch"—or call it as it is—the kill. Which adds to the matter of the "how?" and "why?" of the thing.

Well here's the situation: my father was an inveterate deer hunter for quite a while. But in contrast his only son had never pursued the pastime of wearing his license to kill and then going out to use it.

Philosophically, if you will, while I have never been a hunter in the usual sense myself, I have known many who were. Further, I have come to reject any notion or need to "conquer" any person, no less any beast, as if to somehow draw upon myself its primordial spirit or power–especially via blood-sport. Surely enough that was an idea likely shared by many others from the days when primitive man challenged beasts with rocks or sharp sticks. And just as surely there are those today who embark upon the "hunt" equipped with portable weapons suited to the destruction of any creature, be it of two or four-legged stature. But I am not here to lobby against those sportsmen who populate my own state and so many others.

But notwithstanding any hunter's desire to exterminate rabbits, pheasants, quail, large cats, boar, deer, bear, rhinoceros, wildebeests or elephants, there is of course the challenge of going after something even larger. And at its extreme, here again is that category relegated to creatures of a monstrous kind in the extreme. Here too the challenge is magnified a thousand-fold when the prey itself is not merely endangered or extinct, but possibly non-existent. Which leads us to the subject of those long-necked beasties said still to exist in oceans and deep-water lakes around the globe.

I realized early on that the pursuit of Scotland's most fabled creature, "Nessie" reflected a much older and broader tradition within the British Isles. And that tradition even today represents a depth within our psyches far darker than the deepest Scottish loch. It is instead archetypal and elemental. It is symbolic and numinous in a way that few of our present-day wonders are. But to our forebears these things were greater, mightier, tinged with divine otherworldliness.

I have come to understand that my serial quests at Loch Ness are all that, and more. For here and beyond even this enigma's status as a largely water-born specie, what we are talking about is something wondrous, if not frightening. Not uncoincidentally, both of those descriptions might well be applied to the related subject of dragons.

Were one to proclaim himself a "dragonologist," it would be necessary for them to conduct a lion's (or dragon's) share of historical and folkloric research. This would doubtless serve to present them with a picture of a time and many places at which at least the belief in dragons was quite real.

But when we recede in time to those mythically-blurred accounts, there are a handful which suggest the relationship between a monster and its hunter. First off to be understood, I think, is whether such depictions ascribe the beastie to be of a real, zoological nature, or of some super-natural element? Sadly for that specie of *draconis,* time has done little than besmirch its qualities, equating its scaly, fire-breathing nature to something quite naturally of an evil origin. In specific terms at Loch Ness, a 6th century description of the seemingly demonic aquatic creature finds it pitted against no less a one than Adamnan's *Life of Saint Columba.* There a scene is portrayed in which the holy man repels the monster from reaching a swimmer by invoking the holy name. And like the reputed effect of a cross upon a vampire, the great beast, or "water horse" sank down into the deep. It is, I think, the aquatic version of the chiefly land-based theme of St. George and the Dragon.

There are of course a share of medieval tales depicting the malign shapes of dragons on land, in the air, and as we have seen, in the water. But perhaps none gives us such a profile of the dragon-slayer than the British narrative of the Worm of Lambton. Here we find the young Earl of Lambton returned from the wars, then going head to whatever with the creature.

> *The news of this most awful Worm*
> *And his queer goings-on*
> *Soon crossed the seas and reached the ears*
> *of brave and bold Sir John.*
> *So home he came and catched the beast*
> *And cut him in two halves,*
> *And that soon stopped him eating bairns*
> *And sheep and lambs and calves.*

And speaking of St. George. Known to the East as George of Cappadocia (within a Romanized Asia Minor) his legend drifted West, as did the Roman legions who claimed him. His associations also include Persia, Britain and Nicomedia, where it is said he was executed by Diocletian's persecutors in 303 A.D. The date of his death ultimately became his *dies natalis* and festival day. Coincidentally, St. George's Day in Britain and beyond is also coincidentally the date of Shakespeare's alleged birth and death.

Within the annals of Christendom, there is no greater hero and slayer of dragons. And to me, I think, even better than his arch-angelical compeer, Michael. By compare these two are Batman and Superman respectively; the former possessed of a bit of try-harder prowess, and the latter with the unfair? advantage of talents supernatural.

By repute George is also a military saint, patron of chivalry, if not a member of the *Tropaiophoros,* wherein the trophies of battle are celebrated. But of course, he is also the conqueror of the dragon, and for the fact of this both the beast and its slayer have become the emblem of Britain's own patron saint. Very like St. Catherine's Wheel or the Lion of St. Mark, St. George became the icon of the 19th century British Empire and the model for all "true gentlemen" on and off the sceptered isle. And yet his fame began much earlier. By the Middle Ages the *Golden Legends* of Jacobus de Voragine described many saintly lives, with George's portrait high among them.

Originally conceived of as a tribune in the Roman legion, later tradition would escalate George into a chivalrous knight in shining armor. Such complimented those earlier stories of his encounter with a horrible dragon "in a deep lake as large as an ocean" in Libyan Silena. To date this beast had repelled the best efforts of all men to oppose it, and therefore it had actually been appeased by the citizenry who offered it two sacrificial sheep each day. However, when the supply of mutton fell short, a human sacrifice was offered, with the prospective victim drawn by lot.

The story continues as to how the King's own daughter had drawn the metaphorical short straw, but no one wished to take her place, or try to save her. Here then is where the heroic George rode by and upon hearing the maiden's plight, proclaimed he would challenge the monster in the name of Christ.

The Georgian theme is one of Christian conversion as well, for the hero enjoins the town's folk to believe in Christ and in return they were baptized, says the legend, some twenty thousand men and a multitude of women and children in one day. And with that task achieved, Saint George drew his sword and summarily slew the dragon. Here then there is a strong spiritual metaphor: put on the armor of your faith and evil will fall to your sword.

On my own youthful experience, apart from Communion that most powerful of post-baptism Catholic rites in which I participated was that of confirmation. And as is the custom, one picks a "confirmation name." And while at the time I suppose I might have favored "Christopher" (for I'd just "met" my literary influence, Christopher "Kit" Marlowe), it was decided that I would be confirmed in the name of George. First off, that was a saint's name. Secondly, it was my grandfather's name. And thirdly, and doubtless most important to my somewhat anti-Roman father, it was his name as well. Ergo, I was marched toward adulthood bearing the name of the mighty Dragon Slayer. Had I been informed at that time that the day would come when I would actually hunt one—well, that's hard to say. But I've never since regretted the nomenclature. In fact, at the height of my Arthurian researches, I began wearing a rather sizable silver ring blazoned with the relief of a dragon. Archetypal indeed, and emblematic of the Pendragon line of "great dragons" ruling Britain's isles. Without a doubt, Dark Age Arthur was said to be one of those. Theorists also believe that royal ensigns of dragons moved from the East to the West. Also that the Red Dragon of Wales may reflect a "true" Arthurian heritage passed down even today to the bloodline of the Windsor Royal Family.

It's always interested me to find a number of unknown or unrealized "nexus points" in our lives. For instance, the Clan MacPherson is known to belong to the Gaelic "Clan Chattan," or "Clan of the Cats." Likewise, there is a rampant Scottish wild-cat in our heraldry, and the tribal motto is *"Touch Not The Cat, Bot A Glove."* In other words, wear an iron gauntlet if you're going to stick your hand in the lion's mouth. And speaking of lions, which are probably the most prevalent among medieval heraldic bestiaries after dragons, I think of them in feline terms as only a step up or down from my ancestral land's fabled feral cats.

And in my own case as well, being of the Clan of the Cat, it is not perhaps un-meaningful that my zodiac sign finds me on the cusp of Leo the Lion. And of course, the ensign of St. Mark is—you have it in one—the lion. All of which I suggest brings home my archetypal affinity for things leonine, if not distantly dragon-related. For such an additional reason have I long cherished two keep-sakes, often worn: the first is a silver ring blazoned with the signet of the rampant dragon, and the second a Greek pendant coin that displays an archaic image of the mounted Saint George, his lance impaling the open mouth of the *draconis.*

Upon my arrival in Inverness-shire, I could find no report that the creature of the Ness had ever terrorized or preyed upon anyone. There were a few isolated reports from the Thirties which claimed a land-siting or two, and even some poor sheep which had supposedly fallen afoul of the beastie. But no rampaging of villages or ravaging of maidens.

Nevertheless, on my first foray to the loch I interviewed at least a dozen people who'd had their own "close encounters of the Nessie kind" over the years. Most of the eyewitnesses were now elderly, but owing to their sincerity, and in many cases their backgrounds, they provided what I believed even Sherlock himself would have considered reliable accounts. And what sort? Well, how about a clergyman, a policeman, a retired naval officer, or a veteran fisherman? All had seen something decidedly large and strange and atypical in Loch Ness.

But among the most memorable of my subjects was Winifred Carey, who lived with her husband Basil at Strone Point, overlooking Loch Ness. From what I had heard Mrs. Carey had claimed more than a dozen sightings of the beastie in her life, and only a handful of them when she was alone. In fact, so persuasive had her reputation been that Robert Rines, the Academy of Applied Science head, not only met her, but experienced his own sighting by her side. Were that not enough, his scientific unit had quietly cooperated with "Winnie," whose rep included claims as a seer, a dowser, and a pendulum-user. And that had involved as strange a tale as anyone might imagine. Officially speaking, it had necessarily gone untold. This fact, owing to the potential threat of discreditable practice which might have been aimed at the Academy's research. Unofficially however, it was a water horse of another color. And like Lord Byron's famous comment, in this case the truth was indeed much stranger than any fiction.

It was in the matter of Mrs. Carey's use of her swinging pendulum over an ordnance map of Loch Ness that Bob Rines got his first technological "hit." The mapped field was broken into numerical grids, and one night when Mrs. Carey made a reading, she indicated where the strongest energy was. Accordingly, a car on the hillside flashed its headlamps to signal the number of the grid, while a boat down below made its nocturnal way to that place.

And 'lo and behold! Arriving at the "hot spot" Winifred Carey had designated, the research vessel's sonar locked onto its target, and the underwater cameras snapped off some strobe-lit photos of something big. Later when these images were assessed and computer enhanced at the Jet Propulsion Laboratory in California, the results were staggering. For what they seemed to describe, once the gizmos had removed the obscuring layers of bubble and disturbed water, was the presence of a diamond-shaped aquatic fin, six to eight feet long! (Authorial note: this was the feature made present in Sir Peter Scot's zoological naming of 'Nessiteras Rhombopteryx,' or "Creature of the Ness with the diamond shaped fin")

After talking to Rines about this in Boston I was naturally eager to interview Winnie Carey. Finally when I got the chance, I recall driving up the winding road to Strone Point. I was now the Sherlockian investigator, about to interview a prime witness in the case. What I also remember is thinking that I would be employing certain skills to get to the core of the mystery. To help in this, I had a tape recorder in my carry-bag. Anticipating some resistance to the interview, I'd switched the machine on, with its 40-some minute tape rolling even as I parked my rental car before "Strone Cottage."

I was met at the door by Mrs. Carey herself, who proved to be a rather gray and stringy haired imitation of Margaret Rutherford. I sensed that this "witch of the hills" as someone had dubbed her, was going to be a no-nonsense subject for the intrepid detective now on her threshold.

So once we sat down in her parlor, I asked her straight out about recording our conversation. She replied that she would prefer that our initial chat just be "between ourselves" so she might gain a level of comfort (and trust) with her interviewer. Hastily I agreed, fully aware that the unzipped bag at my feet contained an already-activated device which had been preserving our every word.

That afternoon with "Winnie" was enlightening, a bit frightening, and highly illuminating concerning the matter I'd come to Scotland to describe. First off, she began by telling me of her youthful sightings of the beast in the loch. This was seasoned with tales of her clairvoyance, and instances when she'd assisted local constabulary in finding a missing child. Then there was her talent as a thaumaturge, or healer, as when she'd psychically removed a cataract from a duck's eye!

And then of course there was the matter of the Exorcism Of The Loch. Here she described the visit by a priest named, if I recall, Father Ormand. A practiced exorcist, he told her that he was certain that the loch had been psychically polluted some years ago, on top of its strong sense of being already "elementally" haunted. His reasoning here focused upon the brief tenancy of the black magician and Satanist Aleister Crowley at an 18th century house near Foyers across the bay. There, even as Crowley himself described in his *Confessions,* he had sought to invoke a number of spirits by using a prolonged magical ritual. As a consequence, the magician admitted to have perhaps awakened more than he could manage. As a result, Crowley experienced weird goings on at his isolated cottage at Boleskine House, which was seated on ground just above the ribbon of shore road and an ancient cemetery.

The bottom line, Reverend Ormand said, was that Crowley, the self-styled "Beast, Number 666" (the numeric sign of the Apocalypse Beast in the *Book of Revelation*) had summoned something dark and eldritch which he could not tame. As a consequence he left Boleskine a man now shattered both in health and spirit. Moreover, he admitted to being "followed" thereafter by some dread kind of elemental residue first stirred up at Boleskine, if not hounded thereafter by both ill health and failing fortunes.

But there was more and worse besides. According to the exorcist priest, Crowley's house had maintained its dark aura over the decades. Its most famous subsequent tenant was the Led Zeppelin guitarist, Jimmy Page, who in the band's heyday was a student of the "magickal" writings of Aleister Crowley. As a result of such interest, it was believed that Page and his lead vocalist Robert Plant had knowingly woven Crowleyesque lyrics into some of their songs. But perhaps there was a price on that, as well. Not long after there were fatalities at a Zeppelin concert, and Plant's young son died in mysterious circumstances.

But the popular interest in "666" had not been monopolized only by Led Zeppelin. Careful examination of the Beatles' "Sergeant Pepper" album cover will reveal the bold and balding features of The Beast glaring out among a collage of the famous and notorious.

As Winnie Carey described it, Reverend Ormand's express intention was to perform the ancient Rite of Exorcism over the loch. Further, he wished to do it from the promontory where Strone Cottage stood. With a level of regret now, she said, the mistress of the house had then given her consent to the ancient ritual.

The grisly long and short of the thing was, according to Winifred Carey, the business of "all hell breaking loose" when the priestly ritual was performed. According to my companion, when it was begun there were strange sounds, temperature changes, darkness, and a massive wind. These, Ormand said, as if performing the bedroom scene in the film "The Exorcist" were the consequences of a reprisal of sorts. "They don't want to go" he explained, with the "they" meaning some form of demonic entities which tended to cling to places as a kind of host.

"He performed the ritual and bad things happened" she told me. "And then, suddenly, it was over." But hearing this and seeing the look on her weathered features as she spoke, I wondered if it truly was?

I discussed many other things with Winifred Carey, including her presence by Robert Rines' side when she'd directed his attention to the sudden emergence of a dark, hump-backed shape risen from the deep waters below Strone Point. And as she told me this, I thought of the high strangeness of scientists working hand in hand with a practitioner of the arcane arts?

After a couple of hours, and frankly feeling exhausted by what I'd heard, I thanked Mrs. Carey. We agreed to meet again before I left, when, in accordance with our agreement, I might record her statements "for the record."

Now here comes the punch, as they say. For as I was driving my way back to the road below, I reached into my travel bag and hit the "REVERSE" button on the tape recorder. When it reached its taped beginning I paused on that serpentined hilltop road, took the machine out of its case and placed it on the passenger seat beside me. And I thought, as I moved forward again, and foolish lad that I was, *Well the old Witch on the Hill was not too sharp for the ace investigator, was she?* And then I pressed "PLAY."

As I wended my way along the decline with the vista of Loch Ness still beneath and ahead of me, I heard the recording begin. First the shuffling of my gear, then the slamming of the rented Cortina's door.

Then the sound of my boots on the gravel path leading to the cottage. Followed by my knocking on the door. Then her voice, followed, a minute or so later by our settling down in the Carey's parlor. And lastly, my overture to record our interview, followed by Winnie's request that I refrain for now, and perhaps before I left Drumnadrochit, that I might return and we would do the interview again? And of course, my agreement with those terms. A compact made. But also broken. In other words, my consent to an agreement entered into with this strange old woman of even stranger reputation.

Backing up a tad—there was the sound of my saying *"Yes, I'd be glad just to chat with you. And I'll come back later and we'll record an interview.* And then the sound of the witch's voice agreeing. And then—*nothing.* Or should I say, nothing more or less than the sound of an electronic burr which continued through the remainder of perhaps thirty-five minutes or so of the tape. And that was all. I was amazed. Angry. And then aware. Smiling to myself, I suddenly knew I'd learned an important lesson even Holmes would have appreciated, even if he refused to accept it in principle. After all, as "The Sussex Vampire" makes perfectly clear, there was no vacancy in the firm of Holmes & Co. which could be filled by the supernatural.

But suddenly, and now quite unlike Sherlock Holmes, I could not say the same. For seemingly the Unknown had found its way to my figurative door. And if so, I had little doubt that it was my own damned fault.

As a postscript to the tale of exorcisms and Winnie Carey, I've decided to tell you one more. This too involves Aleister Crowley and Boleskine House. For a year after the visit as described, I returned on my chronic quest to Loch Ness. One afternoon I did so with the express intention of driving over to Foyers, and from a certain strategic point beyond its famous waterfall, of hiking in the general direction of the house where hell had supposedly been raised.

Suffice it to say it was an otherwise gorgeous autumn day. My trekking took me upwards and past a beautiful glen and forests, and farm fields, and then the higher wood. Marching into it, I knew from my coordinates that beyond it and below would be the damnable House of Crowley*: Boleskine.*

When I gained sight of the place I found myself imagining myself as James Bond in "Goldfinger," looking down at the villain's lair from a wooded eyrie. Using my binoculars, I saw the old house and the outbuildings behind it, fringed by dark clusters of pine and other foliage. Shifting my gaze, I then traced the way down to the road, and on t'other side of it, the old cemetery. There, as I'd learned from Mrs. Carey, a number of dark and unorthodox rituals had been conducted over time. An altar cloth of seemingly ancient vintage had also been found draped over one of the gravestones.

After contenting myself that no one seemed visible in the vicinity of the house, I left the fringe of tree-line behind me and started down. A short while later I proceeded toward the side door of the house, from which once, many decades ago, Britain's "most evil man" and practicing magician had come and gone. But had he truly left? Many claimed to still feel his presence.

Others closer to the place such as Led Zepplin guitarist Jimmy Page, who owned Boleskine, felt its dark allure. Enough so to celebrate Crowley in his music—as did his peers from Liverpool, the Beatles, who incorporated old Aleister's bloated countenance on their "Sergeant Pepper" album cover.

But as is often the case with dark magic, there is a toll. Some took note of a "bad phase" for the Zeppelin group, including a death at a concert and the also surprising demise of one of the band's children. Was this somehow the Crowleyan influence attesting to what he'd raised, but could not put down? And even in the absence of that apocalyptic mage, could there still be the residue of his occult experimentations at the old house on the loch? Sources also remembered that certain elemental entities had lingered, as Aleister Crowley had insisted until his dying day, and which had affixed themselves to that evil psychic laboratory of a place, courtesy of the Ritual of Abra-Melin?

And now, well knowing all of this, there I was, as if drawn by some dark lodestone. To Boleskine. As if to visit with the "other monster" of Loch Ness.

I dared to knock on the door. No answer. So I decided to have a further look-round. In doing so perhaps the oddest thing was the un-curtained scene of a room, perhaps a dining room, which had a table and several chairs around it, something like a smaller version of King Arthur's Round Table. The comparison was made due to the fact that there appeared to be names or plaques on each of the seats. *But none of them the Siege Perilous of the old tales. That was reserved for the finder of the Holy Grail. And the Grail was the last thing one might expect to find in this horror house.*

I thought of the energy presumed to be at Boleskine, and which over the years had been supposedly amplified by "the Beast's" followers. Odd rituals. Even the presence of a young man supposedly Crowley's mentally-defective bastard son. But no joy there, either.

I scouted about for a bit, then took some pictures. I even claimed a black shard of some kind of stone as a souvenir from the driveway. Then I ambled down for a look at the churchyard. But shortly thereafter and through a mixture of tiredness and a kind of mental weariness, I decided to hike down the road and make my way back to where I'd parked my car.

But that was not the end of the story, was it? I ask myself: No, I reply.

Indeed it was not.

We'll make this as concise as possible, and I'll allow you to make up your mind on the matter. I'll pick up the narrative after I returned home and wrote up a feature story on my pre-Halloween "Visit To The Magician's House" for *the Detroit News Sunday Magazine*. Yes, for even on the heels of my "How I Hunted The Loch Ness Monster" a couple of years earlier, I apparently hadn't worn out my welcome. But then too there'd been a change of managers for the magazine. I now remember having lunch on my return with the new editor-in-charge of features, Jim Vesely. Somehow I had persuaded him to take my piece on Crowley's haunted house for a Halloween-time special and he'd accepted.

Now then and cutting to the chase. The Sunday the story ran in that weekend's *Detroit News* I was driving back from my parent's northern-based home outside of Traverse City. I had my friend George with me, and he at least became the unwitting witness of what followed. Best as I can describe it, we were driving in my small car down I-75 South and had only a pickup truck ahead of us in another lane. We were close enough to see that the truck's cargo were several pieces of stacked plywood, presumably lashed down.

Well just as George and I were discussing my recent Scottish trip, and my junket to see Crowley's Boleskine, the weirdness began. This, when we both became aware that the plywood in the truck's bed was apparently not tied down. This became plain enough as one of its pieces seemed to rise of its own accord and to hover before flipping out of the rear, and until-then-closed gate.

Instinctively I pressed the brake as we were pulled back from a possible calamity. I remember keeping a weather eye on the truck's load and even veering over to the far right-hand lane. But that was not enough. For even as I did so, both my companion and I simultaneously witnessed a seemingly incredible spectacle: *suddenly one of those wooden sheets seeming to rise like a kite above the level of the truck's cab.* But as the vehicle moved forward its dangerous cargo seemed to wheel about as if it were being guided, with its very obviously pointed end floating up and toward us.

Once again I employed the brake, but like an otherworldly, heatseeking missile, the plywood sheet appeared to be aimed squarely at us. And in seconds, unaccountably, that wedge of deadly wood arced over and imbedded itself in the grill of my car.

Fortunately there was no damage to either myself, my friend, or to the functioning of my compact vehicle. Apart from some nasty destruction of the grill, the radiator had not, gratefully, been pierced by that missile. And as for its carrier? He was long gone and down the road a far piece, seemingly unaware that his unfettered load had nearly cost someone his life.

That week I had lunch again with my friend the editor. I told him about my episode on the road, but I reserved the thoughts which were now fast at work in my mind. *Had that freak accident in any way related to my daring to trespass at Boleskine, or worse, to photograph it, and then to write about it? Or how to explain what had commenced as a fluke, and then seemed to escalate into a chain of what anyone might write off as episodes of "bad luck?"*

My companion seemed more ill at ease than the last time I'd seen him. Unaccountably (or perhaps very accountably) I asked him "How are you?" To which Jim looked back at me and countered "Why do you ask me that?"

"I just wanted to know" I said. And then I repeated my question.

After a few moments my luncheon date looked at me with a kind of furled expression.

"Well if you really want to know, I've never known a time when so many things have been going wrong in my life." And then he began to enumerate them, from the smallest to the bigger. And I couldn't help thinking, as I listened, *it's my fault. It's that damned Crowley again.*

Think what you will about this, and I can probably guess what you might say. Imagination. Power of suggestion. Preconceived ideas. I get that. But at the end of the day, or the week, or the month, or the chain of days that followed, I too felt strangely victimized by my brief, but unauthorized stint at Boleskine House. And yes, things continued to go wrong in my own world. To begin with, I felt lousy. Certain of my financial matters were going south. And my wife suddenly decided that "when thoughts about her job changed, so too did those that concerned her marriage." In other words, she wanted no longer to be married to the Great Investigator. And I thought to myself, *who could blame you?* And then, like the final barb into the bull's shoulders, there was the matter of the marriage counselor we saw. My dubious wife picked him out of the book. And his name? "*Dr. Watson.*" Go figure.

It's safe to say that my life changed over the course of that year. Physically and emotionally I suffered. My wife ultimately asked for a divorce. My work suffered. And I felt like a prize-fighter who goes into the ring with his arms down. Getting over all that required a spiritual exorcism of sorts. That, and a decision to try and stay clear of those very things which had once seemed so darkly fascinating.

By the next year, even while things seemed to have resumed their strangely usual order, I was now mindful of what not to do, where not to go. And it's funny in a way, but charted from that very point in time until my last sojourn to Loch Ness, I cannot say with certainty that the "Crowley Curse" was not working its sinister power even yet.

That autumn I returned to Scotland, undaunted. And apart from my now somewhat habitual routines, I decided one afternoon to make a circular tour around the loch. In doing so, I naturally became aware of Foyers just ahead, and also the spectral presence of Boleskine House. With that in mind, I made my plan. For even as I would come within range of that damned place, I planned to gun it, not stop, not pause, but to drive past Crowley's ill-fated manse with as much haste as possible.

When I came within the Foyers limits, I kept my eyes on the road and felt my foot pressing the accelerator pedal, just as planned. Within minutes I saw the grim landscape of the Boleskine burial ground ahead and to my left. And there on its higher plain as I knew, hovered Boleskine House itself. I thought of "Hell House" in the movie of that name. And I also began to replay what I'd remembered of Winnie Carey's tale of Father Ormand and his banishing ritual. Had it worked? Or not? Frankly, I had no way of knowing whether Boleskine's demon-fouled atmosphere had been cleansed and cleared by the likes of that unorthodox cleric. And what in fact if the attempt had only served as a taunt, like forcing a stick into a lion's cage?

Now however all I did know was that the only power I personally possessed involved steering clear of trouble. And yet here I was again, quite literally on that rustic highway to Hell.

And just as I came in sight of those two uncomfortable visions to my left and right, it happened. Suddenly, and as some like to say, out of nowhere, a large lorry loaded with timber pulled out of a side lane. Literally lumbering its way forth, the combination of the vehicle's huge presence and its rising speed had left me trapped. And now, as if some great Monty Python-ish hand had come down out of the clouds to say "*You Shall Not Pass*," I was slowed to a near stop. And then the lorry hit its air-brake. I braked as well. And there all at once I sat, at the very place I most dreaded once having been. Between, as you might say, the devil and the deep black lake. *Boleskine House. Hell House.* Now a strange inner voice seemed to be saying, *Welcome back. We've been waiting.*

When I got going once more the thought impressed itself upon me that perhaps indeed there was something inexplicably elemental about the world's most monstrous lake? And if there was not, perhaps it was just the belief that this atmosphere was redolent with darkness and fear and something quite old, almost risen to the surface. And whatever it was had taken root long, long ago. In those wooded hills. In that water. And yes, even in myself. For I had little doubt that I had been infected and somehow hurt, psychically and emotionally, in the wake of last year's now publicized episode. How then to explain the bad luck, the emotional sadness, even the ending of a marriage? Was it the fault of some external entity, or merely the by-product of my own stubbornness or need to play the Hero Game, and to insist upon going down into the darkness?

If indeed I ever fancied myself in the Heroic mode of Joseph Campbell, I was always aware of the risks. What if I did succeed in penetrating the depths, but then couldn't rise up into the light to tell the tale? That thought occurred to me early on, and upon that afternoon before the old house, even as it did some six years later, when I nearly drowned in the loch's peaty depths. And perhaps for those reasons, my feelings regarding this particular chapter of my investigative career have been tempered by a kind of new awareness. I have carried this sense through a number of strange experiences. And as you will see, one of those nearly left me completely unable to continue.

As far as Crowley the Mage and his magically-infested Boleskine, I have no problem admitting no desire to see them again. Matter of fact, upon returning home after the last exploit as described, I took that small black shard claimed a year earlier and hurled it into the deep river water before my house. They say spirits cannot cross running water, and I'm counting on the fact that the currents which move out to Lake Erie will seal the deal.

Or so at least I'd hoped at the time.

AN IRREGULAR POSTSCRIPT: Only days after writing my "Boleskine" chapter, I learned that upon the afternoon of December 22, 2015, plumes of dark smoke were seen emanating from Boleskine House, clearly visible from the adjacent shore of Loch Ness. In consequence, Aleister Crowley's damnable manse went up in flames— supposedly on account of faulty heating equipment. Then in the summer of 2019 another blaze occurred, this time ascribed to arson.

On the heels of these two acts of destruction, the most recent chapter has offered a kind of phoenix-like aspect to Aleister Crowley's wicked abode. In 2019 the so-called Boleskine House Foundation, allegedly a registered Scottish charity was established in consideration of Boleskine as a "heritage landmark." As may be learned even now as work slowly progresses in 2021, the charred stone 18th century structure, now gutted and charred, has been targeted for future restoration. From the haunted locus of its flame-ravaged shell, its present proprietors have expressed their aim of re-creating the "wickedest man on earth's" demonic sanctuary and have aimed to reinstate Boleskine to its "historic symphony."

One cannot help but wonder whether the organized efforts now afoot are not rooted in re-establishing a renewed "sympathy" not with history as much as the Devil. That they should do so fully aware that their hero, the Great Beast himself, admitted to failing to contain and control the evil he's succeeded in summoning. And there are those no doubt who might agree. Further, and at the risk of sounding like one of Dennis Wheatley's devil-defying fictional characters, any price must be paid to forestall such demonic works. That may even include the second-phase of Boleskine's trial-by-fire, possibly by the hands of someone who was other than a vandal bent on arson? I suspect more the latter possibility. Moreover, I find no joy or keen interest in someone's wishing to raise, instead of razing, Crowley's destroyed occult laboratory. I mean, didn't we see this in the wonderful old Rathbone-Lugosi film "Son of Frankenstein?" For even as the mad doctor's lab was restored, so too was the horror it originally inspired.

So much then for the living and/or posthumous memory of Crowley (pronounced as in "un-holy") the self-styled apocalyptic Beast 666 and Arch Magus of Loch Ness. I suppose that only time will present us with the possible postscript to his story.

In closing, to this writer Boleskine House has always represented nothing but a nest of perverse darkness waiting to be re-awakened. Much like Britain's be-legended Borley Rectory, which after its destruction (by fire, by the way), its nefarious influences lingered on.

Likewise, the memory of whatever elemental forces once lurked on-site overlooking the loch may suggest that in future time something like a black phoenix might be summoned up from the ashes.

As a sort of last thought for now, we return to the matter of how one measures the un-measurable? Moreover, how by making the "unknown" known we achieve something which furthers us as intelligent beings?

Notwithstanding the "lure of the hunt" and the damnably perplexing presence of what even now seems to resist the best-laid plans of Man and Technology, the question to be begged is: if we should find the Monster of Loch Ness, what would or should we do with it? As in the case of such seemingly relict hominids such as the Yeti or Sasquatch, its dangerously likely that only by killing one would the questioners have their answers. Short of that it is a matter of trapping or confining the specimen. That on its own presents its share of environmental, if not humane jeopardies. So then, what do we gain by capturing a surviving-presumed-extinct species? Do we clone them, if we can? Do we create a new sort of zoo, or likely, theme park? Remember how things turned out in the "Lost World" films.

So perhaps it's better not to meddle. Or to risk visually encountering something majestic or miraculous without needing to place it within your cross-hairs? After all, just because we've never known the feeling of being hunted ourselves, doesn't mean it might not ever occur.

So let's just hope that if ET or his/its kind ever makes Earth-Fall, they don't decide to pursue, contain, or destroy the planet's denizens. Better perhaps for them simply to enjoy the sensation of the Observer, rather than the Hunter-Conqueror, don't you think?

The author keeping watch at
Castle Urquhart, Loch Ness

16
Farewell to Loch Ness?

Now then, after a rather darkly depressing interlude, one final story about Loch Ness. It's been conjured from a comment which actually began this memoir. Spoken by my grandchildren, in the heat of having seen some suggestion of "The Loch Ness Monster," they were apprised by their mother that their grandsire had not only visited the famous lake, but actually gone in search of its incredible beastie.

But by now I have learned not a few lessons. Among them is an awareness that in its original sense, the word "monster" signified "monstrum," or something rather marvelous. That said, then, allow me now to state that I continue to harbor a number of less difficult, if not far less "monstrous" associations for that most famous of the world's legendary lakes. And one of these concerned a gentleman I'd met on my first trip over in 1976. His name was Alec Menzies (pronounced "Ming-eez") and he was the pier-master of Urquhart Pier, near Drumnadrochit.

Old Alec had become a vital part of the Academy of Applied Science efforts to "pick the loch." In his capacity as owner of the pier site from which much of the computerized sonar, strobe, and photographic apparatus had been based, he had many stories of his own to tell. One of these he shared with me on a rainy day as the two of us sat alone in a weathered Quonset hut along the water's edge. I remember looking through its small window and seeing the tethered frame raft bobbing in the Scottish wind and rain. Inside the hut the two of us were dry, even as we listened to the steady tattoo of the drizzle beating down upon the corrugated rooftop.

I'd asked Alec Menzies, who was 75 when I last saw him, if he'd ever "seen the monster?" His answer was disappointing, at first at least.

"No, I never have" he said, smiling and shaking his threadbare grey head. "But you know, my father saw it, and my wife did too. But she doesn't like talking about it."

I understood something of Mrs. Menzies' sentiments. There was something about the subjective experience of seeing or encountering something which logic and reason and day-to-day living says cannot exist. But if you have seen such a thing you have been given your *entree* into a strange fraternity. Moreover, by inhabiting that zone you will also learn that no one, apart from others who might share your encounter, would truly understand. This in my view was much akin to religious or mystical experiences, or certainly of those who claimed to have witnessed UFO's or ghosts. But here again it depends upon the "experiencer." There are all varieties of those as well.

Once many years ago I was sitting in the pleasant kitchen of my landlady, Miss Peggy MacKenzie. She was flouring up some scones and I was reclining near the stove. We'd been talking about "the monster." At this point, I think, it was my second visit to that lady's comfortable and rose-trellised bed and breakfast in Drumnadrochit, Inverness-shire.

Aware that it had become a custom of mine to interview any supposed witnesses of the loch's greatest mystery, Peggy Mac turned to me and asked, "Would you like to meet my sister? For you know, she's seen the monster herself?"

Well I expressed a reply in the affirmative. I'd heard mention of Peggy's sister, a retired school teacher. So then, and given the presumption that certain "professional" eyewitnesses might carry more water than others, I agreed. And just about the time I was preparing to arrange the prospective meeting with the other MacKenzie, my companion added a codicil to her statement.

"Yes as I say, she's seen the Monster. But she's seen other things as well, you know."

"Has she?" I replied. "What sorts of things?" I inquired with a modicum of caution in my voice.

"Oh let me see. Well, she once saw the Black Horse of Glengarry. And you know, she once saw Jesus and Saint John walking through the cloisters at Glastonbury."

I tell that story not only for its charm, but also because it signifies something else. Firstly, one never knows who will be available to witness the remarkable. Secondly, of those witnesses, it may not be better that the observer is a "professional" than merely an open-minded and unexpecting beholder. Thirdly and last, even as I well knew by then, often enough witnesses could be "led" by the inquisitor's own seeding their experience with certain questions. *"Did you notice any whiskers on its face? Did you see two or three humps on its back? Was it blackish-blue in color, or a brownish hue?"* And after all this, the key lesson to be learned at Loch Ness, that Mount Everest of "water horse" sightings: *Seeing is not necessarily believing and not seeing is not always conducive to disbelief.* Confusing? You betcha. Welcome to the world of monster hunting.

And now let us return to the scene I began by describing *Alec Menzies and I in the old hut on that gray, rain swept day.*

"But given that so many people have come here, literally to your front yard" I said, "hoping to see Nessie. Wouldn't you like to see her, or it, for yourself?"

The pier's owner turned a weathered eye upon me as he considered my words. I recall we were in a small Quonset at loch's edge listening to the tattoo of the Scottish rain beating a tattoo upon the hut's roof.

Within arm's range was a small barrage of electronic instruments brought here by Dr. Bob Rines for his ongoing monster quest. The bulk of that machinery now seemed at rest, as if hibernating. Still there were a few winking lights which I deduced were in touch with the umbilical line that ran out from the hut and below the peaty surface toward the floating object out there in that dour, dark water. And upon the raft was affixed a barrage of strobe lit cameras which could be activated if anything sizable crossed their path. Of late, Menzies said, there was a good deal of what he called "spurious triggering of the mechanism."

When I asked what that meant, he told me it amounted to the sonar instruments recording the passage of something crossing its field. When that happened, the cameras would activate and record this intrusion before its lens. But of late, the "spurious triggerin'" signified something tripping the mechanism, but with no tangible evidence to show what it had been. This, no doubt, lent credence to what I'd heard of as the Ness creature being a "bogle," or a sometimes insubstantial entity which could be seen or recorded, or which might the next moment just as easily vanish. But how was it that the singer Donovan once put it?

"First there is a mountain, then there is no mountain, then there is."

Likewise, such reports were increasingly being made about Unidentified Objects, seemingly able to appear, singly or in formation, hover, then vanish suddenly, only to reappear elsewhere. But was Nessie an extraterrestrial? No, I mused, more like a submarine zoological anomaly, according to scientists, if she, he, or it was anything. But then again, and as the ancient traditions of my ancestral homeland liked to tell, there were "golochs" and "water horses" of all sorts in these hills and waterways. This was all the more true at Loch Ness, where,

"the horny goloch's an awesome beast,
all supple and scaley, he has twa horns
and a handful o' feet, and a forkey
tailey,"

"Would I like to see it before I finish?" old Alec said, repeating my last question to him. "Oh, I suppose that would be the grand slam, of the thing." Saying this he sighed and I watched his glance leave our place and drift out toward the peaty depths.

"But do you know what I'd like to see most?" he then asked me.

I awaited his answer with a sense of honest eagerness.

"I saw Halley's Comet when I was a wee lad. I was showin' my grandchildren a picture of it in a book. And they say it's comin' back sometime soon, about Nineteen and Eighty-Six. Well, I'd like to see that again." (Author's note: I'm glad to tell you he did!)

The old fellow's remark touched me. Something in his voice, or those bespectacled wizened eyes were both precursors of the future. For on one far-flung day I too would grow old thinking of the mysteries in my life.

But that afternoon at loch-side, speaking to that Scots elder, I as the intrepid investigator and seemingly self-licensed seeker of the legendary creature had an insight of sorts. This was that whatever one chose to look into, the hunter himself was doubtless changed. Yes, or altered by travel and by difficulty and by the experience of taking yourself out of your safety zone, if only to possibly violate it over and over again, even as I had chosen to do. *Och aye, tis so.*

And at the beginning of the beginning, I too had pilgrimed to this legendarily haunted place where Unreality was said to dwell. At first I had sought out those persons whose personal encounters had forever altered them. And made them unique, if not oftentimes, alone. And they in turn had unexpectedly changed me. Although even at the time I would not know what such a sea-change could mean until a year later. For on that occasion and at Loch Ness I had my own encounter. And like those Christian or other skeptics altered into belief and action by their personal experience, I too was transformed from within. And as a consequence, now as Conan Doyle once said of his witness to the supernatural,

"*It's not something I think. It's not something I believe. It's something I know.*"

So it was that my new "investigative" efforts initially found me at Loch Ness. But not only once. No, for in the wake of 1976 my appetites for adventure in the land of my ancestor would return me there, and to the placid village refuge of Drumnadrochit, in '77,'78,'79,' 81,' 82,' 83,'84, and last of all, in nearly literal terms, in 1985.

My final occasion of returning to the land of my forefathers was on its surface, exciting. But at a literally lower level of concern, it proved nearly deadly. Dori and I had recently married, and I was eager to show her that part of the world which had so attracted me, over and over again. So I suppose you could say the trip to the loch was a kind of additional honeymoon.

Upon that final journey, I managed to achieve a great dream of actually scuba diving the loch. However, unwittingly as well I would willfully compromise what my lessons in SCUBA training and underwater navigation in Canada's Bruce Peninsula had underscored: I violated the tenet of utilizing only checked out and expert equipment. Ergo, when I borrowed a leaky wet-suit and a mask, regulator and fins from a chap in Inverness, I had no suspicion my breathing gear would fail about fifty feet down in the murk. Fortunately for me I was not alone in that epic and nearly lethal dive. Keeping me company on that dark and ominous day was Gordon Menzies, son of Alec, the master and owner of Urquhart Pier.

With borrowed equipment I suited up against the chill of that gray afternoon, even as my wife stood above us looking down upon our diving platform. Nor can I lie and say I hadn't been harboring a dozen or so grim presentiments about "going down." But I'd tried to console myself that after a bit of sunnier snorkeling experience in the Caribbean and elsewhere, quite naturally Loch Ness stood miles higher as deeper in mystery, if not in literal terms.

To make the story as brief as possible, Gordon and I both went down. We were perhaps a dozen feet below and making a diagonal course through those peaty depths when it happened. Literally moments after I'd felt my tank shift on my back as I followed my companion down by taking note of the muted beam of the underwater torch in his hand, the trouble began. It's easy enough to describe when the rhythm of your own breathing is your closest companion under such circumstances. Normally it's just a matter of calming down and forcing yourself into a Zen-like state of calm. And as you do this, your beating heart and the wind-tunnelling effect of your own respiration seems to even out. But not then. For suddenly my inhalations seemed impeded. Next thing, I was aware that my borrowed regulator, which is quite literally a diver's lifeline, was somehow faulty.

It's an elementary but vital lesson every prospective SCUBA student learns that you don't survive even at a moderate depth by holding your breath. That is Taboo Number One. And why not? Simply because given your equipment, to do so is tantamount to your lungs being popped like a paper bag full of air.

Short story shorter, I did my best to signal to Gordon that I was having difficulty. He meanwhile continued to head down, which left me hovering there, the only visible sight his phantom beam and the scant form of my own gloved hand before my mask. So I did the only thing I could, even as I heard my breath rattling through the oxygen tank's mouthpiece. I sensed that in only moments my literally last breath would signal a deadly moment. And so I did my best to paddle upwards toward the already dark light of that late summer's afternoon. But even as I did my best to power the long fins on my feet I'd become aware of a leaden feeling in my thighs, as if something were pulling me down. That's when I also became aware of two things. The first was the sight of Gordon, an experienced diver known to dangerously dive these waters alone. Now however he seemed to have taken note of my distress, and he was moving toward me. In the golden beam of his torch however, I could see something else which disturbed me nearly as much as my own dilemma. For Gordon appeared to be experiencing some problem of his own.

The second thing I knew was that the makeshift weight belt tied to my waist and the tank on my back were both now ballast of a sort. I needed to shed both of these if there was a chance of reaching the surface. Struggling and trying to push back a wave of panic, a few words entered my mind. *Is this how it was all meant to end?* I asked myself.

Yet even as I felt Gordon making welcome physical contact with me, I noted something else he too seemed to be flailing about, as if we were both in the grip of something fearful. Yes, he the seasoned expert and I the adventurous holiday diver. But now both of us seemingly in the thrall of perhaps the most mysterious lake in the world.

I did my best to honor those possible final moments of my life. And truly, I tell you here that that business about "your life flashing by" was genuine to a degree. For in those dangerous seconds I witnessed images of my first trip to Scotland over a decade ago, and of my many returns to the loch. But now that lethal newsreel was also accompanied by the sound of my expelling breath, if not the chaotic notion that after so many forays, this one was bound to be my last.

Before my borrowed regulator failed entirely I managed to shed the anchor-like weight digging into my shoulders. Then with the borrowed tank and the damnable belt of iron undone I somehow managed to churn to the surface, having negotiated about ten feet from where we were when hell had broken loose. Gordon had reached the surface as well, but there was something in his aspect that betrayed his loss of cool.

Finally I remember the feeling of standing on drier land at last. Moreover I was also borne down by the sensation of having failed in this, my self-imposed and long-awaited mission. Also there was a tidal wave of damning my own insolence or bravado for making a SCUBA bid after such a while, and of having memorized how it should be done.

For years I'd compensated my own doubts by reminding myself that I'd chosen the Bruce Peninsula training program simply because it bore a close resemblance to diving the Ness. Murky, chilly waters. Low visibility. The very opposite of those sun-gilded balmier waters of Jamaica , Bimini, or Barbados.

My inner anger subsided slightly when I allowed Gordon to check out my regulator. When he did so he looked at me with a face resembling a blank mask.

"The regulator's jammed" he said. And no doubt as he said it he recalled that the chap he'd sent me to in Inverness had provided the equipment supposed to safeguard my life.

A day later I returned the recovered tank, weight belt and regulator to the garage in town. Indignant to say the least, I described what had happened on my first attempt using his gear. When I finished by asking my middle-aged listener if he hadn't checked the regulator out, he merely replied, "Well, ye said ya wanted to rent some gear. So I rented it." And that was it. No, "sorry you almost lost your life monster hunting." But spoken or not, I knew that to be the grim reality. And when and if I rarely hear it said that "the loch never gives up its dead" I think of that day.

I sometimes look back upon the exploit as described and freely admit that I have never gone back to "pick the loch." But I do still have the occasional waking or traditional nocturnal nightmare about diving into that golden vat of ginger-ale colored water, and of going down where a man doesn't belong. And of nearly paying the price for my presumptions. And all for what? For having the opportunity of being down in that night-blind world, if only to be alone there with my ancient and chronic quarry? That was probably it. An ounce of bravado seasoned by a tincture of fear. In other words, the perfect recipe for adventure and or death.

It's been years since I thought seriously of going back to Scotland and to that near disastrous scene which nearly became the grimmer postscript of a memoir which would never be written. But perhaps as we grow older and possibly wiser we come to understand our limitations, if not to feel free to record them. And yet still I find myself wondering if something about that great, primordial lake had a lesson to teach me from the start? Also, whether by meddling at Boleskine or elsewhere I had let myself in for a metaphorical hand-slapping? Yes, as if something had said to me all along, *there is something here which is deeper and darker than you've allowed for. Trifle with it at your own expense.*

But there is no getting past the fact: I did choose to "trifle" with whatever existed (and exists) at Loch Ness, beneath those haunted hills and waters, so beautiful but in a trice, so elementally fearful. And I did so willingly going beyond the vale of my comfort zone, if only to see and hear something else. And because I chose to do, that place continued to summon me back again and again, like some banshee-like siren calling me home.

But there are moonlit nights when I sit on my Grosse Ile porch and stare out at the expanse of the Detroit River which passes between the Canadian shores of Amherstburg nearly a mile away and my own "Gray Gables." And there are times when I catch the midnight, phantom shape of something out there, swimming its way toward Lake Erie and the darkness. Often enough that is a log or even a deer chancing the currents. Nevertheless this inevitably and always reminds me of another, more legendary lake an ocean away which now seems full of ghosts.

And there are also times when as I squint back at the darkness I imagine the ghost of a young fellow togged out in a hooded khaki jacket and wool cap, alone in a rocking boat with little more than a modicum of electronic equipment to keep him company. That, my friends, was me. And in a way in my mind's eye that specter of myself is still out there. Younger, certainly. Perhaps less wise. But I know him well. He was also ironically and Catholically confirmed with the Christian hagiarchic name of George which he would wear in secrecy for many years to come. Yes, long before he could ever harbor the slightest thought of that saint's connection with his own quest for a modern-day dragon.

But of course that day would arrive. And then, quite voluntarily, my *doppelganging* younger self would choose to cross the ocean for the chance to cling to the surface of a nearly 126 fathom deep lake, in hope that something out of legend would choose to sound from its night-blind haunts. If only as if to say, *yes, I am here after all. Even as you have believed.*

And here again another of those strange Doylean nexus-points which have roped me into their odd radius. For as a Sherlockian I went to Loch Ness, as if to further Sir Arthur's own umbilical, exploratory reach. And by doing so I had carried his speculations, begun on a rugged and unexplored South American plateau to an ancient and glacial fresh-water lake, where what his skeptical colleague E. Ray Lankester had described as "extinct animals" might even now reside.

And like Challenger I had chosen to visit that not lost, but still undiscovered world, and once, even to probe its depths (at the risk of my life) to better understand its secrets.

For such feats of foolishness, or as some might once have termed them, gumption, I have to state that I both like the shape of my younger incarnation, much way a father might value a son. Nor can I fail to credit that same lad who in his own fledgling moments had been sorely tried by nightmares; enough so in fact, to dare them to come forth. When they did not, he chose to edge further into the darkness as if in pursuit of those night-gaunts. And looking back at that shadow quest now, it feels like the recollection of something one was meant, if not born to do.

That young man's path had also been paved along the way with imagery, upon the page as well as the cinema screen. Those then were his gauntlets, tossed down before he'd known why. But he remembers them as well as yesterday. Many of them he'd absorbed within a twenty-minute walk from the house on Wakefield to the darkened, Saturday afternoon chapel of the Berkley Theater. And there in darkness, amid so many other scarifying tableaus, he would be marked forever by flying saucers, a man turned into fly, if not by the hulking "Beast From 20,000 Fathoms." And had he not thrilled as he saw its saurian head rising up before him in black and white from the depths? Did he not see it scaling a rocky shore and assailing a lighthouse like a toy? He had. And as a consequence nothing had so literally baptized him in its terror in days to come when he would find himself in any sort of deep water. Nothing, in fact, until the later advent of "Jaws," but in a safer, chastened time.

Curiously too and as I must confess, childhood evocations of the Beast were re-conjured as I'd first prepared for Loch Ness. Even more so, when initially finding myself in a boat, in the wee hours, and with a Grand Canyon's worth of night-blind water beneath me. For then as Baskerville once warned, were those "powers of evil exalted." Accordingly, I had visualized my own version of prehistoric horror suddenly invading my reality. And it had all begun, explicably enough, when that many-fathomed beast had stalked across the screen. Which makes me marvel all the more how little that open-mouthed youth could suspect that in the far-flung future not only would he be befriended by the great writer Ray Bradbury, who had conjured the story upon which "The Beast" had been based.

My reveries of Loch Ness are many and extremely personal at their quick. I find myself musing sometimes whether their panoramic imagery really occurred, or if it were all but an enfevered dream? And sometimes, conjuring it all back, I wonder if, were I back there in an instant, who and what would I now find?

Bob Rines, the founder of the Academy of Applied Science team is gone now, and so is his lovely wife, Carol. As is Tim Dinsdale, the archetypal Nessie-hunter who gave up everything to re-claim his experience of having known his first "close encounter" with the incredible. Joining them now is Winifred Carey the old seeress on the hill, who claimed she could use her magic pendulum to "spot" the creatures in the loch below her lofty cottage. Constituting that advance retinue as well is dear Peggy MacKenzie, who like her cottage-turned B&B sanctuary is no longer here. There as well is Alec Menzies, who with a submersed monster in his front yard, longed only to re-view the comet of his youth.

Oh yes, now season this choir invisible with all of those colorful, elderly witnesses who once shared with me their brushes with something that is not supposed to exist. I value all of their ghostly voices even now, and see myself joining them some day, and perhaps setting out on another black loch in search of adventure. *And once again, St. George setting out in quest of his dragon.*

And as for that "six degrees of separation" which seems ever to relate my disparate spheres of interest, what about Sherlock Holmes and the Loch Ness Monster? Well by now we've considered the ill-fated plotline of Billy Wilder's unrealized masterwork, if not its appropriately "sunken monster." But there in closing is another connection. This one comes close to the source, *vis a vis* the Baker Street Irregulars gathering, and for many years one of its most illustrious members.

I speak of no less a one than that wizard, scientist, novelist, prophet, and as his calling card still informs me, "Natural Resource," Isaac Asimov. For you see that 20th century *carte d'visite* was given to me by the man himself. We made one another's acquaintance at the 1979 BSI fete. Someone commented to Asimov that I had a curious pastime: namely, hunting the Loch Ness Monster.

I'd come prepared to answer the monster-queries, for not that long ago a New York tabloid had pictured me, my Michigan version of "221B," and an inset mock photo of "Nessie." In my pocket I had a folded copy of another similar story, this one from *The Detroit Free Press* entitled "SHERLOCKIAN DEDUCTIONS TO TRY TO UNLOCH NESSIE."

Asimov seemed intrigued by my mild repute as a Sherlockian questor of *Nesiteras Rhombopteryx.* Yet he never mocked me, or even asked if I thought the beastie did exist? And then, I'm not sure how it happened, this great man of science said "there ought to be a limerick about Holmes and Nessie." I agreed. And challenged him on the spot to come up with one.

The Great Man then asked for a piece of paper. I reached into my suit pocket and withdrew the *Free Press* article. Then undaunted, even as anyone who knew him might expect, Asimov took out his pen, thought a moment, and then began to compose on the blank side of the folded article A minute or so later he handed it back. And there, even as it remains, albeit protected under glass today, was his handiwork beside his card. It reads:

> *To Sherlock Holmes, Loch Ness's Nessie*
> *Was delightful, attractive, caressie*
> *'It's by logic and thought*
> *The dear thing will be caught."*
> *(When he caught it, what followed was messy.)*

But limericks aside, the entire chapter(s) involving my many expeditions to Loch Ness are perhaps the most evocative of my life. For it was there that fantasy became real and adventure too with a tang I'd long to scent, again and again.

And speaking of a conjunction of memories. I'm made to recall one late-night, autumnal telephone call to my friend Ray Bradbury. Somehow the subject of my Nessie hunting exploits came up, and fortunately I remembered to make an observation. This had to do with finding myself earlier on at the famous loch for the purpose of my first baptism there—and nearly my last, as my description in these pages will allow.

At any rate, I remember telling the sage figure at the end of the Los Angeles long distance line that one of his stories—among a legion of others—had seen me through from fantasy to reality and back again.

"It occurred to me as I contemplated my first SCUBA search for the lake's famous denizen, that ever since my younger days the prospect of deep waters were tempered by at least two bits of media imagery. The first of these I'd witnessed at a Berkley Theatre Saturday matinee showing of "The Beast From 20,000 Fathoms," based on Ray's classic of the same name published in 1951.

"The image of that dinosaurian beast making landfall to chew on a lighthouse stayed with me" I laughed. "It also scared the dickens out of me until the sensation was renewed when I saw "Jaws" in the late 70's. Both of those 'creature films' had threatened my sense of ever going into any water deeper than a swimming pool. However later when I snorkeled in Jamaica and even later than that, when I dared diving Loch Ness, the primal image of something huge and prehistoric continued to haunt me. And I have you to blame for the tail-end of that adventure."

At the end of the long-distance line my friend laughed with one of his "Well by God" or "I'll be damned" retorts. He also was I think impressed by my daring do, if not by the sort of child-like wonder we'd both managed to cling to. *Ghoulies and ghosties and things that go bump in the night, and even within the darkest of fathoms.*

Then of course there were the repetitive litany of my seasonal returns to Scotland's Loch Ness over the course of nine, or was it a decade's worth of years? But my I tell you, I did and still do value the memory of each and every one of those celebrations—those self-appointed Grail quests--those embarkations upon the Great Nessie Quest.

And even now I can still re-savor the drill, conjuring up the look, the scents, the tastes of those times, from beginning to end.

First the transatlantic flight from Detroit to London, followed by the night train from Euston Station. The chilly evening departure, the snug sleeper compartment. Tea and a fresh copy of THE INVERNESS COURIER and some "bikkies" the next (usually drizzly) morning as I prepared to re-enter the old world of my ancestral blood. And if only for the purpose of taking up the challenge as those before and after me would and had—to seek out the most famous of our globe's most mysterious of creatures in its own native habitat.

And next thing, with Inverness Station said to be perhaps a quarter hour away, you pull down your case from the overhead rack and extract a pair of jeans and boots and heavy corded sweater. Also the now-vintaged khaki hooded jacket as well as your favorite woolen cap. That stalking headwear had been purchased at Beauley years earlier, not far from your native hunting field. And as you well knew by now, it had been baptized by Celtic showers and Scottish mists, if not perhaps touched by a gunwale's splash of the famous loch's surface.

Before you knew it you were prepared to disembark at the station, walk 'round the corner to the car-hire agency, then to drive out of that old city where, many centuries ago, your own great granddad six times back had been allegedly kidnapped and transported to the New World. Ah God as the poet once said, I see it all now. I'm once again in the driver's seat, tooling down the seemingly wrong side of a ribbon of road through tree-clad roadways, past cottage and weir, then eventually, around a series of sprung-coiled byways against the brown rocky face of the inclining mountains. Soon everything has retreated in time and place. Home. Wife. Job. The Every Day Routine. For suddenly it's Adventure Time. And with the great Scot's city now also at your back, you are headed for the real-life equivalent of Brigadoon, dubbed Drumnadrochit, the "place behind the bridge." Before you now and just down the village road stands Hawthorne Lea, with its floral borders and neat fence. And within the house stands a rotund, gnome-like figure. This is Peggy MacKenzie, chatelaine of so many of your bed and breakfast destinations. And she will be there as always, her slippered feet slapping over her stone kitchen floor as ever-aproned, she makes the ten thousandth scone.

But it is just beyond the outskirts of "Drum Village" that the legend lives. For there as you also know is a skein worth untangling worthy of Mr. Sherlock Holmes. But now and in his stead, you are a combination of the self-appointed untangler, and the seeker. And here just as on previous occasions, you are once again Quixote, willing to trade your present for a storied vestige of the past. Yes, as once again you have donned your leaking and dented armor as you aimed your damaged lance at a cipher.

I suppose sooner or later the Loch Ness Quest reminded me of what it also was: the search for a dragon. And there I was, like my titular and spiritually confirmed namesakes, my grandfather and father, both Georges, and now I myself, entering the lists like the Christian dragon-hunting saint himself.

And at last you are there. Standing upon a mossy loch-side pier, staring outwards at those gunmetal waters, trying to scry out what paddles beneath. Or as you perch yourself off the edge of the midnight parapet of Castle Urquhart's centuried battlement, with nothing below you but night-blind waters. Or seemingly a second later, you are on them, a part of them, as your hull telegraphs each lap of the waves and perhaps something else, seemingly lurking through the veils of those limitless fathoms below.

That then is now part of my history. And just so did I once choose to take up the gauntlet and accept a self-commissioned challenge. If only to renew it with a personal supply of what Churchill likened to "blood, sweat, and tears."

And while perhaps never quite prepared to lay down my life in the name of a dangerous pursuit, I suppose I did in fact risk it often enough in the land of my kith and clan. But that was all "part of the deal." And it was part of steeping one's self in the very act of becoming one with the fantastic. That is a sensation, my friends, which I highly recommend. But only if you have what they used to call "the stomach" for it. Short of that, hug tightly to your armchair!

Farewell to Loch Ness? I hope and think not, at least as far as what I have been able to glean of its dark magic. For it was mystery that brought me there, and a growing need to delve deeply into a great enigma which summoned me back to it so many times. And why? Well perhaps only for the sake of sharing John Donne's vision, when he wrote *"Teach me, to hear mermaids singing."*

Such a siren song, if you are lucky, will hold you fast. Therefore I believe one should have at least the chance to both listen to, if not to seek the wondrous, whatever its shape may be. That then is perhaps my legacy and lesson for my grandchildren—seeing as how they asked me to teach it. So then, may they know wonder and magic and the joy of the quest.

And that perhaps is also the true secret of the loch. Just so then, even these words do not signal a final parting. But rather, *Auf weidersehn,* perhaps.

On that somewhat romantic note then, here ends my account of how both Sherlock Holmes and I willingly went up against what might well be dubbed, my dear Watson, "The Napoleon Of Monsters."

Henry Ford Community College
presents

A Trio of
Mysterious Evenings

Photo: Jerry Sadowski

featuring **Mark McPherson**
founder of the Daedalos Investigative Agency
An agency dedicated to the study of the paranomral
and the great mysteries of our world.

Henry Ford Community College
Adray Auditorium • MacKenzie Fine Arts Center

Please see reverse for program specifics

"The Man From Daedalos"
(In ghost-hunting mode)

17
ENTRE ACT:
"You Are What You're Eaten By"

Over the years I have learned that there are lessons to be learned in the pursuit of what Conan Doyle himself dubbed "the psychic matter." Some of those have been pressed upon my mind and heart in what you might well say was "the hard way." To wit, my experiences in the wake of having deliberately sought out the rustic, if not bedeviled manse of Aleister Crowley, who had been dubbed "The Most Evil Man Alive." That had left me with what might metaphorically be called some psychic scar tissue. Moreover, the Boleskine excursion came as an ancillary matter to my purpose in being in the Highlands. Perhaps something about the often dour and elemental Scottish backdrop had served as an amplifier to my curiosity, if not my fears.

It remains a fact, now seen all the better in retrospect, that I had always felt compelled by the darkness. This sensation is clearly traceable to a childhood that was riddled with my dread of the Unknown. But so too is that unexpected moment when that boy elected to dare down his demons. In fact, it seems that because I chose to challenge my nightmares that my daylit explorations of such things became expansive.

That then was no doubt put to the test in adulthood, and charted from my first venture to Drumnadrochit and the waters beyond its aged pier. For it was also then that I came to truly believe that I had arrived for a reason; moreover, that in almost duel-like fashion, I had chosen to go where the majority of my peers had and would not. Willfully then, I had moved away from the herd. That in turn would not only challenge me, but it would threaten my existence on more than one occasion over a decade's time. Consequently, the lessons I would learn were not experienced at a distance, or from the security of a comfortable armchair. No, for "you had to be there" as they say. And that for me was energizing; to go solitarily into the realm of mystery.

But back home and on dry land, I pursued the quest of seeking out the quaint and curious. Unwittingly as well I would encounter something equally monstrous far from a haunted lake in Scotland, in the form of what I've chosen to call "The Adventure of the Haunted Bookstore."

305

On this somewhat later occasion the matter at hand involved my making use of the services of another "psychic sensitive." Now however the location was an old former warehouse-turned-bookstore which still exists at the junction of Detroit's Fort and Third streets. For there and amid its other curious collections, was a recently obtained grouping of objects and personal effects hastily purchased from the estate of a woman who had committed suicide. But prior to taking her own life, she had killed her dog and then her lover. And then the final deed.

I was told by the bookstore's owner that when they had entered the posthumously grisly scene of the crime, it had been necessary to step over large bloodstains in the living room. And from that place the items which were, you might say, purchased with "blood money" had been transported to the store downtown.

But what was involved in our mystery seemed to reflect odd goings-on within the four-storied structure overlooking Fort Street. Odd noises, temperature drops, if not a general feeling of un-ease had emanated from the floor where the suicide's personal belongings had been collected and kept in a kind of metal storage cage.

I had been called into the matter and had brought with me a woman whose paranormal talents had been demonstrated to be genuine. I'll call her Marjorie. And on that given evening in late October, we entered the old building and wended our way up the old staircases through the mazelike edifice. This took a bit of time, but when at last we reached the fourth floor (where the mystery objects were kept) my friend the medium (who had not been previously informed of anything relevant by myself) suddenly "homed in" on the place, including the caged properties.

"There is great and sudden sadness here" she said. "I feel it now, and strongly."

I have failed to inform you that inasmuch as the investigation being described was on the verge of All Hallows' Eve, I'd been contacted by a major television affiliate looking for a story. They in turn had sent a camera crew to accompany my colleague and myself. That had been permissible to me at the time, but only until things seemed to feel very,

very wrong. This turnabout occurred when I'd noticed one of the camera crew inside the "suicide cage" making a comment about "what a lot of old junk." I can't tell you why, precisely, but at that time I felt, as the old saying would have it, as if we were "walking on someone's grave."

"That's it" I suddenly announced. "Kill the cameras. Shut it down. We're done here for tonight." And for whatever reason, I saw little regret on the faces of my companions. Only the look on my friend Marjorie's usually pleasant countenance, which seemed to resonate increasing discomfort and a veil of great sadness. I remember as we went downstairs and traded the inner darkness for the outer, that she turned to me and said, "Mark, I believe we may have stirred up a hornet's nest." But I didn't fully take her meaning. Although to tell the truth, I did feel as if I'd been complicit in a kind of sacrilege. That is the only word for it. A trespass. But I had no idea whether we had indeed trespassed into something forbidden or not. Not at least until the following day.

I was contacted by the bookstore's owner the next morning. He informed me that despite the fact that his building had been empty after we'd left, "something went wrong here last night." In simplest terms, what he meant was this: upon our leaving and his locking up the premises, he'd believed he'd heard strange noises from the floor above. And then of course there was the damage.

There can be no real explanation, even now, of why the fourth-floor iron doorway to the roof had been seemingly blown outward and nearly off its sturdy iron hinges. Stranger yet, whatever force or velocity had pushed at the riveted and fortified portal must have been major. But weirder yet was the fact that the industrial gauge plastic secured to prevent drafts on the inner side had been disturbed only in terms of a long vertical line or incision, running from top to bottom. And then there was the obvious fact that whatever had pushed at that door had literally propelled it open *from the inside out.*

In the days to follow our grim vigil in the bookstore, seemingly everyone involved had been affected. The station had decided against airing the piece as a bit of Halloween preview. And a member of the crew, the one who'd been pawing through the dead woman's belongings, had grown depressed to the point of resigning from his job.

307

My friend the bookstore owner quickly divested himself of the "suicide collection," which seemed at least to quiet down the nocturnal high-jinks a bit. I couldn't help wonder who or what would experience that lethal group of objects next?

My colleague the psychic sensitive told me that she had been absolutely certain that our visit had only ramped up a kind of "turbulence," which was her word for it. Later she confessed that she'd returned to the site alone, if only to try and offer a sense of peace or consolation, if indeed there had been an angry, sad, or regretful spirit still present.

And for myself? Never in my life again, I hoped, would I ever again feel a sense of that sort of "trespass" as experienced in the upper level of the "haunted bookstore." For over the course of days and weeks and even months later, I felt as if I'd been somehow wounded, or infected by a certain depressive darkness. So much so that I sought out a clerical friend of mine, and told him of the abortive investigation. Moreover, I informed him that I had felt "bitten" by some psychic element encountered in what was intended only as a casual enquiry for a holiday "pumpkin piece." But instead of that, it had managed to morph quite literally into "The Nightmare on Third Street."

It took a good bit of spiritual focusing, prayer, and meditation to get myself clear of the demons riding roughshod in my head. Moreover, there was a newly-made resolution to henceforth relinquish all efforts to walk, willingly or not, into all forms of strange and unknown darkness. *You should have learned your lesson at Boleskine,* I'd told myself. *Now is the time to get smart. And as in life, you need to choose your company carefully. Remember that line in Ian Fleming's Bond book? "He disagreed with something that ate him." In other words, you are what you're eaten by.*

And for that reason, and charted largely from the matter just described, I vowed that as a psychic investigator in the days ahead I would limit my interests to overviews and consultancies. No determined attempts at ghost-busting, or anything close to it. And why? Well here I couldn't help but to reach back to an early episode of "The Odd Couple." In that one Felix Unger is certain that his air-conditioner is haunted. To seek an answer, he visits "Dr. Clove" the supernatural expert, who was wonderfully played by Victor Buono.

After consoling Felix best as he can, Dr. Clove ends his summary by shifting gears and saying, "But keep in mind, Mr. Unger, one thing: that what you don't know can hurt you a whole lot."

And indeed, my good doctor, I believe it certainly can.

"Sherlock in Drag" A rare glimpse

18
Jack The Harlot Killer

Having embraced certain of those mysteries which appear tinged by the otherworldly, perhaps it is time to come back to earth. Or better, according to some, down to the gutter-level of the sort of horror which may be perpetrated by monsters who walk on two legs.

In other words, now let us move from the specialized realms of cryptozoology and para-psychology to what is without doubt at the apex of criminological interest. But more than that, for how to account for an evil-doer or his doings which so exceed the usual as to become of a truly archetypal level of dark power?

Like the redacted Sherlockian case of the fabled Scots "water horse," another Everest-sized and related subject is that of Holmes and perhaps the best-known serial killer of the Victorian era. But here too there are dimensions which have seemingly gone beyond the bounds of a homicidal or psycho-sexual predator. For here is a miscreant who lives on even today within the cold amber of his dark deeds. He has been imagined, glamorized, psychoanalyzed, complimented and immortalized by his many names. Call him "Saucy Jack," "Red Jack," "the Whitechapel Murderer" or what you will, but at the end of the day "Jack the Ripper" has become larger-than-life.

As we have already said within the context of "famous monsters," not all of them have snaky necks or are capable of scaling the Empire State Building. Nor are they all blood-sucking *nosferatu* or of the lycanthropic, lupine breed. Evidence instead might suggest that the greatest and truest monsters of history have been of the *genus homo sapiens*: Hitler, Dahmer, Vlad the Impaler, and of course that much-publicized but still unknown villain whose very name is legendary. This is that officially un-caught and myth-shrouded villain described by Sherlockian author William S. Baring-Gould as "Jack the Harlot Killer,"

Now I feel it's safe to say I've been closer to the Ripper than most of you. Lethally close, in fact. And while this is somewhat of a lurid and dubious claim to infamy, as you'll soon see it's true enough. And once again, I had Sherlock Holmes to thank for the experience. But such a grim association carries with it its own share of past-tense energies, if not contemporary irony. For as every faithful reader of the Sherlockian canon knows, there is nothing known to officially tie Baker Street's master sleuth to the investigation or apprehension of "Bloody Jack." Moreover, despite a number of pastiches in which Holmes takes an active interest in helping Scotland Yard find their arch-nemesis, within the official Watsonian context, Sherlock Holmes seems not to have participated in the hunt. *Or did he?*

But of course to think that (*a*) Holmes was unaware of the Ripper's atrocities, or that (*b*) he turned a blind eye to them, or (c) refused to assist the official forces in tracking down this serial-murderer makes no sense. To believe so is to refuse to acknowledge the Holmesian premise of "The Adventure of Silver Blaze," and the now proverbial "dog in the night-time." To wit, what is most significant is not what the detective did in this matter, *but what he appears not to have done* within the year of 1888.

Nevertheless the seemingly and presumably factual alternative is there, looming large. *For from all appearances, London's greatest detective and master sleuth apparently did nothing to find or stop Jack the Ripper.* To accept such a premise is definitely not only problematic, but puzzling as well. It ranks in the area of a major and inexplicable oversight with another looming question of literary note: why did the legendary William Shakespeare write nothing at all in sorrow or tribute to Britain's Queen Elizabeth I upon her death? For in 1603 when the artistic ground of London was heavy with tributes and eulogies from scribes of all ilk, why utter silence from the man posthumously saluted as the "Soul of his Age?" Unless of course all was not quite what it seemed.

If you're wondering why Mr. Shakespeare has suddenly raised his spectral head, I'll tell you. For as the subject of an ongoing series of inquiries, I've been fascinated by what many have dubbed "The Authorship Question;" *vis a vis*, "did Shakespeare write the works which bear his name? It is a conundrum which outranks a score of others. Moreover, and given the scope of what it suggests, neither can I dismiss the thought that Sherlock Holmes himself would have considered this a mystery worth looking into.

Now I suppose putting Shakespeare and Sherlock on a par is a possibly bad idea. Both have become the stuff of contemporary legend. Each has attracted a coterie of appreciators who even today freely quote their words. Both have become the subject of a tidal wave of scholarship, biographies, fictional treatments, filmed renditions, if not purely historical assessments of their skills. And in the case of both "Gentle Will" and Holmes, both leave in their wake a sort of secular worship. Oh and there is of course one final, and I think, quite vital point to be made about these two gentlemen: *according to many observers both past and present, at least one of them was a fictional construct.* But which one?

Notwithstanding of course the additional fact that there is more evidence to substantiate Holmes' existence than remains in provable form to bolster the life and affairs of the legendary "Sweet Swan of Avon."

Nevertheless a cursory perusal of bibliographic information reveals a great dearth of publications asserting the ilk of *Sherlock Holmes was fictional, Sherlock Holmes never lived,* or representing *The Case Against the Existence of Mr. Sherlock Holmes of Baker Street.* Contrarily however, there are today and in greater volume what began more than a century ago: countless overtures to suggest that Mr. William Shaksper of Stratford-On-Avon and London, England was either a *nom de plume,* a contemporary ruse, or ultimately the greatest literary hoax of all time. But more about that in a trice.

Returning now to that other enduring criminological conundrum in the person(s) of Jack the Ripper, we might ask a couple of basic questions. Literarily to start, why within his proper fictional context, did Sherlock Holmes *not* play a documented role in the Ripper investigation? To believe that he either did, under a veil of confidentiality, did not, or resisted the urge to resolve that mystery, demands a suitable explanation. Given his profession and those boundaries within which he operated, it seems unlikely, if not impossible to rationalize a lack of involvement here. Unless…

Secondarily there is the matter of why the Ripperologists and criminal experts have not been able to state "case closed?" Is this because the centerpiece of so much bloodshed was, to press the point, so bloody clever? Or did London's Metropolitan Police know the identity of the Harlot Killer, and suppress his identity?

In the latter regard, many conspiracy theorists have insisted that Saucy Jack was in fact a person of high ranking royal or diplomatic station. Was this then why revelation of the murderer's identity was not revealed?

In keeping with the notion that the truth was indeed outed, but placed under wraps, there is a comparable thesis suggesting that Holmes did in fact participate, but under a kind of *sub rosa*, rather than Inverness cloak of secrecy. Were this indeed the case, then who might have created that cloak? For an answer here there are two candidates which might be considered in their "official" and "unofficial" capacities, respectively. The first of those candidates is represented by the officialdom of Scotland Yard. They, if not their secret masters on any number of escalating levels of authority within the kingdom, may have harbored reasons for keeping the Whitechapel murders under a tightly guarded wrap.

The second and comparatively more modest purveyor of a well-kept secret concerning Sherlock Holmes may well have been the detective's friend and authorized biographer, Dr. John H. Watson. Here as well and at the extreme, perhaps we might factor in Watson' literary associate, Dr. Arthur Conan Doyle, or even Sherlock's brother Mycroft, who represented not only a filial connection, but also what we have been told involves an integral service to Her Majesty's Government. Each of these figures were privy to Holmes' criminological efforts, and it stands to reason that this information would doubtless have concerned the detective's possible role in the Ripper affair.

All in all, the absence of Holmes's connection to the expansive Ripper File at Scotland Yard may ultimately suggest a complicit agreement to shroud his presence in the matter. But if indeed this was so, then why?

There have been fringe theorists who believe there may be one or two explanations, *vis a vis* what may be dubbed a "Ripper cover-up" involving Sherlock Holmes. The first of these, and harking back many years to Michael Dibdin's *The Last Sherlock Holmes Story* or others, was the explanation that Holmes himself was the Whitechapel Killer.

And the second option, nearly as heinous, is the more recent thesis that it was Watson's supposed "literary agent" Arthur Conan Doyle who now stands as Suspect Number One. For in a public sense, it was he who would ultimately seem to control the flood-gates to the Holmes canon of works.

But being as it is, tantamount to blasphemy, suggesting that Holmes, Doyle, or even Watson himself was the Ripper's alter ego is to scamper down a dangerous trail in more ways than one. And without the evidence to support it, to believe that the detective or either of those two doctors possessed, like Stevenson's Doctor Jekyll, a secret and monstrous inner life.

At present there are efforts which strive to support the Doyle-as-Jack thesis, such as the fictional *The Strange Case of Dr. Doyle* by Daniel and Eugene Friedman. However sensational its premise, such novelistic presumptions do not a mass-murderer prove. It is also important to remember, I think, that as Holmes himself points out there are always hazardous consequences with guess-work. And ultimately, guessing is all those hip Ripperologists who believe in the Holmes-Doyle Connection have. And as tantalizing as the premise may be, it cannot help but resemble the far-reaching suggestions of "Who Was Shakespeare?" which have included even the "outing" of Queen Elizabeth I as the artful culprit.

But as ever, sensation often reigns as king. Moreover, the controversy of suggesting that any "hero" is subcutaneously a king villain is always good for ticket sales. In other words, to suggest that that which is deemed one thing is in reality something else. We find this in the extreme within literary quasi-religious tradition, as when Nikos Kazantzakis' *Last Temptation of Christ* made Jesus a reluctant victim of his own humanity, or D.H. Lawrence's *The Man Who Died* as it offered up a Jesus who despairs upon failing to die on the cross. And of course there is that greatest bit of fodder for alternate possibility, Dan Smith's *Da Vinci Code,* wherein Jesus of Nazareth survives crucifixion and becomes a man with wife and family. As such, I cite this trio of literary and fictive works purely as the extremity of presenting something presumably sacred as profane or mundane.

For a good many reasons we don't like our myths or our facts tinkered with. But without a doubt and within the criminological realm, it is the historical and evidential dearth of closure in the Jack the Ripper Case which has allowed it to grow incrementally since 1888.

315

Earlier I mentioned the 1965 film "A Study In Terror" as an attempt to place Sherlock Holmes squarely within the Ripper inquiry. Likewise in 1979 "Murder By Decree" starring Christopher Plummer as Holmes and James Mason as Watson took up the matter once again. But this time, and echoing a controversial line of country echoing author Stephen Knight's sensationalized 1976 work *Jack the Ripper: The Final Solution*. Here was the seminal linkage coupling Saucy Jack and the Royal Family for all to see. Moreover, an equally longstanding contention has existed that high-ranking Masons within the British Government, if not the Royal Family itself, had fostered their own peripheral purpose in the slaying of at least five London Street whores to keep the truth from being outed.

I have long been intrigued by the idea of "how would Sherlock Holmes have tracked the Ripper?" One of my first inklings here reflected a period Victorian engraving showing two gentlemen on the trail of a rather scurrilous looking character. But it is the fact that one of these trackers is wearing a deerstalker cap, cloak, and bears decidedly handsome and Paget-like features. Was this, I mused, an early clue of Holmes' participation? Perhaps not. For we have already discussed the how and why of Holmes's particular headgear, and how it was introduced, *vis a vis* his *Strand* illustrator's own partiality for the fore-and-aft, ear-flapped bit of headgear. Adding confusion to coincidence here as well is the fact of an early eyewitness report of a Ripper suspect, who was described as wearing—you guessed it—a "Sherlock Holmes cap."

Now unless you aren't aware of the true and iconic provenance of the Sherlockian deer-stalker, or you might reach to the theory that artist Sidney Paget was the real Harlot Killer, then one needs look elsewhere. Consequently and as Bob Clark, who produced and directed "Murder By Decree" suggested, that direction might very well have led to the stately gates of Buckingham Palace, if not the regal corridors of Whitehall itself.

One theoretical school of thought has purported that Queen Victoria's grandson, Edward the Duke of Clarence had trifled with at least one prostitute and possibly impregnated and married her. Ergo and to cover up such a royal indiscretion, a chain of the streetwalker's confidants were serially exterminated by the Queen's own Royal Physician, William Gull. And further masking such low going's on in high places, it was allegedly a corps of high-ranking Freemasons in their roles as police and governmental officialdom (including Randolph Churchill, Winston's papa) that supposedly put a lid on it all. But not of course before the outraged consulting detective in "Murder by Decree" ran the risk of revealing his dark knowledge to the culprits themselves.

While I liked John Neville's somewhat crisp Rathbonian severity in "A Study in Terror," I confess to harboring a true and chronic affection for Christopher Plummer's more pleasant-yet-stern Sherlock. Abetted by an avuncular and somewhat unwitting James Mason as Watson, these two excellent actors assayed the famous friends in a slightly humorous light. For his sins however, Plummer was adept yet perhaps too good looking for S.H., if not inadvertently humorous in its own pawky fashion. This quality had already been well presented by Robert Stephens, who offered an affable alternative to Rathbone's earlier and Jeremy Brett's later laser-sharp demeanor.

But as for Christopher Plummer's key strength in "Murder by Decree?" I believe that was demonstrated by his decidedly heroic demeanor and ultimate sense of justifiable outrage at the picture's end. That and the emotional chinks in his otherwise firm armor spoke highly for this unusual performance. And for the sake of that I believe he succeeded in promoting the value of Sherlock Holmes as one man willing to risk all to go up against a Mount Everest of evil. Moreover, taking up the quest in presenting Holmes the avenging protagonist, Clark's film evokes a bygone time and place seated on the cusp of a moment where the Devil might still be opposed by one true and angelic champion. But only barely. For as the Defender of Right, Sherlock Holmes is himself not without flaws and his own umbrous nature. Nor is he immune to realizing that even Good must acknowledge the existence of Evil, which is capable of working its own devices.

I had the personal good fortune to offer an introductory course in Sherlock Holmes a few times at Detroit's Wayne State University in 1979. The curriculum here involved the standard Holmes Canon, as well as a limited number of those re-workings and pastiches which had existed since Conan Doyle's day. Involved here were Sir Arthur's friends Robert Barr, John Kendrick Bangs and even his brother-in-law, "Willie" Hornung, each of whom played fast and loose with the sage and saga of Baker Street. Such efforts were followed into the 20th century by such revisionist Holmes vehicles as Nicholas Meyer's *Seven*

317

Per Cent Solution, which offered a neurotic and drug-bedeviled Sherlock Holmes seeking salvation at the hands of another master deducer, Sigmund Freud.

I was very pleased indeed to welcome director Bob Clark as a special guest for one of my evening classes at WSU. In Detroit to promote his film, the director and producer of "Murder by Decree" was affable and eager to talk about his Baker Street researches. Ironically as well, little did I know that the following year I would have the distinct pleasure of meeting Clark's "Sherlock Holmes," Christopher Plummer at the annual Baker Street Irregulars meeting in January. That meeting, coming on the heels of my brief audience with Rathbone in '64 and prior to confronting Brett more than two decades later, felt momentous.

Harking back to Baring-Gould's *Sherlock Holmes of Baker Street,* I might point out that the Ripper matter was therein ad*dressed* (in literally transvestite fashion) when Holmes disguised himself as an East End drab and is approached by "Jack" himself, who turns out to be Scotland Yard Inspector Athelney Jones of *The Sign of Four.*

And speaking of a real Ripper hunter, while in London in 1979 I had the eagerly awaited privilege of meeting Donald Rumbelow, author of that well-respected compendium, *The Complete Jack the Ripper.* Our relationship was friendly and reflected a mutual liking for Sherlock Holmes. Moreover, Rumbelow, who was a warrant card-carrying member of the City of London Police and curator of the City of London's Black Museum, was a respected author and remains today a frequent media commentator on the subject of Jack the Ripper.

Years later when we were discussing his book, Don Rumbelow shared his own opinions as to the "best candidate" for Jack the Ripper's identity. His suggestion surprised me, frankly. But no more so than when, after dinner in his home in London's suburb of Catford, my companion left the room and returned with a long object wrapped in protective cloth. He placed it in my hands. Sitting there, I rested the concealed object on my lap.

"Unwrap it" my host requested. So slowly, but with a sense of trepidation, I did exactly that. What lay beneath was a long and thinly bladed knife, its blade in two separate pieces upon the cloth now on my lap. I looked from it to my companion in stunned silence.

"What you're holding is a very dark relic, indeed," said my host. That is a post-mortem knife, and there is compelling evidence that it was connected with the Miller's Court slaughter of the prostitute Mary Kelly, the Ripper's last official victim. She was found in her squalid room, her leg slashed to the very bone. Her breasts had been removed, as were her kidneys and arranged in orderly fashion upon her bedside table."

Hearing the author of *The Complete Jack the Ripper* offer this grisly narration, my mind returned to certain of those incredibly horrific photographs which had been taken of Jack's victims. Many were postmortem mortuary shots, but the one of Mary Kelly had been captured in that "squalid room." Once you saw something that terrible it was difficult to forget it. And I could not.

But moreover, having poured over Don's book too many times before that occasion, my gaze fell once again to the broken-tipped article on my lap. *But could this be the very engine of destruction which had literally cut short the lives of one or more of those unfortunate harlots? Very possibly, given its provenance. And here was I, unexpectedly afforded the dubious privilege of holding this instrument of so much prospective evil, courtesy of a curator of the Black Museum himself.*

I left Donald Rumbelow's home that night after thanking his wife for dinner and he for what amounted to the most unusual post-prandial display of my life. And as a matter of more cheerful recompense for a pleasant, if not unsettling evening, I'd also brought out my gift for my host. It was a Hungarian periodical from 1908. In English the name SHERLOCK HOLMES appeared in a diagonal banner beside the famed detective's image. But it was the illustration below which captured one's attention. For it featured two figures, a hatless man and a woman in a bonnet, both of them struggling beside a tall gas lamp. The man was moustached, and was aiming a dagger or knife over the woman's head. To her credit, she clutched at her would-be killer's arms, as if to ward him off. That she might be capable was a possibility, given that both figures were of an equal height. And then the purpose of the cover illustration was made plain, as was the until-now undecipherable sub-head of "*Jack, a hasfelmetsző* ." And there it was, spelled out for the reader in literally graphic terms: *Jack the Ripper dueling with a cross-dressed Sherlock Holmes!* What a premise. And coming from a publication issued in 1908, only twenty years after the atrocities, what an inference. First off, the suggestion that Holmes was a Ripper hunter, and secondly, that he'd gone out in drag, as a prostitute, as a decoy to attract the murderer.

But now I also wondered, had this bit of Hungarian pulp fiction been the possible key to Baring-Gould's similar description of the sleuth in skirts in his 1965 *Sherlock Holmes of Baker Street?* Here too, if only as a valedictory remark, it ought to be mentioned that one of the theories offered concerning the Ripper suggested that "he" was in fact a "she." A woman killing other women? Not so astonishing a premise. Mightn't "she" have had access to others of her sex? Additionally, could she have had medical training? That was comparably rarer in Holmes' day, but possible nonetheless. And in the latter regard, it is important to cite that it was none other than Dr. Arthur Conan Doyle himself who suggested the notion that "Jack" might have been "Jill," with a hypothetical background as a mid-wife!

Needless to say, Don Rumbelow was very pleased with my parting gift, which he eventually included within a future edition of his *Complete Jack the Ripper.* We vowed to meet again, and I left his house and stepped into the darkness, wondering *Had I actually held Jack the Ripper's blade?* Then I seemed to hear another voice saying, *"the facts would seem to aim in that direction, Watson."*

I tried to shake off the mixture of excitement, tinged by a somewhat sickly feeling as I headed for the Underground station. And all I could think of, my head still full of the image of that swaddled blade fading in and out of those literally atrocious post-mortem photos, was *God rest those poor unfortunate women.*

Looking back on it, I enjoyed my time with Donald Rumbelow. I found our meeting not only scintillating, but a fascinating way of bringing an interest in Sherlock Holmes as well as the police of his day into a contemporary view. And how was that, you might ask? Well for one thing, and as Holmes himself said, with regard to his encyclopedic knowledge of the historical chronicles of crime, often enough that history tended to repeat itself. Therefore, and in almost archetypal fashion, what were ultimately referred to as "copy-cat crimes" often found their genesis in earlier, and possibly more "successful" criminal enterprise. And without a doubt, the main feature of those days tended to concern the serial killer dubbed by the modern-day media the "Yorkshire Ripper.

On the heels of my talks with Rumbelow, in the early autumn of 1980 I had the opportunity of consulting with a second member of London's police force, but on a purely unofficial basis, if you will. This was my reunion with fellow Holmesian Philip "Pip" Dalton, whom I'd first met at the Strand Hotel gathering in 1967. Here then was what constituted my first and last brush with Scotland Yard, which in collective fashion might be considered productively memorable indeed.

Apart from our mutually savored love of the Holmes stories, my friend the detective and I had much to chat about concerning the topic of the Victorian Ripper. But more than that, what seemed to spark our conversation was the matter of a five-year long spree of murders which had so far perplexed the police. So we'd begun to theorize over to what extent the modern day "Ripper" may have taken pride in becoming the 20th century avatar of his Victorian namesake? For indeed, and as the case files indicated, that grisly epithet had been awakened when the killer of eleven female victims in West Yorkshire used this as his signature.

Not unlike the extensive police dragnet for Jack the Ripper back in 1888, the West Yorkshire officials were hotly criticized for a failure to produce the culprit. This, even in the wake of supposed witness reports, letters, as well as a telephone call to the head of the investigation. In other words, the Yorkshire murderer appeared to take an obvious degree of pleasure in taunting his hunters.

I made this observation to my colleague at the Yard and offered the notion that it was perhaps not unlikely that the Yorkshire "Ripper" derived a twisted sense of honor, or even was compelled to pursue his bloody tour on the strength of Jack the Ripper's fame, or better, infamy.

"And isn't it possible," I added to Pip, "that he draws a perverse, albeit long-distance degree of archetypal energy from the deaths of those five women during the late autumn of 1888?" Moreover, I continued, had not the first of the modern-day killer's victims been taken on October 30, the eve of the eve of All Hallows? If this meant anything at all, was there a possible occult significance to his rampage?"

Now even at the time I knew that such assertions might well sound a bit off-the-grid to a police professional. And yet, and even as the Metropolitan officials of 112 years earlier had learned, no leads should be ignored, however wacky. Ergo the idea of using a psychic medium to find "Jack," or even the hypothesis that in their final moments of life, the Ripper's victims might have preserved a retinal "photo" of their killer in their death-glazed glare?

But what, as I presumptuously insisted was likely, was that the unfound killer did in all probability pride himself on being compared to his great and un-apprehended predecessor. Moreover, nor was it impossible to think he may have familiarized himself with the history of the mystery, given the fact that there'd been a number of books (Rumbelow's at their fore) to date on the case. Or was it illogical to think that in a media-based age, Yorkshire's serial killer had more of a grisly inspiration for his doings than had "Bloody Jack."

"What kinds of inspirations?" my friend asked.

"Television and the cinema" I replied. "And films, specifically." And had this conversation taken place today, I might have added, "via social media." But my remark was specific to a sort of personal study of the Ripper I'd already made in conjunction with my university course. One of those installments considered "*Jack the Ripper in cinematic fiction as well as bloody fact.*" In this same respect I'd also paid a bit of attention to how the killer had been portrayed in the movies.

As I now endeavored to demonstrate to my professional colleague, it was not beyond the level of assumption to suggest that Jack the Ripper's modern-day equivalent could well have been inspired by seeing his namesake at the local cinema. There for instance, he might have taken in a "retrospective," which could have run any of five filmed versions of Marie Belloc Lowndes' Ripper tale, *The Lodger*. These were as early as 1927 and as recent (at the time in question) as 1953.

Then of course there had been "Room to Let," a 1950 echo of "The Lodger," and ranked as one of the first "Hammer Horror" flix. This was followed in 1959's "Jack the Ripper" and another of the same name a year later. In 1965, Adrian Conan Doyle's Sir Nigel Productions released "A Study in Terror," and in 1964 a German film "The Monster of London City" was seen by a European audience. By 1971 "The

Hands of the Ripper" came out, again by Hammer Studios, and featured a plot line involving murderous Jack's daughter taking up the "family business" on her own.

Like "Study In Terror," the 1979 "Murder By Decree" pitted Sherlock Holmes against the faceless Harlot Killer. There were others to follow along this vein (bad pun, there) as well, but in 1980, the moment of my comments to my official friend, the chronological list of options were deemed "those films the Yorkshire Ripper might have seen."

As has been mentioned, by 1980 and the period being described, no one could suspect that less than a year might elapse before the moment that the "new Ripper's" reign was suddenly to end. By this time however the West Yorkshire Police believed they might have a candidate for the "Ripper" in Peter Sutcliffe, a former gravedigger with a pronounced sense of dark humor. Curiously as well, despite having been detained and interviewed nine times during police inquiries, Sutcliffe walked free. In the meanwhile the officials found themselves mired in a media circus, and nine times during the course of their inquiries, they'd held and released Sutcliffe. In the meantime, however, and not unlike the dilemma faced by their predecessors, the Yorkshire police continued to receive alleged messages from the killer, as well as conflicting reports from self-described witnesses.

Intriguingly and echoing my 'Holmesian" discussion with my friend the detective, his team had known not a few of those Victorian "echoes" in the days before they got their man. For just as the long-ago killer had sent Scotland Yarders a number of letters, some of them including the greeting "Dear Boss" and signed "From Hell," they'd luridly described his last victims and predicted his next. Of course by now it had also been established that not all of those late-19th century missives had been genuine, or even from the same person, be he the Ripper or not. Unwittingly however, those letters established a precedent of sorts. Just so then when 91 years later a taped message was received by Assistant Chief Constable George Oldfield, chief of the longstanding Yorkshire investigation. On the tape a man's voice said *"I'm Jack. I see you're having no luck catching me. I have the greatest respect for you, George, but Lord, you're no nearer catching me now than four years ago when I started."*

Like a prophecy fulfilled and seemingly reflecting my fanciful discussion with my "official friend," other messages, including two from 1978 were received vainly boasting of the killer's conquests. Significantly as well, one of the last of those letters was actually signed "Jack the Ripper" and claimed responsibility for the recent murder of a 26-year-old girl three years earlier.

But it was not through any vainglorious association with his murderous predecessor that Peter Sutcliffe was finally taken into charge. Instead, in April of 1980 he was arrested for drunk driving. While awaiting trial, he killed two more women. One of his associates reported him to the police as a prime suspect. In January of 1981 Sutcliffe was stopped by the police in the company of a 24-year-old prostitute in South Yorkshire.

A cursory check revealed that his vehicle was fitted with false license plates. Sutcliffe was remanded into custody and questioned again. Further investigation discovered a knife, hammer and rope which the suspect had discarded. After obtaining a search warrant for his home, officials continued their enquiries and after finding more condemning evidence were surprised when Sutcliffe suddenly declared that *I am the Yorkshire Ripper."* Thereafter he appended his confession by giving a calm description of his numerous attacks.

At his trial Peter Sutcliffe pleaded not guilty to 13 counts of murder, but guilty to manslaughter on the grounds of diminished responsibility. He was, he said, acting as "a tool of God's will." And he claimed that the voice in his head urging him to murder had emanated from an old tombstone.

In 1981 at age 35, Peter Sutcliffe was found guilty in the deaths of thirteen women and sentenced to life imprisonment. At this time he also admitted to two further attacks. Thereafter and despite a series of abortive appeals, his conversion as a Jehovah's Witness and a series of debilitating health issues, Sutcliffe the Yorkshire Ripper remained under charge at Broadmoor Hospital where he would end his days in November of 2020.

And that concludes the story of how, in very loose terms, of course, it might be said that both Sherlock Holmes and I had our tenuous connections with "Jack the Ripper." To this day I think of how very real the Victorian mystery became for me, and especially so after my hands-on contact with that dreadful post-mortem knife. Then of course for the rare opportunity of trading theories with detective friend about how Holmes would have handled things?

It occurs to me that the Master might well have reminded us at present, just as he did his colleague back in the day, that "you can tell an old master by the sweep of his brush." Also that, as Holmes expounded in what was titled, appropriate to the time, *A Study In Scarlet,* "There is a strong family resemblance about misdeeds, and if you have all the details of a thousand at your finger ends, it is odd if you can't unravel the thousand and first."

Chronologically it is interesting to note that Sherlock Holmes made his public debut in 1887, on the brink of the societal uproar over the century's most lurid mass murderer. As if to answer such clamor over the inefficiency or ineptitude of the police, Holmes strode onto the stage. Ironically however he did not do so to take up the hunt for the Ripper. *Or did he?*

And that, to a certain extent at least, is how a 20th century avatar of the world's most famous serial killer did in part betray himself. Here too was my "brush with the Ripper," if not my private-most consultation with Scotland Yard.

And as for the original "Red Jack" himself? Officially he remains uncaught and unknown. That is, unless the truth has been deemed by "those in the know" as untellable. Nevertheless, some days I cannot avoid thinking of that blackguard, particularly if and when I chance a glance at my library corner. For there hangs a framed and printed rectangle of newsprint blazoned in blue and black. This relic was purloined (I confess it!) by me late one night in 1980 a day before I was to return home. It was the facing sheet on an empty *Evening Standard* kiosk on a lonely London corner. Given the recent substance of my interest, I took it as an omen before I decided to take it, quite literally!

And there that *Standard* broadsheet reposes today in my shadowy library corner, even as it continues to silently proclaim in glaring message in four-inch-high lettering:

THE RIPPER —NEW VICTIM

Today and gratefully so, that lurid headline no longer represents a current news event. Which makes me all the more glad it's now only a part of my own little "Black Museum."

Another Authorial (Retrospective) Aside:

Given the passage of years since my London-based efforts to pursue the dark specter of Jack the Ripper, the much-hoped-for "final solution" concerning the fate or true identity of the Victorian "Harlot Killer" has not been forthcoming. Which is not to say, however, that there haven't been claims made to the contrary.

But the Ripper chapter(s) in my own "case-book" of inquiries has something in common with certain others. In this regard I look back again to such issues as "Is the Loch Ness Monster Real?" or "Was There An Historical King Arthur and Camelot?" or enduringly today more than ever, "Who Wrote Shakespeare's Plays?"

In each of the foregoing matters, I have spent a number of years trying to try each of these cases in my mind. And as you will learn if you stay with me, within the realm of what I would christen The Great Shakespeare Duel, I have actually managed to prosecute the world's greatest and possibly fraudulent literary enigma.

So now then, moving from the subject of that immortal describer of kings to the most famous monarch of all, let's turn to King Arthur, the fabled "Once and Future" ruler. Arthur Rex. His name is redolent throughout the realms of both legend and reality.

Nurtured by that moment in the mid-Sixties when the Arthurian legend seemed to be stepping forth from the mists into bright reality, I like many others, chose to be excited by both history and mystery coming to life. Moreover, I found the notions of historical myth and its roots grounded in truth to be an amazing possibility. Ergo the idea *that there was an Atlantis. Or that there was a mysterious living creature in*

Scotland's Loch Ness. Or that there were UFO's in our skies. Or that we had the capacity to find the R.M.S. TITANIC at the bottom of the sea.

And as for whether there may have been a British king, chieftain, or war-lord known as "Arthur" or "Arthurius," or "Artorious?" One might accurately say that after a world's worth of wondering, and after compartmentalizing a staggering amount of data, my verdict is "for," rather than "against" the issue.

But perhaps the major distinction from my views of Once Upon A Time and Now, is my ability to synthesize or harmonize what I've learned. And on that basis, I do believe in an Arthur, albeit not necessarily the Excalibur-flaunting medieval monarch popularized by Malory or T.H. White. Fervently, I do ascribe to the idea of a leader among men, most likely a post-roman figure, who pushed back the tide of "barbarians" who flowed into and eventually settled within Britain—including those "pastures green" the poet Blake wrote so finely about.

Moreover, my Arthur, like my idea of Sherlock Holmes, has become rather homogenized. He is not Richard Burton or Harris. Nor is my "Once and Future King" purely British in the usual sense. Instead he is a Celt, but one who may have been best known to the Scots or the Welsh, which means in turn that the Tennysonian notion of an anachronistic and many-turreted Camelot may have been something and somewhere entirely else.

So what I'm seeking to tell you is this: while my thoughts about religion may have congealed in a legion of traditional ways, my views on 19th century murderers, Dark Age kings, or even Elizabethan poet-dramatists have been tempered by justifiable doubt based upon not only evidence, but the lack of it.

Ergo, I can believe in Jesus of Nazareth without any conflict of heart or soul. But dramatically speaking I might now prefer the Earl of Oxford as "Shakespeare." Not on faith, but upon the evidential "pro's" and "con's." Such are the by products of age, experience, and I hope, wisdom.

But I suppose it's a kind of double-edged Excalibur we're talking about here. For even as the last Presidential administration demonstrated, our 21st and supposedly enlightened century has become besieged by the unbelievable; namely, in confronting the idea that there may be more than one truth. In fact, as we were told, there may be such things as "alternate truths." In other words, "real" and "fake" news which is tailored to fit. And that, my friends, is terrifyingly Orwellian at its core.

So then, I resist falling into the comfort zone of the Stratfordians who offer us an effigy (literally as well as figuratively) of their true Bard and Sweet Swan of Avon. Forget the need to prove him. Settle back into what feels good and tempered by time and repetition. In other words, "believe what we say and trust that we're on the side of Truth."

More and more today in our much-troubled world, the matter has become "which truth?" or "whose truth?" It is an onerous burden I feel will be thrust upon my grandchildren. What remains is whether they will be able to separate the wheat from the chaff?

J.B. Rhine ("The Father of ESP") and the author (1974)

19
Why Build These Cities Glorious ...?

Throughout this memoir I've more or less confessed to what many have suspected: I took the notion of "acting on my fantasies" seriously, and often to a deep degree. Among those departures, as you now know, was the idea of imagining how Mr. Sherlock Holmes may have set his wits against any number of mysteries which surpassed even the backlog of his sixty or so recorded cases.

Therefore and as I would see the aforementioned mysteries, they might have included the likes of the Great Egyptian Mysteries, a variety of paranormal experiences, the prospect of a modern-day dinosaur alive in a fabled Scottish lake, or even the key to unlock the question, who was the provable author of the works which bear the name "Shakespeare?"

Further along as well I suppose there would be a host of other fascinations, but perhaps few of them so richly wrought or so well rooted in my earliest consciousness than the subject of the "real" King Arthur.

Now I know for many who know me and a legion who don't, certain of my interests might seem either flighty or unconnected to their brand of daily reality. That has long had the effect of "cutting me out of the herd" to a degree. Further, no one knows better than yours truly that by seeking the Unusual one cannot help but to become what researcher Colin Wilson once called an "outsider." Moreover, the very act may be considered *de rigeur* in the pursuit of the odd, the controversial, even that element dubbed the "supernatural." Here the reason also involves the fact that few among the many will empathize or share your belief, unless of course they have become "believers" themselves.

As for myself, I prefer the term "para-normal" rather than "supernatural." This, on account of the fact that I do not believe that Nature exceeds itself, any more than God out-Gods Himself. No, for that is the work of their presumptive explicators and often, despoilers.

So then and perhaps not unlike Mr. Sherlock Holmes himself, I became aware early on that the cost attached to stepping out of the line of my "normal" fellows was likely to evoke malignment, criticism, marginalization, resentment, jealousy, or just plain rejection by those ordinary persons or groups who pretend to comprise our world.

And yet there will always be those who ask "why?" or better yet, "why not?" Voluntarily, I now admit, I became one of those early on.

In discussing these things, my mind retreats back to the autumn of 1975. This era is significant to me for a major reason; namely, it may have been the final phase of my own long-term "normality."

But in that November of some five decades ago, I was newly married, had a job as a collegiate publicist, and was involuntarily ready to join the legion of my peers. There were no monsters or castles or sunken kingdoms on my horizon. No, nor ghosts or Elizabethan mysteries or religious shrouds, or even, to tell the simple truth, any beyond-the-usual fixation with the creator of that chronic literary hero of my youth, Sherlock Holmes.

As a non-traditional wedding gift from my bride's New York Uncle Doug, who happened to be a social worker, photographer, and part-time astrologist, his inspired nuptial present to us both was not surprising: it took the form of two specifically researched and well-tailored astrological charts.

I remember that day when Doug Quackenbush and I sat down at our dining room table so he could "read" my chart to me. He'd also done so for his niece, but all my attention was now drawn to what the paperwork before me suggested. This in effect was a story—my story, the reader stated, concerning those stars which had been in alignment at the time of my nativity some twenty-eight years earlier,

So I'll cut to the chase here and get to the meat of the matter. After explaining the various angles. declinations. ecliptics and whatever else astrologers like to consider, my now familial interpreter began to recite what he saw written upon my chart. And this was the gist of it.

"You like mysteries" Doug began *"You always have. Secret things. Dark things. And because of that, everything is now about to change for you. For now you're going to start looking at those things more closely. You are going to want to study them. And to see them at close range. And to do that you are going to travel far. But you will also pay*

a price for the journey. For in order to gain the knowledge you seek, you will give a great deal up. You will walk away from a good deal of what now surrounds you. In other words, you will learn to sacrifice much in order to gain much."

In its abbreviated form, that was my personalized gift. The awareness of my—what should we call it? Destiny? Fate? Prearranged course? Karma? Now and in retrospect it seems to me that upon receiving Doug's portent I was very like the fairy tale princess who was saluted, indirectly in her infancy, by a seer who came bearing news of her impending happiness and subsequent tragedy.

But the message concerning my future seemed at the time merely an oddity. For frankly enough I have to admit that at that time I suppose I was simply ready to smile knowingly if not skeptically, to nod, and to think to myself, *well, credit crazy Doug with his part-time work as a hippy-dippy star-gazer."*

But you see, more than that in that hour of time, what I had not expected to hear, or couldn't feasibly make much sense in hearing, was something that couldn't have run so at odds with my apparent new life. Marriage to my long-term *enamorada;* a terrific apartment with a lake-front view; a job I could handle, and quite literally, an uncluttered prospective future awaiting my discovery. But certainly nothing at all to do with looking for deep-diving answers to mysteries, or daring to trade away my new and normal life for the imaginative drill of tilting at windmills. And after all, why in the world would I want to give up any of the things I'd not yet had the chance to enjoy? *Home life. Walking the dog. Maybe even the prospect of starting my own family.*

But I suppose, looking back, all of that as a combination was simply "not in my stars." Or as Shakespeare, whomever he was, did write and confirm, *"the fault...is not in our stars, but in ourselves."*

And that may well account for what my longago astrological reading had portended. I cannot say for absolute certain even now. And yet if indeed there is credence to be lent to that ancient system of scrying out one's destiny from the heavens, perhaps I ought to lay the blame on the celestial framework above, rather than my new bride's counter-cultural uncle for having planted crazy ideas in my head?

But now I have no doubt that those "crazy ideas" had been germinating for quite a while. And just no doubt as Mrs. Holmes' boy Sherlock had absorbed a good deal and kept his young eyes open, so too had I. And when the time came the switch was simply flicked. Unexpectedly. Without fanfare. And in my case, all it had taken was following a series of stories in *The New York Times* concerning how a team of scientists were now in Scotland to hunt the legendary Loch Ness Monster.

And the long and short of the thing? The prophecy of those stars, if you like, came true. I became fascinated, if not fixated upon the exploration of a parade's worth of worldly and otherworldly enigmas. Ultimately that fixation took me to the deserts of Egypt and the moorlands of England and even down to the peaty depths of Loch Ness. And along the way many other Indiana Jones-ish interludes as well. And they did indeed all come with a price. What kind? I'm reminded of the wonderful Sean Connery film "Entrapment." When he shows his gallery of treasured artworks to his beautiful guest, played by Catherine Zeta-Jones, he's asked if they're all paid for?

"With blood" Connery's character sardonically replies. And I guess I might say the same. For that "price" connected with the self-made compact signed and sealed between myself and my metaphorical monsters over the years did not come cheap. No, for it was meted out instead in a marriage, in friendships, in a job, and at the expense of old lessons unlearned, and newer ones as if committed to heart. And all of this sea-change, may I add, took place not from the comfort of a snug armchair, but by seeking my quests, as my astrological chart said, "at close range."

So and without knowing it, I was involuntarily volunteering to become one of anthropologist Joseph Campbell's "heroes," who willingly went down like Theseus into the darkness after the Minotaur, then hoped against hope to return to the light to bear witness to his mysteries.

For such reasons then I suppose I could not find a better model for either conscious or sub-conscious emulation than Sherlock Holmes. Also like Holmes, but without the clinical gifts of his great brain or its application, I have sought over time to interest myself in matters which I believed others found of interest as well. Yet by doing so I have often run a gauntlet which might easily have ended with death, oblivion, or simple obscurity.

To the latter point: years ago I was approached by a local journalist who rang to say he had "heard about me" and wished to write about my peculiar and self-created avocation. Immediately sensing something troublesome here, nevertheless I allowed the meeting to take place. And when it did, and when the erstwhile reporter met that "Man From Daedalos," (the name of my investigative agency) he had an ultimate confession to share.

"You know, I write about people's jobs: he said, "and sometimes those take on odd dimensions. But none so unusual as yours. For I heard you were an author and a traveler and a kind of historical detective. Also that you dabbled in the occult and that you lived in an old house that was probably haunted. But when I got here, and I met you, I realized something else."

"And what exactly did you realize?" I asked.

"Well I realized that you were, to put it bluntly, everything you were supposed to be" the reporter confessed. "And while your house is old (Author's note: "Gray Gables" was built in 1849), it's charming. A cross between *Better Homes and Gardens* and a museum."

"But not quite the Addams Family," I couldn't resist countering.

The scribe then went on to tell me that in a strange way he was really pleased not to have been disappointed. Although as he confessed, he'd hoped for the chance to 'de-bunk' my credentials or what had been claimed on my behalf.

"For instance," he continued, "you said you were in Egypt. Well anyone can lie, or even travel there on a tour, but that's a framed photo of you with Anwar Sadat on the wall. Isn't it?" It was, I confirmed.

"And some articles said you liked going on stage as Sherlock Holmes or Sir Arthur Conan Doyle. But I find that you actually worked with Doyle's daughter. And there's another picture of you and Jeremy Brett, the actor on PBS who played Sherlock."

Another nod in his direction, then a correction.

"I have never appeared onstage as Sherlock Holmes," I said, gently informing my guest.

"But you act like him all the same. The mysteries you've investigated, and all the wonderful stuff here in your library. I've read the stories. I know that he lived in Barker Street."

"Baker Street" I inserted. "Yes, I guess there are a few similarities.

And that's how it went. And my point? Merely that sometimes when someone does something out of the usual mode, he is distrusted or even doubted for his claims or his actions. And often enough, quite rightfully so. I mean, this had to be true for Sherlock Holmes, didn't it?

And while I make no such claims, it was in choosing to interest myself in any number of mysteries, and then re-presenting them in print, or on television or radio or elsewhere, I decided indeed to "act out my fantasies." And never did I doubt that had I seen someone else do such things, I too would be interested. But also skeptical. Just as I was back in 1981 when I saw a film about a fellow named "Indiana" Jones.

That so-called "raider of the lost ark" and in subsequent exploits was either out there on a self-commissioned mission or sent out clandestinely by the government. But wasn't that the traditional image of those secret agents of the old school, who were chosen to be such on account of their solitary prowess, or because their unusual "covers" might allow them to mask a true purpose? Ergo Baden-Powell, the Boy Scouts begetter, or Richard F. Burton, the white trespasser of Mecca, or Somerset Maugham or even Noel Coward. Such fellows, known principally for certain pursuits, had also embarked on a shadowy peripheral course of danger and adventure. And for that reason, I suppose, I felt I understood those gentlemen, and maybe more than you, dear reader, could know.

But what that small corps of seekers also knew involved the price attached to adventure and to what any number of Grail-seekers know to be "the quest" in its un-ending form.

But as I've said before, you can't truly immerse yourself in a mystery unless you get your hands dirty. That proved to be my case in the mid-Seventies and for one very important reason. For if indeed you were

335

merely all talk, bombast, and a failure-to-deliver-the-goods, you'd be discarded, rejected, and reviled as a faker or worse. Or worst yet, you'd know yourself to be a failure or a fake. Therefore if you wanted to "walk the walk" you just needed to start walking. And I believe I did exactly that. And lo and behold, before long I found myself being introduced on one of Detroit's highest rated radio chat shows as "Michigan's own Indiana Jones." High praise that was, of its peculiar sort!

But this is always the bottom line: you need to leave the armchair and get out to where the people and places connected with the matters at hand are to be found. Be a news maker rather than a news reader. And after that you need to get your facts straight and keep a mind open to possibility. In this sense even Sherlock Holmes, who was capable of remaining in his seat and mentally roaming far-flung landscapes, such as Dartmoor to deduce an answer, needed to "get out of the house." And he did so, rather famously.

After removing one's self from his domestic comfort zone it is always easier to expose yourself to what may come. After that, and if you're lucky enough, you may have something to regale an audience with, or perhaps one day to share with the grandchild who may wind up on your knee. And after that? Perhaps and most importantly of all, as you draw your last earthly breath it will be in tandem with witnessing a parade of images, and of crusades new and old. Of the people and places you've known. Of the darkness and the dawnings you've witnessed. And sometimes, of the revelations you have been given to experience. And all because you once chose to strike out, to forsake the Known, and to seek instead those foreign territories of the Unknown.

In the case of Sherlock Holmes I don't think there were grand-kids in his mind, but of course he did have his Watson. And for that reason someone to state for the future, "and then he did this…"

I have been very fortunate to have met some incredibly fascinating people in my life. By my own admission I've felt something akin to Woody Allen's 1983 cinematic enigma "Zelig," whose fictive specialty seemed to involve his chameleon-like ability to meet and to merge with a score of his heroes or intimates. Or much nicer perhaps, as the Sherlockian critic Philip Shreffler wrote in *The Saturday Review of Literature* of the present volume's first edition, "…here is the life of a man who out-Peter-Panned Peter Pan and found the subtle and elusive key to playing boyhood games in an offbeat adult context. At one point he writes, 'William Shakespeare and James Bond. Throw in Sherlock Holmes and you begin to get the idea of what goes on in my mind.'"

There were and remain three figures who factored into my Never Land existence who, while not being "Sherlockian" by specific intent, were in manner and nature much akin to being a master detective. This trio includes Conan Doyle, Harry Price, and Joseph Banks Rhine. But in these cases as well, the context involved is, while that of an investigator, one largely of the psychic variety. In fact, collectively they offered the real-life counterpart in the paranormal realm to William Hope Hodgson's *Carnacki, The Ghost Finder.* And in the examples of Doyle, Price and Rhine, we also encounter what might well be deemed a trio of paranormal pioneers in the burgeoning realm of psychical research.

As I well knew however from the start, the realm of paranormal investigation was nothing in truth that Sherlock Holmes aspired to professionally explore. No, for that became more the later purview of Conan Doyle's other literary monster, Professor Edward Challenger. Like Holmes and Doyle's mentor Dr. Joseph Bell, it's said that Sir Arthur based Challenger on Sir Edward Rutherford, a real scientist. But in Challenger's case, this hard headed and bombastic gadfly would move from the topic of dinosaurian survival to Survival after Death. In this respect he was most certainly an avid convert, as was his true begetter, Conan Doyle himself. Moreover, Professor Challenger's conversion to the Spiritualist persuasion was said to be Doyle's means of promoting the cause he himself held dear. Here too we ought to be grateful that Challenger moved willingly into a sector which Holmes would deny to the end, despite his being in all probability more a student of metaphysics than even Dr. Watson described.

But here for a moment I'd like to return to that other and very real "psychic sleuth" and man of rational science I have hinted at. This was none other than Dr. Joseph Banks Rhine. I first met him in person in 1974, upon the occasion of seeking out a kind of cornerstone speaker for the Institute of Human Resources, which was established by my own Wayne County Community College. Officially speaking, it was within my role as an informational publicist (again, *Ave, Bill Rabe)* that I contacted Dr. Rhine at Duke University in Durham, North Carolina.

J.B. Rhine. His name is engraved in the metaphorical annals of those men of science who've sought to probe the Unknown. And in his case, here was a man whose legacy includes the first experimental research in 1931 into the matter of Extra-sensory Perception, the acronym of which has since become a household world. Add to that this young former botanist's exploration of many aspects of parapsychology and its professionalism throughout America and abroad. Deemed the new discipline to be an important branch of psychology, he furthered its study by founding a parapsychological laboratory at Duke University, as well as creating the Foundation For Research On The Nature of Man in Durham, North Carolina and the Parapsychological Association. Author of many books including *Extrasensory Perception* and *Parapsychology: Frontier Science of the Mind,* Joseph Rhine was indeed a pioneer. And as someone even said, "Where would the Ghostbusters be without him?"

To my own great amazement, one moment I was sitting at my desk trying to ascertain if indeed Dr. Rhine was still alive, and the next of picking up the phone and finding myself speaking to the very man himself. In cursory fashion I informed the man who was once dubbed "the Father of ESP" and "the Original Ghostbuster" that we were hoping he might be available to come to Detroit as our keynote speaker. In other words, imagine the thrill of actually meeting the paranormal equivalent of Sherlock Holmes!

The voice at the end of the line began asking me questions about my own interests. I told him about my unofficial penchants for the history of parapsychology, and of a special fondness for the Sherlock Holmes stories of Arthur Conan Doyle. And while as I said I did not believe in everything Sir Arthur espoused as perhaps the leading Spiritualist crusader of his day, I was mightily intrigued by psychical research. And of course, by the doctor's own experimentations in this unorthodox field since the 1920's.

"You know, I'm seventy-nine" Rhine replied on the long-distance line "I don't get about so easily any more. But why don't you fly down to Durham and we could discuss this speaking business in person?"

Well who wouldn't have jumped at this chance? Cut to the image of me packing a bag, flying to North Carolina, and then actually meeting the one man who had popularized the investigation of all kinds of paranormal topics? For even as my recent research told me, it was Rhine and his scientist spouse Louisa who had indeed been pioneers in this field, and who'd been instrumental in establishing the paranormal laboratory at Duke University, which became a template of sorts for other institutions around the world.

I found J.B. Rhine a charming and elderly gentleman, who despite his reliance upon a powerful hearing aid, didn't miss a trick. And feeling rather like the interviewee myself, I became aware after two days of our meeting in Durham that this man desired to get a sense of me as well. Moreover, when I'd begun to describe my interest in exploring the supposedly "para-normal," the old man smiled. "You remind me of myself at your age" he said. Which I in turn took to be one of the greatest compliments of my young life.

Without directly over-describing why I wanted him in Detroit, or even what our burgeoning, social science-related Institute for Human Resources might become, I felt Professor Rhine's interest in our cause growing. This no doubt was aided by his sense of my own long-term attraction for so many things mysterious. Also there were my enthusiasms concerning Conan Doyle's greatest creation, Sherlock Holmes. Here ironically, the creation was not as credulous as his creator. In this respect Rhine was like the great detective, who, in the fashion of Houdini, would have been at the vanguard of those seeking to debunk fraudulent psychical claims. Included here were Sir Arthur's own sincere intentions, however credulous.

"He found my need to analyze the idea of ghosts and voices from the Great Beyond nettlesome" explained Dr. Rhine. "In fact, the great man became so incensed over my criticism of one of his favorite mediums that he reviled me in print. There was actually a newspaper headline in Boston that read *"J.B. RHINE IS AN ASS—A. Conan Doyle."* I treasured that statement as a kind of back-handed compliment," laughed the wonderful old man before me.

I learned a good deal with my acquaintance with Professor J.B. Rhine. But not merely about the need to measure, as best we can, what seems impossible or unbelievable. Perhaps it had more to do with the matter of keeping an open mind and considering the rich panoply of what he called the "Nature of Man."

But even Rhine was to have his share of personal disappointments. But not with unproven or willing voices from the beyond, or the reliability of an ectoplasmic flash produced on a developed negative. But rather, with living individuals. For example, not long after I'd gone to Duke and been given the rare chance of a tour through its updated parapsychological lab, things came apart. For it seemed that a fellow whom Rhine had entrusted to take his legacy further, turned out to be caught committing the crime of falsifying experimental data. And data, as Sherlock Holmes knew, was paramount. But it needed to be authentic. Otherwise reputations were at stake and possibly even more.

And in case you're wondering, yes Professor Rhine did accept my invitation. He came to Detroit and assisted our community college's planning to launch what it called its "Institute For Human Resources." For its logo, I'd borrowed Da Vinci's image of the Vitruvian Man. But to officially christen this academically metaphorical "vessel," J.B. Rhine came to Michigan and spoke to us like the sage he was.

I now treasure my preserved correspondence from Dr. Rhine over those years before his passing in 1980. Sometimes I like to re-read his letters, as if to find some undiscovered nuance. And often enough I succeed.

"Now what about you in our world?" as he wrote to me immediately after his successful appearance at our event in Detroit.

"You need something to show that works faster, is fairly simple and tangible, and gives everybody a chance to nod his head instead of shake it...I could perhaps play some little part, but you had better consider my age and look for people with a lot of energy, like yourself...Your kind of college is doing something that is obviously needed. How they got you and how they are going to keep you will keep me wondering. But not the need itself—that is too evident. If you can keep up your enthusiasm, your belief in what you're doing, and your patience with what you have to do it with, I think you will discover your own potential in the next ten years right there to a degree you will be grateful for the opportunity you have had...In the meanwhile and while I may not be able to help out directly, I will be watching your progress, even from afar."

I think of the Professor's statement, *"I'll be watching you from afar"* from time to time, even now. And I cannot help but to muse, with gratitude, on my ability to have met and in turn be inspired by this remarkable man, so admired by so many. Further yet, of his actually complimenting me by saying he felt a certain kinship with me.

Each day in my study I pass a framed eight by ten photograph. In the clearer foreground sits J.B. Rhine, in crisp white shirt and tie, expounding to a small group of us at that long ago seminar in Detroit. Slightly behind him, somewhat less sharply defined, is myself. Dark haired, thinner, and certainly younger, drinking in the words of the master. Like a Greek acolyte in the Academe listening to Socrates.

Below that photograph I have also framed a portion of Dr. Rhine's notes, which I requested, that he'd used at our event. One of those included a folded bit of note card, and handwritten upon it a maxim he greatly valued. It says:

"Edwin Markham:
Why build these cities glorious,
If man unbuilded goes?
We build in vain, alas, unless
The builder also grows!"

I take courage from the thought that perhaps, even as he promised, Dr. Rhine is still keeping an eye upon me. Also that he may well be in that Elysian "Summer Land," where perhaps he's finally come to happier terms with Sir Arthur. And by now, both of them may have rubbed ectoplasmic shoulders with their contemporary Harry Price.

Of the aforesaid trio of psychic questors, Price was perhaps the most controversial and entrepreneurial of the lot. Here the reason involved Harry's penchant for not only investigating, but also writing and broadcasting his paranormal exploits. Imagine Sherlock Holmes doing remote radio broadcasts of his cases! But that was the Ghost Hunter of the Thirties and Forties. Yes Price, whose apex of casework ultimately involved Borley Rectory in Essex, that so-called Mount Everest of haunted houses. In fact, the sleuth himself dubbed Borley "the most haunted house in England" and penned a number of books to prove it.

Sadly however, Harry Price's critics have long since charged the arch Ghostbuster to be a king-sized Ghost Booster and Huckster.

Furthermore, they've leveled the charge that the investigator had cooked up, if not staged many of the seemingly otherworldly effects he'd claimed to expose. So then was the seeker himself debunked--at least in accordance with his nay-sayers. For others however, including, I might add, myself, I deem Harry Price to have worked as a kindred spirit beside the likes of Doyle and Rhine, despite their seeming differences. But more on that in another quarter.

But still now so many years later, I smile at J.B. Rhine's 1974 prophecy, which suggested that perhaps *you will discover your own potential in the next ten years...*" Perhaps. But curiously enough that was exactly the time when I decided to formalize DAEDALOS, my agency for "consultancy and field investigation." And on the heels of that, so many adventures were waiting in the wings, like clients who'd appeared in Sherlock Holmes's sitting room. And all I had to do next was to be present, review the circumstances of the case before setting out, bags packed, and metaphorical magnifying lens in hand!

"For One Brief, Shining Moment…"

20
Camelot Quest

Climbing into the well-worn saddle of Mr. Wells' Time Machine, let us now retreat a year to 1979 to properly set the scene. And with that, a shift of the crystal-knobbed lever as the gears grind, the dials revolve, and we hurtle backward again.

By this point of my life I confess to having felt, to paraphrase Mr. Sherlock Holmes, rather like an engine which was finally connected to its proper work. After all, I was thirty-two, feeling fit, a married man, working at a job which allowed me latitudes of many kinds, and free to travel hither and yon to suit my purposes.

Rash perhaps, I felt certain of my bearings concerning those things that year which had related to my collegiate work, and imperatively, the sudden planning and execution of a PBS documentary film involving a group of Detroiters journeying to Egypt. But more about that in a while.

I believe that 1979 inadvertently provided me with a Guinness-like achievement, but on a lesser scale. And as fortune sometimes favors the clever if not the bold, my flight returned me to America's greatest city only two days before the annual BSI birthday dinner. And on that account I probably earned the dubious honor of "who traveled furthest to get here." But of course, it was not the honor one most wished for at that event.

But that was a rare weekend indeed. The meeting was predictably fun, and although still a stag affair, I was afforded a special honor. It was that very accolade I'd coveted since childhood: the Baker Street Irregulars Investiture. Mine was "Cecil Barker,' a figure from *The Valley Of Fear*. Not perhaps as evocative as my pal Jeff Montgomery's new Sherlockian signature of the canonical "Inspector Montgomery" at that meeting, but who in their right mind would complain?

Now in retrospect it felt as if the Wellsian machine had suddenly advanced more than a few ratchets. For seemingly just over my shoulder the year had been 1965 and I was trailing, Wiggins-like behind Bill Rabe, and introduced to the BSI. Holy of Holies. But now seemingly a click later, I was fourteen years older, "full grown" and

344

with a few Holmesian rite-of-passage notches on my belt. Strangely as well, those began to feel like tableaus out of someone else's life.

Finding Baskerville Hall. The Baker Street's plaque. The Houdini-Doyle Séance. The Napoleons of Crime. The lectures. The articles. And all those ancillary, Holmes-styled adventures, ranging from the Pyramids and Loch Ness to Camelot. And now, seeming to cap those early side-trips to Baker Street off, the official investiture!

It was, of course, the most singular honor of all to be taken into the Irregular fold. In my case, the years which had prefaced my investiture had been full of wonder and I admit it, excitement. Moreover, my own self-made plan of "activating" my Sherlockian/Holmesian interests had, I hoped, served me well. To wit, then, and rather than talking about Baskerville Hall, why not go out and find it? And rather than debating with one scion society claque or other about the location of Number 221B, Baker Street, why not return there and place a plaque on an approximate location? Such had become my own *modus operandi* of living the tenets of a Sherlockian life. And then of course, there was the matter of putting the matter into practice. Ergo those increasing matters involving any number of such "little problems" that had long gone unanswered. *The Ripper. The Most Haunted House In England. The Shakespearean conundrum. The enigma of Scotland's most famous lake. Charting the landscape of the "true" Camelot. Or perhaps even an attempt to contact the world's greatest magician at the séance table. And other matters of course, both "quaint and curious" as well.*

But I've never believed that if you were lucky enough to ever be given a laurel wreath, you need spend much time wearing it. File it away. Put it on a shelf or in a scrap-book. And then get back on the trail where "the game's afoot!"

Carefully then, and without making false claims either going in or at the point of summation, I have tried on the role of the historical, literary or even psychical sleuth and liked it. For that reason and upon looking back upon a great deal in this memoir, I've smiled at both the witting and unwitting dimensions of how I may have taken my love for Sherlock Holmes quite literally to heart.

Upon the acceptance of my BSI Investiture, "Cecil Barker" from the hands of Dr. Julian Wolff himself in 1979, I found yet another little mystery. It is predicated upon its allusion not only to the aforesaid character in *The Valley of Fear,* but also to another of that surname in "The Adventure of the Retired Colourman" within *The Casebook of Sherlock Holmes.* More than ever these days I find myself thinking that whether by design or application I have chosen to occupy the space described for my societal namesake, who was first described in *Valley* (1915) as a "tall, loose-jointed figure" who "was a frequent and welcome visitor at the Manor House" of Birlstone. He is described as "straight" and "broad-chested" "with a clean-shaved prize-fighter face, thick, strong black eyebrows, and a pair of masterful black eyes which might, even without the aid of his vary capable hands, clear a way for him through a hostile crowd." Ultimately Watson summarizes this Barker as "an easy-going, free-handed gentleman" of pleasant mien but capable of action, if and when needed.

Barker the Second of twelve years later bears some possible traces of the first of his name. "The Retired Colourman" (1927) describes him in Holmes' own words, as "a tall, dark, heavily moustached man…with gray-tinted sun-glasses…and a Masonic pin." This then is the chap the detective assayed as "my hated rival on the Surrey shore." In other words, Barker is also a sleuth, at large, and practicing his trade in Holmes's own territory.

"He has several good cases to his credit" Holmes says. "His methods are irregular, no doubt, like my own." (An inadvertent pun?)

And therein, I think, an auspicious clue from the past. For the two Barkers are both tall and dark haired. The detective wears tinted spectacles and sports a moustache, both of which might be a disguise. Neither of them within our canonical context are disparaged by Sherlock Holmes. In fact, one hears a jocular tone when the latter alludes to "my hated rival." For it is apparent in "The Retired Colourman" that Holmes trusts this rival to follow his lead. One senses that there may well have been other occasions upon which the two conspired, just as it might not feel totally unlikely that Cecil Barker of the Birlstone case might have been kindly received at Baker Street in later days.

And as for that "auspicious clue?" I choose to take its meaning largely from the line about the investigative Barker and his "irregular" methods. Hopefully then, my own investiture may have originally, or now does in part at least, reflect my application of such techniques over the decades. With that in mind I continue to ponder "the two Barkers." And the more I think on the thing, I believe there might be a reason for Holmes' fondness for both individuals: *what if they were in fact, one and the same man!*

From 1979 through 1984 a good deal of my time was occupied with two, if not three central figures from my youth. Apart from Holmes, the first of those was King Arthur, and the second was Secret Agent James Bond and his creator, Ian Fleming.

By the autumn of '79 my collective interests in the fabled ruler of Camelot had become rather more substantial. Over the past decade I'd been aware that all of a sudden both history and archaeology had taken a more serious glance at whether there ever was a "Once and Future King?" Charted from the early Sixties onward, the new verdict suggested that there might well have been. But, as even Churchill himself said about the Round Table's founder, there was "more and better besides" to be learned.

For those reasons I'd been welded to reports and books and articles concerning the quest for Camelot in Britain's rural Somersetshire. For it was there, by the growing accounts, in the storied "Summer Country" that excavations were beginning to literally home in on the myths, if not provide a map for the legends. In other words, the effort to summon Dark Age "King" Arthur out of the mists of myth seemed to be succeeding. And with that success came a new image of Britain's champion in the face of its greatest early hour. No less a hero for it, new indications made Arthur a *dux bellorum,* or "leader of battles," and a figure who managed to purchase his island a slim era of peace in the face of the barbaric and Saxon invasions. Whatever the case, it was now becoming seemingly apparent that that "one brief shining moment" known as Camelot had actually occurred.

I was hungry to know more, if not to visit Somerset and Glastonbury, where allegedly King Arthur and his Guinevere's grave had been dug up by Benedictine monks in 1191. Moreover, I wanted to stand on the terraced promontory of what was dubbed Cadbury Castle, where a decade's worth of excavations had aimed at reconstructing a 5th or 6th century hill fortress atop that Neolithic British mound.

From my swirling Sherlockian annals what often came to mind was one of Holmes' cases, which concerned a certain "ancient British barrow." Had the master sleuth ever interested himself in things Arthurian, or the so-called "Matter of Britain?" To the best of my recollection the oldest artifact the Master had found had been cited in "The Musgrave Ritual." This involved the old and fragmented circlet which had once been the "ancient crown of the kings of England." But given his interests in medieval motets or his knowledge of old charters, who knew? For like Watson himself, the Sacred Writings never professed to reveal the unbounded "limits" of Mr. Sherlock Holmes.

But I'd elected to interest myself in the Arthurian research on my homeward route from Inverness-shire and my favorite monster-haunted lake. Therefore I planned a detour to the warm climes of Somerset, and set my cap upon locating another man I'd long desired to meet. This was the author Geoffrey Ashe, who apart from his many books on "the real King Arthur" had been a member of the initial Camelot Research Committee in the Sixties. Working in tandem with Professor Leslie Alcock of Cardiff University, Ashe became part of this most historically dedicated effort to locate the possible prototype of "Camelot."

And if Geoffrey Ashe was himself dedicated to, as Sherlockians like to say, "the sake of the trust," he was certainly in the right place for it. Many years earlier he had passed through the old market town of Glastonbury with its romantic ecclesiastical ruins, and made a decision. That was to come to this place and is said to live under the shadow of Glastonbury Tor, that great and terraced emerald promontory which has been explained as everything from King Arthur's "hollow" hill to the final resting place of the Holy Grail. For that most unappreciated of Christian relics and even older tradition was also associated with the "Apple Isle," as old Glastonia was also called. For indeed this pagan-worn and mysterious locus was regarded as weird by religious and secular types of all colors. Some of them regarded the remnant of Glastonbury's great Abbey as the *nexus* point for the first above-ground Christian shrine in Britain (and the West), made there by that New Testament figure of mystery, Joseph of Arimathea. Both history and myth seemed to attest to the notion that following the Crucifixion and his imprisonment, Joseph had brought a contingent of refugees out of the Holy Land and westward, to the "White Land" of Britain. And there, landing near the island-like Tor which was then surrounded by a marshy terrain, Arimathean Joseph planted his staff. And not only did it bloom, says tradition, but so too did the *vetusta ecclesia,* or "Old Church" of eldritch Christian traditions. There too many believe Joseph brought the cup of the Last Supper, in which accounts tell that he caught the blood of the executed Savior. Thus was the Holy Grail, descendant of eons of sacred and archetypal cauldron lore, now materialized in the minds of its beholders. Supposedly it was hidden in a spring near Glastonbury. To this day that place, Chalice Well, abuts the ground below the Tor's labyrinthine surface which itself looks across to the former Abbey grounds where the monks found Arthur's Grave.

Allegedly the "Avalon" of old, it was to Glastonbury that legend insists that the mortally wounded king had been brought to be healed of his wounds. Failing that, it was here that Camelot's lord was interred with his reputedly unfaithful lady.

For all of these reasons and even apart from what the diggings a dozen miles away were revealing, I wanted—needed, more like—to find myself in Glastonbury. And ultimately my decision to go there would repeat itself, just as my pilgrimages to the Ness. But here, at the heart of the Summer Country, I was going in search of—what? My religious faith, perhaps. That and the curious vestige of Christian symbolism and "Avalonian" mysticism which had grown, or been grafted onto the lore of the Arthur Country.

And there was even more to stimulate my interests in that old market center. For Glastonbury had also been the home of the occult writer Dion Fortune. A "white witch" you might say, this author's *Avalon of the Heart,* which was a paean to the town and its magical environs, had jump-started any number of my fascinations. Arthur. Joseph. The Grail. Atlantis. Merlin. The Tor. All of that and more. And then of course that serendipitous element of rightness in my voyage to "The Apple Isle." For you see, as I've said, Dion Fortune lived, wrote, and performed her rituals here. And as a matter of coincidental curiosity or unrevealed purpose, I had learned that Geoffrey Ashe was now residing in her house!

Up to the present moment, I have known Geoffrey Ashe and valued his expertise on the subject of King Arthur. A pioneer of the Sixties Camelot excavations, a few years ago he was accorded the accolade of being included on the Queen's Honours List. Gratefully and despite the passage of time I continued to hear from him, glad to know that he has continued to write and affirm an image of a vaguely Merlin-like figure for pilgrims who chance to visit the Apple Isle. I was even pleased to arrange a state-side lecture for "Geoffrey of Glastonbury" through the auspices of my role as a trustee board member for the Cranbrook Institute's auspicious Writer's Guild.

But in 1979 both Ashe and I were younger, and so was the world. And in due part it was not a few aspects of that world which constituted our first discussions. But in the main most of those gravitated to King Arthur. And as we sat that first afternoon in his front room, or his garden beneath those rather appropriate apple trees, we each mused a bit on what was to come.

At this time I had begun to conjure with the notion of not only a real King Arthur in bygone terms, but also, and by virtue of his lineage, his successor. To make matters all the more exciting, it was obvious in '79, even as it was for at least the next few years, that Great Britain could well see another "King Arthur" on its throne. This of course, in the prospective person of the Heir Apparent, H.R.H. Charles Phillip *Arthur* George, Prince of Wales and "next in line."

So intrigued by the idea of a 20th century King Arthur's "return" that I broached a fictive idea to Ashe. "What about a tale about a young prince of the Arthurian blood-line who suddenly becomes a young king?" I asked Geoffrey. "Taking it a step further, what if this 'Arthur' marries a sweet young thing who becomes, over time, a harridan and undoes his plans for the future?"

"As did Guinevere" my companion stated with a smile.

"As did Guinevere" I repeated. And then I began to reach back into the present day reality of Prince Charles' options as "the world's most eligible bachelor." True, it's hard to envision that now, when like myself His Highness is of an age to collect his equivalent of Social Security. But back then Charles was still being touted as Britain's great hope. And for such reasons as well, all kinds of match-makers were opining on who "Charley" would settle upon as his future Princess of Wales, and thereafter, Queen of England?

Now consider again the framework of time. As Ashe and I discussed my fanciful idea, Lady Diana Spencer was somewhere in the wings. But within only a couple of years she would become the "favorite" in more ways than one. And then of course and as the world would remember, "Lady Di," and "the People's Princess" would be consigned by tragic memory as "England's Rose."

But in 1979 my imaginative scenario concerning Charles' fictive alter ego or even the real prince's yet-to-be-announced royal bride was not of any issue. But I do recall my discussions with Geoffrey about my novel's protagonist, who might find himself in a sort of Jungian, archetypal labyrinth of some ancient design.

That initial visit to Glastonbury and my epic meeting with Geoffrey Ashe set a tone for me for the days ahead. That, and standing as I'd envisioned, upon the crest of Cadbury Hill, with no other companions than a company of grazing livestock. And of course, the hawk. We'll close with that.

It was perhaps six-thirty on a sunny autumn morning. I had purposefully driven halfway up the wooded, mud-rutted track to Cadbury's summit and then hiked the rest of the way. For I wanted to be up there and to commune with—well what, exactly? Perhaps the ghosts of the past. For I'd heard the story from Ashe himself that on Midsummer Eve the specters of Arthur and his mounted huntsman could be seen and heard, the tips of their spears glowing as if afire. Once, he confessed, he had kept tryst on that night of nights, but seen nothing. But he claimed he had heard something in the darkness, sounding like a Pan-Pipe in the distance.

But on that given morning there were no spectral figures, and no music of any sort. And by the time I got to the top, I reveled in getting my bearings. All around me was a sort of patchwork of countryside, the fields looking exactly like that. And in the faraway, at least I gained sight of Glastonbury's Tor, with its ruined tower rising up like a megalithic marker.

It was about this time, even as I was trying to establish certain points of geography, that a small sparrow hawk darted out from seemingly nowhere. I immediately became aware of its presence, and then it vanished! But I suddenly remembered two things. The first of these reflected a conversation I'd had with a friend of a decidedly "re-born" Christian persuasion. We'd been talking about my going to Loch Ness to look for its fabulous creature.

I recall my Christian friend suggesting that I ought to try and commune with "Nessie."

"Speak to it. Call her up" he suggested. In other words, invoke this possibly sentient thing which was more than likely far beyond some ghostly, elemental "beastie."

I thought of that matter of "communing" as I stood there atop what was supposedly Arthur's hillside. And secondly, I found myself remembering Mary Stewart's wonderful musings about Camelot and its wizard. Thinking this, rather spontaneously I heard myself say out loud to the sunlit skies and that lone sparrow hawk a single word.

"Merlin!" I said. And then I repeated it again, louder this time, as if to be heard even higher in those sunlit ethers. For as any self-respecting Arthurian buff knows, legends say that the old magician taught Arthur to be many things. And that he himself could shape-shift into a hawk.

And as I uttered that talismanic word, once again the small gray hawk seemed to materialize before me. But this time it continued to circle me, even as I visualized my own lone form below it. And suddenly like Arthur in T.H. White's *The Sword In The Stone,* I had momentarily become the darting form in the sky, looking down upon that poor sot below him!

I began sighting again upon the faraway Tor, my arm extended before me to gauge the distance. Strangely, this was a precursor to my later SCUBA training certification at Canada's Tobermory. Now however, I was orienting myself to the quilt-like vales of storied Camelot.

And just as I was doing so, I saw hovering out there and seemingly levitating above the level of my fist, the hawk! And in those seconds it seemed that his winged presence had seemingly frozen in time and was poised just beyond my raised hand. Old Merlin once again!

My recollection of that solitary morning and of my possibly wishful evocation of King Arthur's famed magus remains with me, fresh. It continued to return to mind and memory on other occasions of visiting what the scholars and sages wished to crown as Camelot. But truth to tell, and in the years which have intervened, other experts have downgraded their hopes for having found any true trace of Arthur at Cadbury. Surely, they've chanted, the dearth of hard and fast evidence is enough to perform a kind of exorcism. *An old, even Neolithic hill, undoubtedly. And an outpost for someone, well fortified, circa the 5th century, yes. But "many towered Camelot?" Unlikely at best.*

But we've all lived long enough to see the "experts" make their claims and then recant. And we have heard the "official" pronouncements of scientists and politicians as they've come and gone. And especially in the latter regard, we might put teeth to Winston Churchill's earlier definition of the politician's job: to say what will happen tomorrow and next week. And then to explain why it did not happen at all. That's my paraphrase, but you get my gist, don't you?

But I for one am at a point where for much that I revere, my belief is founded upon a considered "choice to believe." And in light of Camelot, wherever, if ever it existed, I tend to fall back on that other statement, which is my favorite made by Sir Winston. In his *A History of the English Speaking A People,* and speaking of King Arthur and his heroic retinue and their places within the hearts of his nation, he said,

"If we could see exactly what happened we should find ourselves in the presence of a theme as well founded, as inspired, and as inalienable from the inheritance of mankind as the Odyssey or the Old Testament. It is all true, or it ought to be; and more and better besides."

With such a thought in mind, and with Churchill's words still fresh in my ears, I have returned to the Summer Country many times. I have placed a spade and trowel into loamy earth, beneath which are the memories of the long ago. I have been where legends come to life. And to that extent, by making contact, I have been able to live them.

That said, I think for now I'll choose to hang my deerstalker cap on that particular peg. *And yet as I say this, something in me hears the old clarion call. This time from Wales, from which a wealth of the old lore harks. Perhaps....*

And that was 1979. To my mind, I now had the best of two worlds to explore: first there was the Gas-lit Age and its most formidable sleuth. And now as well the Dark Age, legend-haunted world of post-Roman Britain and its most fabulous *Dux Bellorum,* or "Leader of Battles."

It is odd how some things find a kind of synthesis in retrospect, don't you think? For instance, years earlier I'd met my Arthurian idol Richard Harris, whose magic seemed to extend from MacArthur Park to Arthur's Camelot. Ultimately too, when I met Geoffrey Ashe he had recalled joining the Camelot Research Committee. One of its earliest meetings included the lovely Vanessa Redgrave, whom my friend couldn't refrain from citing for her Guinevere-like loveliness. She after all had played that role to Harris's courtly king.

And I think of Richard Harris inevitably whenever the subject of Camelot comes up. Also of the year 1981. I look back upon that moment in time years ago as my "Arthurian Summer." First of all, I was on my way back to Glastonbury for more digging, both literally and figuratively, and to see my friend Geoffrey Ashe. Secondly, I was teaching a course at The University of Michigan to do with the legends and archaeology surrounding Camelot's king. And last of all, I was commissioned to write a cover-story for *The Detroit News Sunday Magazine* on King Arthur in conjunction with the imminent arrival of "Camelot." With that article in mind, I proposed to my editor that I go to Minneapolis to write a side-bar interview with my colleague the Roisterer from Limerick. How indeed things change with time! Another editor, of course, but with much less "argy bargy" involved over my requesting permission to fly elsewhere for an assignment. And while Minneapolis was not Loch Ness, there was, I believed, a story there. And with the man in charge agreeing with me, he nodded. And I did go.

When I had my reunion with Harris and evoked a bit of the distant past, the actor said he remembered my showing up at his door. I'm not sure I believed him. But we did talk a good bit about the show and Arthur, and what the star called "the curse." This, he stated, was the fact that every actor bringing Camelot's founder to life on stage came down with some illness. He backed this up by alluding to Richard Burton's early illness on Broadway, then Laurence Harvey's and Burton's again. After that, and in due part because Harris was offered the reprisal of his film role, he was mindful of whether or not he too would be affected?

That was the last time I saw Richard in person. On screen however, I found myself charmed at his transition from King Arthur to Arthur's Merlin, in the evocative role of Dumbledore in the first two "Harry Potter" films. He said he did those for his grandkids, and these days, I understand why. But for me, even now, he is still standing there at the end of "Camelot," Excalibur raised to the mists, yelling "Run, boy!" to a young Tom Malory.

Every few days I pass the shelf where two pictures sit side-by-side. One of those is of my terribly younger self, at 22, leaning over a marble throne occupied by King Richard in his medievally-appointed home. In a sweater and tee-shirt he looks frazzled, and I, youthfully naïve. But the second shows a literally marked difference. There are Harris and my now 34-year-old incarnation in Minneapolis. But a sea-change has occurred. Now both of us are looking bearded and dashing, Richard's got his arm around my shoulder and I'm looking into the lens, arms folded. There's no way around it: we looked like a couple of rogues bent on trouble.

And that's really the last of my Camelot story. Oh yes, except for the post-script: for you see, almost midway through his Arthurian run in Detroit, Harris was rushed to the hospital for an undiagnosed ailment. Was it the every-present "curse?" I'm hard pressed not to believe him. And for the record, I don't think my favorite King Arthur returned to the Fisher Theater's stage exactly unchastened. Nor for the record were two of Harris' successors to the role, in the persons of Robert Goulet and Michael York. I had the chance to meet both of them. And yes, the matter of "the curse" came up. Goulet found it amusing, and later signed a picture of the two of us, with the former "Lancelot" now turned "Arthur" inscribing it, *"Mark, Stay Well!"* Sadly, not too much longer, we lost Bob Goulet. And as for York? He'd expressed an interest in the old story, and never loathe to ignore theatrical tradition, told me that the fact that he'd required a doctor's care while in Detroit "might mean something."

And I couldn't help thinking to myself and remembering my initial conversations with friend Harris, *"Yes, Michael, I think it might."*

But unwittingly and only five years later I would add yet another passion to my quiver. This one had been fostered, ironically, at about the same youthful moment I'd begun to explore the by-ways to Baker Street.

But first another detour, and this one to the Land of the Pharaohs.

President Anwar Sadat and the Author
Aswan, Egypt – 1979

21
An Egyptian Odyssey

1979 was indeed a pivotal year for me. With a good many irons in the fire, Sherlockian and otherwise, I'd been, as already cited, presented with a unique opportunity which came to me rather involuntarily. Perhaps now is the time to talk about it, for this involved my first and only sojourn to the Land of the Pharaohs. And why? I was about to make a PBS documentary film in Egypt.

The circumstance evolved in sudden and somewhat problematic fashion. It began when our collegiate Vice President for Finance wished to capture the idea of a business articulation then in the works. This involved a computer software company which was about to partner with our institution. But further, and once those cogitations went a bit further, these two master-minds launched a plan: why not create an Americanized corporate and academic means of selling a specialized program in Egypt?

But why Egypt? You may well ask this, but the answer here, my dear doctor, is purely elementary. For you see, the vice president I've referred to happened himself to be Egyptian, and with family and purported contacts back in the old country. That then was sufficient warrant for him to temper our discussion of going to Egypt, and somewhat legitimizing the business aspect of it by taking a touring group from the greater Detroit and metropolitan region. Now all that remained was the "how?" and "why?" of the thing.

Well my administrative superiors felt they had the "why" down. They would go over to Cairo and pitch their collegiate-corporate-computer package to their counterparts at Egypt's prestigious Ain Shams University. But what was lacking was one key element: my masters also wanted a film made to chronicle this historic venture for posterity.

We had no in-house mechanism for shooting such a documentary. Naturally I suggested that Detroit's own Public Broadcasting affiliate, WTVS, had the means. I could discuss the matter with them, I said, but what about the *quid pro quo?* I asked. What could we offer the station to merit their lending a crew and equipment to the venture, if not the means of making and then airing the film after the junket? Without hesitation, my vice president had an idea; "What if we offered them an interview with Egypt's President Anwar Sadat?" *What indeed?*

I heard the offer and wasn't certain I believed it—not entirely, at any rate. Yet I was encouraged to bring the message to WTVS and to make the offer. Which I did. And to my surprise, excitedly they agreed. And before you could say Tutankhamen, next thing I knew I would be spending my post-Christmas holiday in the desert, given that my new role was as titular head of the joint college and PBS crew. In other words, I would be the point man for "An Egyptian Odyssey."

But apart from the way the entire project was coming together in rapid strides, my internal Doubting Thomas-like instincts were ringing like a fire alarm. On that note, I took an extreme measure, or a diversion as some would call it, to find out the truth. To achieve that end, I covered my tracks by taking a personal day one Friday morning and flew into Washington. And there, if you can believe it, I kept an appointment with the Egyptian attaché at that country's embassy.

I explained my place in the impending project. Also the word which had been passed down to me that "everything was arranged." The Sadat interview was set up. Now all we had to do was to get to Cairo. *Wrong.*

For you see, what I actually learned from the Egyptian representative was anything but assuring. No, he told me, there was no such interview scheduled or even proposed. No official international arrangements made. And as for those Egyptian contacts supposedly making this possible from Cairo to Detroit, such promises were, shall we say, groundless. Nor, was I told, did those prestigious "contacts" even begin to carry enough clout in his country to make such a plan as was proposed happen.

I flew back to Detroit feeling despondent. For already the Egyptian plan was made on paper, the tour had been arranged, registrations for the trip made, and even my script for what was to be dubbed our "Odyssey' begun in outline fashion. Little could I know how peril-fraught the way ahead would be. I suppose I should have asked Odysseus. And then of course, concerning the lynch-pin of the proposal, i.e., the visit with

President Sadat, there was nothing beyond a bit of one-sided planning afoot.

I'll make a long and somewhat unpleasant story as short as possible. Knowing what I now knew, I was hoping against hope that, even as my employers advised, "something will work out." And on that lame assurance did I muddle through the Yuletide and pack my back. And as far as WTVS was concerned? They were about to secure a unique interview with Anwar Sadat, which in turn would doubtless seal the deal at Ain Shams University where the computer plan was to be pitched. *That's right. We were about to sell a computer program to the people who invented the abacus and built the Great Pyramid. How excellent was that?*

Upon our arrival in Egypt it was chaos from the moment our luggage was lost somewhere between Geneva, our first stop, and the bazaar (and bizarre)-like confusion of Egypt's major airport. Likewise, and in rapid strokes over the next few days, things went from bad to worse in a click.

My PBS cohorts were growing antsy, for they suspected (justifiably) that something was up. Meanwhile, we needed to go about the business of following the group of Detroiters to a number of local and more distant sites. This in real terms meant that we would need to precede that aggregation. Toward that end we'd been promised private and efficient transportation by which our five-person crew could get from here to there. Instead of that, but in keeping with promises made thus far, we were compelled to ride with a loud and disagreeable bus-load of tourists, our $90.000 Ikagami camera equipment in the aisle, even as daily excursions became less endurable by the hour.

But we did keep track of those Detroiters. Eventually we managed to secure a hired car, often riding in its opened trunk. And then of course there was our "ground" and "water" transport, which in translated form meant my experiencing riding a camel, a horse, a wagon, a truck, a *felucca,* or sailboat, etc. Factor in that during that odyssey we were compelled to board at least four Egyptian-based airlines, and each time I felt we were desert bound, but nose-first.

Often enough one of our major dilemmas was arriving ahead of the Motor City entourage. On a couple of occasions by the time we got there, they never did. I recall compensating for their absence on shooting days by filming other American tourist groups at the Cairo Museum and the Mohammed Ali Mosque. I got the idea at the first stop when I saw a woman who seemed a sunglassed twin of one of our own. Ergo, we filmed her against a tableau of strangers. To the best of my knowledge, from that day until this, no one ever twigged to the ruse.

The focal point of the trip was to be the Sadat point-of-contact. By now however, the sad truth that no officially-orchestrated meeting existed had become painfully known to my PBS cohorts. In no conceivable way was this satisfactory. Adding to the angst of this, Jack Caldwell, the station's point man, was ready to pull up stakes. He'd developed a dislike of certain of my collegiate chiefs and had never wanted to leave Detroit to begin with. In fact, this assignment was to be his last before he ended his term at WTVS. Now and worse yet, upon learning that all was not as promised, he was on the verge of ringing home and booking the next jet for the Motor City.

It looked bad, as I'm sure you would agree. But somehow I tried to keep the team together. For by now we'd shot a great deal of background footage. But sadly and not exactly as planned, our upcoming arrival at Aswan was going to be earmarked by big news: President Sadat was going to meet there with Israel's premier Menachem Begin. In its way this would be an historic meeting, for earlier on as the world had known, Sadat, Begin and America's President Carter had entered into an accord which seemed to promise new peace in the Middle East.

As for our group however, all that had been arranged at Aswan was a special meeting with the president's wife, Jehan Sadat. But sadly, not with her husband.

With my camera crew ready to abandon our sinking ship, I struggled over how to plug the leaks. The best I could do was to rely on instinct and a few prayers to the effect that all would be well. And it was on that basis that I assured Caldwell and team that "everything would work out." But who, I wondered, was going to give me the pep talk? Already I'd nurtured an evolving distrust for the ones who'd brought us this far. And knowing what now teetered in the shadow of the Pyramids, I urged my colleagues to trust me. And for some unforeseeable reason, they did.

Meanwhile I cajoled and finally bought a moment of time by persuading Jack Caldwell him not to do anything rash until Aswan was over. I might add here that there was also a palpable level of tension in the air when we arrived, for that week word of Anwar Sadat's summit had begotten an unparalleled level of security forces on Egyptian and Israeli sides. So I suppose it was with a degree of self-advised cold comfort that I weighed the stakes of what was going on, telling myself that in contrast to world peace, one little interview amounted to a hill of beans. However I also realized that everything involving the "how?" and "why?" we'd been brought so far from home depended on whether or not we might soon find ourselves in the company of the Supreme President of Egypt.

On the weekend ahead the star players were to be only Menachem and Anwar. The only Americans known to be within range of the compound were to be ourselves, and no doubt some members of the international press, including our own countrymen. And that was that. Once we arrived in that ancient city, all we had to film was the equivalent of tea-time in the Egyptian Rose Garden.

Meanwhile, the much-anticipated meeting at Ain Shams University came and went. Imagine an elephant making time for an ant who wants to make a presentation supposedly designed to benefit Elephant Kind? So at least it seemed to me that day when the collegiates and corporates made their petty pitch to the professors and governmental reps assembled that day. And I couldn't help but think, "here we are, in the place and among people who advanced civilization." Yes, a nation of people in many ways as sophisticated or more than their American opposite numbers. And by that day's end, clearly one thing was plain; *we had nothing to teach them.*

And as for the Egyptians themselves? They had endured us with an extremely polite form of deference. Tolerance or something like it had been written upon that great room-full of foreign countenances. But clearly, it was all akin to saying, *No sale. Enjoy our country. And have a good trip home.*

A couple of days later when we arrived, Aswan was crawling with security when we reached the Presidential Compound. Members of the Israeli Mossad were thick on the ground, as were their Egyptian counterparts. I remember the mood as I presented our permission papers at the gate. And just as when I'd needed to flash our Arabic-designed permits in the recent past, I often wondered if they actually said *"These idiots are Americans. Overcharge them as much as possible and give them a hard time if you can."*

So it was we entered a verdant part of the compound where, in a matter of two hours or less, our group was to have a meet-and-greet with the lovely Jehan Sadat. I'd seen the President's wife interviewed before, and had been struck by what a charming woman she was. Physically she bordered on being beautiful, and at the time I found myself likening her to another comparatively regal first lady, Princess Grace of Monaco.

It was while our crew was setting up within a sort of garden-like plaza that I saw something strange. This took the form of one of our guides seeming to assume a kind of rigid stance as he stood at the crest of a nearby flight of stone steps. Now it's hard to explain what I mean, but it was a strange sort of visual sensation in someone that you just take note of. *He's seeing something* I thought to myself. *But what?* To find out I began to ascend the steep flight leading to an upper level of the presidential grounds. But only when I reached the top and stood there looking down with my companion did I have my answer.

Approaching us and now within a short flight of where we stood, was God Himself. Which is to say, the seemingly larger-than-life figure of the one man whose pictures flanked the boulevards along Cairo's traffic-choked main drag. Sadat in military uniform. Sadat in dark suit coat. Sadat in portrait. And here he was in the flesh. *President Anwar Sadat, suddenly only a few yards away from where I stood.*

The rest of it happened almost unthinkingly. I yelled down to one of our team members to get out his camera and aim it up here. And then I turned about just in time to greet the man now joining us where the guide and I stood.

In person the President of Egypt was very like his various presentiments. He was a handsome man attired in a dark suit and immaculately dressed. Like myself, he wore sunglasses, and I suppose when I stepped forth and dared to extend my hand, I probably looked like a CIA contact. Blue blazer, gray slacks, a pair of Ray Bans.

Sadat received my greeting with a smile. As we shook hands I did my best to calmly explain our presence, and the fact that our group would shortly arrive to meet with his lady. But importantly, I stressed, we had originally hoped to arrange an interview with the President himself. Sadly, that had fallen apart through what I described as "bureaucracy." That seemed to ring a bell. The President nodded as if in commiseration.

To his credit and mine as well, that great man took the time to listen to my words before telling me what to do. This in fact involved seeing someone specifically before our departure. I thanked him, and then did something which continues to surprise me even to this day, but which I'm glad I did. I asked the President of Egypt if I might detain him further by introducing the members of my crew? He nodded his agreement. And that was how Jack, Cecilia, Simon and Jim got to find their moments with history.

Circumstantially and as Egypt's leader had informed me, he was even then en route to meet with the Soviet Ambassador. Nevertheless, he agreed to my request. So then, before sitting down with the Russian envoy, President Anwar Sadat had deigned to make time for his Yankee guests.

One by one the four members of our entourage came up and got to feel the touch of the man who had recently furthered the promise of "peace in the Middle East." For he, like Menachem Begin and our own Jimmy Carter, were giving every impression of beating those proverbial swords back into plowshares. Would that they all had the renewed opportunity of doing so.

When our surprise guest left we were all stunned. I gave my WTVS colleague Caldwell the information which Sadat had passed on to me. And as it happened, as a result of this the much-discussed interview did occur, but it required my dour friend Jack to stay at his work station, and even to return to Egypt within six months' time. Somehow, for that opportunity he did not thank me.

When our group showed up before Madame Sadat's arrival there was excitement in the air. The word of the President's appearance moved through the crowd, and ironically the only one who refused to believe it was our Egyptian vice president. Yes, the Man of Many Promises himself. But when he eventually saw me greeting Mr. Sadat in hard photographic form, he eventually had to believe. I wonder how difficult that might have been for him?

The Rose Garden meeting went off like clockwork. After that the group left Aswan and my crew finished up our 10-day shoot by having one afternoon to go our separate ways. After being fused at the hip for what seemed like months, here at last was pure relief. For myself, I celebrated the opportunity by returning to the Great Pyramid of Giza. There and only days earlier I'd come upon the brain-storm of how to get from point-to-point before our tourist group's arrival. The idea wasn't mine to start, but I'd heard a slight and heavily accented young voice say to me, "Hey Mister, you want a horse?"

The lightbulb had literally illumined over my head when I'd turned to see a young fellow holding two Arabian stallions. Both of them were gorgeous creatures. Quickly I negotiated with my companion. And I asked him, "What's your horse's name?"

"His name is Prince Phillip" he said, grinning.

At any rate, Prince Phillip and I cut a dashing figure that afternoon for the second and last time. I gleefully recalled the first instance, as our tourist-filled coach rumbled up to the Pyramids in gassy fumes. Inside it were its denizens, hot, bus-sick, and doubtless complaining as they had throughout most of our time spent together. Now however, I was free of them. And having hired a horse instead of horsepower, I was in my element. And you know, I actually guided that stallion up upon a slight rise above the road, and when those by-now-painfully-familiar faces passed by, noses pressed against their dusty windows, what they saw was something which might have been part of an Indiana Jones film. But remember, this was a couple of years prior to "Indie's" arrival. Now all they had was me. And there I was, saddled up like

Hopalong. And you know, I actually persuaded that beautiful steed to buck a bit, like the Lone Ranger and Silver as those miserable Michiganders edged their way to the coach stop. And watching them from higher up I mused, *small pleasures sometimes loom immense, under the proper circumstance*s.

At any rate, on that last free day when I returned alone to Giza, I found my young friend and once again climbed into the saddle with Prince Phillip raring to go. But this time out we were not bent on any reconnaissance of any errant group of Motor Citizens. Instead, now we were about the business of simply tearing off into the desert side by side, like Peter O'Toole and Omar Sharif in "Lawrence of Arabia." It was, simply stated, one of the most exciting afternoons of my life.

In post-scripted fashion as well, my personalized Egyptian odyssey was possessed of its own Sherlockian/Holmesian connection. En route for Detroit, I found myself remembering the detective's explanation of his "missing time" after Reichenbach to his chronicler. He told of how he had existed under the pseudonym of Sigerson, a Norwegian explorer. In such mufti he had gone to Lhasa and travelled through the Middle East, stopping at Khartoum. Yes, well out of his usual element—even as I had been myself!

We returned home and I made a detour to New York. As luck would have it, I was only a day away from the BSI meeting. Upon attending and being accorded the honor of my long-awaited investiture, it occurred to me that someone at the meeting should have paraphrased Holmes in *Study in Scarlet*. But instead of saying to Watson, "You have been in Afghanistan, I perceive," they might have intoned, "You have been in Egypt and two weeks of hell, I deduce." And you know, they would have been right.

But as a postscript to this somewhat exotic chapter," I'd like to close by sharing an even odder reflection, no doubt typical of my sometimes-unusual take on things. You see, it occurred to me many years ago that often we engage in opportunities which are not at the time fully realized for their potential. One of those, I thought, had been the epic opportunity of my meeting Anwar Sadat.

But what, I asked myself, however ridiculous the idea might have seemed to some had I shared it, if I had gained the President's attention to tell him something? And what if that "something" had been a warning about a singular day in his near enough future?

Had I been able to hold that great man's attention long enough, might I have been able to at least have planted the seed of a warning? And that would have involved a yet-to-be-realized event, at which President Sadat would be standing and reviewing troops. But what if I had made him remember my warning, and upon that fateful day he had heeded my warning, and taken action? And impossible as it must seem, what if, given my meeting and my warning, Mr. Sadat might have avoided being mowed down by militant assassins? Had he but lived. Then what?

I have every faith in the man's prowess to think that President Sadat would have persevered in his quest to bring peace to the Middle East. And had he been given the chance to do so, what different shape might there be over there today? No Desert Storm? No "shock and awe?" No hatred in unparalleled fashion among so many within the Arab world? No ISIS or Taliban or super-evolved Al-Qaeda. Perhaps no "weapons of mass destruction," and ultimately, even theoretically, no Twin Towers disaster? Perhaps not even a "War on Terror" in all its abstract or tangible elements. And best of all, the preservation of so many lives, American and foreigners alike.

In short, how might our world of today have been different, had one good man but lived? Strangely enough and to this very day, the question weighs upon me in a haunting fashion. And however wild or fantastic its implications might seem, still an inner voice occasionally asks itself: *What if you had known the future, and could have re-shaped it with a few words exchanged with a great man?*

Ian Fleming's faithful factotum of eighteen years,
Violet Cummings and the author at "Goldeneye," Jamaica

"ACD" where Bond was born - the author at "Goldeneye,"

The Car I Never Owned–The author and 007's Aston Martin DB-5

London 2016 ~ "The Writer and The Muse"
The Author and Blanche Blackwell

22
"The Name Is Bond ... "

With Egypt now behind me and our ill-fated documentary film completed and aired, there were new considerations ahead. For myself, the next couple of years passed pleasantly enough, notwithstanding a divorce. But down the road I found my bearings once again. And when I did, I seemed to make a faster acquaintance with another old friend from my childhood. To do this, I was also required to wing off to the veritable island paradise of Jamaica. There I would do so in order to seek out the creator of yet another literary giant whose exploits had blurred the lines between fact and fiction. For in my sights now was the ghost of a clever and erudite English gentleman named Ian Fleming, and reflected in his artistic shadow his own larger-than-life creation whose name was Bond, James Bond.

And speaking of authors and their images. Don't we all like to imagine the psyche or personal demeanor of those artists whose spun words have evoked a kind of greatness in ink? And don't many of us as aspiring writers find ourselves ready to put down our poor pens forever in the face of such genius?

There are also any number of peculiar dimensions to authorship. For example, how many of the world's great literary masterpieces have been sired by "Anonymous?" Precious few. And yet, what of those lasting works which have offered us the benefit of doubt, but without incontrovertible provenance? Take for example the Synoptic Gospels. Or better yet, what of the greatest enduring literary conundrum in the history of our world, the "works of William Shakespeare?"

Since my youthful days as a died-in-the hounds-tooth Sherlockian, I confess to reading about another super-hero. This was the British secret agent 007 created by Ian Fleming. Moreover, as I poured through the paperbacks and watched Sean Connery as the first (and I think, best Bond), 007 Mania was everywhere. A survey of President John Kennedy's favorite bedside reading included a Fleming novel, and I later learned that Fleming and Kennedy had met and discussed a bit of spy-craft. I was also entranced by knowing that Bond's creator had been himself an intelligence agent during the Second World War. Ergo, as the Bond Wagon was slowly beginning to suggest, there was more

371

than a slight degree of parity between James Bond and his creator. This notion had been vested by years of press blurbs featuring a close-up of Fleming's rugged profile, even as he had a pistol poised near his lips, as if he'd just blown away the gun smoke. And with those layouts was the legend "IAN FLEMING IS JAMES BOND."

At the time I wondered how Conan Doyle would have taken it, early on, had the *Strand's* adverts trumpeted the theme, "ARTHUR CONAN DOYLE IS SHERLOCK HOLMES." But in point of fact, such an association did come, despite the author's own public dismissals. Paradoxically in his Memoirs ACD made the admission that "if anyone is Sherlock Holmes, it is I." Earlier on however, the author placed credit for Holmes with his old teacher and mentor, Dr. Joseph Bell of Edinburgh University.

Bell was something of a deductive savant, capable of glancing at a patient as his subject and telling him much more than his physical malady. Most often he was capable of deducing the person's profession, aptitudes, living conditions, etc.

And when Joe Bell was asked about who the "real" Sherlock was, he turned the table back on his former out-patient clerk. And that left Conan Doyle saddled with one of the earliest chronic cases of celebrity association with a fictive character. In something of a similar vein, a bit later Basil Rathbone inherited the "Doyle curse" by having his lion's share of dramatic roles overshadowed by more than a dozen cinematic outings as Mr. Holmes. He came to hate his deductive alter ego, as did Doyle himself, who ultimately decided to kill off his sleuth before the latter did the same to him.

As for Ian Fleming, however, there are mixed opinions as to how he handled his own accusations of "being Bond." The facts were there, nevertheless. Commander Ian Fleming had served as Assistant to the Director of Naval Intelligence during the war. He was undeniably involved in any number of "black ops," and dirty tricks. Moreover, he earned the respect of his peers and his superiors, including Winston Churchill. Therefore when I discovered James Bond, I felt I'd found a modern-day equivalent for my hero worship of Sherlock Holmes.

In the case of James Bond, my fancies were spawned early on by the paperback series and of course, the genre of the "Bond movies" which commenced with "Dr. No" when I was fifteen. And just as young men of my age in Conan Doyle's day found exciting currency in reading the Sherlock Holmes stories, so did I in similar fashion.

It was simple enough to constitute the 007 Formula. Take one heroic, risk-everything fellow and season in derring-do, king villains, fast cars, and beautiful women. Shake but do not stir this recipe and then practice your Sean Connery burr, intoning such lines as the immortal "My name is Bond, (*pause*) James Bond." Or that other line which, as I have repeated often enough, came to my lips on two rare visits to the hospital. In the first of these I was about to be anesthetized, and the second, as I was being wheeled to my room in post-operative fashion. In each instance however, I intoned the (to me) familiar question, "*Do you expect me to talk, Goldfinger?*" Yes, so deeply ingrained are Ian Fleming's words, or at least, those of a Bond screenwriter.

But such was James Bond's influence upon myself and many of my peers that I suppose it was natural enough to want to be him. And then of course there was the "next best thing," in the living, breathing person of his creator, Ian Fleming. Known to have been in intelligence during the war, it was often said that without Commander Fleming's wartime exploits, Commander Bond would have had none at all. Meanwhile, the creator himself, like all good ex-spies, denied what his flatterers and exposers liked to say, and merely smiled sardonically, either behind the smoking barrel of a handgun, or more often, clenching his cigarette holder and looking like a true keeper of secrets.

But as I had now learned, Ian Fleming had known the scent of danger and on that score had written a fair account of it for his fictive alter ego. Moreover, he was reputed to have also known gorgeous women, was a good shot, and liked noting better than to be depicted in an open Bentley and looking across its bonnet with its Amherst-Villiers supercharger. In "real life" however, an American Thunderbird would have better fit the bill.

Years later and chiefly in conjunction with Sherlock Holmes, I was fortunate to spend a long afternoon with the British author John Gardner. At the time John was completing his second novel about

Moriarty, told from the point of view of Holmes' arch-nemesis. In short order however, Gardner would be commissioned to "continue" the Bond adventures in the literal wake of Ian Fleming. But what he told me about my second favorite childhood author came somewhat as a surprise.

"In the later years Fleming began to take both the myth and the Bond mystique literally to heart" the writer explained. "While he was able, it wasn't unusual at all for Fleming to take off in a fast car, find some beauty to accompany him while his attention span lasted, and then to roar off to some exotic destination in a cloud of alcohol and tobacco smoke. In point of fact, I think he came to believe he was James Bond, just as so many wished to insist to me. And as I say, taking the game literally 'to heart,' he eventually died of his excesses, with his foot on the accelerator. But maybe that's not such a bad way to go out, is it?"

All I myself knew was that as a stripling envisioning an exciting adulthood for myself, Ian Fleming's world of gilt-edged Bonds were a major source of inspiration. Here however my desire to enter into a bit of "bondage" was never designed to replace my own persona, or to entirely sublimate my fantasies. It was instead to imagine myself as my hero's begetter. They were two of a kind, up to a point of diversion.

And not unlike Conan Doyle's Holmes, Agent 007 led an exciting life. He didn't worry about tomorrow, as much as the quality of the moment. In other words, this was a man with the goods who enjoyed fast living, exquisite tastes and the exotic company on the female front. Ergo, I wanted some of that--or all of that--for myself.

So I guess you could say I was a bit of a time traveler. Thus, courtesy of a few clicks on the old Time Machine dial I could envision myself in the Victorian Nineties, even as I could zoom ahead on into the Swinging Sixties.

But needless to say and as I suspected early on as well, my inclinations to emulate such a figure as 007 must rival those felt by earlier generations of Victorian and Edwardian lads (or lasses) who aspired to be a criminal avenger in the cut of Holmes.

And even without knowing it, I'd begun to enter into a world of imagination in earnest, For example, there was the matter of my automotive exploit as an eighteen-year old Bond fan. This when I wrote to the Aston Martin Lagonda Company for the purpose of putting in a bid on the "Goldfinger" DB-5. Or of how its managing director wrote back, saying that my kind offer of $238 for a vehicle then valued at $47,000 (it was recently auctioned a couple of years back in the millions) might not be my "firm offer." Or of how, years later, I was photographed standing next to that very vehicle, thinking *I should have offered more.*

But as has happened, gratefully to me over the years, I somehow found the means of realizing many of my more youthful pipe-dreams. No, I didn't become a special operative with a "license to kill." But I did eventually know my share of beautiful women, fast cars, a few life-risking adventures, and not a few exotic locations. All of which segues nicely into my voyage to Ian Fleming's Jamaica, if only to deliberately step into his sandal-prints.

The adventure had commenced one late winter in 1982 when I saw a small ad in the *Saturday Review of Literature*. It offered a holiday property for rental—but not just any fun-in-the-sun type. No, for this fanciful escape to Paradise featured none other than "Goldeneye," the house Fleming had built, lived in, and where he composed his James Bond sagas.

Suffice it to say I jumped at the chance. And in order to make the $950 weekly rent, I contacted two pals of mine, Greg Maronick and Dr. Danny Bloch to share it, as well as any other adventures at "the house where Bond was born."

It was a fun and adventurous and informative week. I'd made it plain to the agent that I wanted to write some sort of feature piece on Commander Fleming, and being in his house would obviously be food for thought. And it was. In fact, I slept in the man's bedroom, worked at his desk, and was served a gin and tonic ("one o' de Commander's favorites") by Violet Cummings, "Goldeneye's" major domo for eighteen years.

That week sped by before it was time to hie back to a chilly and slushy Detroit. But before it ended I had the opportunity of chatting with "Goldeneye's" owner, Blanche Blackwell. As I'd already known, she too had spent a considerable amount of time with Fleming. But perhaps much more than that, as my on-site researches were indicating. And because of that, either instinct or just common sense produced a new resolve in me. Already fantasizing about possibly returning to the jungle-surrounded house with its sunken garden and terrace overlooking the beach, I told Mrs. Blackwell I'd made a decision. I'd made up my mind to wait awhile before trying to write about some new bit of country, a' la the creator of Commander Bond. She seemed surprised, but somehow pleased by that statement.

Sometimes the decisions we make have a way of returning to us, retroactively, don't they? Well just so mine of that first, glorious time at "Goldeneye." Ergo, the following year when I rather nervously asked the New York agent and Blanche Blackwell's friend, Barbara Cuddy, if I might rent the place again, she astonished me.

"Yes Mark," Barbara replied. You can have it again for the week. And the price will be...."

I braced myself for the fiduciary blow. You see this time around it was not my plan to take two buddies, or even one. Something informed me that if I went alone the experience would be even better.

"Well, how about $150 for the week?" Barbara stated. I paused, obviously having misheard her.

"Not $150, did you say?"

"I did, Mark. You see, Mrs. Blackwell appreciated what you did." I remember when she said it the word "appreciate" had the British "c" instead of "sh" intonation. *A-ppre-cee-ate.*

"But I didn't do anything" I said.

"And that was what she appreciated" Barbara replied. "That's one fifty all inclusive, with Violet and the staff."

I couldn't believe my ears. *She appreciated what you did.* And that was that. My second tour to "Goldeneye" was more memorable than the first. On this occasion however, I was flying solo. No other moonstruck chums. On my ownsome. And quite frankly, I needed the getaway. In short, I was ready to step into Ian Fleming's sandals, for a week, at least.

The unreality of my real-life fantasy had commenced once I landed at Montego Airport. I picked up my rental car and found my way out of the maze-work of what passes for the commercial sector. Then it was a clear shot headed for the North Shore of the island. The day was fine. I was in a good mood. I mean, who wouldn't be? You find yourself fancy free, pushing the accelerator down and headed for Paradise. And ready for adventure. But I didn't have long to wait for that.

I took note of the other car about half a mile behind me not long after I'd set out. Traffic at that hour and part of the world was anything but congested. Therefore even the presence of a car in my rear view seemed a kind of singularity. So I put the proverbial pedal down. Strangely however, despite my increased speed, I noted that the car behind was also moving like a bullet. Moreover, it seemed to be eating up the distance between us. So I pressed down again.

It went on this way for many miles. Before long I was irritated and also concerned. Who was it that was trailing me? And why didn't they come up and pass? Unless…

After a bit more of this cat and mouse, I decided to slow up and let my pursuer pass. On the whole I much preferred the idea of feeling entirely alone as I made the stretch between Montego Bay, Boscobel, and my destination. So I reversed my Steve MacQueen-at-Le Mans attitude and began to decelerate. But to my further surprise, so too did the car in the mirror.

This went on for another quarter of an hour. Now I could see the dark face of the vehicle's driver and glancing at my own shaded eyes in the mirror, suddenly I heard the old familiar guitar thrumming to a voice in my head.

Bond was used to being followed, but he knew how to handle it. Then of course there was the matter of why someone should be pacing him here, in the middle of beautiful Nowhere. Making a snap decision he decided to confront his pursuer rather than to wait for him to act. If there was going to be trouble, he wanted it now, and on his own terms.

I gunned the small Ford and shot ahead on the tarmac. Surveying the beachy shoulder for a good place to make my stand I finally saw it just ahead. Keeping an eye on the shape homing in ever closer behind me, I suddenly accelerated and came to the spot I'd chosen. Quickly I wrenched the wheel to the right and braked to the accompaniment of cloud of dust. Coming to a rapid halt as I did, I glanced in the rear-view mirror.

Bond braced himself for the confrontation. Reaching for the handle on the door, he sprang out of the car, ready and willing for whatever would come.

I was out of the car in a trice and standing there, legs poised for who-knew-what, when the other car, now nearly white with a hot sheen of dust, also came to a full stop. And just as I had done, now the driver, a black man in wraparound sunglasses, also bounded out onto the shoulder. *He was ready to dance as well*, I mused.

There wasn't enough time to wondered if or whether there would be trouble. It seemed to be here and now. I regretted not getting more of a head start if only to retrieve the dive knife from my luggage. I'd packed its sheathed, serrated blade along with my mask, snorkel and fins. But of that trio, now only having the knife available would have been a comfort. Too bad.

I now faced my pursuer and waited. We two stood there in silence as the dust had yet to settle. I decided to meet the issue head-first.

"What do you want?" I demanded. And I waited. And I wondered what I'd do at the first sign of a weapon in the stranger's hand.

"Mon, I been tryin' to catch up to ya" the man said. "I'm from de rental hire and dey tink mebbee you got an oil leak in the car." *Oil leak? Rental agency?*

"Then why the hell didn't you try and give me some sort of sign?" I demanded. "You could have honked the horn or waved to get my attention, couldn't you?" But for answer only a kind of dumb, embarrassed shrug.

What followed next was a cursory inspection of my car. After that, and determining no apparent leakage, we nodded at one another and parted. No handshake. No laughter. There hadn't been enough reason to merit either of those, I thought.

I took my time climbing back into the car as I waited and watched my lone companion wheel about and head back in the direction of Montego Bay. After a few extra moments I started up my engine and eased back onto the road that would eventually lead me to "Goldeneye." After a while I picked up speed, but not the kind of velocity I'd employed in trying to out-distance the man at my back. Thinking about it all, I suddenly heard myself swear and then laugh. And then I said to myself, *Well you wanted a bit of Bond adventure, didn't you? And you certainly got it.*

By the time I reached those familiar blue stone gate posts surmounted with their stone pineapples, I was truly excited. Yes, and prepared for a wonderful, sun-clad week spent alone writing and snorkeling and asking Violet, "what would the Commander be having about now?"

But from the moment I took the jungled drive up to the main house, I sensed something was wrong. As I switched the Ford's ignition off, listening to the heated engine simmering against the sounds of the heavy foliage around me, I saw the car.

It was a dust-furred convertible MG parked halfway beneath the shady palm-fronds within about twenty yards or so from the screened back door house. As I got out and knocked, I was met by the friendly face of Violet Cummings. I was especially pleased when she greeted me, and not as a stranger.

Once inside, I asked Violet whose car that was? Obviously the last thing I wanted was visitors or tourists, or anyone. "Oh, dats de car of a friend o' Mrs. Blackwell's. She's a painter lady who's got permission to be here and do a picture of de beach." *Just terrific* I thought, hearing this news. And slowly I began to envision spending the week watching Margaret Rutherford with an easel waddling up and down to the beach.

Still miffed, I crossed the main living area and headed for the welcome sight of the Commander's (and mine for the week) bedroom and unpacked my gear. Hot, a bit tired as well, all I now wanted was to strip down, get into some trunks and race down the steps to the beach with my snorkel and fins.

And that is exactly what I did. But it was only when I was standing in about a foot's worth of water looking out to the reef that it happened. I can't say what it was, exactly, but just as I was spitting into my mask I saw some movement within the rocky arbor beneath the cliff. I turned and studied it, only to see a vision.

Her name was Prudence. Prudence Lovell. Youngish, British, very attractive, and togged out in a summer shirt and khaki cargo pants. She was barefooted, nails painted a kind of pink, and slightly tanned. And did I remember to say, the lady was damned attractive without being showy? Try thinking of a Bond Girl, but for real.

I walked back up the beach and up to the concave bit of rock. "De painter lady" smiled at me, looking up as if she were entirely aware of my presence. I imagined that in that moment she too might have been considering how to deal with an unexpected intruder? If so, I did my best in turn by introducing myself, which she did as well. And then we began to chat. The first of countless others to follow that week. Eventually I got back into the water and let her finish what she was painting.

Over the course of those seven days I was anything but alone, and now entirely by choice. And in curious fashion it occurred to me that in a way here history was repeating itself. I'd read that when Ian Fleming set to creating *Casino Royale*, the first Bond book, he'd brought his new bride with him. And while he spent the days writing a gold-mine-in-the-making, Ann Fleming painted on the beach. And yes, possibly even close by that very same spot which Prudence had chosen.

And that was my second return to Paradise and to the house "where Bond was born." It was marked in a way which seemed nothing short of Providence looking down on me and saying, "give him a break." And it was that, to say the least. A week spent seemingly following a golden thread. Playing Fleming. Playing Bond. And the ritual was repeated, day by day. And like the Commander, I wrote by day, punctuating my efforts with a swim. The lady also painted while the Jamaican sun was high. But when it sank into the sea, everything changed. And in the evening there was dinner and long conversation and watching the moon rise over Cuba, out there somewhere in the faraway. It was a memory I'll cherish as long as I'm able.

My third time to "Goldeneye" was also memorable in a wonderfully heightened way. For the next year I was fortunate enough to bring my own bride to the North Shore and its most famous house, where again I savored its pleasures.

And now for the incredible/incredulous? postscript to my story.

Once again the Time Machine lurches forward as our surroundings whirl like a mad carousel.

In an expanse of, say, four years prior to this writing, I sat down to finally write my "new bit of country" concerning Ian Fleming. It took the shape of a novel, entitled *Shame Lady,* and it's set in Jamaica, Cuba, and across the Caribbean. But here's the point. Keeping faith with my promise thirty-one years ago to Blanche Blackwell to "hold off" on my idea, this year I felt the time had arrived. With that in mind I asked a new colleague, Andrew Lycett for a favor. Fortunately the author of the excellent biographies *The Man Who Created Sherlock Holmes: The Life and Times of Sir Arthur Conan Doyle* and *Ian Fleming: The Man Behind James Bond* was willing to comply. I hoped we'd be in sync for this. And the reason involved a mutual, albeit long ago acquaintance of mine, and a more recent one for Andrew. Our subject in common was Blanche Blackwell, "Goldeneye's" former owner, and as most Fleming aficionados probably could learn, Ian Fleming's long-term paramour and great, final love.

Visiting Mrs. Blackwell, now 103 years old, at her London home, Andrew Lycett presented her with a note from me. This informed her that indeed, I'd kept my promise to her, made in gratitude back in 1982. Also that my new and fictive *Shame Lady* featured her own good self, but under the pseudonym.

To the best of my knowledge and judging from what Lycett told me, he'd successfully relayed my message. I felt at the time he was therefore the perfect go-between, and truth to tell, my "last, best shot." After all, how often can one call upon an accomplished writer who'd written two *magnum opuses* concerning the two major and influential writers in one's own life? So he and I had discussed the matter. I handed the ball to him, so to speak, and I waited.

Nor was I exactly encouraged when I spoke to Andrew Lycett again, several weeks later. "I gave her your letter" he said, "but I wouldn't expect you to hear back" he added. His words did little other than dampen my spirits. Why would she not reply? And then the reality of the thing hit me,

First of all, if as I trusted, Blanche Blackwell had received my communique, had it been read to her? I'd heard that these days the lady was nearly blind. So then, had my go-between said something like "I was asked to pass this onto you," but what did that suggest? Nor had I asked him to read it to her, which may have asked a bit much.

And then of course there was another suspicion lurking unaccountably, in my mind. Would my surrogate have any reason to wish to further my contact, owing to the fact that I'd told him I'd been working on "something entirely new" about Ian Fleming? Artistic altruism notwithstanding, the phrase, "honour among thieves" (and writers) had popped into my head at the time.

At any rate, the seeming end of the story found more time passing with no indication from Mrs. Blackwell that she'd received my note. That then was enough to compel me to face facts. This was the end of the line for an exploit which had commenced more than three decades ago. And now? "That's the end of it" I told myself. *Or so at least, I thought.*

Now then, envision if you will, just as in one of those old Forties films, a sort of desk-top calendar, the pages of which are being flipped as if by some unseen breeze signifying the passage of time.

So then, picture if you will your humble scribe in the year 2016. After spending eight days following old Arthurian pathways around Glastonbury and Wells, he finds himself with one spare afternoon in London. Trying to decide on an endless *smorgasbord* of options in that city of so many memories, he opts for one odd choice. He will visit Paddington Station. And why? For the sake of photographing the terminus' famous statue of its eponymous symbol, Paddington Bear.

As an aside, I happen to love the Paddington stories by Michael Bond. In fact, on one occasion I was so imbued with enthusiasm that my terrier Bradbury and I decided to write the famous bear's creator a fan-letter. Enclosed with it was a snapshot of Bradbury, my own plush Paddington, and myself on the sofa.

Well wonder of kind wonders, a short while later we received a reply. It was a lovely note from Bond—Michael Bond—telling us how much he enjoyed our letter and how nice it must be for Bradbury and I to live in such a place as Grosse Ile! But wondrous too was the writer's own enclosure, which was an autographed photo of Paddington and his creator.

So then, fueled by that recent memory, there I was in pre-Brexit England, and now entraining to Paddington for my special mission. One day, I mused, perhaps Isabella and Christian would share our love for the little ursine waif from Peru! And adding to their interest might be a picture of the bear and their grandfather, long ago!

Well as they used to say, despite "the best laid plans," my own to get off the Metro line at Paddington, went pear-shaped. It chanced that work was being done on the line and would require a change at another station. As it chanced, that stop was going to be Sloane Square. In that moment of decision I recalled two things; first off, that this was the very stop-off point I'd experienced on many occasions over a decade. The reason for this had involved my going to visit "the daughter of Sherlock Holmes," Dame Jean Conan Doyle at her Cadogan Square flat.

Now I've told the story of Dori and my own first foray to meet Sir Arthur's daughter. But "the rest of the story" spans out for a long bit of time which more often than not didn't necessarily involve my play. Instead, it involved two friends, and one of them a great lady whose own accomplishments were stellar. There was of course the fact that she was the only girl-child of Sir Arthur, and by ways of literary paternity, also the "sister" of Holmes, who was perhaps the most prominent of Doyle's issue.

It was with a kind of bittersweet recollection that I got off at Sloan Square. I remembered my last visit to see my friend. And then something else occurred to me. Suddenly the voice in my head said *You know, Sloan Square is not all that far on the map from Lowndes Square, is it?"*

Lowndes Square. This happened to be, as I also recalled, where I'd heard that Blanche Blackwell, my much-sought-after contact, resided to this day. The only problem to date had involved this quadrant of London as a kind of very large hay-stack containing the "needle" no one had been able to pin-point.

And it was then that I made my resolve: I would hop it to Lowndes Square and, as Indiana Jones once said, "make it all up as I go." Imagine then my eventually arriving at my destination, in the form of a huge and sprawling crescent of some of the most expensive realty in all of Her Majesty's capital.

Standing there, I viewed the stretch of handsome old structures flanking the Square. Sighing, I remember looking up overhead and saying "God, I'm here. If you can do anything to help, I'd be grateful. And if not, then that will be the proper end of my search."

I proceeded along the angled walkway and took note of a certain reality. For within or beyond the endless porticos there were numbered and copiously buttoned panels for each of the building's residents. However and contrary to what was common practice in the States, here the numerical buttons did not bear the names of the building's denizens. Also and upon closer notice I also saw that every panel provided a button marked CONCIERGE.

With a sense of trepidation I depressed the concierge's button. I followed the disembodied "Yes?" with my request.

384

"I'm seeking a party by the name of Blanche Blackwell" I said, bending low to the speaker. Seconds passed. Then the distant-sounding voice.

"No Blackwell here" it said with a dismissive tone. "Try further down."

Undaunted, I walked down the crescent past a number of other buildings. Feeling like a participant in some random game, I finally turned toward the next portico on my left and ascended its flight of steps.

Locating the CONCIERGE button I depressed it and waited to re-experience a sense of disappointment.

When the metallic voice asked my purpose, I repeated my query.

"I'm looking for a resident named Blackwell" I said. Another succession of silent moments. And then.

"Flat Seven, Fourth floor" the voice said.

"I beg your pardon" I stammered. "Is that Blanche Blackwell?"

"Flat Seven, Fourth floor" the voice repeated. *Unbelievable.*

Once inside I gained sight of a friendly looking Indian-seeming young fellow seated behind his desk. Uncertain of whether or not he was the visual equivalent of the invisible speaker, I faced him and announced "I'm here to see Mrs. Blackwell."

"Very good" the young man said. "May I ring up to announce your arrival?"

"Quite honestly, I'd rather it be a surprise" I said, surprising even myself. And it was just then I noted the open-door of the lobby's small lift. Advancing toward and then entering it, I waved at the young chap and said, "thanks very much" as the lift door closed.

In a trice the door opened again to the Fourth Floor. Stepping out, I surveyed the small corridor and noted Number Seven to the left a few yards away. Approaching that much anticipated portal of my long-awaited destination, I paused and drew a breath. Then I depressed the bell near the door.

In short order the door was answered by a crisply uniformed woman, whose island-lilted voice greeted me. *Jamaican, I deduce. Possibly Montego or Kingston* I heard Sherlock Holmes suggest.

In calmed but rapid-fire order I explained that I was calling upon Mrs. Blackwell, who had kindly allowed me the use of her "Goldeneye" on three occasions many years before. Being in London for only that afternoon, I'd decided to offer my compliments, even as I apologized for arriving unannounced.

And while I suppose the gist of my remarks sounded like some Georgian caller having pulled up in a brougham before this handsome structure, it was all true enough. And could it really be possible, I asked myself, that after so many endeavors over so much time, that I'd reached the purpose of my quest at last?

The dark lady nearly smiled as she asked if I would wait a moment? I agreed, even as she turned about and left me quite literally on the threshold of my long-intended purpose.

Perhaps twenty seconds or so later the guardian reappeared.

"Please if you would follow me, sir?"

And follow I did. Into the handsome foyer and outward into an *Architectural Digest* caliber of London flat. I'd heard that possibly the city's most gorgeous and expensive of the city's sophisticated dwellings were seated here, along Lowndes Square. Now as I followed, I had little doubt this was true.

The maid, as she seemed to be, extended her arm toward the small figure on the couch around the flat's book-cased corner. And there in that moment I was reminded of Holmes's quotation of Shakespeare's words: "Journey's end in lover's meetings." Lovers? Not mine, at least. But Ian Fleming's own lady love, as most interested parties by now had learned.

And there, facing the very near large screen of her television, which was showing some sort of tribute to the Queen, sat the 103-year-old Blanche Blackwell.

I remember looking down upon that cheerful, rather bird-like lady, who looked up toward me as I described what amounted to our longago first meeting. And of how I'd come to Goldeneye with the aim of writing "something new" about her friend Fleming. And also, as strategically as I could, I alluded to what I'd told her only the final evening of my Jamaican sojourn; namely that I'd decided to "hold off writing, until the time was right."

As I well recalled too, my second return and even my third successive stay at the House Where Bond Was Born had much to do with my decision not to write. And of how I'd been told that second winter that "Mrs. Blackwell appreciates what you did." And when I stated, "I did nothing," I was informed that "that is what she appreciated."

So then, there I was once again, I explained, and after more than thirty years, I'd reappeared at last, armed with the news that I had at last written something worthy of sharing about "the Commander."

"But I certainly didn't think it would take so long" I laughed, which prompted a risible response from the lady herself. She asked me to sit down there on the divan next to her. Which I did. Even as we began to speak about my longago visits and ultimately, my yet-to-be-published novel *Shame lady,* which rather dramatically involved Ian Fleming. And as I added, but not without some degree of trepidation, the fact that I'd created another of my book's characters, Maeve Steadwell, cast in the image of her real-life alter ego!

Over the course of the next hour or so, I sat next to the figure of so many of my day-dreams. And she in turn shared aspects of her life, both before and after meeting and loving Ian Fleming.

She was also very candid about those "old days" when Jamaica had experienced a kind of liberal and artistic Renaissance. Also about others such as Errol Flynn (who once proposed marriage to her) as well as such Fleming/Blackwell friends like Noel Coward and Ivar Bryce.

Both of those had also danced through the pages of my novel, I told Blanche, as she asked me to call her.

Suffice it to say, the miraculous weight of that incredible experience on that rare afternoon made me kindle a myriad of thoughts. Included among them was my recollection of the old Sinatra version of "A Foggy Day in London Town." And while my impromptu visit was in no way fog-bound, the lyric evoked another cogitation, when it said "how long, I wondered, could this thing last? The age of miracles has surely passed." Or had it? Apparently not, I mused, over and over again after I'd taken my leave.

Finally en route to Paddington Station and its two life-like effigies of its namesake, I could not cease to be amazed at my good fortune. Or was it more than that? Had my decades-ago meeting of the younger love of Ian Fleming's later life represented something deeper, if not prophetic? All I knew is that long, long after I'd set out to seek her, I'd found my "needle in the haystack." And all it had taken was what a friend liked to call a "God incident," which may have taken the shape of some maintenance in a portion of London's Underground.

One day in another place I'll reveal more of that golden afternoon's long-awaited assignation, and what I learned from one remarkably seasoned woman. To James Bond's only begetter, "Mrs. Blackwell" was Ian Fleming's equivalent of Sherlock Holmes's Irene Adler. *The Woman,* Dr. Watson had called her. And just as "Pussy Galore" and "Honeychile Ryder" in the 007 saga had been reputedly based upon the object of my admiration and chronic questing, so too had her real-life counterpart become unwittingly immortal within the cinema, if not upon the pages of popular literature.

2016 marked the prelude to Britain's controversial choice of opting out of the European Union. Thus was Brexit added to history's vernacular. But for me, that British escape had signified not a few turning points. Some of those were disappointing, but others, such as my homing-in toward Lowndes Square, just shy of miraculous. For that impromptu detour had rendered the unmistakable impression that I'd been led to a seemingly destined answer, but only after demonstrating my loyalty to its purpose. That as I have found throughout the course of my life, is often the way. And lucky me in consequence.

That well-remembered Spring afternoon in London had signaled a great deal, indeed. For even as I did then and still continue to realize, I had found my Grail, in the person of the first of the Bond Girls. Who in turn seemed glad to be "found," and invited me to sit down once again by her side.

Blanche Blackwell passed from this life the year after our reunion. Surrendering at the age of 104 in 2017, I've little doubt she was ready to move. Yes, even as my late friend Jean Conan Doyle once described the sensations of age, and of "standing at the station, your bag packed, but the train just does not arrive."

But I do like to think, based upon our conversation concerning Ian Fleming the man, rather than as the Begetter of Bond, and on that note I knew she had greatly loved and now missed him. Enough so to more than likely look forward to her own possible reuniting with "the Commander." I'd imagined as much in the final page of my novel. The two of them arm-in-arm, staring out at sunset's falling curtain even as the surf surged on, as if beckoning to those two statue-like figures on the beach.

In any event, I hope they're both together now, free of age or illness, perhaps strolling the unspoiled sands of some wonderfully Jamaica-like stretch of beach. That's something to conjure, isn't it?

Time now to move along, if not backward on the calendar. The juncture of time upon our Wellsian machinery's chronometer is now re-set for the past. And given that the name of Herbert George Wells has a tendency to crop up within these pages, perhaps an "aside."

I have always felt a strange sympathy between "H.G." and "ACD." This no doubt reflected a true liking between the two men, both of whom were fine fantasists, but also forward-looking, would-be social reformers.

But both of these top-flight writers had to earn their stripes after a considerable time, if not a considerable output of words. Over time this found both authors finding success when something they'd written seemed to click with a vast readership.

Given the period and world they shared, I have never quite divorced the images of Doyle and Wells, respectively. No doubt the personalities of each had much to do with their creations. Also I am sure that in reflection of any scribe's attempts to re-conjure the Past, each in their ways is himself a "time machine."

However in the year 1894 H.G. Wells wrote his novella *The Time Machine,* which, you might say, started the clock running. Himself already married but separated from his spouse, Wells embarked upon an unusual adventure involving his extra-marital relationship with Amy Catherine Robbins, whom he had tutored for her bachelor of science degree. Unusual too was the fact that the smitten swain brought not only his mistress but also her mother to a rented holiday dwelling in Kent.

So it was that Wells, Catherine, and Mrs. Robbins shared engaged rooms at a semi-detached residence seated on Kent's suburban Eardley Road, Sevenoaks. There over the course of a fortnight the author wrote *The Time Machine,* which like Conan Doyle's 1902 *Hound of the Baskervilles* was destined to always be equated with the author's name.

For obvious reasons then, on one of my forays to see Dame Jean Conan Doyle, Dori and I made haste to enjoy our own holiday. One Holmes-unrelated stopover was Sissinghurst, the world-renown garden and house once created by Vita Sackville-West and her diplomatist husband Harold Nicolson.

Through some stroke of luck, now rather hazy, I managed for our Sissinghurst visit to include a private tour of the grounds, guided by none other than publisher-journalist-historian-and-author Nigel Nicolson. The fact that we were being ushered about by "Vita's" son was a thrill, and the special access he offered Dori and I of the house and its environs was to be envied.

Also and in related fashion, I'd wanted to visit Knole, the Sevenoaks Kentish estate associated with the Sackville-Wests and immortalized by Virginia Woolf's novel *Orlando.* The book itself was a sort of love letter to the estate in question, by way of being its author's paean to Vita, who for the sake of being female could never inherit the home of her ancestors. So instead of that her paramour, Mrs. Woolf, penned a gender-bending saga with her *enamorada* at its core. Ergo, "Orlando"/Vita's connection to the home of her forefathers would be indelibly fused.

But after enjoying our meander through the magnificent house and grounds of Knole, including its deer-park, I made an announcement to my wife.

"I want to see the house where H.G. Wells wrote his *Time Machine.*" It's in the town portion of Sevenoaks and I've got the address. So off we went to that not-all-that-well-known literary landmark.

When we got to Eardley Road the house for all intents and purposes bore no marked connection to Wells or his literary masterpiece. No blue plaque or other designation. In fact, had I not originally seen the photo of the house in Peter Haining's *H.G. Wells Scrapbook,* I wouldn't have known it on sight.

When we got there I paced back and forth across the hedged front walk-way before the semi-detached edifice, which seemed the twin of its neighbor. Then I made bold enough to go up and peer into the house. It seemed for the moment at least unoccupied. So, resigned to the moment, I knocked on the house next door. But likewise, no answer, So I re-resigned myself to "having been there" and minimally contented myself with a series of photos of what I thought of as The Time Machine House.

That then was going to constitute my adventure concerning H. G. Wells. At least until I returned home and realized my egregious error: for despite or on account of my great excitement, *we'd visited the wrong house.* That's right, for as it turned out Number Twenty-Three, Eardley Road was the building adjacent to the one we'd reconnoitered!

Upset but only temporarily daunted, I filed away that erroneous attempt until the next trip to London, Fast forwarding to the following year, allow me to state that "the second try was the charm." Armed with research, pictures, as well as a revitalized will to see where one of the world's classic books had been sired, we made the second attempt— and succeeded.

And here's the strange postscript to that trip. Standing once again on that stretch of Eardley Road and confirming the small numerals upon the door's small portico, I felt like a climber returning to Everest to complete his formerly unsuccessful ascent.

I recall also being tempted to see more of the place. Once again, after knocking on the sheltered front door, it appeared no was at home to hear it. This led me to think that despite being offered a tour, or even at the risk of being tossed out on my ear for trespassing, I had a chance to spy things out. This notion was furthered by a glimpse of the gate to the modest back garden.

So then, emboldened like Raffles, I tread softly to the wooden portal flanking the house from the adjacent foliage. Before me I saw a wrought iron ring serving as the head-level heighted gate in question.

Reaching for the ring I was startled at once and also a bit alarmed. For the circlet of old black iron had come off in my hand!

I cannot in all good conscience recite what was going on in my mind in those moments. All I knew was that I was standing there, red-handed, you might say, in an attempt to voluntarily trespass upon someone's vintaged property. Worse yet, I had technically damaged that property, or a small part of it.

Looking down at the seemingly forged bit of iron in my palm, I suddenly registered an inner and solitary voice in my head. "The ring to H.G. Wells' garden gate has come loose, or broken off" it said. "You need to protect or preserve this artifact, lest some bounder comes along and does who knows what."

And that is how one of the most contentious decisions I've made in yonks, as some not-so-great Briton once said, came about. For as if to heed that Greek chorus of one, I made no attempt to replace the garden gate's ring. I thought instead, "when you return here sometime, you can bring the ring-handle with you as you explain why you purloined it, however temporarily."

And that's the end of the story. And that is why, even as these words are written, the Time Machine House's gate's handle reposes only a few feet away. In fact, and perhaps appropriately, it has been placed in situ with a small model I made years back of the Wellsian Time Traveler's conveyance. Before that it hung from a small hook within the glass globe which protects my old hunter-case pocket watch. As if "charging" it, you might say, with the residual energy of something which H.G. himself might have once touched.

And here's what I call the "cherry on the top" for this story. For you see, before leaving Number 23 for the second time, 'lo those years ago, I re-shot any number of photographs. But more interesting to me than anything else was the wrought iron gate which stood between the two nearly hedge-covered brick posts. One sees that gate in the oldest of photos I've seen. But what they did not reveal is what I took note of as I was close enough to touch that gate. I'm speaking of the gate's designed motif, which seemed to resemble compass points, or some form of chronological dials. But what, I wondered, might this mean?

In short order I fantasized the answer, which is as good as anyone's guess, I believe. And that has to do with (1) from the look of it today and (2) from the indication that the longago first depictions included this very gate, then (3) that gate must have confronted H.G. Wells every day for weeks back in 1894.

And if indeed Herbert saw those dial-life shapes, might they have somehow reminded him of time, clocks, and chronometers of the past and possible future? Here then, had I viewed the precursor to the Time Machine, the works and totality of which had been assembled within the ground-floor front room of Number Twenty-Three? Perhaps. And once again, so I have come to believe, at least in conjunction of what I've come to term the Churchillian Principal: to wit, "it's all true or it ought to be; and more and better besides."

That then is my reflection upon literature's greatest of all travelers through time and space. And once again, of how sometimes persistence wins the day. As does, I think, honor.

So perhaps the next time I return to Sevenoaks I'll make that self-promised detour to Eardley Road. I mean, by then I'll have "charged" a sufficiency of relics with the power of the "Wells House," its curious history, if not each of its gates. Time then to "return in time" on my own, if only for the sake of restoring that weathered wrought iron ring to its former home.

Which now leads us here to a remembered succession of years including 1979, 1984, 85, and 86. These in turn would also serve as a prelude to yet another little foray, and this one involving the name of Shakespeare. William Shakespeare.

I suppose my interest in the "mystery" involving the name and life of he who is regarded as the world's greatest dramatist began early on. In particular my attention was piqued about my time in junior high school when I read a book entitled *The Murder Of The Man Who Was Shakespeare.* Like a clarion call which would later become a sort of battle cry, I became fascinated by its author, Calvin Hoffman's conjecture that it was not Shakespeare, the acclaimed poet-playwright who wrote "Hamlet" and so much more—but his contemporary, that gay, Elizabethan James Bond himself, Christopher Marlowe.

Hoffman's premise was that Marlowe's death by stabbing in 1593 was in effect, a put-up job. More intriguing was his hypothesis that Marlowe was in effect a spy who could not come in from the cold. Ergo, his death was falsified so the man himself could live on, under an assumed name. And that name? You guessed it: William Shakespeare!

The "facts of the case" as Holmes himself might review them, are scarce for William Shakespeare's life and dramatic career. Such a scarcity has been trumped by Mark Twain, Freud, Bismarck, Dickens, Orson Welles and others. In effect, all we may presume to know "factually" is that one William Shaksper of Stratford was born and christened. He eventually married an older woman, had children by her, and presumably, left rural Stratford for London. In London he supposedly worked at the Globe theater as a horse-handler before he became an actor, and then a playwright, and then, if you listen to his idolators, God. But this came only seven years after "Shakespeare's" death in 1616. We don't know a whole lot before that. Not if you skip over the fact that there was no factual testimonial to "Gentle Will's" early or later education, or his training by profession or travels to write the things he did. Moreover, a Shakespeare does act in London, but we don't know if it's the same chap. All we do know is that when Great Elizabeth dies, there is not a word in tribute from Shakespeare, later called the "Soul of his age." Nor was there any public or overt mourning in London when the man dies in Stratford, presumably in his bed, in 1616. No tributes, no recollection of him as in any way being artful. He leaves a thoroughgoing businessman's will, with no papers, books, manuscripts, rights to plays, etc. He leaves his wife his "second best bed" and behind him, an illiterate daughter.

All we know about "Shakespeare" of Stratford is that he was a man of business who liked suing for his rights. He sued to keep the poor folk off the village common. He had debtors. He had business affairs. But none we can see which were in any way artful. And then, seven years after this "soul" passes on, great tributes and a collection of his works in the First Folio are released.

I always thought it was convenient that Shakespeare strode on stage, both literally and figuratively, just as Kit Marlowe took his exit. And if you listened to fellows like Calvin Hoffman, there were all sorts of clues which proved that Marlowe was Shakespeare. These in the main, he said, came in echoes and copies and paraphrases of Marlowe's work and those of the "Immortal Bard." Coincidence? Plagiarism? Who knew?

The mystery was however sufficient enough to make me a young Marlovian. I was not aware then, nor could I have known, that old Kit would lead me into the quasi-legal duel to come. Ironically as well, many years earlier, in similar fashion, a sea-change of sorts had occurred to the youthful Myron Wahls, who would become my older and stately friend in the Eighties.

Mike Wahls became a Court of Appeals Judge in Detroit, and he was handsome, erudite, and fascinated, as was I, about the Shakespeare Authorship Question. But there was a reason for that. For you see, in his own youth he'd written a term paper about something he was suddenly passionate about: namely, the possibility that Francis Bacon, rather than Will Shakespeare, had written "Hamlet."

Mike's account of his own brash, attempted brush with anti-establishment thinking resonated with me. And the reason for that?

Well coincidentally or not, I too had penned a youthful *magnum opus*, but mine suggested Christopher Marlowe as the culprit, rather than the man from Stratford. But in each of our cases, and even as Judge Wahls grew up accepting the usual party line about the "Sweet Swan of Avon," our paths were accordingly paved—both as friends as well as literary adversaries.

At any rate, I enlisted my friend the Judge in a couple of Shakespearean debates, and again in 1989 for "The Great Shakespeare Duel," a PBS-aired, dramatically mounted "trial," complete with a celebrity jury, a judge, defense and prosecution councils, and a kind of *vox populi,* audience jury ready to make their verdict. I took on the Prosecution role, and Wahls the Defense. But this time, even as he'd announced in a media-grabbing press conference a few days before our "Duel,' "I shall be stepping down from the altar, so to speak, to enter the arena." And in his earlier stead, I had a well-known female appeals judge wearing the magistrate's white wig.

There was a great deal of press on our "Shakespeare Duel," and rightfully so. For even as Mike Wahls and I both knew, the issue of our respective childhood was no longer akin to religious anathema. Perhaps it had to do with a growing public distrust of authority, of someone's traumatic experience in a Shakespeare class in school. Whatever the reason, to question the Bard on the basis of evidence was, I realized, a matter of escalating academic scrutiny.

Mike and I pounded away at one another, traded jibes, and questioned our witnesses. And at the end of the metaphorical day? While I was told that the celebrity jury were on the edge, they chose to side with tradition. But not the "audience jury" in attendance of 300-plus. They voted "Nay!" on the basis of reasonable doubt. And Shakespeare, whoever he was, lost the day.

I recall many things about our mock "trial." Chief among these was the fact that I'd battled bronchitis for more than a week, and even days before our event I had difficulty speaking. Also, acting in my Orson Welles-like capacity as producer, director and performer, I was a bit nervous, chiefly because my parents were sitting up front.

But when the verdict came in, I was elated. I had called the facts into question in this literary investigation, and I believed even Sherlock Holmes would have been amused, if not intrigued.

There was also another rather fascinating upshot of my squaring off against the Establishment view of Mr. Shakespeare. I knew there would be, charted from my earlier conversation with the press rep for the erudite Folger Shakespeare Library in Washington. Hearing of our intentions in Southfield, Michigan, he actually asked me to cancel our event! He then threatened to bring the matter of our heinous doings in Michigan to the attention of the Folger's Director. "Please do!" I implored.

But within a month or less of our victory for the Prosecution, I was contacted by none other than the collateral descendant of the present Earl of Oxford, whose Elizabethan ancestor was now perhaps the best "candidate" for the Shakespearean authorship. Moreover, having heard of our success, Charles Vere and his team in London wished for us to join him at the Middle Temple Hall, where a British "Shakespeare Moot" would be held. Asked if I would come, I replied "you betcha!" or words to that effect. And I went. And again, saw the Oxfordians lose by a hair.

The Shakespeare "vindication" did in fact prove one important thing: the Opposition was gaining on the phantom horse so long in the lead. Moreover, as each year passed, something new served to awaken the public. The mood had changed. And just as I recalled my friend Wahl's story about his youthful challenging of the Bard, there'd also been my own much later. Consolingly however, today there were many reasons why there might be fewer teachers categorically stating, "everybody knows Shakespeare wrote it." Because not everyone does.

So I suppose I can lay claim to participating in "the trials of William Shakespeare." And if you were to ask, "well where do you sit with it now?" I'd probably describe my posture as leaning more than ever before in the direction of the Earl of Oxford. And that's not faith, friends, but an opinion based upon evidence which supports it.

But time has a way of either making us think, or it simply gives us more to think about. This I confess to be true with my evolved belief in a

Welsh rooting for the actual person of King Arthur and also a grudgingly retained belief that something of a mytho-historical nature still prowls the depths of Loch Ness.

But these days I cannot ignore the tantalizing "absence of evidence" concerning the chimera the literary establishment calls "Shakespeare." And while I am aware that here the true value of the matter depends upon the "work" ascribed to the Sweet Swan of Avon, it remains an intellectually-directed necessity that we measure authors, past and present, on the basis of their lives and talents.

Ergo, and at the risk of making this sound like a Parthian shot, I am more than ever disposed to focus my interests upon Edward DeVere, the Seventeenth Earl of Oxford. For it was as scholar, patron, dramatic producer, agent, and co-author of some at least presently deemed "Shakespearean" works (possibly within league of certain of his talented contemporaries) that Oxford fits the Shakespeare Template rather nicely. His family background, his education, his peccadillos, his travels, his contacts, all of these conspire in his favor. Moreover, he offers us a sort of nexus for those other "authorial claimants" over the centuries, such as Kit Marlowe (always a favorite here) and Sir Francis Bacon.

Moreover, I remain convinced that as a disservice to history, literature and drama, clinging religiously to the Stratfordian assumptions is not only dangerous, but simply wrong.

For today, and for this moment of writing, if pressed to put my pension on the bet, I'd likely put my money on Oxford. There are just too many factors that lean in his favor, and to enumerate them all here would be to be writing an entirely other book. Suffice it to say, and in concert with the theme of this memoir, that had Sherlock Holmes been made privy to what we now do not know about 'Shakspere' and do know about Edward de Vere, I'd wager he'd fall in with the Oxfordians.

But that's a matter you'll have to take up for yourself. As I've said, it's long been a knotty problem, and over time and experience, one may well tend to take a new perspective. Or as the popular guru Wayne Dyer once sagely stated, "sometimes when you look at things differently, they begin to look different." I value the meaning of that, and am not reluctant to state that I have willfully looked at things "differently," and in consequence now see them in a new or clearer light.

And on that note, for the moment at least, the Prosecution rests.

William Shakespeare and James Bond. Throw in Sherlock Holmes and you begin to get an impression of the strange choir which still chants in my mind. That, as well as those "strangely serendipitous connections" which always exist. One of those deserves mention here. Take Christopher Marlowe, whom we now know served in Her Majesty's Secret Service. Moreover, one of his contacts was Elizabeth I's court magus and astrologer, John Dee. Well at the risk of trying to explain it, or offer up a "how?" or "why?" I'll just say it: one of Dee's coded identities was—brace yourselves—007!

As I look back upon that time, and upon the heels of my fascinations with William Shakespeare and Ian Fleming, I wonder if they might they have unwittingly prepared me for another foray into investigation? But this time the human subject involved would exist between 16th and 20th centuries, respectively. This time around I would find myself returning to another and bygone era I had found remarkably familiar as a youngster. Now however I was about to draw even closer to the radius of an unmet friend. And little could I know it at the time, I would manage to do so through the friendship, courtesy, and patience of his daughter.

And that man's name was Arthur Conan Doyle.

"A Certain Gracious Lady"
Dame Jean Conan Doyle and the Author

Henry Ford Community College
and
Daedalos Productions
in conjunction with
Dame Jean Conan Doyle

presents

An Evening
with
Sir Arthur Conan Doyle

A Memoir of
Mystery & Myth
with
Mark McPherson as Conan Doyle

November 16 & 17, 1990
Adray Auditorium
MacKenzie Fine Arts Center
Henry Ford Community College
8 p.m.

LIVE...
ON STAGE!

WORLD
PREMIERE!

Tickets available at:
The HFCC College Store
and the
Little Professor Book Center
(West Dearborn)
or at the door

Welcome to "An Evening with ACD"

"The Daughter of Sherlock Holmes" – The Shape of Things To Come

23
"The Daughter Of Sherlock Holmes"

I found the old magazine in an Ann Arbor bookstore one rainy Friday evening. On my own, I'd treated myself to a solitary dinner and then made my way to the familiar shop on Main Street.

Upon discovering the periodical in question, I'd been immediately drawn to the magazine's cover. This featured two figures, an older man and a younger woman beside him. Despite their ages and gender, there was a strange and intentional similitude between them. This was emphasized by the fact that both of them wore a rather feminine and peculiarly canary-hued brimmed cap featuring a black ribbon which encircled their headgear, respectively.

More peculiar yet, while the attractive younger woman's ensemble also featured a matching yellow bowed cravat, her companion's attire was dark, as was the ebony curved stem pipe he had clenched in his teeth.

Nor could there be any doubt as to the identity of the couple on the cover of the July, 1933 issue of MYSTERY Magazine. Its title was sufficient to tell that: "The DAUGHTER OF SHERLOCK HOLMES." And inside the magazine's contents page led with a rectangular black and white photo of the lady on the cover. It was titled "The MYSTERY SCOOP OF THE YEAR!" And below it, "Introducing—SHIRLEY HOLMES THE FAMOUS GIRL DETECTIVE."

Well, sparing you any further information concerning the MYSTERY feature entitled "The Adventure of the Queen Bee" by Basil Mitchell and Frederic Arnold Kummer, I hark back only to the story's title. Unknown to me then, this existed as an unwitting preview of an as-yet-impossible-to-know coming attraction. But as the future would subsequently reveal, "THE DAUGHTER OF SHERLOCK HOLMES" would become an enduring reality for me several years later and for nearly a decade after that. But unlike the idea of that Thirties pulp adventure which pitted the daughters of both Holmes and Dr. Watson against an insidious plot, more fascinating yet was their creator's living offspring, in the person of Air Commandant Dame Lena Jean Annette Conan Doyle, Lady Bromet, DBE AE WRAF ADC (1912-1997), known to the Holmesian world as Dame Jean Conan Doyle. But to me she was always "my friend, Jean." And before continuing, here is another of those irksome asides.

As I often consider it, there is a peculiar affinity of sorts between the great literary successes of Sir Arthur Conan Doyle and Commander Ian Fleming. In essence this amounted to two of the most successful literary creations in the history of the world's popular literature. Moreover this also had much to do with the curious manner by which each writer found himself overshadowed by his own fictive creation. As a consequence, the lives and careers of both Sherlock Holmes and Secret Agent James Bond would assume a level of reality which at times seemed to exceed that of their artful makers. But more than that and their mutual successes notwithstanding, both Holmes and Bond would take on the trappings of a self-made monster for their respective Frankenstein creators.

By 1985 what I considered to be my "investigative method" had found me getting very close to my subjects. In most cases this was often based upon being at the places, walking where my subjects walked, and if and whenever possible, of my associating with others who had direct or most often indirect "proximity" to my interest.

And of course, there must be a modicum of normalcy in this portion of memoir, don't you think? On that note then, allow me to interject: *1985. Another marriage. A fascinating and beautiful woman. And another chance at renewing my odd, if not irregular existence.* But never to date had I been brought so close, or enabled such a privileged sense of access as I did in the autumn of 1987.

I had been in Glastonbury "carrying coals to Newcastle." Or to state it factually, I'd been asked by my colleague Geoffrey Ashe to deliver a lecture about King Arthur at the virtual heartbeat of that place where British interest in Camelot's king had long simmered. But on the heels of this event and upon my return to London I was slated to pay a very special social call. This had been arranged through the auspices of my friend John Bennett Shaw.

Even at this time in my life, I felt the strange magic which had culminated in my relationship with John. We'd first met at Bill Rabe's garden party back in 1962, and now, nearly a quarter of a century later, here we were, old enough to be equals, but never, I presumed, upon that level of respect and enterprise which my friend had drawn to his southwestern headquarters.

J.B. Shaw was already a legend of sorts within the Sherlockian Irregular movement. To date his prowess as a speaker, humorist, bibliophile, and of course, the begetter of the Brothers Three of Moriarty of Santa Fe, New Mexico. His annual "Unhappy Birthday, Moriarty" fetes had become legendary, and nearly as much as Shaw's own stature as one of the country's most illustrious Holmes scholars.

In the Spring of 1979 I'd had the honor and pleasure of coordinating a two-and-a-half day Sherlockian conference, "Sherlock Holmes: Alive and Well" at Detroit's Wayne State University. This unique event involved John as keynote speaker, as well as another Holmes acquaintance of mine, the popular mystery and western author Loren Estleman. Nine movies and a film strip were included in the weekend event, as well as many presentations, contests, prizes, cocktails, and a "Sherlockian banquet." It was great fun and there was more time than usual to see John and his lovely wife, Dorothy. It was also a wonderful opportunity of renewing a friendship which had begun back when God was younger, and so was I. But each of our meetings had set a special tone of sorts. And unbeknown to me at the time, eight years later there would be another meeting in the offing, and this one largely due to John's efforts.

Now cut to 1987. Dori and I arrive in London and at our hotel we find flowers, with a card reading, *"Welcome to London. Warmest Greetings, Jean."* The words thrilled me, for as I knew, the writer was an old friend of Shaw's, with whom I now had an appointment to meet. And the lady's name? *Jean Conan Doyle.*

We arrived on schedule to Dame Jean's flat at Number 72 Cadogan Square. I have often found, and to my chagrin, that certain people or events tend to go unappreciated in full at the time, but only in retrospect do we gain a full sense of their value. This may be a good thing or not, or may even be a blessing in disguise. For, let us say for example, if you meet someone whose accomplishments are enough to freeze you into inaction, then maybe it's better that you didn't know it all. And that to a certain degree was certainly the case with Jean Conan Doyle, *a.k.a.* Lady Bromet, who despite her personal accomplishments, was often better known for filial connection with the creator of Sherlock Holmes.

In this instance however, what we were talking about was the second daughter of Conan Doyle who'd once been dubbed a tomboy by Harry Houdini. An early childhood spent proudly wearing her nickname "Billy," she used to sign letters to her father "Your loving son." This however lasted until scarcely her tenth birthday, upon which she announced to one and all that she'd decided to be a girl.

After attending school Jean would go on to serve for three decades in the Women's Auxiliary Air Force, or "WAAF, where her specialty was military intelligence during the Second World War. She was commissioned a section offer and them temporarily as a flight officer in 1942 and subsequently to a temporary squadron officer in 1944. In 1947 (the year of my birth) Jean Conan Doyle became Acting Wing Officer Conan Doyle and was eventually appointed OBE (Military Division) in the New Year Honours List of 1948. She would then be granted a permanent commission as a wing officer in the renamed Women's Royal Air Force (WRAF), and group officer in 1952. Eleven years later she was promoted to air commandant, the highest rank in the Women's Royal Air Force. And in the Spring of that same year she was appointed an honorary Aide-de-Camp to Queen Elizabeth II. In the 1963 Birthday Honours, she was elevated to Dame Commander of the Order of the British Empire (DBE) prior to her retirement from the WRAF and subsequent marriage to Air Vice-Marshal Sir Geoffrey Rhodes Bromet. Therefore, in addition to her distinction as Lady Jean Conan Doyle, she was also officially rendered Lady Bromet.

This then was the charming woman who opened her door to us on that early autumn afternoon in 1987. John Bennett Shaw had paved the way for my meeting with the lady in question. He'd told her something about my enthusiasms and of our work together. That may have piqued her curiosity, or perhaps she was merely being polite. In any event, when our meeting occurred, I don't think she was entirely prepared.

Now I'm only going to describe this as Dame Jean herself later remembered it. Because, she said, "from the first moment I saw you, all I could think was how much you reminded me of my father."

With regard to her compliment, I have to state something that was somewhat obvious to myself, and obviously so to the woman who had known Sir Arthur Conan Doyle for approximately seventeen years. To his daughter, however, he was "Pops," and her mother and namesake's greatest and undying love. I say undying, chiefly because even upon Sir Arthur's passing in 1929, Jean Conan Doyle, his wife, insisted that the spirit of her late husband remained in contact with herself and the family. So much so that on one of his later visits he diagnosed the malady that would end Lady Doyle's own life. However, and given her nearly religious faith in the principles of Spiritualism, there was more than consolation in speaking to a familiar voice from Beyond.

I once asked my friend Jean, as she would become, when the family ceased to commune with the discarnate spirit of her father? She told me when, but more importantly, the "why?" behind that "final transmission.

"Do you know how it is at times, when a loved one visits you, and you say to them, 'when you get home, do ring me?'" I said I did. For this was often a practice among many people, including my own. "Well then, Mark, once you know they've reached home, there's no point in ringing again, is there?"

My future friend's words made sense, particularly if one accepted the belief in Survival shared by her late parents. And indeed, it would be a great consolation, I mused. But harking back to that first visit, when we were warmly beckoned into her tasteful flat overlooking the fenced garden in the Square, I had the sense that I was being studied by my hero's daughter. Over the course of a couple of hours we had tea and chatted, and Dame Jean made a point of addressing Dori as much as myself. She also professed herself to be very interested in what John had told her of my early forays to Loch Ness, my work at Glastonbury, and perhaps, I think, my research on "contacting Houdini." In other words, a template of interests which more than slightly resembled those of her "Pops." To wit, ACD's passions for the medieval era, as with his *Sir Nigel,* his notion of a dinosaurian survival, i.e. *The Lost World,* and of course, his great crusade on behalf of the Spiritualist movement.

And then of course there was the "curious case of the physical resemblance" between us. I make no apology or explanation for this, but the fact remained that in 1987, at age forty, I bore more than a passing resemblance to Jean Conan Doyle's late father at about that age. And encouraged by a closer haircut and the removal of my beard, even I found it strange how much I favored Sherlock Holmes' creator in his youth, middle age, and with any luck, my senior years. Add to this we were both "big men" in the physical sense, with craniums that would have fascinated Dr. Mortimer, who had coveted Holmes' own in *The Hound of the Baskervilles.* And in point of fact, I was tempted to risk an impropriety, even as I faced that attractively dignified white-haired lady, taking note as I could help but do of her own "Doylean" features. A certain slant of the eye, a steely look, and a sort of—how shall I say this, kind of flattish skull (no disrespect meant to that lovely lady!)

At the risk of a *faux pas*, I said nothing. But it was Dame Jean herself who remarked, "you so much resemble him. Your eyes, the way you carry yourself, and even the shape of your head!" Saying this, that charming lady made a brief pass at her own well-managed snowy *coiffeur. Bingo!*

Nor do I now have any doubt whatsoever that that first, historic meeting was as an interview of sorts. Which is also to say, the lady was counting my guns, gauging my mettle, and probably seeking to ascertain for herself whether the "press" that had preceded my visit had been accurate?

I have often thought back to what that initial visit of so many subsequent returns actually signified. I mean to say here, that once again it was proven out to me that life is often more dramatic, if not "romantic' than any creative scribe might conjure. Just so, think then of the prospect of Sir Arthur Conan Doyle's daughter suddenly encountering a fellow who, in my friend Shaw's own words, "looked like, acted like, spoke like, and was as close to the real ACD as possible." Further, here too the embodiment of that presentation of Jean's father in his more youthful middle age, at a moment which she herself had not experienced. Ergo, and save for photographs or other chronicles of the *fin de siècle* Doyle, there I was, as if materialized upon her threshold!

We spent a couple of hours in the lovely front room of her flat, and I was mindful from the start that behind me, in larger-than-life aspect was a portrait of Sir Arthur, as if peering over my shoulder. Nor did I evade the sense that even as his beloved daughter was chatting with me, behind me she was also able to make contact with the most famous man in her existence.

The upshot of my first meeting with Conan Doyle's daughter was the suggestion of an idea. This had germinated a bit in our conversations about how ACD had been portrayed over the years in film or the written word. I suppose this was the genesis of my evoking the dramatic work of America's fine actor Hal Holbrook, and of how he had long ago decided to re-create Mark Twain's presence for the stage. We also discussed another one-man dramatic vehicle playing at that time in London, which had to do with the British war hero, "Bomber" Harris.

And that, I suppose, was the pivot upon which a casual suggestion depended. What about the notion of a dramatic "evening with Sir Arthur?"

"And would you be interested in portraying my father?" Dame Jean asked the seminal question, scarcely skipping a beat. I heard it and I felt the room shift. And then the words that followed.

"Because you know, from the moment you arrived all I could think of was how much you reminded me of him."

That comment, repeated by me many hours later to my wife, signified an enormous and incredible opportunity. A one-man play about Conan Doyle. *But could I write it?* And more than that, could I "become" Dame Jean's "Pops" on stage before an audience?

The opportunity, like certain others which seem to have a sense of "rightness" attached to them, could not, and would not be avoided by me. This at first was rather nettlesome, because by agreeing with Dame Jean that this might be a tremendous thing, I also realized how much its success might be dependent upon my own abilities.

At this point in time I felt very comfortable as what used to be called in Doyle and Twain's day, a "platform performer." By this juncture as well I had also written the script for a PBS documentary, "An Egyptian Odyssey,' in which I had done the on-and-off camera narration. For that reason then, and although I lacked what might be called "acting" experience, I was not averse to giving it a try. But more than that, suddenly the notion of researching, then writing an abbreviated and dramatized "Life of Sir Arthur Conan Doyle" became a consummation devoutly to be wished. So I decided to plunge ahead.

By the time I'd returned home I collected every Doylean biographical resource and set to creating what in the old days used to be called a "prompt book." This in effect amounted to a journal-cum-compendium of every notable dimension of Conan Doyle's life, from birth to death. With special emphasis upon the man's character, his foibles, his shortcomings, his humor, his quirks, his frustrations, etc., I sought to get the pulse of my subject.

Upon assembling a rather thick and bound "Casebook, Prompt Book & Log" for "AN EVENING WITH SIR ARTHUR CONAN DOYLE," I set my sights on writing a script. This would ultimately prove a true maiden voyage in many respects. To begin with and as I have come to learn over the years, the average length of a two-act drama has amounted to between sixty and seventy pages. In other words, such would constitute what amounts to two, forty-five minute monologues in which you are out there on-stage, in effect talking to yourself in the direction of the audience.

But I confess, full of ideas and enthusiasm as I was in 1987, my initial script for "AN EVENING" ran in excess of one hundred and more pages. This then, the first fruit of my inspiration, was in turn sent overseas for my friend's review.

Suffice it to say and as I well knew, the best means of explaining my words was to explain them. For that reason there was a short period between Jean's receiving my script and once again finding myself there on her doorstep.

The week we spent together going over the project, word for word, has been shared by me with audiences and friends many times over.

However, and for the sake of not scrimping and better, for preserving that rare opportunity, I will try and describe it once again.

We sat down in the parlor of her flat overlooking the fenced gardens of Cadogan Square. We both had copies of the script, which I intended to read to my subject, including addendums which were either hers or my own. But before we jumped into the proverbial cold water, I inadvertently added the caveat, "but if you feel there is any reason to stop, or to question what you hear, just ring a bell or something." To my surprise however, I had not expected my companion to take my remark so literally. Nonetheless, she got up off the chintz sofa across from where I sat and left the room. Moments later I took note of the small china bell in her hand. She had a broad smile on her face, as if to say *well this is what you asked for, isn't it?*

The measure of our work over the course of some twenty accumulated hours that week can be represented, I think, by that china bell. This, largely because we seemed to get on so well, and with such perhaps undeserved candor, that by week's end I could easily say, with mock intensity, "don't you dare ring that bell!" That in turn would provoke the lady's laughter, and mine as well.

The fact is, we got on very nicely from the beginning. Not to say there were not a few mine-fields, such as when I read the line, "so I said to that fellow" only to be interrupted by my listener.

"Oh no, my father would not have called someone 'that fellow'" she said. And I took note. Then of course there was another instance, early on. I read out my line, but not yet with the Doylean burr which would eventually become necessary on stage. This time again she erupted, "Oh no, my father would never have put it that way." At which point I reached into the bag at my feet and withdrew *The Memoirs of Arthur Conan Doyle.* Searching through it at last I came to the passage in mind. And then I quoted it, repeating to his daughter precisely what her late father had said. Which, by the by, had been my source in setting down the line for the script.

"Oh" Jean said, sitting back against her cushion. 'Well, I suppose he did say it after all."

Such a parade of wonderful interludes comprised the singular process by which I sought and believed I'd found, Arthur Conan Doyle's tenor of "casual" speech. In other words, that style, apart from his written words, which reflected his manner and ability to engage his lion's share of audiences over the years.

And then of course there is the secret which is one no longer. This derives from the one and most singular event which I believe baptized my friendship with Dame Jean Conan Doyle. It occurred one early afternoon in that week we were together. Taking a much-needed break, Jean actually apologized to me to the effect that she "had nothing to give me for luncheon." I said it was not important. She then told me rather ruefully that she had not had the opportunity to get "out to the shops" for her grocery run. This as I discovered, meant a trip down the street to Sloane Square where she picked up her occasional comestibles.

"Well why don't we go together?" I suggested. "We can stretch our legs, and I'll carry your groceries back here." Well I might just as well have suggested we charter a plane and head for Jamaica. The lady's face brightened.

"I couldn't ask you for such an imposition" said the daughter of Sherlock Holmes.

"No trouble at all" I said. "I'm a bit peckish and we can get something together while we're out."

And that is exactly how it went. We walked down to the square, found my companion's favorite shops, went in, and made purchases. And rather than stopping somewhere for a bite, Jean suggested we return to Cadogan Square for a minor feast. And we did that as well.

Now I tell you this only because it is often the small things which are magnified over the years. And in my case in over the course of nearly a decade, my friendship with she, to quote Holmes, speaking of his country's empress, who was indeed "a certain gracious lady," was founded in part upon that afternoon's shopping trip.

I also remember two incidents, one of them at the time in question, and the other years later. The first involved my departure from London that week when we'd gone over my play. Jean returned her manuscript to me, with her own annotations, which she'd entered earlier. At any rate, the afternoon I took my leave, she thanked me profusely for my kindness. To which I involuntarily replied, "the Armstrong Shopping Service is always at your disposal." She laughed at this as we hugged good-bye. And I am pleased to tell you as well that over the ensuring years, the "shopping service" often became the "birthday service," the "Christmas service," the "ACD remembrance service" and more. And all because of that simple and shared shopping excursion.

That first vignette was never lost upon me, as a second anecdote will show. This was a few years later, and as was my custom before heading for the night train at Euston, en route for Inverness, I had time to kill. Moreover, my scheduled call or calls on Jean Conan Doyle were certainly high points, and by that time it was more the matter of seeing a friend rather than meeting with the daughter of Sir Arthur Conan Doyle.

At any rate, it was an early evening and I had hours yet before I took the taxi over to Euston Station. Jean and I had talked about the trip to Scotland, which she loved, and about my earlier forays in quest of "Nessie." Nor did she look at me in that strange way that some might on hearing that you've traveled a thousand miles to get into a small boat at night to look for a still-possibly alive Mesozoic survivor. But this in the main had to do, I suppose, with the identity and caliber of my friend. She after all had grown up knowing adventure, and her father had always harbored the notion of how wonderful, if not possible it might be to discover a supposedly extinct species of dinosaurs on some remote, if not "lost world?"

So there we were. This time around Jean insisted that she whip up a slight repast of soup and sandwiches for me on the spot to have before setting out on my way North. I confessed to her that I wouldn't mind the chance to kick back a bit, for my day's journey to reach London had been a bit tiring.

"Now then, just you sit back in that comfortable chair and put your head back" said the mistress of Number Seventy-Two, Cadogan Square.

"The food will be ready in a short while, and I'll wake you if you doze off."

I thanked my friend and hostess and closed my eyes. There, comfortably seated in my armchair in that now familiar room. Overlooking us both was Sir Arthur himself in the portrait upon the wall. Yes, I knew that place, I thought, even as I registered the slight sound of a vehicle passing by Number 72, if not the closer rustle of a pan in the nearby kitchen. And as I allowed myself to relax even further a panoply of images began to race through my mind, like coloured clouds. Moorlands, giant hounds, gaslit streets, and before long, misty autumn weather and a vast black lake, with something incredible possibly swimming within its fathoms.

And then too again the recollected image of where I was, and in whose house I now sat. And of the remarkable circumstances that had brought me here, years ago, which in turn had set me upon a number of the world's stages, where my primary mission was to recreate the persona of the man who now kept vigil over this room, and no doubt, over his beloved "Billy."

It was then I suppose that I nodded off. *And shortly you will leave this place and go off alone, in quest of yet another mystery. Like Holmes on a case. Like Sir Arthur packing his bag once again for another crusade.*

I cherish the memory of that early evening and the identity of the pleasant faced lady in the kitchen. And even as I'd found myself surrendering to sleep, the thought occurred to me that the former Adjutant to Her Majesty was only a few steps away, preparing a pot of soup for her American guest.

Now, so many years later, I reflect upon my good fortunes. And at their vanguard stands my friendship with "my friend Jean." Over the course of time I had made her but one promise: *I will always disappoint you.* This brutal admission was uttered early on, even as with great trepidation I scouted out the territory I was about to inhabit as Arthur Conan Doyle. And blessedly, just in case you're interested, I never heard a word of real criticism from that gracious lady.

414

However, I take comfort from the fact that certain of my varied interests did nothing but reinforce my plan to play out the game by following the Rules According To Doyle. In that respect I had met Jean on the heels of my demonstrated passions for medieval research, prehistoric survival, criminology, and even "the psychic matter." She was unsurprised years later when I rang to tell her, "I have a new subject." She was always politely amused at the range of my dramatic choices on the heels of "ACD." Churchill, Shaw, Dickens, Earp, Twain.

"Will it be political?" she asked me. When I heard this, I was immediately struck by another of those odd correspondences between my intentions and those of her father so long ago. Doyle had announced to his brother that he was planning a new career shift. And the question was asked, just as now, "will it be political?"

"No" Conan Doyle had replied, just as I did now. "It will be religious." That then had been the official spark which had fueled the blaze of Sir Arthur's crusade for Spiritualism. And as for my own "new direction?" This "religious" context was about to take on the shadow of C.S. Lewis. Nor had I forgotten my association with Narnia's creator back in 1988, when I'd stayed the weekend at Richard Lancelyn Green's ancestral Poulton Hall.

The conception of bringing the persona of Professor Lewis to the stage seemed an apt means of airing out my chronic views concerning the Christian faith. These had germinated for quite a while and charted from my childhood days as a confirmed member of the Catholic Church. However, "time and tide" had taken their effects, and from my university days onward I'd found no precise means of acting upon my faith. That took a while longer, and at the end of the metaphorical day it required me to re-embrace certain of those mystical trappings I'd so long ago felt unnecessary to my spiritual well-being. Perhaps like Waugh's Charles Ryder in *Brideshead Revisited* I'd needed the crucible of life, love, death and sadness to put my soul's journey into its proper perspective? Ultimately I found that by not only "becoming" Clive Staples Lewis on stage (or behind the pulpit of a multitude of ecclesiastical settings as my "theater") but by listening to his message.

And again, and very like Arthur Conan Doyle, I had been driven on, by either God or his Adversary, to ask the question *Does true life ever end?* My conviction at the end of my searching was that it continued, and well beyond this mortal arena. Moreover, like that young man educated at Stonyhurst and tempered over the spit of the Jesuits, I had needed to part from the Church in order to see it plainly. But unlike Doyle, who found no solace in orchestrated Christianity or its doctrines, I could not fully embrace Spiritualism. That such a thing as Human Survival was possible, I had no doubt. Or even, perhaps, that the veil between the Living and the Dead is at times rather thin, I did in fact believe. For myself however, it was enough to believe that those who have shuffled off this mortal coil did in fact wind up elsewhere, and to my way of thinking (and Doyle's as well) it was a place not unlike the very best of what we'd seen on this side of things.

I state the evolution of my interests in King Arthur, Loch Ness, Jack the Ripper or even C.S. Lewis only to chart what I knew to be Jean's notice of what my "journey" had involved. I am also content to know that my friend recognized one of my life's passages to have happened by circumstance and early choice, rather than as an attempt to emulate another man's course. That is enough, I believe.

For reasons such as these then, I fondly look back upon my association with Jean Conan Doyle with gratitude. At times it even seems as though the experience belonged to some lucky person other than myself. And I think *what a bloody fortunate fellow you were. To sit there, with Sir Arthur's huge portrait hanging behind you, alone and with the ability to ask this man's daughter questions of a serious or even mundane nature. Such things as "how did he hold his pipe? Or how did he stand and speak to an audience? How did he read a Sherlock Holmes story to you?"*

Ultimately of course it required a crucible of sorts for me to reach the point of making dramatic contact with my version of Sir Arthur. This over time took on the shape of following the research, be it first-hand, autobiographical accountings, or a cornucopia of third-person descriptions of the man called Arthur Ignatius Conan Doyle. But as I say, it took a bit of musing and consultation. Then of course there was also my awareness that at times one can actually be too close to his subject. To wit, stand directly before the Shroud of Turin and you will not see its finer outline. But stand back and get your perspective, and you do. In fact, you see wonderful bits of detail.

I also recall the advice given me by two friends at similar, but ultimately different ends of the Doylean measuring stick. The first of these was my American Irregular peer, Jon Lellenberg. Jon had earned his stripes in the field and had vast knowledge of the BSI and the nascent Sherlockian organizations worldwide. These he would later put into context with many excellent publications, as well as a novel, the personae of which constituted a veritable *Who's Who* of earliest BSI players. More curiously yet, the future would find him banished from those club-ranks, and his name attached to not a few curious incidents.

But in terms of a unique access to Jean Conan Doyle which preceded my own, Lellenberg by then had gained the trust of this "certain gracious lady." Moreover, he became a trusted advisor to her with regard to the legal aspects of the Doylean estate and its literary treasures.

I'd initially valued Jon Lellenberg's advice early on, as when he gave me what I still consider to have been wise counsel indeed.

"Listen to everything she (JCD) tells you," he advised, *"and factor into this what the scholars and others you talk to tell you. And after that, go ahead and do it your own way."* Which, for the record, Jon, I did.

My second confident was the eminent British scholar, author, bibliophile Doyle collector, invested Baker Street Irregular and fixture of the Sherlock Holmes Society of London, Richard Lancelyn Green. Our friendship over the years always maintained a certain warmth for the excitements we mutually shared in Sherlock Holmes and his creator. In strange part as well, I never quite overcame the feeling that by virtue of my positive connection to Dame Jean, Richard felt rather like a spurned suitor who relies on news of the former object of his affections via a go-between.

Such a matter became obvious upon my learning that Lady Bromet and my young friend had had a falling-out of sorts, which had to do with the future disposal of certain Doylean manuscripts. So strong was this on Jean's side that there was little Richard could do to brook their disagreement. Yet all the while I had the keen sense that he yearned to be back in that lady's good graces again. Moreover, I also recall a minor

417

trace of suspicious empathy in my friend when I told her of my own connections with Lancelyn Green. And when this occurred, I took note of a certain sense of—what shall I call it?—intractability in Jean Conan Doyle, *vis a vis* my friend Richard. Nor would this be the last time I would experience it, if not to see it pointed elsewhere, even closer to home.

I suppose I do have the distinction of a curious historical footnote, in that I was perhaps the last guest to be shown Richard's personal and carefully assembled presentiment of Holmes' 221B in the upper story of his family home, Poulton Hall, in Cheshire.

I say the "last" observer of that quaint and curious chamber, in that the weekend I'd been invited to stay, Richard's tenancy at Poulton was about to change. For upon his father's death, his brother's seniority made him "lord of the manor" in the legal sense, and on that count, Richard was about to re-locate to London.

But the weekend was itself a wonderful adventure for me. To begin with, there is that curious business of how things tend often to happen without your awareness of their future context. A perfect case in point here involves Richard's father, Roger Lancelyn Green's great friendship with C.S. Lewis, the great Christian apologist. For it was Green who was an enduring colleague and supporter of Lewis' work, and in particular, his series of the seven "Narnian" stories. These were those very fictional endeavors which Lewis' other chum, J.RR. Tolkien had despaired of, even to the point of suggesting that the tales of Aslan and the Pevensie children be put into the fire. As I understand it, Tolkien, or "Tollers" felt that C.S. Lewis' children's stories did not carry overmuch weight. And by inference, we might well presume that JRRT was not equating the seriousness of the Narnia saga with that implied by his own growing installments of his Middle Earth tales of the Hobbits and his *Lord of the Rings*.

But it was Roger Green who advised his chum Lewis to press on. And not only that, he christened what now we recall as the "chronicles" of Narnia.

The full impact of my August, 1988 visit to Lancelyn Green's ancestral home would not be impressed upon me for perhaps seven years. This,

418

when my first Doylean dramatic venture had expanded to include other favored subjects, such as Churchill, Shaw, Dickens, and even Wyatt Earp. But midway through that repertory of historical friends was Clive Staples Lewis.

But in 1988 I had yet to bring Sir Arthur to the stage, and had no inkling (a perfect pun here) that the future would find me attempting to "become" the author of *Mere Christianity, The Screwtape Letters,* and of course, *The Lion, the Witch & the Wardrobe.*

And strangely as well, nor did I fully appreciate that future project when I'd been informed that the bedroom given me for that weekend in Cheshire was the very one that used to be occupied by C.S. Lewis in his infrequent stay-overs at Poulton Hall. And there in that stately home once visited and cited by Nathaniel Hawthorne, I took my place as one of the family's weekend guests. Unlike the few others however, my mission involved a certain passion by gaslight shared chiefly by Richard and myself.

In similar fashion then, I did not realize, or even take full advantage of the fact that August, that my hostess, June, Richard's mother, had known both C.S. Lewis and his wife, Joy. Or that she and her late husband had spent the last holiday shared by CSL and his spouse. But I suppose that some things must go unknown at the time, until their proper moments of revelation.

As for my "Evening With Sir Arthur," Richard vetted my script and pronounced it much to his liking. Also, and based upon my self-imposed drill of elocutionary exercises, I offered him "a bit of Doyle," a' la McPherson. This preview of sorts included my attempt to mimic the muted burr of Conan Doyle's actual voice, transcribed from the surviving film of ACD.

That then was my trepidatious debut, rehearsal-styled, for my friend the Doylean scholar. But to be truthful, more potentially nerve-racking was the prospect of presenting my rendition to the subject's daughter, *The time for that would come,* I told myself. *So for now, why press your luck? Deep breaths now. Take your time.*

When Richard heard my first descriptions, *a' la* Doyle, his face brightened. And when I'd finished he did his own impression of my impression and we both laughed. Somehow it reminded me of seeing the impressionist Rich Little on the Tonight Show years ago, and watching Johnny Carson's pleasure, even to the point of mimicking the mimic. High praise, indeed.

I will always remember Richard Lancelyn Green showing me his version of "221" which would shortly be dismantled prior to its transfer to his Scarsdale Crescent home in London. It was with a visible sense of sadness that I heard him talk about it leaving this place, and I suspect that also reflected his own *tristesse* over departing his childhood home so that his brother could take charge of it.

As a kind of parting token Richard had given me a copy of *Sherlock Holmes Letters* which he had edited. Somewhat timidly and as was his way, upon presenting this he said "there is an inscription that describes this weekend." It was with a special sense of gratitude that we shook hands as we parted.

I did not examine the fly-leaf of my friend's volume until I was on the train back to London. Choosing to savor it along with my other recent memories of discussing a multitude of all things Doylean, finally I opened the cover and read. The inscription was there, penned in Richard's minuscule hand upon the frontispiece. It said:

> "*For Mark*
>
> *'There was no mistaking the poise of the head, the squareness of the shoulders, the sharpness of the features ... It was a perfect reproduction...'*
>
> *With Conanical regards & best wishes*
> *From Richard Lancelyn Green*
>
> *Poulton Hall, 8-8-88."*

I knew the importance of the passage, and it made the honor of being critically appreciated all the nicer. For you see, my colleague had merely quoted Conan Doyle to the American actor William Gillette, who became the Jeremy Brett of his day as Holmes. Or perhaps we ought to say, Jeremy became the "Gillette?"

And then of course, for those numerologists among you, there is the curious matter of the date: "8-8-88." I am certain it had some greater, latent meaning. But for me, it made things merely all the more special, signifying a time unlike any before or to follow it.

I also think of my first meetings with Richard, and then the visit to his family home, or to others in its wake, including my visit to his new London digs, and of his being part of my audience when I would perform as Sir Arthur at Tunbridge Wells as a tribute to Dame Jean. Yes, many memories. Nor can I help but to recall having shown Richard the draft of my sequel to the "Evening," which I'd entitled "The Untangled Skein." This work, as I told him, would only be produced upon Jean's passing, if only for the sake of certain intimations or assertions I would make concerning ACD and the Edalji case. And as the play would show, Conan Doyle struggles with his inability to help his client as himself, but succeeds only when he grudgingly gives in to Holmes, and "becomes" his fabled detective.

Ironically, and sadly for me, Richard Lancelyn Green was the only person to vett the script of "The Untangled Skein." And like its predecessor, he pronounced it of enough value to be mounted on a stage.

It is with certain sadness that I continue to register a sense of surprise at Richard's loss. He was many things, beginning with being a true lover of Holmes and his begetter. After his untimely death it was suggested that the biography of Sir Arthur said to be on this young man's short list of objectives, now would never be.

But indeed, I valued sharing work, and thoughts, and even casual conversations with one of the world's great collectors of Doylean memorabilia, including manuscripts and other relics. In closing I will allude to one of the latter chats. In its way, it is typical I think of my subject.

We were at his London home and for some reason we got to discussing the subject of pipes and Sir Arthur. At this juncture Richard stopped me, raised a finger as if to say "Wait!" and left the room. Moments later he returned carrying a silver salver, upon which was a lone briar.

"Was that his?" I asked, my voice a bit whispery.

Lancelyn Green merely nodded. And I had that chill of a feeling. Not perhaps as chilling as when Donald Rumbelow had handed me the Ripper's post-mortem blade. But instead, a feeling that might only have been out-rivalled by, say, Geoffrey Ashe handing me the Holy Grail (which he has yet to do!) But it had been a kind of True Cross moment, holding that pipe. And what it meant for me was having that rarity; a mutual friendship with a man who had gone his own unique path to find Sir Arthur Conan Doyle, even to the point of acquiring his writing, his spectacles, his pipes. *And what else might he have in his private vault? I couldn't help but to muse.*

Sadly, Richard Lancelyn Green passed away in 2004, the victim of a mystery which at its heart might have been taken up as a case by Holmes himself. In effect, Richard was found in his home, in bed, garroted and surrounded by books about the great detective. The matter of what is called "foul play" is still being debated by Lancelyn Green's friends and family, and there are even some who have theorized that the scholar had in fact asphyxiated himself. However the prospective verdict of suicide runs at odds with Richard's own span of worry and even paranoia over the matter of how certain Doylean documents were being disposed of. In fact, it was known that distressed over this issue as he was, Richard felt in danger of his own life.

The odd circumstances of the Green Case have been considered to elaborate effect in journalist David Grann's book *The Devil and Sherlock Holmes*, subtitled *Tales of Murder, Madness, and Obsession.* In truly morbid fashion, what the book describes is not only an unsolved matter that abuts upon many features which have brought so much entertainment in fictional terms to Holmes' readers, but as a real-life exercise, Richard's passing leaves in its wake cavernous questions. Moreover, it also takes into account what many of us have encountered in somewhat whispered terms. This, in effect, is what some have called the "Doyle Curse." It involves certain pit-falls encountered by some who have gotten "too close" to the subject at hand. It seems also to be comprised of a roller-coaster of Everest-like "highs" and the prospect of certain subterranean "lows." Imagination? I might think so, were it not true that I have seen something of that "curse" at close range. Later I will return to this matter.

But as for whether, like that ancestral "Curse of the Baskervilles," there was a correlative "Curse of the Doyles," we may never know for certain. Moreover, for the question of "was Richard Lancelyn Green one of its victims?" the jury may never say. Regretfully as well, all that I personally am able to surmise here is that my clever and talented friend died unshriven, by Dame Jean Conan Doyle, at least. I haven't the slightest doubt that he would have liked being able to make peace on that front, and further, I'd like to think that perhaps by now they may well have. Finally, I take great comfort in hoping that Sir Arthur's own confidence in the Summer Land's existence is now being shared by one, if not many of his greatest admirers.

24
The Siren's Song

This chapter comes as an unexpected addendum to its kin. I blame its appearance purely upon the autumnal season, as well, of course, due to certain ghosts that like to hover about now. For me, historically this has been the best and the worst of times. Nevertheless, there is a clarity which is palpable when one enters into what my friend Bradbury dubbed his "October Country." And I've followed its many routes, and continue to do so, feeling a good many shades by my side. Poe. Lovecraft. Fleming. Bradbury (of course). And Doyle.

But the other day I suppose I unwittingly summoned two discarnate specters in the familiar persons of Arthur Conan Doyle and Harry Houdini. This evocation of sorts was serendipitously occasioned by my discovery of a wonderful new book by David Jaher entitled *The Witch Of Lime Street*. Its subject matter not only fit into my mood, but coincided nicely with my mental excursion into the season.

So why don't we begin with Houdini? I've spoken of the legendary King of Cuffs earlier on in this memoir. That episode had largely to do with our daring attempt to place a psychic call to the mage forty-three years ago as of this writing. Moreover, whether or not Harry's voice on that Long Distance line upon that now distant Halloween Day is to be credited, it was certainly a weirdly exciting adventure. Even more so, I dare say it with a certain sense of pride on behalf of all Hallows purpose. And that purpose? To conjure up Houdini from the Beyond, to meet with us in the room where he met his death at Detroit's Harper Grace Hospital.

And then of course the clever notion of what I'll call our "parapsychological plan." That by intention involved a kind of paranormal "trunk call," not only to the Great Houdini, but also to two of his former colleagues in the persons of British ghostbuster Harry Price, and the better-known Sir Arthur Conan Doyle, Ghostbooster Emeritus.

For the better part of its story, *The Witch Of Lime Street* involves Houdini and Doyle as key players. It is also a re-telling of their relationship, which initially found them admiring friends and ended by pitting them as what might be called eschatological adversaries. In plainer terms, both the magician and Spiritualism's 20th century St. Paul had been attracted and then repelled from one another over the issue of Survival After Death.

Conan Doyle had become a firm convert to the spiritual cause with the First World War. Houdini found his own *cri d'coeur* for challenging the mediumistic creed in 1913. Its occasion was the death of the magician's beloved mother. As the lion's share of Houdini's biographies agree, the passing of Cecilia Weiss was her son's tipping point. For it was from that juncture of time that her son's mourning found itself amplified by his quest to convince himself that his late mother was not lost, but now existing happily upon another unearthly plane. So indeed insisted many of the performer's psychical contemporaries, including Sir Arthur. But of that crowd, and despite Harry's own demand for proof of a Hereafter, he remained disappointed.

It has always been of great interest to me to recognize the true motivation behind The Great Houdini's tireless plowing through countless psychical mediums. Some believed that he did so only to oppose charlatanry, while others suggest it was merely the trickster's own means of gaining what he loved best of all; namely that commodity called publicity.

But even superficial examinations of Houdini's life demonstrate that his rabid determination to destroy all mediums was very possibly connected to the notion of actually finding one capable of providing him with the secrets he sought. In other words, to be persuaded that indeed the dead were capable of communing with the living. If so, *ipso facto*, among them might be his own "dear little Mama," waiting on her side of the veil for the sound of her youngest son's voice. And as for the son himself? If psychic contact could be made with the Hereafter, it might afford him the chance to say what he had not been able to before his mother had expired. That he had not reached her side in time continued to haunt him. But so too did her livid and loving memory, which doubtless served to beckon him onward, as if to say "find me, Ericha." Then of course there is the part played by Arthur Conan Doyle in Houdini's later career of decimating those ranks of prospective messengers to the Beyond. Interestingly, I think, Doyle's own case and his seemingly Quixote-like efforts were doubtless sublimations for key missing elements in his early makeup. In Houdini's case it was the unprovable reality of that posthumous existence he secretly hoped for.

This was the dark dynamo that drove Houdini on, even to the point of mocking those who chose to believe. Similarly and to a degree, Conan Doyle's youthful dispensation with Jesuitical Christianity had been replaced with a temporal veneration of what constituted his "code of honour." That had been his moral compass since his youth, when his own beloved mother would tutor him in his family's chivalrous and even noble past. Later however, that mortal platform would give way to his fledgling belief in the divine spark of the soul suddenly re-kindled by Spiritualism.

The notion of Doyle's "conversion" did in fact strike many of his admirers as shocking and disappointing—even as Bruce Jenner's recent sea-change as "Caitlin" represented for many a kind of public betrayal tarnishing his better-known past.

But might any part of Arthur Conan Doyle's newly professed spiritual convictions find themselves marred by a sense of guilt, as with Houdini? While some might say this is a hard bow to pull, something curious occurred to me in this respect while I was writing "The Untangled Skein." The moment of its beginning finds the author now a widower after more than a decade of watching his wife Louisa waste away with consumption. And as all who have studied ACD's biography must be aware, it was during this period of time— approximately nine out of the thirteen years of Lady Doyle's illness—that her husband had become infatuated with another woman.

The facts of the case are these: while he was in the throes of being a celebrated author, sportsman, social commentator and reformer, Conan Doyle found himself the victim of Cupid's ill-timed arrow. The cause of this dilemma was Jean Leckie, a beautiful young Scottish woman who (to our subject at least) had stepped out of the pages of Sir Walter Scott's romances.

The long and short of the thing is simply this: during the duration of his wife's sickness, Arthur Conan Doyle conducted a platonic relationship with a younger woman who was not only sensitive to his situation, but who in her way was as strange as he. In the latter regard I speak of Miss Leckie's own penchant for the moral course, if not her belief that the honorable track was the best and only to follow. And yet.

As was explicitly portrayed in the televised version of Julian Barnes' novel, *Arthur and George* concerning the Doyle-Leckie relationship, the post-script of Louisa Doyle's passing found her husband bound by the chains of guilt. So much so that he may well have entered the emotional realm of a breakdown, had he not found a form of sublimation for his anxieties. This was the Edalji case, in which Conan Doyle struggled to vindicate a wronged man. But in order to do so, he needed to call up talents better utilized by his fictional counterpart, Sherlock Holmes.

Long ago in "The Untangled Skein" I suggested that coming as it did so fast on the heels of his wife's death, the psychically inclined Conan Doyle was more than at sixes-and-nines. In other words, struck by the feelings of betrayal of his late spouse occasioned by his now-chronic affections for Jean Leckie, the man himself felt fragmented. On one hand he could not help but to have mourned his wife's passing, particularly given her stoic reserve over such a painfully long haul. Moreover, and while he'd done his best to console and help her, the man knew where his divided heart tended to flit. Therefore and upon Louisa's death, what some might call relief became a grim and fearful sentence. This I think was compounded by Sir Arthur's growing belief in a survival beyond the earthly realm. Given that, was it not likely that even now his wife still existed, looking on from Beyond? And were this the case, was it not possible to communicate with her? But here, as Hamlet said, was the rub. Were he to speak to the mother of his children from beyond the grave, what would he say? What would she say? Did she remain aware of his earthly doings? And to what extent had she been aware, while alive, of his relationship with Jean Leckie?

Opinion remains divided as to the question of whether Mrs. Doyle was aware of Miss Leckie's place in her husband's life over that near decade of time? In reality however, we know that Arthur's mother not only was aware of Jean's presence, but liked her and felt she was a tonic for her worried son. Similarly, others in Doyle's family were aware of the young woman's presence, for he had invited her to certain public events and at least once she had found her way to the Doyle family dinner table. But as what? As far as we might gather, only as one of Louisa's husband's many friends and admirers. And indeed, she was that.

In my play I explored Conan Doyle's psyche at that juncture following his "Touie's" death. Believing that she was now in that "better place" which he had thought so much about, could it have occurred to him to try and reach her? Dramatically speaking here however, he does not. In point of fact, he is not only reluctant to reach her in her Summer Land domain, but is afraid to do so. And why? Simply because his guilt will not allow it.

Therefore, and presented merely as my own hypothesis, I believe that Doyle's eventual movement toward the ranks of the Spiritualists was a kind of double-edged blade, especially for he whose sword was always allegedly brandished for the noble cause. Further, that he may have found guilt edging his transformative beliefs is not entirely unlikely. Ergo, like Harry Houdini, the context for his adopting an aggressive stance over the matter of Survival may have had its share of paradox.

And then of course as the years passed and with the new Lady Doyle by his side, the great man suffered his share of slings and arrows. Not unlike the man from La Mancha, many of Sir Arthur's dragons were indeed revealed to be windmills. Nevertheless, the creator of the world's greatest literary detective dismissed naysayers and even rationalized examples of psychic fraud masquerading as truth as necessary evils. Nor did successive condemnations or exposures of persons he had championed deter him. He moved on like a juggernaut through troubled waters. And throughout it all what many deemed his over-credulous catechisms on fairies, spirit guides, or a new liturgy concerning voices broadcast to and 'fro from the Summer Land continued.

The purpose of David Jaher's *Witch of Lime Street* is ably fulfilled in its skillful telling of the controversy surrounding the psychic abilities of Mina Crandon, dubbed "Margery" the sensual medium who vied for the financial prize offered by *Scientific American Magazine* in 1924. Her story is one replete with jealousy, wonderment and incredible happenings, if not the decided hint that there might well be things incapable of measurement by either science or logic. These were also the very phenomena which many in the Spiritualist movement, with Doyle at its vanguard, had espoused.

Jaher's novel constituted a kind of serendipitous reminder to me of my earlier interests in Houdini and his zealous attempts to discredit "Margery" and others. Yet it also evoked my more youthful inquiries into those spirit-charged days of the Twenties when séance room antics were a perfect complement to flappers, the Charleston, if not an era chock-a-block with a number of larger-than-life characters. Included here of course was Conan Doyle, lumbering out of the Victorian and Edwardian eras onto the modern stage *sans* his implied Sherlockian alter ego. Paradoxically as well, the "who and what" he now espoused involved a cause if not a client-list which Sherlock Holmes would have never allowed within the confines of his Baker Street sitting room.

Curiously, my own *entrée* into that psychical battleground of nearly a century ago had also been spurred by my interest in the British investigator Harry Price. Inexplicably I'd found myself gravitating to this man's own *modus operandi* for making a living out of what his colleague Doyle referred to as "the psychic matter." No university grad or academically trained scientist himself, nevertheless Harry Price was a dab hand at mechanics, photography, and the unpractical arts of conjuring. His bibliographic interests lent themselves to his numerous collections, files and scrap-books which were reminiscent of Doyle's Holmes. Moreover, his latent cleverness became the driving force for what began as the National Laboratory of Psychical Research in London. Here his efforts frequently involved devising controlled measures for testing supposed mediums and their paranormal talents. Advanced for its day, the National Laboratory became a seminal point in the fledgling discipline of parapsychology. Testifying to his adeptness in this field were friendships Price maintained with a number of European pioneers who shared his quest to explore the Unknown. In addition, research compiled and studied by the likes of Britain's Society for Psychical Research (SPR) or America's equivalent agency relied early on upon efforts such as Price's own.

Despite what certain of his later detractors might say, it was Harry Price's successful creation of a scientific apparatus for gauging supposedly "supernatural" activities which became the basis for later academic endeavors, as were promoted by Joseph Banks Rhine and others. Today as a result, the game remains "afoot" not merely for the sake of ascertaining the existence of paranormal phenomena or its practitioners. Moreover, and despite the passage of years and the developments of technology, one fact apparent nine decades ago remains; namely, *that the only predicable aspect of psychic activity continues to be its unpredictability.* Secondly, the abiding, if not unpopular prospect that much of what is deemed "extra-sensory" is in fact perceivable only through a human filter. Also, that dimensions of what may be dubbed "paranormal" may reflect (a) a reflection of human personality, or (b) an external, discarnate or dimensional plain of existence. In short, that very "borne from which no traveler returns."

Frankly I always felt an inexplicable kinship with Harry Price. Truthfully, I have regarded him as an unmet friend, flawed and dramatic, but fueled by the romance of the Unknown. This liking has endured, despite even what some of his critics have offered up as reasons not to regard the intrepid, pipe-smoking psychic Sherlock in favorable light. I've read Price's memoirs and their equivalent "casebook" accounts. I have even been amused and excited by this man's own "Watson," in the person of Professor C.E.M. Joad.

Therefore and probably because I not only identified with him, but liked Harry Price, I've continued to cut him a good bit of slack. And why? Well perhaps it has to do with what you might term my mindset in affording that self-made, self-promoting and decidedly enigmatic figure what's called "the benefit of the doubt." Flawed certainly, and aware of his own limitations (and those of others), Harry Price remains a pioneer in the now primitive-seeming era of dancing tables, ectoplasmic energies, haunted manses, if not their curious purveyors. Cutting a swath through as many of those as he could, seemingly only on one occasion did the investigator himself seem persuaded of a Life Beyond. That was enough to rattle him. And in similar fashion, both before and away from the cameras and reporters, Harry Price's long-term fascination with Borley Rectory, that Mount Everest of haunted houses, abided until his death. And indeed, if one considers the paradoxical "evidence in the case," some insist that Harry's penchant would eventually include him among its ghostly retinue!

I consider myself incredibly fortunate to have come "within range" of not only Conan Doyle (via his daughter), Harry Price (by being accorded the privilege of working with his private collections at London's Senate House) and J.B. Rhine, *vis a vis* my friendship with the great man himself. Without such proximities I suppose I would never have entered into their worlds to such an extent. Nor I suppose would I have emulated those gentlemen in my own course of a lifetime of studies.

Yet truth to tell, there was something about each of those figures that I found myself identifying with. In the case of ACD and JBR, this may have largely to do with their innate curiosities and how they acted upon it. Beyond that as well was how those men grappled with the spiritual aspect of their makeups. And it was in that latter, somewhat wispy realm that they grappled and they found ways of reaching out to the seemingly unreachable. Intriguing as well, in the instances of Doyle, Price, and Rhine, each man was both well regarded but also vilified by later generations of observers. Doyle was reviled as a crank. Price was accused of being a master hoaxer. And Dr. Rhine lived to see the repute of his scientific achievements at Duke University sullied by falsehood and lack of academic integrity.

Despite the obviously Doylean-Sherlockian ilk of this memoir, would it surprise you to learn that in many respects I have personally identified with Harry Price? By comparison to Doyle and Rhine, Price was at heart a showman. He'd discovered early on that there was literally a market for promoting the Unknown, which he did again and again. His books, his radio broadcasts, and of course, his establishment of his laboratory to measure the unmeasurable were all noteworthy. But on a personal level, I recognize that Price's major talent was his ability to promote himself via his subject matter. Just so, when he set out to investigate Borley Rectory in Essex, dubbed "the most haunted house in England," he conjured an avid audience to follow his adventures. And in such fashion was he able to continue adventuring.

But also key to this discussion, I think, is the subject of human fallibility. In this sense, we might risk two other terms such as "deception" or "chicanery." I find that in the instances of Doyle, Price and Rhine, each of those elements would figure into their mind-sets, consciously or not. And in terms of many of those psychic strangenesses they were all intrigued enough to scrutinize, it's safe to say that no history of the Psychic World exists without its share of implications of deceit or even outright fraud among the best and worst of its population.

It is one of the most damning elements of psychical research that there have existed few examples of "true ability" that have not been tinged or tainted by a mediumistic subject's seemingly final (or even first) resort to trickery to establish, replace, or amplify their supposedly uncanny abilities. Daniel Dunglas Home. Eusapia Palladino. Margery. And as a consequence, this negative tradition has whetted a kind of double-edged blade for a host of those "physical" or "mental" mediums who have been studied. Likewise, and related to the Heisinger Principle, wherein the investigator taints what he examines, there is a plenitude of evidence revealing the willful chicanery, unwitting gullibility, or even outright credulousness by a legion of psychic Sherlocks, ranging from Houdini and Doyle and Price to a core of lesser-known promoters or debunkers.

Which brings us to an important question in this "psychic matter": should someone capable of exerting allegedly paranormal ability be discovered in the act of exerting fraudulent behavior be irrevocably dismissed? Or, and dependent upon the medium's previously tested record of achievement, should such a lapse from honor be perceived merely as a dimension of human shortfall?

Human shortfall, indeed. For does not fact often seem transformed into fiction? Do not heroes often become villainous before our eyes? (or vice-versa?) In the latter regard, should Sir Thomas Malory, the chivalrous author of *Le Morte D'Arthur* be outed as a cattle rustler, molester of nuns, and all around "bad hat?"

Or how in more recent days does one view Harper Lee, the celebrated author of *To Kill A Mockingbird*, that seminal work of legendary liberal attitude, when its recently published prequel reveals its formerly beloved familiar central character Atticus Finch as now steeped in attitudes of racial inequality and seemingly justifiable bigotry? Or lastly, how does society accept the prospect of a handsome and virile male Olympian who became a role model in his youth, suddenly

432

expressing him/herself by assuming a woman's name, clothing, body, and mindset?

With such questions in mind we might ask whether either today if not nearly a century ago an individual capable of evoking discarnate voices, telekinetically moving objects, or providing the living with messages from the dead should be forever condemned for resorting to parlor or magic tricks to fill in the gap when the "real thing" was not do-able?

Such no doubt was the reason that many of those Jazz Age mediums may have felt compelled to enhance their unusual abilities, or even to sublimate them through trickery or legerdemain. Here and perhaps in the mode of the Devil's Advocate, it was often stated that a subject was unable to perform under the auspices of certain prescribed and "scientifically" restricted conditions. Along such lines there is a genuinely mixed message, particularly if the medium had been capable of psychic effects under alternate conditions.

In direct relation to gauging the allegedly extra-ordinary talents of a target individual, also to be considered is the mindset and motive of those employed to monitor them. Often and like a director's influence upon an actor, the psychical investigator may temper his inquiry voluntarily or otherwise, for good or for ill, in accordance with the Heisenberg Principle

In the latter instance there are a legion of critics today who claim that Harry Price's chronic exploration of Borley Rectory was from its inception a complete fraud. Which was therefore to suggest in outright and posthumous terms that the king of ghost hunters had made the conscious decision to falsify such mysteries as might be translated into both his book sales and his public popularity.

In fairness however, and even in the face of Price's many critics who have attempted a de-construction of his persona, his motives, his methods, and his achievements, there is still, I think, more to be considered. What for instance of the fact that the alleged paranormal events constituting Borley's "scam" did in fact *precede* Harry Price's chronological involvement with it? Or consider the fact that after the psychic sleuth's own demise and the razing of the Rectory itself, certain of its paranormal activities remained. And what of those reports of Price's own ghost being seen or even photographed within Borley's environs?

From a purely psychological perspective, at this juncture of my life I believe I can at least understand to a degree the motivation behind, or temptation toward what in essence is fakery, either for attention or to bolster what may indeed represent a genuine mystery. Here I am compelled to confess that as an early teen, a companion and I shot a series of Polaroid photos of a supposed UFO hovering over our summertime suburb. When eventually asked by a reporter from *The Daily Tribune* if I could swear that I didn't toss that Frisbee-shaped object into the air, I so swore. For indeed, it was my friend who tossed it upward, and I who took the picture! But should this forever ban me from the ranks of other intrepid and serious UFO mavens? Some might say so. But perhaps they never found their own roads to Damascus?

Decades later and during my early sojourns to Loch Ness, I confess to considering the prospect of creating a humped, elephantine back and photographing it as the "monster." And why? Well possibly, as I rationalized, to keep the subject matter at hand and before the public. Or by gaining a "new" Nessie photo, I might gain attention translatable toward furthering my genuine inquiries. In other words, might there be some kind of convoluted merit in calling attention to this phenomena by "replicating" it? Similarly I have viewed many episodes of a program called "Fact or Fake?" in which anomalous phenomena are studied and then replicated. The flaw in their premise, as I take it, is that "if they can build it no one will come." Which is to say that because someone can take a picture of an extraterrestrial vehicle over your garage, such things cannot be real.

Speaking for myself and in consideration of the purely fraudulent dimension of such an ill-conceived plan as tossing a pie-plate or building a *papière maché* monster, I can only apologize and move on. Maturity teaches one that it is a high price to risk all credibility as, say, a full-fledged monster-hunter by "faking it.' And yet nevertheless I seemed to understand the motivation which is often associated with deceit.

Paradoxically as well, it is incumbent upon those seeking to assess prospective tricksters to know their way around tricks. It just is! As I'd discovered, often enough as at Loch Ness, where the incredible invades the daily atmosphere, the idea of keeping an enigma alive at all costs "until the real thing comes along" has become part and parcel of things. There the dividing line between the Real and Unreal is slender indeed. But that is no excuse for air-brushing a photograph of a bit of decaying vegetation (as I discovered that certain "experts" I once respected did indeed do) and calling it "Nessie." To do so is to make one's best attempt at getting away with metaphorical murder. In other words, to promote fiction as fact. Sadly however, often enough the effect of such a premise serves only to confuse or discredit what might be true. Moreover, if and when that "real thing" does emerge from the depths, certain of those true believers may be left feeling like the Boy Who Cried Wolf. And even then, someone from the wings is going to cry "fraud!"

And then of course there is that famous relationship between Conan Doyle and Houdini to return to. Here we find a study in friendship gone fascinatingly wrong in the most highly publicized of senses. Initially, both of those famous men harbored a seemingly genuine respect for one another's talents. In Sir Arthur's case however, he continued to embarrass the renowned escapologist by inferring that Houdini's abilities were of psychic, rather than physicalized, show-business value.

Up to a certain point Houdini listened to the great Englishman's high praise of his talents, even as he consistently demurred as best he could. However when Houdini ultimately believed he had been gulled by both Sir Arthur and Lady Doyle in an attempt to reach his dead mother, the magician lashed out. The line had been crossed, altruistically or not. Diplomatically at first, and more aggressively thereafter, the conjuror dismissed Doyle's well-intended efforts in psychic affairs as the workings of a credulous and foolish old individual. And when things were at their worst, nor did the magician find any compunction at aiming a deliberately low blow at the man he'd once called "friend."

Reacting to Doyle's criticism of the Handcuff King's own dismissal of what in general terms now could be considered his church, the magician's sense of envy, petulance and latent talent for treachery rose to the surface when he assailed not only Sir Arthur, but also his greatest creation.

"Well all right, if I am ever such a plagiarist as Conan Doyle, who pinched Edgar Allan Poe's plumes…" Houdini said. Yes, he actually said that. And while the thought may not have been original with the speaker, its accusatory words carried a certain kind of damning and lethal weight.

I have no doubt that upon hearing his former colleague's comment about plagiarism, the usually avuncular Doyle was now ready to enter the lists of combat. But no longer as a doting admirer of The Man Who Could Walk Through Walls. Now however he'd become his full-fledged and able adversary. Impelling him to do so, I believe, was the famous Doylean code of honour. This, taken in tandem with a perception of his accuser's lower social and ethnic station were sufficient unto the day for Conan Doyle to demand satisfaction. Doubtless he still rankled since having heard Houdini's earlier critique of Lady Doyle's ill-fated performance on his behalf as a self-styled medium. That in itself would have given sufficient cause for a personal affront. But then came the ultimate assault upon Doyle's greatest literary creation, which, despite its creator's stated enmity for it, had commanded the world's affection. For now Sherlock Holmes had also been defamed. To deny him his birth-right, and worse, to accuse him of bastardy was heinous. Moreover, loosely veiled in Houdini's taunt was the implication that Doyle had purloined his veritable milk cow from Poe, an arguably greater writer. But perhaps there is still a bit of cold comfort to be found here; for had the magician's jibe been made a century or less earlier, both discussants may have met upon the dueling field.

Last of all, there was Arthur Conan Doyle's sincere fidelity to the Spiritualist cause to be considered. Over the last fifteen years of the author's life this was the greatest truth he could profess concerning this world or the next. As the cause's ardent champion, Sir Arthur lent his talents to the trust. But as he did so, he remained the chivalrous lad who believed in "might for right" and a noble battle worth fighting. Now however, the old knight was exactly that. Set in his ways. A great friend. A keen enemy. A sometimes-childlike believer in the ilk of Peter Pan.

And yet also a dangerous man to run afoul of.

Therefore for anyone, be they friend or foe to denigrate the Doylean context for Spiritualism was tantamount at least to sacrilege. And for the sake of such a trespass, no one had the right to poison the well. To do so was to violate a taboo, if not even as a corps of Doyle's Spiritualist cohorts suggested, to invite the greatest of all prices to be paid by Harry Houdini.

Before closing this portion of our discussion, I feel it is incumbent upon me to say something about the subject of Survival. Here and notwithstanding measures employed back in the heyday of Spiritualism, the game of Psychical Pursuit is not so changed as in the days of Doyle and Harry Price. Ironically, I think, and despite the slew of Ghostbuster-type technologies out there today to measure motion, temperature, radiation, infra-red imagery or electronically-snared vocalizations unheard by the human ear, the drill remains largely unchanged. Which is to say, the belief in the Unbelievable continues, even as it has done since pre-Old Testament days until now. It is the formative content of the key religions and it involves the hope or belief that what we call the soul, or kernel of the human spirit, may well be death-resistant. Further, that what we deem to be death as the Ultimate Ending is in essence as the saying often has it, "only the beginning."

Reflecting the maxims of the world's many cultures, the endurance of the human soul has continued over the eons. From ancient-most times until today, there remains the sense that this world, this existence of ours, is not the only one on offer. In effect, that there may indeed be other worlds and other dimensions, if not a spiritual terrain which has only been hinted at by the world's greatest of philosophical and religious sages. Viewed in Platonic terms or not, that Other World may be a better and amplified version of our own at its best, but in more eternal terms. Also the possibility of "many levels" of spiritual progress, each with its own "schoolroom" for those seeking to "matriculate." But such psychic infrastructure may also accommodate the prospect of a darker, perditious realm.

The notion that Arthur Conan Doyle was either convinced or gulled into believing in a Spiritualistic credo remains the fact. For him it constituted a thinking man's philosophy concerning not only the meaning of life, but what it presaged. And while in retrospect Doyle's belief in a Summer Land, where whiskey and soda and eighteen rounds of golf might be enjoyed seems naïve, if not foolish to many, we may only consider the alternatives, if any. There is also the fact that while the credos of our recent longagos may seem primitive, so might our own of the 21st century one hundred years hence.

For now however, and addressing the question of whether ghosts, poltergeists, demonic entities, angels, Heaven or Hell exist, these things to my mind remain to be disproved. Or not. Much in the vein of contemporary fascinations with Bigfoot, lake monsters, extra-terrestrial intelligences or UFO's traversing our skies, there will continue to be suggested proofs and evidences, just as there will be debunkings of the miraculous by a revitalized corps of Arch Skeptics.

But what does any of this mean? Will it, for example, have an effect upon that proverbially mysterious tree always falling in the metaphorical forest? For in truth, whether or not there is someone to hear or see it does not take away that it may well have fallen. Or does it?

For such reasons and more, I've no doubt that having willfully, artistically and imaginatively affiliated myself with such characters as described, I continue to feel a kinship with their passions. Like Houdini, I have lost those I might like to see or hear once again. And somewhat like Doyle, I have reconciled myself to a synthesis of belief which does not preclude me from existing as a Christian who holds certain of the Spiritualist tenets to be true.

So then do I profess, even as my creed allows, to anticipate another world to come, if not a form of personalized resurrection. What state or form that may take remains to be seen. Here as well, and at the risk of violating some liturgy or other, I find myself comfortable with the notion of communicating from Here to the After through the agency of prayer, meditation, intuition, or whatever route you may call it. I remain therefore a "spiritual" person and seek to embrace that notion without wedding myself to any one denominational divide or other.

For the record then, and for those who might care to wonder, I do believe in a Creator and that he, it, or they had an only son. Moreover, that my faith in such has and will bear me into the days ahead and even beyond. Such a certainty has been built over more than seven decades out of a medley of faith and fear, wonder and doubt, all of which have led me to the threshold of belief at which I simply choose, as C.S. Lewis once put it, to subscribe to.

Undoubtedly to some, at its heart the present memoir may well present a parade of credulous beliefs deliberately embraced by its author. Upon reflection I suppose this may only emphasize my curious disposition to "the rules according to Doyle." I make no apology for this, or for the fact that without the inexplicable or mysterious, the mythic or the miraculous, my personalized cosmos would be a smaller, darker place. I can only say with some sense of certainty that much of what has grabbed hold of me and clings tightly even now began as a kind of Siren Song. And I, like Ulysees before me, have willfully set sail if only to hear it. In such an attempt then have I brailled my way along the storefront of Life's most curious inventory of gifts.

"Right out of Paget"
Douglas Wilmer as the Great Detective

What happens when an author becomes a detective

25
Who Becomes the Legend Most?

The title for this chapter is purloined from those memorable Blackglama ads for fashion furs, in which portraits of famous ladies are poised and draped in mink. I suppose the signature question which accompanied them all was meant to be rhetorical, given the already legendary status of *les femmes fascinateurs.*

In somewhat comparable terms, I suppose the matter of trying to assay the "best," "most realistic," or "authentic" of a century's worth of Sherlock Holmes portrayers is likely a moot point. For very like anyone's opinion of which dame looked best in a certain brand of mink may well depend on a number of factors: degrees of beauty, talent, classic film or artful achievements, etc.

But in the case of Sherlock Holmes, much of the analysis must come down to how true to the Sacred Canon of Doylean/Watsonian works the portrayals in question may be? In other words, can we succeed in believing that this is the great detective before our eyes, and were it so, would we be measuring him on levels of handsomeness, nastiness, humor, or even manic behavior? In the latter realms we may gauge any number of dramatic Holmes incarnations, even apart from the fact that should the real Sherlock have signed in on that now vintage program "What's My Line?", how many of today's viewers would either recognize, like, or even enjoy him?

This has been much in my thoughts whenever I've been asked, *"Who's your favorite Holmes?"* My reply here is most often more honest than diplomatic, for truth to tell I do not specifically see any of the actors of the past or present day when I re-read the stories. But as I say this, I also wonder whether anyone reading the Sherlockian tales for the first time has not already been somehow tempered in advance? Which is only to say, for example, how might someone seeing Basil Rathbone's cinematic portrayal eighty years ago decide to read the official chronicle and not be duly influenced?

There is of course also the cult of personality today which sometimes finds actors portraying characters well beyond their wheel-house. A case in point is also not without a share of paradox, as in the two Guy

442

Ritchie Sherlock Holmes films featuring Robert Downey as our sleuth. I say paradox, because while a good many of us enjoy Downey's work, we cannot be persuaded that the Iron Man is also Mr. Sherlock Holmes. And why? Well, for a good many reasons. To start with, Downey is not physically right for Holmes, despite the fact that Jude Law makes a rather fine Watson. Secondly, Holmes was not slovenly unless he wished to appear so. Downey's Holmes carries eccentricity into the vales of grunge, as if to collect on the popular sensitivities of a 21st centuried more youthful crowd.

Therefore when we ask for, or are told that a "new Holmes" is on the horizon, we do in fact have standards for apt comparison. Moreover, given the technical developments of our day, we are fully capable, say, of watching William Gillette in his seminal (albeit silent) dramatic performance, or of seeing Holmes come to life, courtesy of Arthur Wontner, who in retrospective terms is even more true-to-Paget's illustration than even Rathbone, God bless him. And of course, old Basil's presentiment as the Victorian and Edwardian Holmes is frozen in the amber of those two pre-war films in which we see our man in deerstalker and cape, trudging through the mists. Curiously too, thereafter the string of Rathbone-Bruce films were anachronized war-era vignettes set to an earlier archetype.

One cannot help but believe that inappropriate "props" notwithstanding, even Sir Arthur would have enjoyed both Wontner and Rathbone, despite his iconic paternal benediction upon Gillette's image, which was in turn sealed in stone—or in ink, by Frederic Dorr Steele.

There were of course other yeoman-like cinematic presentations, including Clive Brook's trio of impersonations, as well as Cushing's finely-tuned sleuth or even George C. Scott's traumatized Judge Playfair-turned-Holmes in "They Might Be Giants." And of course one must pay special tribute to Ian Richardson, who turned his talents toward Sherlock in 1983 with "The Sign of Four" and "The Hound of the Baskervilles." However and like Christopher Lee's alternation of Holmesian roles, Richardson is unique in that in curiously *apropos* fashion, he played not only the great detective but also his real-life inspiration, Dr. Joseph Bell. To wit, in 2001 "Murder Rooms-The Dark Beginnings of Sherlock Holmes" series launched six episodes involving the youthful Conan Doyle and his deductive mentor, Bell.

Therefore, whether presented with Scot's brogue as Bell or with that fairy twinkle in the Holmesian eye, Richardson's reserved but insightful manner offered us a prototypical Holmes from another perspective which was close enough to be his creator's own. His Holmes was mercurial, but more importantly, more likable than many before or after.

My purpose here did not begin as an elaboration upon every Sherlockian portrayer, or to gauge the comparable merits of Eille Norwood against Reginald Owen, or to pit Leslie Howard against John Barrymore, Peter Cushing, Douglas Wilmer, John Neville, Ronald Howard, Tom Baker, Raymond Massie, Frank Langella, Ian Richardson, Christopher Lee, or Robert Stephens. Or even perhaps to reach into the "what might have been" grab-bag to opine upon actors who never played Holmes, but could have.

Yet it's always tantalizing to risk a bit of "Sherlockian casting," isn't it? Along such lines, it was once rumored that Peter O'Toole and Peter Sellers were to be the original detective duo in Billy Wilder's "Private Life," but they were not. However O'Toole did lend his voice to a couple of animated Holmes adventures, and best as I know, Sellers never got closer to Watson than playing his contemporaries, in a comedic take on Fu Manchu, in which he became both Nayland Smith and his king villain adversary.

In the Sellers vein you might be tempted to add the "Carry On" style of the Peter Cook-Dudley Moore version of "The Hound of the Baskervilles," which succeeded as an incredibly bad campy but madcap romp.

There is also a category of the Holmesian impersonation: "those who perhaps never should have been." Here, and with all due respect to many fine actors, we could have done without the saintly and Adonis-like Roger Moore, or even the stocky and blond Nicol Williamson trying out the fore-and-aft cap. Yet ironically in both of those cases the stars found themselves nicely complimented by Patrick Macnee and Robert Duval, respectively, as two quite visually serviceable Watsons.

Infamously as well, there was Reginald Owen, coming in an inappropriate second as Holmes, just as he'd done in the wake of

Alistair Sim's more iconic outing as Scrooge. In Owen's case, his much better Watson with Clive Brook as Holmes in the 1932 "Sherlock Holmes" gave the impression a year later in "The Sign of Four" that his portly medical companion was cavorting about in his friend's deerstalker while Sherlock was away!

Likewise in the 1959 "Hound," we might have happily survived a turnabout in casting by featuring Christopher Lee as Holmes and Peter Cushing as Sir Henry, rather than the other way 'round. Their partnership as opposites had already been honed by the Hammer Dracula sequels in which they'd played the Count and Van Helsing, respectively.

But who's to explain the intricacies of movie casting? Why did Billy Wilder, for instance, prefer Christopher Lee as Mycroft, when years earlier Robert Morley fulfilled the Pagetized image to a "T"?

And since we're playing the game, what about "future, or alternate casting?" Here I'd like very much to see Bill Nighy as Holmes, or perhaps over time, Tom Hiddleston. And putting the Time Machine into reverse gear, I'd like to have seen the young Michael Caine (who brilliantly played an actor playing Holmes in "Without A Clue") as Dr. Watson. Just so, I think either Sean Connery or Charlton Heston would have been worthily nefarious versions of that old *shikhari*, Colonel Sebastian Moran. And speaking of Mr. Heston, who considered acting as Wyatt Earp in a script of my own entitled "The Last Knight," I recall him writing to ask "how I liked his Sherlock Holmes?" Here of course he alluded to his role on stage in Paul Giovanni's "Crucifer of Blood" in 1981, where he was abetted by none other than Jeremy Brett as Dr. Watson! Heston's performance in "Crucifer" is commendable, rather like a larger-than-life, well-fed, sharply aquiline automaton cast in the image of Holmes. But that, according to many purists, is right on spot!

In the present day there are actually two versions of Holmes on television, with Jonny Lee Miller in "ELEMENTARY" and Benedict Cumberbatch in "SHERLOCK." Ironically, but for the clever need to conjure Holmes forth into the modern day, either actor might well have played it straight in a Victorian-set piece. No need, therefore, to give Sherlock a week's worth of stubble, or to make Dr. Watson an Asian-American woman. Closer to the mark, if you have to do it, is

"Sherlock's" pairing of Cumberbatch and Martin Freeman as his amiable Watson, an army doctor invalided (appropriate to our own day), out of Afghanistan. *(Authorial addendum: The producers of "Sherlock were wise enough to try a bit of time-lapse photography with the special episode "The Adventure of the Abominable Bride." There Cumberbatch and Freeman were unfettered and suitably attired to bring Holmes and the good doctor to life—even as fantasized counterparts of the contemporary duo.)*

And as a final aside, let me make a last observation. This has to do with the now-cancelled "Forever," in which a forensics specialist who happens to be immortal employs methods which are, to say the least, Sherlockian. Here Iaon Gruffudd, the once youthful Horatio Hornblower of the popular BBC series, could just as easily have been sent back to Victoria's day and presented us with a quite adequate Holmes.

And while we're on the subject of doctors playing a detective written about by a doctor and created by one as well, there are two to consider. The first was Ben Kingsley's superb Watson in "Without A Clue." And the second? Hugh Laurie, who was the curmudgeonly modern-day diagnostician in "House." So obvious here was the connection that there were not a few barely-concealed Sherlockian allusions in that program. Moreover, but for the era and the plot-line, the former "Bertie Wooster" could well have presented us with a worthy Holmesian model, had the detective been more than a student researcher at St. Bartholomew's Hospital.

Ultimately however we find ourselves reeled back to the essential, if not difficult original question of *"Who is the best Holmes?"* Failing to give you an answer satisfactorily tantamount to the Mirror On The Wall, I can only offer up my own opinion, which to me is well-founded.

For if indeed I "see" Holmes come alive through the stories, I envision *no one particular portrayer,* but perhaps, a morphed medley of many. To wit, I see the clinical severity of Rathbone without the manic sofa-vaulting of Brett; I see Wontner looking Sherlockian to suit the illustrations, and I see Brett again, if only for the sake of a kind of hauntingly wistful Holmes. All of these I stir well into the mix, if only to conjure a Sherlock Holmes who has never appeared on the large or small screen or made a radio broadcast. As I say here, for myself alone perhaps the best defense for "seeing" Holmes is somehow reminiscent of the Irregular axiom, "they never lived, and so can never die." Just so then and from my point of view, the immortal problem solver of Baker Street wears no completely recognizable face. He is, in demonstrably canonical fashion, "a man of many faces." And at the risk of incurring ire by contrasting the great detective to Jesus himself, perhaps no other character has been so envisioned or physically assayed than Holmes for the masses.

So at the end of the day, perhaps we are all merely seeking to peer behind a number of popularized masks in our quest to meet "the real Sherlock Holmes." And even as we do our best to sort through a catalogue of physicalized Master Sleuths, we may be fated to find another, rather Oz-like countenance. For the man behind the curtain, or lurking behind the disguise presents us with the broad face, slanted eyes, sportsman's build and walrus moustache of a burly Scotsman of Irish descent. And his name? *Arthur Conan Doyle.*

However as we consider the histrionic or cinematic Holmes, I believe there may be another possibility for us to consider or standard by which to measure him. This one has much to do with the fact that fidelity in portraying the detective must also take into account his deliberately dramatic nature. In other words, the panache and delight in his capabilities at misdirection, if not his positive elation at the dramatic *denouement* of a case. Here we cannot ignore a certain streak of extroversion worthy of finding no better outlet than the stage itself. This factor may also be indicative of what has often been considered of Holmes; namely that he may have spent a portion of his younger life as a member of the acting profession. And it is likely there, according to Baring-Gould and others, that he acquired his ability to assume characterizations and become proficient at make-up, if not to acquire an ability to quote from the Bard and others.

From a strictly physical perspective it is intriguing to consider the propensity of both Sherlock Holmes and his creator Conan Doyle for blurring the lines of appearance. Clearly the stories themselves reveal a propensity for disguise and even transvestism. The sixty stories themselves are ripe with deception. They are graphic and depend upon our (or Watson or others) buying into Holmes's mastery at disguise. And just so is the detective himself temporarily foiled by a gentleman masking himself as a street beggar, an American adventuress posing as a young man, or a nefarious agent donning a false beard, so too does he aspire to physical transformation. Just so he may choose to identify as a laborer, groomsman, clergyman, bookseller, seaman, tramp, or even an old woman!

Helping to confirm this suspicion there is Conan Doyle's own known desire to appear as someone other than himself. We have it on his sister's own authority that so caught up in his character of Professor Challenger of *The Lost World* that Doyle reveled in donning whiskers and full make-up, if only so as to deceive his relations. Sadly however, it does not seem that the famous author had mastered the inviolable talent for disguise practiced by his deductive creation. Nevertheless, it was perhaps not for wanting to do so.

And speaking of "the best disguise," one of the more fascinating elements in Sherlockian speculation involves the aforementioned matter of cross-dressing. Moreover, and as was so amply surmised by Sam Rosenberg's controversial 1974 book, *Naked Is The Best Disguise,* there does exist in Conan Doyle's *opus* more than a thread of gender-shifting and transvestism beyond the norm—if norm it was indeed.

In other words, suggested Rosenberg, the Doylean desire to deceive, or "cross over" from one persona to another is apparent enough in the stories, as well as "real life." Shocking? Perhaps, if indeed the sexual element is to be introduced into the matter. Here and alternately as well is the level of intimacy involved between our "players." I will not seek to over-explore the lingering hypothesis that alike Batman and Robin in later days, such cheek-by-jowl companionship must suggest something more than camaraderie.

Far simpler, or "elementary" perhaps is the basic trope of Holmes' seeming ability to consistently deceive his friend and companion Watson. The friend-and-biographer is often his cohort's acid test. This, largely on account of our taking the doctor to be somewhat adept and in his own professional way, observant. Ergo to fool such a one suggests a real victory.

But in realistic terms, one must question even the great detective's ability to physically dissemble, given the rudimentary theatrical and cosmetic tools of his day. More so as well, there is once again his seemingly consistent ability to gull his friend and fellow lodger. Thus, whether presenting himself as a waiting client or even on his death-bed, Holmes appears to succeed in his part-playing. To wit, fooling strangers is one thing; fooling one's partner is highest praise. Daring to stretch the parallel here, how many husbands (or wives) might so convincingly and often have managed to deceive those closest to them?

In Holmes however we are presented with an exception on many levels. Ergo, his skills as an actor would have lent to his ability to disguise himself, even as we might presume Sir Henry Irving, their day's greatest actor, might have pulled the trick off. I suppose it's all down to experience, as well as one's ability to transform his expression, gait, voice, posture, etc.

At the end of the metaphorical day, much of this aims us again in the direction, I believe, of (*a*) Sherlock Holmes' own skills as an actor, and (*b*) in similar fashion, certain actors with a specialized ability to "become" Holmes.

On one hand, the detective's training for his profession was much in line with that of a professional actor. As if in confirmation of this thesis, Michael Cox, producer of the Granada Holmes series said of his star Jeremy Brett, "*What was right for Holmes was the classical actor's Hamlet factor, if you like. The fact that he could play the role; that he had the voice and the actor's intelligence, the presence, the physique, the ability to jump over the furniture, handle the horses, do the disguises and whatever may be. To me he had the best combination of all those.*"

Cox's comment does indeed speak to the needs of a detective as well as an actor. Moreover, should an individual (such as Holmes himself) happen to be both, then all the better. Ergo, this "Hamlet factor" was certainly in play with not only Jeremy Brett, but a lion's share of the "best" Sherlockian portrayers, of whom some seventeen out of twenty-one were themselves British. This fact may confirm that the preparation of an actor able to play Prince Hamlet might also abet him in re-creating the persona of Sherlock Holmes.

But if indeed my Hamlet Premise is valid, might we ask how recently it can be put to the test? For answer here, perhaps one has no further to look than London at the moment this chapter was initially drafted: Autumn of 2015. And one of the hottest tickets in the City's West End? It was "Hamlet," starring Benedict Cumberbatch, *aka* Sherlock Holmes in the stratospherically popular PBS program "Sherlock."

And if this is not enough, I have discovered supportive evidence a while back from two other gentlemen who also brought the Prince of Denmark into the picture. The first is Matt Frewer of "Max Headroom" note, who also starred as Holmes in a series of Hallmark Entertainment Sherlockian adaptations. Interviewed, he said that "... *playing Holmes is rather like Hamlet. It's a horse that has been ridden by many jockeys and there's a certain responsibility with it—particularly to the audience, because they have certain expectations. But I think once those preconceptions are satisfied, then you can bring your own stuff to the dance ...*"

And finally there remains the great Basil Rathbone himself. Like Brett ultimately finding himself seemingly dominated, if not consumed by the character of Holmes, nevertheless early on the multi-faceted actor said of him: "*Ever since I was a boy and first got acquainted with the Great Detective I wanted to be like him...to play such a character means as much to me as ten Hamlets!*"

Here then is curious evidence in support of the notion that some actors believe themselves to have been "born to play the part." Brett's comment would not necessarily apply across the board. For instance, did Sean Connery ever believe he was meant to play James Bond? Doubtless not.

But sometimes the notion seems likely. To wit one early critic pointed out that "Basil Rathbone had seemingly been born to bring life to the Paget illustrations of Sherlock Holmes." It's all a matter of perspective, I suppose.

Yet perhaps like the Melancholy Dane, Holmes is often remembered for his meditative soliloquys, as he is for his declamations. In other words, for his actor-like demeanor. Perhaps it stands to reason then that a dimension of his persona(ae) may well find itself grounded in a love of the dramatic arts.

What I mean to say here is that in obvious terms *Sherlock Holmes comes across like an actor.* Therefore such a resonance, if emphatic in his portrayer, may offer a kind of concentric series of tricks. And yet we know that Holmes is not by trade a professional thespian, but in effect, a thespian-like solver of real-life problems upon the world's stage. Or perhaps, as some have hypothesized, *an actor who became a detective.*

Canonically speaking and as some degree of support for our contention, what better means of attesting to it than the words of "old Baron Dowson on the night he was hanged?"

"In your case, Holmes, what the law has gained the stage has lost."

Or by Holmes' own admission in *The Valley of Fear,* "… *some touch of the artist wells up within me, and calls insistently for a well-staged performance."*

And that performance, stylized over the course of a crime-solving career, did not go un-noted even by members of the official force.

"You would have made an actor, and a rare one."

These words of praise, from Inspector Athelney Jones in *The Sign of Four,* upon his being duped by Sherlock Holmes walking into his own Baker Street flat in full disguise.

So then, with thoughts of detectives as actors or vice-versa, we come to assess their amalgamation in the most powerful Sherlockian avatar of the past three decades. And on that note, surely one cannot escape the obvious fact that the seminal, if not controversy-free achievements of Jeremy Brett as the Great Detective cannot be avoided. Not of course that one should try to do so, for the theatrical and filmed achievements of this remarkable, if not troubled man allowed him to become a master at his craft, and ultimately, recipient of the accolade as "the definitive Holmes" before his death in 1995 at age 61.

Fans of the PBS Masterpiece series will recall Brett from an early version of "Rebecca" in 1980. Theater mavens might well have seen him as Dr. Watson to Charlton Heston's Holmes in "The Crucifer of Blood," or speaking of blood, as the sanguinary Count Dracula in the play of the same name. But it was as Sherlock Holmes that he inhabited the archetypal mold by which a future generation would recall him best. Moreover, finding his place in a parade of at least two dozen earlier portrayers, Brett's Sherlock became his own, despite many other approaches to how the role ought to be played. And harking once again to Hamlet, it was perhaps his co-star Edward Hardwicke who put it best when he said *"The role of Sherlock Holmes is like that of Hamlet. Every generation brings something to it. Jeremy brought extraordinary energy to the part and made it his own."*

My own first glimpse of the man who would become Holmes was back in 1964 with the filmed version of "My Fair Lady" starring Audrey Hepburn and Rex Harrison. There he played the smitten Freddy Eynsford-Hill, and I dare say how few might equate the pining swain who sang "On the Street Where You Live" (although Jeremy's own fine singing voice was dubbed) with the chap who would later intone, "the game is afoot!" And yet he did. And the fact that he appeared in the Lerner and Loewe cinematic re-boot of Shaw's 1912 drama "Pygmalion" is not entirely divorced from the subject at hand.

As I endeavored to explore in writing many years back, there are not a few intriguing similarities between Shaw's "Fair Lady" and Doyle's Sherlock Holmes. In what way, you may ask? Well consider: here are two leading gentlemen, in the persons of Professor Henry Higgins and Colonel Pickering. The latter seems to be the sounding board and admiring confident of the former, who has savant-like abilities to deduce (the *mot juste* here) a place of his subject's origins from the sound of their speech. In this regard we are led to understand that Higgins is somewhat unique in his profession.

And then consider Holmes. He too like Higgins is a self-trained specialist who makes deductions right and left to fulfill his role as the world's first and only consulting detective. And by his side is another retired military man returned from the Middle East, Dr. John H. Watson. As for further comparisons between Henry Higgins and Sherlock Holmes (both "H" names) they are each captivated and uncharacteristically undone by a female. In the Professor's case it is his waifish, urchin-like subject Eliza Doolittle. And with Holmes? Well *"The woman"* is better advantaged from the start, and is an American contralto and adventuress named Irene Adler.

While we're at it here, I suppose one might proceed with a monograph's worth of other singularities between the Doylean Holmes and Shavian Higgins. Consider for one their individual but similar milieus. Here are two London-based gentlemen living as flat-mates on Wimpole Street (where Conan Doyle had his London surgery at Number 2) and Baker Street respectively. Each has a landlady and household factotum and both surround themselves with the curious apparatuses of their trades.

In the respective cases of Holmes and Higgins however, there is of course the enduring question of to what exact degree they were touched by the respective ladies in their spheres of action? Here I fear in both instances speculations have become a bit strained. To wit, the musical version of "Fair Lady" lends the impression that after finding and then losing his "Liza," Henry Higgins is prepared to try again, this time appreciating her. But Shaw's seminal version gives no sense of that. Once Higgins' guinea pig is gone and on her way to marry Freddy Eynsford-Hill, her wealthy admirer, that's that. Which is not to say that the Professor might not wax wistful later on, but merely over Liza's utility as a kind of lab rat capable of performing tricks. Is that a bitter take? Ask Mr. Shaw about this line of thought, if you ever chance to meet him.

Likewise with Sherlock Holmes, much has been opined to suggest the detective's deeply emotional attraction for Miss Adler. Some have elevated this into a passion or romantic *idée fixe,* and some have envisioned a later tryst between the two. But nowhere has this game been played out so cunningly as by Rex Stout within the games-playing world of the Baker Street Irregulars.

Stout postulated not only a fixation, but a tongue-in-cheek liaison resulting in the birth of a child whose name signified the "er" of "Sherlock" and the "ol" of "Holmes. Namely then, *Nero Wolfe* (who also assumed the physically broad proportions of Mycroft Holmes).

On Stout's heels, other theorists have conjectured that by technically being bested by a member of the fairer sex, Sherlock Holmes was keen to mark the occasion. To wit, he wears her coin as a token on his watch-chain, even as he keeps her picture. And by virtue of the latter, the lady in the King of Bohemia's worrisome photograph seemingly assumed the role of a medievally inaccessible maiden, forever wistfully admired by Holmes.

But none of this is firmly based upon the foundation which the story "A Scandal in Bohemia" gives us. This does indeed show Holmes' appreciation for Irene Adler's prowess as a clever deceiver who is capable of check-mating not only a crowned head, but also the most deductive cranium in London. But do we have the impression that Holmes spent the rest of his time mooning about? We do not. He has simply marked the page. Just so did he disparage faith in woman-kind when he informed Watson in *The Sign of Four* "I assure you that the most winning woman I ever knew was hanged for poisoning three little children for their insurance-money."

In somewhat inverse fashion, Miss Adler essentially represents the master detective being bested at his own game—not only as a woman, but briefly, as a man. Recall that she passes and speaks to Holmes one evening in the guise of a young man! But on such account we should not cavil over whether or not the detective was capable of admiring others who were adept at their histrionic trades. And most certainly Miss Adler, an operatic diva, was no stranger to impersonation. Therefore in addition to being a serviceable contralto, Irene Adler lived up to her reputation as, (in Holmes' own words) an "adventuress."

Sherlock Holmes never seems to begrudge his rivals their due, or even to overly disparage their talents, unless they are of the fictive variety, such as Poe's Dupin or Gaboriou's LeCoq. In real terms, however, he notes potential and skill where it exists. Take the case, for example, of his "hated rival on the Surrey side, Barker." Add to this professional roster even the best of Scotland Yard were ungrudgingly cited by him as knowing their work. It's really the matter that while he may reflect appreciation for skill, it is rare enough to see him beaten—or for him to find himself beaten to the finish line by a woman. But here, and to quote the famous remark made by the King of Bohemia, "What a woman!"

But for Holmes, there is little more than that. For even as Professor Higgins dismisses Eliza with the final certainty that "she's going to marry Freddy," Holmes has recognized the fact that Irene Adler has engaged in matrimony with another man. And that man, described in her own words, and despite her admiration for Sherlock's failed, but bold attempts, she chose for her husband. Ergo, her ties to Godfrey Norton's far exceeded her brief flirtation with one of the blood royal. This is plain enough given her final word on the subject when she wrote: *"I love and am loved by a better man than he."*

On that literal note, the "better man" seems to have won. Norton emerged as the victor, out-trumping not only a king, but also the king of detectives.

So much then for the Doylean-Shavian aside. Now let us come back to Brett. Forget even to say that the "Higgins" of Shaw's play and the later film sounds a bit like "Huggins," which was in truth Mr. Brett's real name. Or if you wish to become mired in odd nomenclature, the fact that Eille Norwood who played Holmes in the Twenties was born Anthony *Brett*. Mere coincidence? You tell me.

Or what then of the serendipitous fact that following Conan Doyle's success, the Edwardian mystery writer Arthur Morrison gave his detective Martin Hewitt a side-kick named "Brett?" And what of the additional odd happenstance that Arthur Wontner's Dr. Watson was played by an actor named Ian Fleming? *Curiouser and curiouser.*

For the moment at least, let us progress to the question which continues to be debated among *aficionados:* namely, whether Jeremy Brett merit's the accolade of being the "best Holmes of our day" (take note the word *our)* and if so, why?

For the record and submitted as only one man's own opinion, I must admit to having savored Jeremy Brett's performances throughout Granada's early productions. Only later when the producers were compelled to acknowledge the actor's increasing infirmity did the "original" Brett-Holmes find itself sacrificed to a figure who looked less and sounded oddly different from the original template.

But in his prime Brett was superb. *Sans pareil,* as the old expression has it. Over time his youthful handsomeness gave way to that gaunt, ferally hawk-like visage so right for his greatest character and role. However, also owing to enhancing the characterization were a number of external factors which inevitably influenced Jeremy's portrayal. He once told me of some of these in our first interview, and he described how the sudden loss of his wife and his increasing bouts with depression involuntarily tempered what Holmes was going through on the screen. In other words, the collateral effects of Real Life produced or enhanced the detective's becoming doubly isolated and demon-driven. The traits which Brett began to display were notable. The manic aspects of rest and motion, silence and outburst, happiness and melancholy, were all components of a man doing his best to act, even as he was in the iron grip of an elemental darkness which only hugged him more and more closely over time. But was his ability to convey those the by-product of something more?

As a consequence, prior to the final installments of the Granada series, Jeremy Brett was no longer in full control of himself as Holmes. And like Robert Louis Stevenson's Dr. Jekyll before him, he could do little more than to ultimately succumb to his demon. And very like the inscription found upon Christopher Marlowe's alleged portrait at Cambridge, Jeremy may have become a voluntary victim.

"Quod me nutrit, me destruit" says Kit Marlowe's artistic *impresa;* or in translated form, "that which nourishes me, destroys me." An apt phrase that, according to many, which seemingly reflects the Elizabethan poet-playwright-turned-murdered spy's tragic fate. Which only compels me to wonder, do you think Mr. Brett might now agree with such a notion?

At the outset of his debut as Holmes however, in physical, vocal and general presentiment, Jeremy Brett became the very visual echo of the Sidney Paget *Strand Magazine* illustrations. But this was no accident. And just as the actor was mindful of not mimicking, but settling into the established image, he took pains to assure that all was correct in the Granada undertaking. And if not?

"Well I simply said to the producers, if it's not right then I will not be happy" he once told me. *"And if I'm not happy, well..."* Then that low, guttural chuckle.

The sets, the locations, the physical characterizations, and of course, Baker Street itself and its most famous flat—all of these components were scrupulously addressed. The result of such intense desire for accuracy not only re-created Holmes' gas-lit *mise en scene,* but in general terms also Conan Doyle's Victorian cosmos.

As will be discussed shortly, there are some criticisms which have been leveled at "Sherlock" Brett. Certain of those involved the seemingly manic dimension of leaping over sofas, furiously brushing his clothing, or producing a level of rudeness and dismissal that many viewers felt were unworthy of the great detective. Adding a weightier bit of agreement here, I once personally heard such criticisms from none other than Dame Jean Conan Doyle herself. But were those charges truly apt? Of course here we come before the court of each audience member for a possible verdict on the "true Holmes."

As if in a prescient remark, Jeremy Brett himself privately admitted that it was originally a task to play Holmes. This, largely on account of the fact that the actor and the role were so far apart temperamentally. As for whether Sherlock Holmes was someone he might like, the actor was emphatic in the negative. "I wouldn't walk across the street to meet him" he said. Ultimately however, and to our own benefit, Jeremy Brett gave us a lion's share of Holmes to enjoy, again and again. He elected to tackle what he dubbed "the sacred monument," and he scaled it, I believe, fairly close to its summit. But like all mountaineers know, there is always a price levied for the attempt. Sadly, and even in the end and aware of it, Jeremy paid that price for what we so amply received in return.

26
The Man Who Would Be Holmes

The evening I first met Mr. Sherlock Holmes came at the end of an appropriately "foggy day in London town." Or so at least it seemed.

November, 25, 1988. Dori and I had arrived in Britain over the course of the Thanksgiving holiday, which seemed a bit surreal. But rather than this being a negative, the up-side was not merely the early winter weather, but also the imminence of Christmas along the city's avenues and shop-fronts.

And yes, speaking of the weather. Perhaps it would be over-much to say it was a throwback, but given the mood and the place, the chilly, dank air of London seemed to evoke a suitably past-tense world. That and the impression of a misty, street-lamped byway suggested the specter of a Victorian fog such as Mr. Holmes would have known.. I mean to say, there was a kind of grayish, vaporous quality to the evening air, which was all that was necessary for the mind's eye to convert it to a faint reminder of the "pea-soupers" of yore.

But to talk about a rekindled fog as if to greet us might be overgenerous. Today the long-gone miasmas of London are literally frozen in a kind of Victorian amber. That fact, notwithstanding a recent *New York Times* story suggesting that pollution in Britain's capital may well find those noxious otherworldly billows resurrected.

Dramatic as the idea of a Sherlockian world where "the gaslight fades at fifty feet," the reality of those distant decades was quite something else. Nevertheless, like a stage-dressing for mystery, "foggy London" has become a trope for those who have yet or wish to visit the capital and its storied labyrinths.

At any rate, when we arrived in the metropolis at the tail-end of that bleak November, the oddly mist-sodden evening seemed like an omen; that, and a sign that the Doylean gods were now aligned in their proper heaven.

I made my way to Wyndham's Theatre on Charing Cross Road where the production of Jeremy Paul's play "The Secret of Sherlock Holmes" had recently opened to fine reviews. My purpose was to meet the drama's star Jeremy Brett, who by that time had brought Conan Doyle's master detective to life for nearly five years. In that task the actor was more than ably abetted on stage by his television-and-real-life friend, Edward Hardwicke.

But in 1988 I'm certain that no one, beginning with "Holmes" and "Watson" themselves would have anticipated six more years of their popular series, or that which would come in their wake?

Yet as Irene Adler had sung in 1965 in the Broadway musical "Baker Street," I knew I was "in London again." In point of fact I also had certain unrelated reasons to be there, beginning with the follow-up to my own PBS "Great Shakespeare Duel" and the invitation to join the prosecutorial team in the much-vaunted "Shakespeare Moot" to be held at the historic Middle Temple Hall on November 26th.

So then I was in town to see Shakespeare as well as Sherlock, or at least to lend support to this most recent assault upon certain of those lofty assumptions which promoted what anti-Stratfordians called the Myth of the Bard.

But now and paramount to my immediate purpose, I was about to "meet Mr. Holmes," a feat which had been arranged, rather appropriately, I thought, through the auspices of none other than Dame Jean Conan Doyle. That on its own was chillingly right, and was founded in my previous contact with Lady Bromet (as she also was by title), who now indirectly served as a mediatrix for bringing two men together who had sought to embody those two giants in her life. Ergo, *Sir Arthur, please say hello to your creation, Sherlock Holmes.*

On the heels of his great success as Holmes in the Granada series, Jeremy Brett had supposedly had a hand in inspiring and commissioning the dramatic production penned by Paul, who'd previously provided dramatizations for "The Naval Treaty," "Wisteria Lodge," "The Speckled Band," and "The Musgrave Ritual." Ergo, a winning combination of words and action.

I arrived at the Wyndham's Theater about two hours before the curtain for "The Secret of Sherlock Holmes." I was there to meet an actor whom the critics were calling "the perfect Holmes," and whose work I had digested eagerly as the final and fitting re-creation of the world of Baker Street and beyond.

Both Jeremy and I had the good fortune of meeting Dame Jean Conan Doyle earlier. Curiously then, in a strangely similar fashion both of us sought the approval of that "certain gracious lady." Moreover, and knowing that Jean spoke highly of my Doylean dramatic project, without doubt this had provided the impetus for my meeting with Brett.

I believe the actor had known that I'd initially met with and worked on the script for my "Evening With Sir Arthur Conan Doyle" with my subject's daughter. Yes, just as I was aware that the famous Holmes portrayer had been wooing Jean from the start to gain her approval of his work. Moreover as I was shortly to learn, approval of his craft could easily mean the world to Mr. Brett.

I was ushered backstage to his dressing room. And there I found not an actor, but Sherlock Holmes, albeit a modernized version of him with tousled hair, jeans, and a short-sleeved sports shirt. We shook hands. I looked into the eyes of "Holmes." And he at me. Strangest of all in that moment, I found myself imagining who and what the star was now seeing. And from my own perspective from somewhere within me a quiet voice remarked *you are taller than he is, and bigger.*

"Yes, you've got the look" the actor said appraising me, commenting upon what our friend must have said concerning my incipient resemblance to her late father. Doubtless as well she had managed a word with Jeremy, which had resulted in my being given access to him. No, I had no doubt that he'd been briefed.

"I think you can do it" he said, obviously cutting to the chase of whether or not I was worthy of "becoming his creator." But his next words startled me.

"Now then, you must tell me what I can do to help you?"

Such words coming from such a source were, I cannot lie, overwhelming to hear. As was the experience of sitting down in that small room and talking about London, the weather, my play, and of course, Sherlock Holmes as transmuted by the man seated across from me.

I confess that that conversation, monumental in its small way, made me nervous and excited in the way a child feels when confronted by his favorite toy or pastime. And further, I would lie to tell you that at that juncture of time, and on the threshold of my own dramatic project, the idea of simply being on my own for a face-to-face chat with "Sherlock Holmes" felt like the rare opportunity it was.

I asked my companion if he would mind our talk being recorded. He didn't hesitate. Actors are used to being captured on film, in a camera's lens, or even by adoring members of the public who want nothing more than to preserve their moment with "himself."

Nearly two hours had flown by before Jeremy needed his "quiet time" to prepare. I was mindful of that in a general way, but more specifically so in terms of his sea-change into Holmes. As he explained it to me, "I need to squeeze the sponge dry of myself, and then allow it to absorb him."

By this time I've given a bit of thought to that business of "squeezing the sponge." It becomes apparent to every actor unless he or she is portraying themselves. Therefore when one needs make the jump from Jeremy to Sherlock or in my case, from Mark to Conan Doyle, nothing should be left to chance. This notion was perfectly illustrated by Brett's descriptions to me of how he had studied his now dog-eared copy of *The Complete Sherlock Holmes,* which he'd brought to the sets of Castlefield, near Manchester, as if it were the Bible. But it was, as we both agreed. And it had been this singular actor's mission to see that the metaphorical law and the prophets would depend upon on the Sacred Gospel According to Sir Arthur.

"It came up from time to time that we try the story or the lines a different way" he remembered. "But on those occasions I would say, "why don't we just do them according to Doyle?" And judging from the finished product over the course of eleven years, Granada's producers took their star's message to heart. And the result became perhaps the most faithfully recreated depiction of the domestic and greater world of Mr. Sherlock Holmes.

I was left with a headful of thoughts and a great deal of excitement after my first meeting with Jeremy Brett. And were that not enough, our interview and conversation would continue the next night when I would brighten Brett's dressing room with the addition of my attractive wife.

The following evening we went to the Wyndham's Theater to see "The Secret Of Sherlock Holmes." Once again there was its star, and to my great pleasure as well, a few moments spent when he introduced us to his Watson, Edward Hardwicke.

I will always value the kindness and gentle patience Mr. Hardwicke had for yet another couple of visitors. I had barely enough time to spend, en route to Brett's dressing room, to chat, but enough to hand "Dr. Watson" a letter I'd prepared, if only to express my appreciation of his wonderful portrayal of Holmes's friend and confident. In that letter I reiterated something I told him of in person, involving my participation in the Shakespeare Moot at the Middle Temple Hall. Moreover, he seemed amused by the fact that I was to stand on behalf of the prosecutorial Loyal Opposition to the Stratfordians, as the Shakespearean supporters are known. Also, I'd made the point that like Sir Cedric Hardwicke, Edward's father and a great actor on his own, I was an avid appreciator of Christopher Marlowe. He, I was told, had been a "candidate" in Sir Cedric's mind, for the honor of being the "onlie begetter" of Prince Hamlet and so much more. And then it was time to take our leave and move down the hall to Jeremy Brett's dressing room.

From the start Jeremy came across as a mixture of a doting cavalier and the man Dori expected to see and did, without the slightest disappointment, when she met "Sherlock Holmes" in the flesh. I've no doubt that on the heels of his many gorgeous leading ladies, my own fair lady was no letdown. In fact, when we discussed my then-favorite episode, that of "A Scandal in Bohemia," Jeremy began to wax on the loveliness of his "Irene Adler," the Texas born Gayle Hunnicutt.

"She was an absolute vision" he remembered with a smile, and she wore a Penhaligon scent. I think it was 'Blue Bell.'

Before we left London and remembering her new acquaintance's comment, we visited Penhaligon's emporium where a special purchase was made. Soon after and upon our return home Dori sent Jeremy a Victorian lady's handkerchief, scented with—you guessed it—"Blue Bell!"

I still recall a great deal of my first chats with "Sherlock Holmes." I found myself elated by his stories of his early-stage career working for Laurence Olivier and with a host of other greats. I chanced to mention my chronic passion for Diana Rigg, with whom he'd also acted. This in turn made me recall citing my meeting with Brett to Diana a year or so later. To which she'd merely smiled and simply said with a shake of her gorgeous head, "Jerry."

There was a great deal more, but perhaps one of the most poignant aspects was Brett's own recollection of how the sudden death of his wife while filming "The Final Problem" had sent him in a downward spiral. This would only worsen at intervals with regard to the sort of manic depression suffered by a cross section of people. We spoke of Churchill's own "black dog" and his belief that somehow his long-term malaise had been hereditary. For Brett however, he felt that he had absorbed the pain and registered it in different ways—including how he brought what he'd felt to the role of Sherlock Holmes. But always throughout it all I could not help but to think *here I am sitting with Sherlock Holmes.*

I could also be no less than candid with Jeremy concerning certain of my favorite lines, a' la Brett, if not his ability to bring Baker Street's most famous tenant to life. One of those was the passage spoken in the lower bank vault in "The Red Headed League" concerning Professor Moriarty.

Curious as well and in a rare bit of dramatic license by dramatist John Hawkesworth, the lines in question had been transposed from the later adventure of "The Final Problem" to the earlier "Red Headed League," which Granada had broadcast in 1986. But Brett knew precisely what I was calling for. And there, suddenly, for my eyes only in his quiet dressing room, the actor began to intone his lines for only the two of us to hear. He closed his eyes briefly and began.

"He has hereditary tendencies of the most diabolical kind. A criminal strain runs in his blood, which is increased and rendered all the more dangerous by his extraordinary powers. He is the organizer of half that is evil and of nearly all that is undetected in this great city."

Yes, those familiar words. Undoubtably some of the greatest ever written for the world's greatest detective to speak. And I was there to hear them again. As if it had been a command performance for myself alone. I was honored.

Following our privileged time with its star Dori and I enjoyed Jeremy Paul's "Secret of Sherlock Holmes." As I would discover, not only did Brett have a good deal riding on this (he told me "his pension" relied upon it, making me think he was an investor), but he also was the play's sparking plug. Jeremy Paul later told me that his friend had copious discussions and note-making conveyed to the playwright, most of which he hoped would find its way into "his" drama. Curiously as well, near the end-point of his life, Jeremy Brett harbored ideas about a sequel to "Secret," and once again plied Paul with his notions. But nothing came as the result.

In closing here, my memories of my all-too-brief relationship with Jeremy Brett are bitter-sweet in the most literal of ways. As I write these words I look across to the shelf. There within a plastic frame is a clipping. And speaking of how I risked introducing my attractive lady wife to "Sherlock Holmes," I recall a certain kindness he did for me on the evening of November 26, 1988. This involved a favor, conjured the evening before when the two of us had first met. I'd informed him that we'd be returning to see the show the next evening, and that there was "a certain something" he often did as Holmes which Dori simply loved. Seeming to savor the idea, Brett agreed.

Now cut to the next evening in his dressing room. After chatting a bit, the star pleaded his need for some time to prepare before going on, which is every actor's privilege. But just as we reached the doorway I remembered and turned to him, and pointed a finger at Dori, I said, "Jeremy, don't forget." At which the great man adjusted his smile and seemed to straighten into the icon. Then he said, looking squarely at Dori, "Oh yes. Watson, I have something to say to you."

The attractive lady framed in the doorway was quite taken by surprise. She looked back at the star and smiled back, expectantly.

"Hah!" said Sherlock Holmes, sounding exactly as he had on those cinematic occasions of revelation when he would astonish his friend Doctor Watson. And for that favor, I thought to myself I would forgive this man anything. But had I ever truly found a later reason to retract that statement? I wonder now if I did?

A. Conan Doyle — "Sir Arthur"

27
According To Doyle

I am often asked what was involved in the process of readying my portrayal of Sir Arthur Conan Doyle for the stage? In point of fact, it took a good while for me to feel satisfied that I could "become" my subject in theatrical terms. Nor was I moved by appreciative appraisals or any sense that I was "doing it right." To be doing it at all was difficult enough, and I'd moved through some dark and perilous waters to navigate to this point.

I find myself recalling a chance meeting with Roy Pilot, whom I'd met ten years earlier when he'd enrolled in my Holmes introductory class at Wayne State University in Detroit. Now however it was 1989 when we found ourselves in Ann Arbor, and Roy introduced me to his companion, Dr. Alvin E. Rodin. The two of them were mapping out an annotated edition of *The Lost World.* Moreover, Dr. Rodin offered me another surprising tidbit; namely that *he was thinking of dramatically portraying Sir Arthur Conan Doyle.* But of course and as he said, he'd been informed that I had met with Dame Jean in London. *True.* Also that I had gained her co-operation in creating my drama, which was about to be produced. *True again, doctor.* And on that note, perhaps something of an understanding. *Entirely so.*

I liked Dr. Rodin, but empathized with him a bit. For even as we discussed the notion of bringing Sir Arthur to life on stage, I couldn't help but to take note of our physical differences. To begin with, the good doctor was short, bald, and spectacled. He admitted the physical disparity between himself and his prospective subject to me. I replied that the genre of the "one-man show" brought with it a sense of relativity. In other words, in being alone on stage, the actor is therefore in relative position to what surrounds him. Ergo, a smaller man may seem larger. Also, the effects of makeup or lenses can easily compensate for physical shortcomings.

"But you're about Doyle's height" he said to me, looking up into my eyes.

Yes, I agreed, I was Doyle's height, and I'd also acquired a certain "breadth" over the years which prior to this time I might have liked to shed. But not so much now. Then there was my own latent resemblance to Jean Conan Doyle's "Pops" which the lady herself had commented on the first occasion of our acquaintance, if not thereafter. *"You have reminded me of him from the first moment we met."*

Dr. Rodin went on to publish his annotated rendition of Conan Doyle's wonderful tale of Dr. Challenger and a relict species of dinosaurs on a remote South African plateau. Sadly however, he passed away at just about the time the kudos should have been coming his way. But not as Sir Arthur. And that left his partner, Pilot, on his own. I remember saying to Roy, as we reminisced about those earlier days when he was a Sherlockian in the making, that "the time will come when you are the one they will want to meet." My colleague demurred at the suggestion. But when *The Annotated Lost World* emerged as a fine piece of scholarship, my prophecy was proven out. At the time of this writing it's also been furthered, given that friend Pilot has now emerged with an annotated rendition of that Doylean knightly tale, *The White Company.* And at the risk of daring to repeat myself here, "honour due," Roy!

I remember thinking that in the wake of my meeting with Rodin and Pilot I'd been left with the opportunity to do what no one had to date done: to portray Sir Arthur on stage, and to work with his daughter to assure a sense of authenticity. In other words, "the rules According To Doyle."

And among those "last things" concerning the business of "becoming Sir Arthur," a final anecdote. I recall one of my mid-point performances some while after we'd been out of the gate with my play in 1989. On this particular evening at Henry Ford Community College, my friend and dramatic accomplice, Dale Van Dorp, the HFCC theater manager had shot some video-tape of my performance. Taken from the booth high above, it gave a kind of longer distance view of Conan Doyle, but was interesting nonetheless to me. And why? Well the short answer is: for the first time after more than two years, *I felt I actually saw Arthur Conan Doyle.* Yes, a big man, bear-like, prowling about the stage, engaging his audience, his voice commanding them to listen with that curious dulled burr I'd studied when I'd begun the drill of speaking his-and-my words. But that night, it seemed to be the first time I actually "saw" my man, and realized that I wasn't looking at myself. The sea-change had begun to occur!

It was a long and challenging road since my first return from Cadogan Square and the one lady in the world I required to like me as Sir Arthur Conan Doyle. My friend as she became will always be remembered in her own right as "the Woman" in my unique endeavor.

But it took a while to get the research done. The prompt book first. Then that cumbersome script which was sent to Britain, and duly followed by its author shortly after.

It was a bit of fun selecting my wardrobe. I haunted vintage clothing shops and found spats and a gorgeous mauve smoking jacket. I was photographed in our back yard kneeling by the weathered head of Zeus, looking like a caped and cloth-capped Conan Doyle, a pipe clutched in his gloved hand. Ironically and some seventeen years later, I would take note of the costumes worn by Martin Clunes in the PBS rendition of the novel *Arthur and George*. And I thought, *the cap, the cape, the pipe— even as I'd worn them.*

And as for the Doylean voice? That was a matter a bit closer-to-home, or very shortly would be. Importantly here as well I wished to be careful on this count, for a parade of mistakes have been made in the past. Some versions of Sir Arthur on screen made him handsome and British sounding, as in "The Great Edwardians" when Nigel Davenport became ACD. An early Houdini movie made Peter Cushing Holmes' creator, and that didn't look or sound right. In a movie about fairies Peter O'Toole became a rather tubercular looking Doyle, and a year ago, which was a far cry from his wonderful vocal intonations for animated Holmesian versions of the *Hound* and the *Sign of the Four.* An HBO Houdini special offered up a shortish older chap who would have made a great Watson, but a poor impression of his colleague.

In obvious terms I suppose it is appropriately easy to confuse Holmes with his creator; to wit, at times it may be perceived that Sir Conan Doyle and Dr. W. might be seen as interchangeable. To wit, the ACD-JHW meme even includes a fairly recent "Sherlock Holmes Paper Doll" book, in which the disrobed and attired Dr. Watson is in effect also Sir Arthur!

In any event, I am pleased that in visual as well as other terms, Dame Jean Conan Doyle was constant in her approval of my presentation.

Always I will recall her comment upon our first and auspicious meeting.

"From the moment you arrived I could not help but think how much you resembled my father" she'd said. And accordingly, I will preserve the memory of Brett's eagle eye, and of his saying to me *"you have the look, and I know you can do it."* No mean praise from either of them.

All of this I suppose must reflect the fact that I do believe that I quite literally "grew into the part" of my dramatic alter-ego. But not merely in the sense of my "fighting weight." Believe it or not—and you probably won't—but after I began performing in "An Evening With Sir Arthur Conan Doyle" my height gained nearly an inch. I kid you not. But perhaps that's only on account of having such a lofty subject to aspire to become, dramatically, at least. That, at any rate, involved the visual dimension.

The other day I found a letter from my friend John Bennett Shaw, dated 29 November, 1990. It had been occasioned by John's receipt of a videotaped "audition" I'd put together for my "ACD." He wrote:

Dear Conan/Mark
Dear Mark/Doyle
I am not certain who is who…all I know is that I saw both of you on that video-tape. You have done it! No more nit-picking! Get out so that many may see Doyle as he was.
Great show!

As you might imagine, such words from America's "Dean of Sherlockiana" and one of the world's foremost collectors and aficionados were beyond hoping for! And very like my prized Baker Street Irregulars investiture, no one can relieve you of those honors.

Little however did I know that Shaw's high praise would eventually be exceeded by another glowing statement, but this one intended for the general public. It read:

"There have been literally hundreds of performances of plays about the Great Detective, Sherlock Holmes, as well as films, television and radio programs, readings and much more. Surely the adulation of Mr. Holmes is deserved. But justice must be served. Was not Sherlock Holmes a creation of a great thinker and writer, Conan Doyle?

Certainly. And now comes a play conceived, written, and acted by a man who thinks like, looks like, talks like, and is as close to the real Conan Doyle as is possible. He is Mark McPherson."

With my well-tailored armor now polished, I felt prepared at last to enter into the lists of battle. So I forged ahead. Early on the newness, if not strangeness of my project brought with it certain pitfalls. These I tried to cover over by the device of portraying Sir Arthur being coerced to go out onto a public stage for the sake of describing his own life and times. But moreover, as the author himself freely admits to the bust of Holmes in his study, *"the question is, who or what do they really want to hear about? 'The War In South Africa: Its Causes and Conflicts?' No. They'd prefer to hear about you!*

In the latter regard I needed to address, whether consciously or not, the matter of portraying a public figure uncertain of how to reveal his private-most inspirations. Here the fact of the matter was that Conan Doyle would not have taken that path. But in dramatic terms, it was necessary to allow my protagonist to share his highs and lows. This then was the trick: of being able to offer up a candid, if not soul-baring monologue in which the creator of the fictional Sherlock Holmes confesses in a way the real man never did.

But over time the exercise felt more and more comfortable. I sensed I was slowly finding my way to the world of Conan Doyle, and oddly, given those coordinates I sensed a certain wind-shift in my orientations. In other words, while it may have been Mr. Sherlock Holmes who had led me to "discover" Sir Arthur, once that discovery was made the great detective became a kind of literary vestigial organ! Which is freely to admit that I became more steeped in the doll's maker rather than the doll or even his doll-house. That epiphany was rather major for me, and appreciated by no one better than Conan Doyle's daughter.

Over the years which followed my Doylean debut, I would see Jean somewhat regularly and ring her up or write. She in turn would kindly post me articles or items, such as a set of commemorative Holmes stamps put out by the Royal Post, a magazine article about Diana Rigg, or a holiday postcard featuring a be-whiskered gent in a top-hat who vaguely resembled me. And inscribed on that card was Jean's message, "Long Live Beards!"

When we had the good fortune of meeting in person we would talk about many things, which never had anything much to do with Sherlock Holmes or even in direct terms, Sir Arthur. That, I believe, was the key to her sense that I liked her for the woman she was and not simply as "the keeper of the sacred flame." And as I also knew, being that "keeper" grew at times to be exhausting. She also heard from more persons than she cared to in this regard, and frankly found herself more often than not wishing not to be bothered.

She was also irritated by the constant slew of re-creations, parodies and pastiches about Sherlock Holmes. "Why can't they simply make their own characters instead of my father's?" she asked me.

But I knew I would always value the memory of my first meetings with Dame Jean, and that seminal week we'd spent together vetting the lines from the over-sized prototype of my drama. And over time I found myself feeling increasingly protective of my friend as well. The time we'd spent together was too precious to waste, or even to over-discuss with strangers. Therefore it was quite a while before I would reminisce about our first meeting, of her taking me to luncheon at her club, or of our very frank conversations about life, death, or her father's penchant, Survival Of The Human Spirit.

We also discussed my ideas for a sequel to my "Evening." This was a project I'd envisioned once I felt comfortable enough in Conan Doyle's skin. Moreover, I wished to set the drama, to be titled "The Untangled Skein" at the point in time just after ACD's first wife's death. This to me represented a time of true emotional testing. First of all, he was more than flirting with "the psychic matter," as he called it.

Secondly, I found myself artistically considering whether or not the man I admired felt a sense of guilt in the wake of his wife "Touie's" passing? Here the guilt aspect reflected the very human fact that for the last decade Doyle had maintained an ongoing friendship and perhaps more with Jean Leckie, whom he would wed. Furthermore, this same period of time signaled the moment when ACD would "become" Sherlock Holmes for the public. The reason here involved a young solicitor named George Edalji, a son of a Parsi vicar who had been charged and imprisoned for cattle mutilation. Incarcerated and stricken off the law lists as a consequence, Edalji implored Sir Arthur to help to clear his name. And Doyle's response? *"I am not Sherlock Holmes."*

Sir Arthur's admission as it related to separating himself from his creation would find yet another strange echo in my relationship with his daughter. Upon one of many of our discussions concerning my dramatic quest to strike the truest tone for my subject, I recall once hearing myself make the most blatant of admissions.

"You know" I said, "I will always disappoint you. For try as I might, only Conan Doyle could be Conan Doyle."

Furthermore and at the core of my play stood the idea that Arthur Conan Doyle as the creator of Sherlock Holmes was distinctly *not* his detective. And paradoxical as it now seems, he always drew a line of distinction between what he called "the doll and its maker." No doubt this came as the upshot of the public's assumption that if you could create the world's greatest detective, then you could be him. Moreover, according to some, the creator himself may have been affected, wittingly or not, by the notion. For it is a fact that Sir Arthur did choose to embark upon certain casework which, save for the Holmes association, was disconnected from his career as a writer. Or was it? Here I could not help but remember an anecdote told to me by British author John Gardner, who was once commissioned to continue the late Ian Fleming's James Bond series.

"He went through a phase when Fleming seemed to believe he was Bond" Gardner explained. "Fast cars, pretty women, and a great deal of excess. In effect, he believed the myth he himself had created."

On a perhaps somewhat valedictory note, perhaps we might gauge Conan Doyle's intent in concert with a comment made by his son, Adrian Conan Doyle. "If anyone was truly Sherlock Holmes, then it was my father" he firmly stated.

However and dramatically speaking, I wanted to progressively demonstrate that particularly at the moment of his greatest emotional and cerebral tests, Sir Arthur was on the verge of being a shattered man. He was in effect like his fictive character complaining of feeling somewhat torn apart like a racing engine unconnected with its true purpose.

Therefore and in order to bring those pieces together, Arthur Conan Doyle finally accepted George Edalji's plea to help him. But and as my un-produced drama "The Untangled Skein" would demonstrate, the protagonist found himself quite unable to function—as himself. Ergo and like Stevenson's Dr. Jekyll, Doyle seeks to induce his Mr. Hyde-like side, by chemically stimulating himself into the persona of his "monstrous" alter ego, Sherlock Holmes. He does so by the stimulus of not only drugs, but through the act of surrendering to the nearly demonic spirit of Holmes who in nearly schizophrenic fashion had secretly possessed his maker for so long.

And it is only by that such a self-surrender that Arthur Conan Doyle did in fact aid and vindicate George Edalji, married Jean Leckie, and in the process succeeded in breaking the emotional chains which had been his self-imposed fetters. As a result I could not help but to wonder whether by doing so the author and his Frankenstein-like creation might somehow come to better terms?

I recall discussing my imminent sequel with my colleague Richard Lancelyn Green, and in particular, of how I did not wish to incur Dame Jean's anger by portraying her father in anything but a noble light. To date this had become the recognized "straight road" taken by John Dickson Carr, who had partnered with Jean's brother Adrian Conan Doyle, to write *The Exploits of Sherlock Holmes.* Which is to say, to present the "blade straight, steel true" rendition of Sir Arthur, rather than to risk enmity, patronage, or in this case, friendship with the Doyles.

Therefore I elected to continue to perform my "Evening" and to refine it. I suspected that the day would eventually come when "Untangled Skein" would be revealed. In jocular fashion as well, I remarked to my friend Richard that as I grew older, balder, grayer and more infirm, ideally my resemblance to the "later" ACD would only become more authentic!

Ironically and sadly as well, in making that remark I probably envisioned Richard, whom I felt was more than capable of one day penning the end-all, be-all Doyle Biography.

But "time and tide" once again played their unannounced roles. Neither my colleague nor I could have known or even imagined what the unknown future would present to us both.

And as for my already mounted, if not still-to-be-produced play "The Untangled Skein" today?" Truth to tell, and perhaps like Dr. Watson's stored works at Cox and Co. Bank, it lingers in that repose which await dramas dreaming of their times. For the moment then the stage is dark, save perhaps for that single and customary "ghost light" which metaphorically holds it at bay.

But perhaps even now, as I exceed Sir Arthur's own time on earth, the moment for resuming my guise as himself will arise. Short of that, there may be wisdom in taking a breath and waiting for a celestial, comet-like sign, as if to say "all right, take your turn once again."

As of the present, there have been not a few other rogue comets hying into view. Time has witnessed new takes on the character of Holmes, and new films, new pastiches, and at least, a new generation to experience the magic. If not a new freedom, more unbound in legal terms than ever to make the Master Sleuth of 221B Baker Street a permanent denizen of the public domain.

For these and other such reasons I suppose I have felt more compelled than even at the onset of this memoir to share what I have learned and experienced within the Doylean/Holmesian World. Moreover and as I've tried to suggest, it somehow feels imperative to capture voices I have heard before all of us vanish into the mists.

For by re-membering and re-presenting those I have encountered within this beloved niche of literature, I feel its occupants (even present company included) may seem to be re-animated, however briefly. And for that reason I have elected to tell a number of separate and sometimes interrelated stories in this memoir. From it the reader may or may not choose to make their own deductions about the author, much as Holmes suggests in *A Study In Scarlet*.

"From a drop of water" said the writer, *"a logician could infer the possibility of an Atlantic or a Niagara ..."*

Here then in these pages, if you like, is an ocean's worth of remembrance. Draw from it as you please.

In describing the composition of *An Irregular Life* I have mentioned the occasional appearance of "signs." One of those was perceptibly recognized more than half a decade ago when I first set these words to the page. It was then , as I've noted, September 21, 2015. On that evening I watched the third and final installment of the new PBS season's airing of "Arthur and George," based upon the novel of that name by Julian Barnes. As you may recall, this teleplay dramatized the Doyle-Edalji relationship and starred Martin Clunes of "Doc Martin" fame as "Doc Doyle," if I might risk the liberty!

Moreover, and despite the need to go beyond the novel to induce a sense of *uber*-mystery, if not to present ACD as Action Man, the story of "Arthur and George" was tight enough. Importantly, it presented the author's own interpretation of Conan Doyle at a cross-road. Most importantly to me, at any rate, was that this dramatic juncture in our hero's life was akin to, but different from what I have suggested. And on that note, I feel there is more than enough room for us to re-present the strange case of George Edalji, and the role of Holmes' literary "father" in resolving it. There will be more to come on this front, to be sure.

External Shot of "Windlesham," Crowborough

"The Ghostly Staircase" Windlesham

(*Top*) Dame Jean at Crowborough
(*Bottom*) Crowborough's Lord Mayor and the Author

Sir Arthur according to Paget

Sir Arthur according to McPherson

"Sir Arthur" In The Garden

28
The Ghost On The Staircase

By 1989 my production of "An Evening with Sir Arthur Conan Doyle" was up and running. I'd begun slowly with a number of performances on college stages and in private theaters. Over the course of the next few years I was privileged to be invited to bring my drama to a cross-section of performance venues. Another specie of "being Sir Arthur" involved exporting my work to a variety of scion societies across the country.

But in the latter regard there was a bit of irony afoot, and that reminded me of the line in John's gospel about a prophet having honor, but not necessarily within his own community. And that community, as I was given reason to learn, began the organization known as the Baker Street Irregulars.

I recall a difficult conversation with Thomas Stix, the then commissionaire of the BSI. Caustic, brusque, even outright rude as I thought, he'd questioned the authenticity of my claim to have worked in conjunction with Dame Jean Conan Doyle. Time would only exacerbate our slender relationship, as when Stix threatened to de-invest me if I did not become a regular attendee at the annual dinner. My reply to him was direct: my investiture ("Cecil Barker") had been presented to me by Julian Wolff in 1979. Ergo it was not within his purview to strip me of my shilling.

I cannot help but to admit that I was a bit hurt by the seeming lack of interest toward the notion of entertaining Holmes' creator (or Watson's agent, if you like) at the annual dinner. I did not press the issue at the time, knowing as I did that there existed a kind of paradoxical dislike for things Doylean. Not merely that Conan Doyle's name would be raucously booed (most often in high spirits) at club meetings, but that for some reason, among some people, there was an enmity between Sherlockians and Doyleans. This was much more pronounced back then than in successive years. But I recall ruing this fact with Christopher Rodin, who had also known Jean Conan Doyle, and had been the sparking plug behind the Arthur Conan Doyle Society.

But as they say, one "goes where the work is," and best of all, where one is most wanted. On such a note the overall welcome to "An Evening With Sir Arthur" was warm and frequently emanated from the Holmes societies across the country and beyond. Just so, I was both challenged and glad to perform for The Bootmakers in Toronto, at its excellent central library with its magnificent Doylean-Holmesian Collection. It was also a pleasure to meet such Canadian specialists as Chris Redmond and Cameron Hollyer, and later to be praised by both for their kind after-the-fact reviews.

And I did indeed come to appreciate the value of that "specialized" appreciation for one's hard work. On one level I suppose the reaction of the general audiences who are kind enough to come to see you perform means a very great deal. More difficult, perhaps, is the sense that there are some seated out there in the darkness whose acumen rivals, if not surpasses your own. Therefore, one goes into the arena with loins girded. And as I've already said, armed with the sense that you are walking out there not as yourself pretending to be someone else, but *as someone else.* This aura is bolstered if you've done your work, touched the essential bases, and are prepared to offer your observers even more than they expect. Such became the most valuable gifts given me by Dame Jean Conan Doyle; i.e., equipping me with a set of unknown traits or quirks or habits which none but the purists could appreciate. But it is rare that one performs for an audience of purists. But that would ultimately become a consummation devoutly to be wished for, even as I later hungered to present the opinions of Professor C.S. Lewis to an audience comprised of atheists and agnostics—and not merely true believers. For you know, while preaching to the choir may be musical and fun, trying to get to the core of the character the longer way 'round is of more value.

Which reminds me of a story Brett told me regarding his "hardest fought" (my term for his) review. This took the form of a certain writer for *The New York Times* who had sat on the proverbial fence regarding his performances as Sherlock Holmes.

"Honestly, I tried best I could" Jeremy told me, and then, eventually, the review came through in print. Moreover, he demonstrated his point to me in our first interview, "Here, let me show it to you" he said. And with that he reached into his wallet and retrieved a somewhat dog-eared relic which he unfolded for perhaps its hundredth time. He handed it to me and I read it. And indeed, it was high praise indeed.

"Let me tell you" the actor continued, as I handed the precious bit of newsprint back to him, "that was absolutely the longest f*** to get to what I wanted to hear. I looked at him and nodded. And I couldn't help but think of our mutual friend Diana Rigg, who had actually put a book together comprised of the bad reviews of famous artists. It was entitled, appropriately enough, *No Stone Unturned.* I was not however certain of whether Jeremy's own appraisal would have made it, *sans* asterisks or not!

But a bit further down the road I heard about the one review which had perhaps taken the longest, but which, when it came was the sweetest. This was Dame Jean Conan Doyle's comment to Brett that *"your portrayal reveals the Sherlock Holmes of my childhood."* That meant the world to him. And I was pleased to hear for his sake that his reward for toiling in the Doylean vineyards had paid off so well. And at the same time I recalled Jean's own first remarks to me about Mr. Brett's rather overly zealous approach to woo her.

"Honestly, I didn't quite know what to think" she told me at our first time together. "Here was this actor doing his best to impersonate my father's character and wanting me to like him. But he was leaping about and bellowing. I did come to like Jeremy down the road, but at times he was a bit over the top. For instance, out of the blue he would ring me up and threaten to show up at my door saying, 'listen, darling, I'm coming over with a bottle of champers!'"

I suppose I did my best to commiserate with my friend. After all, how many people could admit to being pestered by Sherlock Holmes? Not that many. Yet in this case I imagine there was a bit of "the artist in search of his subject." Jeremy had been mad keen to "get it right," and that meant playing by the Rules According To Doyle. If nothing else, he was smart enough to recognize its importance. Doubtless as well, he might have been aware of those who'd run afoul of Jean, or earlier, her volatile brother Adrian.
But credit due, at the time no one to date had managed to pull the rabbit out of the hat quite as well as Brett. And on such a note it would not be unreasonable to assume that failing having Sir Arthur to woo, as

Gillette had done so successfully, there was still the great man's daughter.

And speaking of a creative challenge, there was of course one of my most personally memorable performances, this one given in conjunction with a special "Weekend With Arthur Conan Doyle" in May of 1992. The three-day program commenced at a hotel in Tunbridge Wells followed by a short journey to Crowborough for an afternoon unveiling of The Conan Doyle Memorial at Terrace Montargis. This event was jointly hosted by the Crowborough Town Council and the Crowborough Establishment, which had been initiated in 1989 on the 130th anniversary of Sir Arthur's birth as "a venture to promote the life and works of Sir Arthur Conan Doyle."

That evening a dinner was laid on, followed by our slated dramatic presentation, consisting of "An Evening With Sir Arthur Conan Doyle" featuring your humble servant, as Orson Welles used to say.

My memories of that weekend are sharp for a number of reasons. First off, I enjoyed the great company of Jean and her cousin by marriage, Georgina Doyle, wife of Brigadier John Doyle. I found Georgina extremely knowledgeable and a great deal of fun. We both had a nice time seeing my friend unveil the aforesaid plaque. Lady Bromet looked elegant and in fine fetter and still a considerable pace from the illness which would later lay siege to her indomitable will.

What also distinguished that afternoon was a special "side trip" after the unveiling and luncheon. This found Jean, Georgina, Jean's friend Norman and I motoring out to Windlesham, the house in East Sussex where Conan Doyle had lived for 23 years. No longer a private residence, the house is now owned by another family who ran it as a retirement home for the aged. At the time of our visit however, the place was bereft of anyone other than ourselves.

But imagine the rare opportunity of making a walk-through of a place like Windlesham, with Jean Conan Doyle as your guide! For here was the house in which she and her brothers Denis and Adrian were born and educated in nearby Crowborough. Sir Arthur had brought his bride, the former Jean Leckie, to Windlesham after their marriage in London. The already existing house was broadened by half its size under Conan Doyle's specifications. Here then was a perfect rural haven for writing, rambling, and receiving a legion of famous visitors. And it was there at Windlesham that the immortal Sherlock Holmes's creator died on July 7th, 1930. True perhaps to the real-life love story between ACD and his lady fair, he was found in the garden, clutching the first snow-drop, which was a ritual shared by the gallant knight and his beloved Jean.

He was buried on the grounds near his garden hut and writing room. Over 200 people came for the ceremony, accompanied by an acre's worth of floral coverage from the wreaths and arrangements sent by the famous author's admirers. Lady Jean would continue to live at Windlesham until her death a decade later, when she was buried beside her beloved husband. In 1955 when the estate's grounds were sold out of the family, the remains of the Doyles were reburied at All Saints Church, Minstead in the New Forest, Hampshire.

Upon our arrival, seemingly every step of the way was memory filled, and I reveled in hearing my friend describe her childhood here. Moreover, there were her own imaginative adventures during that epoch in which she'd proclaimed herself her father's "other son" and called herself "Billy." This novelty was to a certain extent abetted by her "Pops" as well, including any number of liberties ordinarily forbidden a child. The most vivid of these was Jean's recollection of a small pistol which she was allowed to keep in her room, regardless of certain prospective hazards attached to its possession.

"My father knew I had that little weapon, but I wasn't doing any harm with it. But there was that one evening, late it was, when I heard footsteps coming up toward my bedroom. Anticipating any number of monsters approaching, I pulled out my pistol and aimed it at the doorway. Fortunately however I didn't shoot, because it was only the man my parents employed to look after the house!" On hearing this I thought, *but for a twist of fate, imagine the prospective headlines, which might have read: "SIR ARTHUR'S DAUGHTER POTS THE BUTLER."* Fortunately for the family retainer, however, Jean never took her best shot!

It was a once-in-a-lifetime experience to have all of Windlesham to ourselves. I found myself drinking in the place, and remembering Brett's comment about "emptying the sponge of yourself," I allowed myself to become one with the spirit of Sir Arthur. I felt a very strong sense of Windlesham's owner, and particularly so in his study, where an antlered stag's head now was hung over the red-tiled fireplace. But perhaps oddest of all was making my solitary way down a staircase. The sunlight from the otherwise bright Spring afternoon was muted by the landing above, and as I descended in silence I must have been somewhat cloaked in shadow. In any event, I didn't realize that at the foot of the staircase stood Jean's friend Norman, who gave a visible start when he saw me.

"I thought you were him" he said, re-composing himself, and we both had a laugh. Nevertheless, the fact that even my off-stage resemblance to Windlesham's creator was obvious was no surprise to me. I'd taken note of certain nervous looks back at the Establishment's premises and during lunch at the Crowborough Cross. But this, as I knew Jean herself might say, was "as it ought to be." I also thought of a comment she'd made when I'd remarked upon how much larger than my companion I'd seemed in examining a picture of myself, side by side with Jeremy Brett. Breadth of shoulders, and even the size of my cranium. I looked like Piltdown Man beside Sherlock Holmes in his off-duty outfit.

"But that is the proper proportion of the thing, Mark" Jean explained. "For like my father, you are a much bigger man than Sherlock Holmes. I'm certain if you and Jeremy walked into a room together, all eyes would go to you." Hearing that wonderful fib, and knowing this would be anything but the case had Brett materialized in my presence, I took the compliment for what it was. Holmes and Conan Doyle. *Physical opposites and ultimately, adversaries.* How little could I have suspected that in only a few years we'd be playing that game for real.

After our return to the hotel I had the chance of sitting down with Julian Symons, the well-known mystery critic and author. We'd been introduced earlier on, but now we decided to have a drink and to talk about Holmes, Doyle, and of course, my evening's performance.

Throughout our chat I could not avoid thinking to myself of who my companion was. For the sake of his body of work, he'd already received the accolade of being dubbed the apt successor of Agatha Christie, the so-called "Duchess of Death." But my own knowledge of Symons' work went back a bit. In fact, one of my great favorites was his publication *The Great Detectives: Seven Original Investigations,* circa 1981. I'd very much enjoyed his description of a visit by a young woman who calls upon Sherlock Holmes in quest of a mysterious solution. The fact that the lady in question was the future's mystery solving Jane Marple made it all the more fun.

And there was of course the aptly-named Symons novel of 1975, *A Three Pipe Problem*. To me, and given the circumstances of the then present, if not the future, what that book had presumed had come true in a way in my own instance. For its plot had involved the work of an actor known for his televised personifications of Sherlock Holmes actually undertaking the solution of a grisly chain of murders. Imagine Jeremy Brett pronouncing himself a real crime-solver! But Symons' 1975 thriller came earlier. And in its way, I suppose it might have been prophetic.

But what was oddly familiar about Symon's *Three Pipe Problem* had more to do with its premise, which involved *an actor turned detective*. And here was I, now having a drink with its celebrated author, who to some extent at least may have been aware that he was sitting with *a detective turned actor!*

Truth to tell, in the latter regard the curious contrast between the author's actor-detective and myself came home only much later. At the time, you see, I had all I could do to calmly make delivery on my friend Bennett Shaw's claim that here was a man *"who thinks like, looks like, talks like and is as close to the real Conan Doyle as is possible."* As I'm certain you'll agree, that's a tall order for anyone to try and fulfill. Nevertheless, there were strange Sherlockian-Doylean parallels between myself and Symons' Holmesian Sheridan Haynes. That character was steeped in the quirks and morays of the Victorian detective, even as I'd come to feel a kinship with Jean Conan Doyle's father. Haynes ultimately proclaims to the media that Sherlock Holmes could solve the current string of murders, and so, *id est*, it's expected by all that he means himself. But well aware of his critics waiting in the wings, he presses on with the thought

"You would have made an actor and a rare one," Athelney Jones had said to the great man once. *If a detective could be an actor, was it not possible also for an actor to play the detective?"*

I've long considered the additional question that might well have been put to Conan Doyle himself: *"if a detective can be a writer, was it not possible for a writer to be a detective?"* Here of course the answer was "yes," and had been fortified by ACD's own record of investigations, both criminal and otherwise.

At the end of *A Three Pipe Problem,* the television Sherlock Holmes embarks upon a new venue for bringing the canonical adventures to life. He is approached in Symons' novel by an American agent and asked to consider a series of platform performances, or lectures, much in the vein of Charles Dickens and Oscar Wilde.

"Now, what I want to ask is whether you would consider doing a series of such readings from the Holmes stories, acting the parts and telling the stories. Can you imagine The Hound of the Baskervilles done like that, with the atmosphere of those dark moors conjured up, and the great hound striding over them?"

And like Sheridan Haynes in 1975, twelve years later I took to the stage as the creator of Sherlock Holmes. And like Dickens, that literary genius turned thespian, I (without the genius) explained to countless audiences at home and abroad how it was that I gave birth to Holmes and even how it came to pass that I eventually decided to kill him, if only as an act of "justifiable homicide?"

That afternoon when Julian Symons and I shared a drink, our conversation was influenced to a degree by that weekend's edition of *The Daily Telegraph.* It featured a generous story celebrating him upon the occasion of his 80th birthday. It was entitled "Three hats for the man of letters." Here he was quoted as describing himself as "a free-lancer and free-living radical" who enjoyed writing non-fiction, fiction and criticism. He was also candid in saying that "My crime stories have been praised as much as they ought to have been praised, but some of my non-fiction books are a bit better than they've been painted."

Given the man's bold ability at self-appraisal, I wondered how I would fare under his own magnifying lens that evening? This came up indirectly when our chat wandered into the territory of Sir Arthur Conan Doyle as a writer. And here, inevitably to be found was my own chronic interest in him.

My conversation with the great man of letters eventually abutted upon my decision to "become" Conan Doyle on stage. Here we both spoke fondly of Emlyn Williams, who like Hal Holbrook's long-running

"Mark Twain Tonight" had made Dickens something of a rock star in his day. For having avoided the pooh-poohing of his cohorts, the author had set his mind to reading—and presenting his written works to a live audience. His work had set the bar, and the future would find actor Emlyn Williams recreating the proper tone in 1951 with his series of Dickensian "readings." Another bar set, and one which has been equaled in my opinion, by Simon Callow's one-man performances in 2000.

"But you must be rather nervous" said the gentleman behind the large white goatee peering at me through the heavy dark frames of his thickly-lensed glasses.

"Nervous?" I repeated. "Why? Do you think I ought to be?" I inquired.

"Well, you are an American" he laughed.

I regarded that great master of mystery and considered his remark. Instantly I was reminded of one of the earliest reviews of William S. Baring-Gould's book *Sherlock Holmes of Baker Street* back in the Sixties. The author managed to dine out on the acerbic words of one of his British reviewers, whose best Parthian shot simply stated "Mr. Baring-Gould is an American." But and as I continued to my erudite companion, that didn't daunt Barinig-Gould, nor would it myself. By now I'd grown accustomed to having knowledgeable appraisers of my work. Authenticity of material, estimations of my physical appearance, and of course, even the sound of Arthur Conan Doyle's voice. I told Symons of how I'd been given advance warning in Toronto that a member of my audience, a certain Professor so-and-so was a noted dialectician in the mode of Bernard Shaw's elocutionist Henry Higgins.

"If I was overly bothered by knowing who was in the judge's seat, I shouldn't get out into the courtroom at all" I jibbed. "Or most certainly, the stage!"

For by now I'd learned that by volunteering to go out there, and to say to an audience "*look here, I'm him. Give me your complete and utter attention*" was the only proper mind-set to embrace. Such has been my philosophy over the past twenty-eight years. Since 1987 A.D. (After Doyle) I have sought to learn the art-form of "acting alone." I've also had the opportunity of following the super-sleuth's creator by inhabiting the dramatic skins of Winston Churchill, Bernard Shaw, Dickens, Wyatt Earp, C.S. Lewis, Theodore Roosevelt and Mark Twain.

The drill is essentially this: *you must become the character and then be him.* It's as simple and as complicated as that. Years ago I recall being hired to present my rendition of Teddy Roosevelt at a special event honoring U.S. Congressman John Dingell on behalf of his environmental contributions. The location of the event was Fighting Island, which is seated west of Ontario and not far from the southerly shoreline of metropolitan Detroit.

At any rate, before my dramatic bit, which would involve my being chauffeured up to the conference center site, shaking hands all the way in, and then taking the dais to salute the guest-of-honor, I'd found myself sitting alone in the back seat of a police car in a wooded clearing. The officers had left me there, just as dusk was about to fall. They promised to return when the time was right.

So there I was. Theodore Roosevelt. Twenty-sixth President of the United States. Now feeling isolated if not insulated, even as the sun was going down and he sat alone with his thoughts.

But as for myself, the actor, what skipped through my mind were not my lines as rehearsed, or whether the performance would be a success? Instead, and rather suddenly, to my own great surprise all that was on my mind were Roosevelt's re-conjured recollections of the night he'd left his wife and children behind to hie off to the Spanish war, and to what awaited him in the shape of destiny at a place called San Juan Hill.

In other words, on that particular evening and seated in the back seat of that police cruiser, I'd found myself deliberately immersed below the water-line of another man's memories. Then seemingly a moment later I was called back to my world. This upon the returned form of my uniformed driver. Peering in at me through the closed window he mouthed the words "It's time."

Slowly "TR" lowered the layer of glass between them, looked out at the policeman through the lenses of his *pince nez,* and said, rather decisively, "Officer, are you in the habit of keeping the President of the United States waiting?" Those words surprised us both. But the copper more than I. Because, you see, in that moment I *was* Theodore Roosevelt.

Therefore it's plain enough, I think, to walk on stage thinking "*I wonder if they'll like me?*" But instead, you need to walk out, loins girded, ready to survey the audience as if seemingly asking yourself, *Who are these people, and what do they want?* But also on the side of valor is the fact that *they have come to see you.* Not an actor (unless he is very famous) but a simulacrum—an authentic rendition of whomever. And for that reason they ought to be the nervous and excited ones. And why? *Because you're about to give them what they expect and something else they don't. Close up and personal. A private audience. And you'll be the one talking. So if they have any problem with you, they'll be having it with the real thing. So excelsior, and get on with it! Now then, let us return to that evening in Britain...*

I took to the makeshift stage that evening in a large meeting room in the Tunbridge Wells hotel where a host of the day's attendees were staying. Among those were Symons, my friend Richard Lancelyn Green and another Doylean specialist and author, Owen Dudley Edwards. Georgina Doyle was also in attendance, but regretfully Jean had been unable to come.

As always, the dynamics of every dramatic performance are affected by physical limitations. Looking back it seems all too rare a thing to be performing a two-act play in a theater proper. Which is to say, top-notch systems for lighting and sound and your own placement on stage with the audience traditionally down there in the dark. However, I long ago learned that to hazard the one-character genre is also to be extremely close to your onlookers, and at times, uncomfortably so. For that, after all, was the *milieu* experienced by many of those bygone "platform speakers." They might well have chanced to speak in great halls, parlours, meeting rooms—and certainly not always beneath a gorgeous proscenium arch!

And as I've said, there is always the risk of being held hostage by the technical side of things. For that reason I am always grateful to those professionals or amateurs who may find themselves drafted into the job of pressing the right button for musical cues, or framing you in the lighting established through many or few rehearsals. But saying this, one has a tendency to reflect on those frequent occasions, when through

493

your own or someone else's mis-attention, things boded ill for the star performer.

Once I remember, I walked out onto the stage suddenly aware of something wrong with my left wrist. This in effect was the fact that I'd foolishly failed to remove my wrist-watch in the dressing room, needing as I did to keep perfect track of my performance time. That required a rather elegant (I hope) turnabout to palm the timepiece from my wrist to my pants pocket. Or then and prospectively worse, there was the time I moved across the stage for the sake of divesting myself of Conan Doyle's gorgeous smoking jacket and trading it for the suit-coat resting on the back of a chair. To my shock and only upon donning the jacket, my fingers spidered down to the coat's buttons, only to Braille out the horrific shape of a cleaner's plastic attachment, as is often affixed upon receiving your garments! Foolishly again, this part of my property had been arrayed on set out of its plastic garment bag, fresh from the dry cleaner's. Ergo, a bit of deft handiwork, *viz* Houdini to remove the offending plastic device and to dispose of it with a quick turn.

There are simply so many things that can go wrong in the course of any dramatic performance. This fact is intensified of course by the performer's own state of mind. *Will I "dry?" Will the next line be there when I need it?* And remember, dear reader, that if you're an actor the masochistic act of embarking upon a "one man play" means you are out there as your own compass. And no one else to talk to who will talk back. And of course, no one to address aside from those shadowy faces beyond the footlights. But there are also those times when you can see them. Smiling. Frowning. Hopefully not sleeping. And depending on the performance venue, at times they are closer than usual, or even all about you if you're performing "in the round." Yes, all of them little perils and prospective minefields. But such things, as I later rationalized were part and parcel of any speaker's life, as was the case of say, Oscar Wilde, Mark Twain, and of course, Conan Doyle.

But still and all, there are dangers in looking out there and actually establishing eye contact with members of one's audience. It might be a certain beautiful lady in the third row, offering you her come-hither or "you are so wonderful" expression. Or perhaps it's her husband or companion, who is or is not most definitely enthralled. Or possibly you see the expert you were warned was coming tonight to vett your

494

performance, or worse, the critic who deigned to come and review your show.

In other words, it's easy to get lost, or worse, let go of your chain of thought. Also perilous is thinking you can read your audience's mind from their aspects. But looks, as they say, can be deceiving. For instance, what may appear to be a seemingly judgmental frown of displeasure in your beholder, or an ideally happy and satisfied visual reflection of what a fine job you're doing. Don't trust them. In actual fact, none of that may be a proper gauge of what the audience may actually be thinking.

Somewhat as a related aside, I recall performing as Charles Dickens one year and was asked by a young man if it might be appropriate to being his mother to the show? I said of course, that mothers were most often present at my annual Yuletide events.

"But you don't understand" he said, and proceeded to inform me of the sad events of the prior year for his family. It seems that his father had passed away, and so great was his mother's grief that she put a damper on all entertainments, as if to say that her son and daughters should reflect the level of her own personal grief.

Hearing that young fellow's sad story, I responded by saying that part of the Dickensian message was to remember those bygone times as fine things, and to celebrate, rather than to rue them as gone. And on that score I added, perhaps his mother would enjoy our "Dickens Of A Christmas." Nodding, he agreed. He would risk bringing his mother that very night.

And when that evening came, I used every bit of my energetic Dickensian radar to reach my audience. Meanwhile, and given the fact that I was playing "in the 'round," I was able to keep account of the audience in that small performing space. Moreover, it became my mission to visually locate the young man's mother, and thereby to direct certain of my heartfelt points to her. And this indeed I did. I found the lady in question, and was pleased, if not unduly proud of myself that I had a purpose in being there that evening, if only to share Dickens's message of remembrance, forgiveness, and of "renewal at that part of the rolling year." In other words, I felt I had entered into the proper "zone." Dickens himself couldn't do better. Oh and wasn't I good?

Well all went spinningly until at a certain poignant moment, suddenly a lady jumped to her feet in the back row. Uttering an audible cry she made her way out of the room. With that it became more than evident to me, as the powerfully motivating star performer, that *I'd been playing to the wrong woman.*

In case you're interested, the upshot of that Christmas performance had a happier ending. At the play's end the young man found me backstage and offered me his apology for his mother's display. I felt embarrassed at hearing him say this, and could only offer my own regrets that my words had succeeded only in hitting a painful nerve. And it was then that he informed me that the lady in question was just outside my dressing room. I got up and we walked out.

The denouement of my story found me sitting with the grieving widow, who in turn offered me her own apology for "spoiling your show." I assured her that it was anything but, and then said little enough, for it seemed important to her to tell me her own recent story. All the while she had taken the hand I'd used to shake her own when we met, but she continued to hold it as we sat there. She spoke. I listened. And at the end of it she said, "but your play makes me think that perhaps I have been wrong, especially for my family." And I said I was glad. Less than an hour later as my friend and I were driving homeward, he said to me, "You know, I have a feeling that apart from all of those other people, you were actually performing for just one person." And on reflection, he might have been right.

But coming back to "being Doyle" on stage, there are always those aforesaid pit-falls. Sometimes those are simply miscues on behalf of those whom you have charged to hold your artistic life in their hands, however momentarily. For instance, there was my Toronto performance in which I instructed the chap who'd been drafted to "douse the lights when I say (whatever the line was) and then turn about as if to leave." Well we practiced that, I repeated it many times, and he proclaimed himself content to do what little he needed to do to close the first act. But when the time came, so engrossed was that gentleman in Doyle's peroration, that when Sir Arthur turned on cue, and the end-of-act music played, *the lights did not go out.* Instead, there was I, as if frozen in suspended animation, waiting for the darkness that never arrived. So I merely exited with a scowl.

Which brings us to the matter of Sir Arthur at Tunbridge Wells. In any event, the specially-abridged version of my "Evening" had been prepared for the hotel audience, and moreover, was being captured by a team of videographers hired by the Arthur Conan Doyle Society. The plan established between my friend Chris Roden, the society's head, was that the video of that evening's performance would be given to the ACD Society as my gesture of goodwill. Ergo, all I had to do was to offer up my best dramatic energies, which in turn would be duly captured.

I managed to embark upon my single act without any undue difficulty. Which is to say, in most cases if one gets to the end of his histrionic journey without any too-obvious gaffs, coughs, hiccoughs or sneezes, etc. he does well. And usually what I deem to be the successful conclusion of what normally constitutes two forty-to-forty-five minute halves is that if anything went wrong, only I was aware of it.

I succeeded, as I say, in running the Doylean gauntlet, full aware of the presence in my audience of at least one Doyle family member, one or more international Doylean scholars, and of course, Symons, the heir apparent to Dame Agatha Christie's legacy. In other words, I had every reason to experience a jitter or two, being as I was a Yankee in Brit's clothing, standing there and doing my best to capture their attention.

Reaching the final word, the lights went down upon me and the applause started up. When the lights returned, I stepped back into the performance circle and took my bows. The audience gave me the "Standing O" which is precisely the sort of ovation every actor wishes to receive. And after that, it was time for the next step. In the case of the lion's share of my audience, this was likely to retreat to the lounge bar for some refreshment. And as for me, much the same, just as soon as I was able to make my way upstairs to "Sir Arthur's" room, blow my nose, change my close, and prepare to make my way back down to join the faithful corps.

However, just as I was making my way to the exit I paused to acknowledge the videographer and his two assistants. It didn't take Sherlock Holmes to see that there was something afoot.

"Everything all right?" I risked asking. And to this I saw the team leader's furled brown.

"Except for a slight difficulty" he replied.

"Such as what?" I inquired, stalled in my tracks.
"Well, sir, it's like this. We had a bit of a problem with the sound. Seems we lost some of it."

"How much of the sound have you lost?" I asked.

"About half of your performance" the videographer announced. He looked down at the floor, perhaps expecting it to swallow him up. Or perhaps, if only to avoid the lead weight of the stare he may have felt emanating from my eyes.

I made a moment's calculation and considered our options. The evening's performance had been the one and only for the weekend. Moreover, I had given my all to be my best, well knowing what had been at stake had I failed. And if that hadn't been bad enough, there I was with edited material, in a hotel meeting room, with a set of parking lot windows behind me and the constant, if not inebriated noises of the Merry Makers of Tunbridge Wells performing on the other side.

So I made the executive decision.

"Have your crew ready and double-check your equipment, especially for sound" I said. "When I come back down we'll shoot the damned thing again."

"You'll do the play another time?" asked the surprised camera man.

"That's what I said" I replied. "Be ready in about fifteen minutes."

And that was exactly how it went. And while there was the sound of merriment and revelry by night in the hotel's bar, rather than joining in I was back on my mark, starting from square one and my first words, which once again unfurled over the course of the next forty minutes. And yes, no one in that room save for myself and the trio of technicians.

Fortunately for all concerned, what the camera and sound unit had preserved was the opening applause, some cutaways of audience members, and the final standing ovation. These bits and pieces were later edited into my version of a Doylean "silent night" and incorporated into the Arthur Conan Doyle Society videotape which became part of the organization's cottage industry of products.

I will always remember that weekend in Tunbridge Wells. Seeing Jean unveil the plaque, seeing Norman's face when he encountered "the ghost of Sir Arthur" on the staircase at Windlesham, of having my drink with the new "Duke of Death," and lastly, of performing twice, and once before an empty theatre. Such then concludes "The Adventure of the Invisible Audience," and on its account an example of this humble player's lot.

Watson:

I have done my best to take it all in to this point. Frankly in the beginning I felt this was only a jest, perpetrated by your own pawky humor to rile me. But then it became obvious that the present manuscript's author is perhaps as singular a sort as any we ever encountered. But more than that. He is not a hero, nor is this McPherson a villain. Or is he demented, despite that penchant which, by his own admission, has become a kind of idée fixe upon the subject at hand.

While I have done my best to dislike or even to dismiss what the manuscript's creator has set down, I am left with a peculiar sense, never pleasurable to me, of having been honoured by the attention of a stranger. That Mr. McPherson has spent such a considerable degree of time under my influence, I feel, albeit involuntarily, that I owe him at least my temporary attention.

Lastly, there is another peculiarity about this "Irregular Life." It is that somehow the writer has touched a nerve, or played a chord which is decidedly familiar. Is it then possible that he is, in his way, a loyal follower who could have been also a valued companion? As one who has earned that rather singular entitlement, my dear Doctor, perhaps it is I who should ask your opinion?

I will read through the last of it. Whether my attention can or will make the slightest of difference remains to be seen. For now at least, it serves to while away a lonely, rain-swept afternoon here in my rustic hideaway.

Holmes

Jeremy Brett and "The Woman,"
the author's lovely wife Dori

29
Stand With Me Here Upon The Terrace

This no doubt is perhaps the most difficult of my memoir's many chapters. It is also one of only a few I decided to re-visit within the revised edition. It also stands as perhaps the most bittersweet among the rest, in that it succeeds my earlier words, and represents the passage of at least five years.

Moreover, this chapter has much to do with a seeming *denouement*, or culmination in my relationship with three outstanding personalities in the world of Sherlock Holmes.

The first of those is Jeremy Brett. Gone now for more than two decades, posterity will yet have his image and stentorian voice to savor. This is assured so long as the visually recorded episodes of the Sacred Canon are available on this planet—or perhaps in future, upon others.

And like so much else, my memories of Jeremy are eerily fresh. All the more so in fact, for as when I initially constructed this chapter, my *aide de memoir* was served in part by two cassette tapes within the machine at arm's reach. Upon those is recorded my first and long conversation I enjoyed with the actor in his dressing room at the Wyndham's Theatre, on November 25, 1988.

As I have endeavored to describe, my relationship with Brett began excitingly and well. Doubtless it was through the cachet of my growing friendship with Dame Jean Conan Doyle that the two of us had met. In simplest terms, as he had wooed that fine lady to accept him as Holmes, so too I appeared upon her doorstep, if only to return as I endeavored to "become" her late father on stage.

Therefore my first and second meetings with the star of the Granada Holmes series were more than I might have expected. This in greater part reflected their context, which had more to do with a common dramatic undertaking, rather than a simply fan-based exercise in hero worship.

In recording these memories I found myself confronting a real problem. This had to do with whether or not to recognize shortfalls in one's self or others, if only as a matter of record? In the former regard I have not shied, but in the latter regard even now, however, I am very aware that it may seem a low-down thing to strike at another man when he is either down, or unable to defend himself. On that very count I confided my concerns to a friend who had also met Jeremy Brett within our shared context of Dame Jean. Earlier on and even more than I, he had experienced an unpleasant side of the actor; so much so, in fact that it had compounded his initial failure to appreciate Jeremy's run as Holmes. In the main here his criticisms had much to do with the Brett interpretation of Sherlock as a kind of manic night-bird, rude and divorced from all but his own inner voices. Worse yet, my colleague said, it became obvious to him that such traits were not merely limited to the actor's on-camera persona.

In such regard it occurred to me that here, unsurprisingly, was a strange and dark key to Brett's Sherlock Holmes. For as those within this talented man's range often had come to understand, over time his performances were increasingly colored by his own mental and physical limitations. These had initially tempered his presentation, and subsequently would tinge and even threaten his ability to deliver his image of the great detective to the camera's eye. Tragically, I think, Jeremy's chronic and unfortunate ultimate surrender to his bipolar and physiological demons had often marred his off-stage life as well. This fact was reflected by a number of persons, many of whom I had known. And then of course, I had my own personal experience to go on, which for me was perhaps the saddest of all.

Upon my return to London in 1989 I was now underway in my own dramatic journey of trying to learn how to "become" Arthur Conan Doyle. In theory at least, I suppose this may have created a slender bridge of affinity between Brett and myself. In fact, one of my fond memories was of walking into his Wyndham's dressing room after a chat with Jeremy Paul, his "Secret of Sherlock Holmes" playwright, and being greeted in novel, albeit typical Brett fashion.

"My friend" he intoned. "And my Doyle!" I heard the words nearly trilled by the reflection of the actor in his make-up mirror, a sweater draped over his bared shoulders. I was struck by the utter privacy of the shared moment, if not by Jeremy's zealous greeting. Truly, I would never forget those words, or how I felt upon hearing them uttered.

At this time I had vetted my play with Jeremy Paul, whose own experiences as dramatizer of several of the Granada productions were solid. Only recently did I discover a letter from "the other Jeremy." It was postmarked "Middlesex" and dated January 30, 1989, many months prior to my return to London.

> *"Dear Mark,*
> *First let me congratulate you on giving me a marvelous read.*
> *You really have got under the skin, and the pictures are excellent*
> *too. I think you've produced a draft which is in fine shape to take*
> *to a director ...'*

Quite naturally and as you might imagine, this was unexpected and high praise, coming from such a seasoned and successful dramatist. Paul's words served to press me on, but more so my desire to refine the drama which I had written and presented to Dame Jean. On that note then, I wanted to refine the characterization of her father even further before taking steps to launch "An Evening With Sir Arthur Conan Doyle" on any professional stage, be it in Britain or elsewhere.

But I was increasingly encouraged by such critical support. In similar fashion, I had the chance to discuss my project with Roger Llewellyn, a fine and lesser-known Holmes portrayer, whose accumulating performances have at present earned him a place in the annals of "the theatrical Holmes" with "Sherlock Holmes—The Last Act!" This was a one-character drama which features Holmes returning to "221B" on return from his friend Watson's funeral in 1916. That then was the device of the work, which was presented with skill and veracity by Llewellyn. Years later the play's author David Stuart Davies, wrote in *Starring Sherlock Holmes,* a compilation of Holmesian performances,

"Roger Llewellyn is the actor who has grasped the nettle of this demanding interpretation of Holmes, and has received stunning reviews for his performance. London's Time Out stated that, 'From Basil Rathbone to Jeremy Brett there have been many fine portrayals of Conan Doyle's greatest creation. The name Roger Llewellyn can now be added to the distinguished list.'"

Upon seeing Llewellyn's portrayal I'd found it brilliant and refreshing for the simple sake that he was not such a "known" or "branded" commodity in the task of bringing Sherlock Holmes to life. Moreover, his ability to direct his remarks to the audience on a one-to-one (or many) basis was something I understood.

I enjoyed hosting Roger Llewellyn at our home "Gray Gables" and of sharing some of my more curious collection items. But perhaps even more so was our sampling a twenty-five-year-old blend of Laphroaig Scotch whiskey which had been reserved for a special occasion. This meeting proved to be that, and only after we grew meditative did Roger make what now seems a rather sage observation about my undertaking the challenge of re-creating Arthur Conan Doyle.

"Doesn't it seem strange, or perhaps fitting, Mark, that the first actor chosen by Doyle himself was an American?" Roger asked me. Of course he was alluding to William Gillette, who became the Basil Rathbone of his day in a play he had written and adapted with Conan Doyle's special permission. Early on when the Yankee actor asked the author if he could marry Holmes in his play, Doyle said, "you can kill him for all I care!"

And yet, I began to take Roger's meaning. He continued. "And similarly, here you are, another American, tapped by Sir Arthur's daughter to become her father!" Hearing this, I could only agree. It was odd. And wonderfully coincidental. Or was it?

My apprenticeship to the spirit of Sir Arthur and the very lively person of his daughter opened other doors as well. In brief reply to a request for an interview with him (which was granted!) the great Christopher Lee congratulated me on my project, if only to remind me that he had played both of the "Holmes brothers" (Sherlock and Mycroft) Holmes in "Sherlock Holmes and the Deadly Necklace," "Sherlock Holmes: The Golden Years," "Sherlock Holmes and the Leading Lady" and "Incident At Victoria Falls." But more than that, he added, he'd played Mycroft Holmes in Billy Wilder's "Private Life of Sherlock Holmes," and in a related Baker Street vein, Sir Henry Baskerville in the Peter Cushing version of "The Hound of the Baskervilles."

As time passed I considered myself tremendously fortunate to have gained access to such superb actors, chiefly through my love of the characters they had brought to life. To date that list has included Basil Rathbone, Christopher Plummer, Douglas Wilmer, Jeremy Brett, Paxton Whitehead, John Wood, Gerald Harper, Leonard Nimoy and

Roger Lewellyn. And as for Watson? Well I have had the additional privilege of spending time with Edward Hardwicke and Patrick Macnee, aka "John Steed."

But after so many performances, so many places, so many audiences, I wonder whether I have gotten any of it right? Which is to say, and to parallel Jeremy Brett's prideful, "Dame Jean said I was the Sherlock Holmes of her childhood," did I in any way become a scintilla of the man she called "Pops?" She told me I had, and had described the reason with the word "presence."

In stature, look and perhaps to a degree voice, I have done my best to assay the great man on stage. Moreover, and apart from what any serious reader may gather to be the "spirit" of the author, there was also a bit of direct evidence to work from. Here the template of sorts was a filmed interview made with Sir Arthur a year or so before his death. And in that, within the garden at Windlesham, the great man speaks directly to the camera and begins

"People often ask me how I ever came to write the Sherlock Holmes stories..."

Unwittingly from my first viewing of it on an eight-millimeter reel, that rare interview became the basis for my sense of the "real" Doyle long before I would meet his daughter. For being able to see and to hear him, I had what ultimately felt like a bit of True North, if not my beginning point.

Initially I spent a great deal of time simply listening to the man's voice. Also to be factored in was the fact that unlike myself at middle age, my subject was three decades older. And like his larger girth, thinner hair, more walrus-like mustache, the voice was obviously tempered by decades of platform speaking, if not by a long and adventurous life, probing this world and the next. Gone by that time was the dashing cricketer, adventurer and reformer with the waxed-mustachio ends. Such an image had been captured rather nicely by Sidney Paget, who'd spent so much time presenting Holmes to his public. In fact, I'd deliberately sat for a "comparison sitting" before the camera, if only to see if I could match the man in the oil painting. These two images appear in this memoir, so I'll let you be the judge.

As for getting a true sense of my subject, I had my game plan in mind. First I elected to translate the 8-millimeter film of the Doyle Interview to recording tape. From that I transcribed the tape to written text. Now and with that in hand, I began to struggle to sound like the voice as I read along. Soon I became aware of certain nuances, cadences, stylistic pauses and more. I also took into account the trace of the Edinburgh burr which was there behind the rest, and an almost flattened out tonal dimension which at times resembled an un-British, almost Americanized accent. Once these were duly noted it became the grueling work of being able to simulate those sounds. Eventually it was an exercise not merely of replicating the Doylean text, but of being able to read anything—the phone book—the Declaration of Independence—the daily paper—or even a Holmes story, as Sir Arthur himself might.

I remember the drill of vocalization to be initially punishing. Early on I would dry out, as my vocal chords were unused to that artificial rhythm. But slowly, eventually, it got easier. And by the time I was to speak Conan Doyle's very first words in my "Evening," I could not only run the race, but complete it!

Ultimately I found "my time with Sir Arthur" to be valuable indeed, *vis à vis* the business of accents. Similarly, my regimen of leaving my own voice behind was expanded for the future when I sought to evoke the sounds of Winston Churchill, Bernard Shaw, Charles Dickens, or C.S. Lewis. I cite these apart from those other members of my dramatic repertory (Wyatt Earp, Mark Twain, Theodore Roosevelt) if only to underscore the objective of an American sounding like a British subject.

The matter of crafting a dramatic, one-character performance is in essence an intimate series of conversational moments shared with the audience. In that sense you might describe my efforts as a dialogue structured to represent a number of such intimacies as might otherwise go unrevealed. Which is to say, here the conceit represents a character who might be otherwise tight-lipped sharing his innermost thoughts to the darkness. And that darkness is, dare we say it, the audience.

In my case such a dramatic series of quests began with what we'll call the Doylean endeavor. There I knew I would be required to be as authentic as possible, if only on account of being judged by members of my audience. Which is not to say that one expected to find the likes of a Julian Symons, Lancelyn Green, Georgina Doyle, or even Dame Jean Conan Doyle in the "seats up front" —but it was always a possibility!

For my general template there now stood the history of the one-charactered solo performance. The first of those to come to mind was Hal Holbrook's enduring offering "Mark Twain Tonight!" which commenced in the 1950's as a cabaret feature after germinating from a brief monologue. Over time both the material and duration of the performance lengthened, even Holbrook's ease with his alter ego succeeded in making the audience feel that here indeed was the author of *Tom Sawyer* and *Huckleberry Finn* musing aloud for themselves alone to hear.

But *suddenly* the fundamental question arose: could I "become" the creator of Sherlock Holmes? Perhaps an easier task, had I been up for it, would have been to portray Frankenstein's Monster, rather than peeling back the layers of the mad doctor himself. And in this case, the doctor in question was not mad, but only hungry for the sort of literary success that could free him from his quotidian duties. So to paraphrase Jeremy Brett's later remark, I began to "climb the monument."

As I also learned in short order, there are many pit-falls in the business of choosing to embark upon a "one man show." This particular genre is presumed by some, and erroneously so, as being easier than being on stage with an ensemble. I cite the simple fact here however, that in being the solo performer you have the advantage (or disadvantage) of being absolutely alone. In effect, your work involves delivering a veritable monologue of two approximately 45-minute halves. Vocally, you don't have much of a respite, and dependent upon your character(s) there is always a potential strain upon your vocal chords. I found this to be especially true when I took on the job of becoming Winston Churchill. For apart from this actor's best efforts, being as he was in 1991 44 years of age, lighter in weight than now, who had more hair than now, and who was still 6'1," all I had to do for authenticity was to become a short, fat, bald 75-year old Englishman! Eezy peezy, as my British friends say.

Another dimension of flying "solo" was my Dickensian Christmas drama, "A Dickens Of A Christmas." In the second act of this I employ the author's own script for Stave One of his *Christmas Carol,* which involves, conservatively speaking, about five distinctive voices, ghostly rants included. Ergo, one needs to spare the voice but use it, and send it out to the back row!

If indeed it is a real detriment, I will share a final anecdote concerning being on my ownsome as Arthur Conan Doyle. I remember having lunch one Bank Holiday Monday with the then-unknighted Derek Jacobi, whose own dramatic record is enormous. At the time he was playing Lord Byron in a one-character vehicle and he remarked that "the only things wrong with that is you've got no one to talk to on stage, and worse, no one to go out to eat with after the show!"

I remember that same trip to London seeing Anthony Hopkins in "M Butterfly." After the show we spoke about my reason for being in town, and of my meeting that day with Dame Jean Conan Doyle. I also told him that given his physical features he might well present a more than serviceable aspect of Sir Arthur on stage. But what I did not say was that, much as I'd thought of Dr. Al Rodin years earlier, it would be more difficult for a smaller man to assay Sir Arthur's girth and height. On such a note the performer would be compelled to rely upon his brilliance, and less upon his seeming height.

Hopkins told me he was flattered to be so well thought of, and commended his best wishes to Dame Jean. However, he said, after "Butterfly" he was "going to focus on the big screen for a while." I'm pleased to say that he did, for the next time audiences saw Sir Anthony (as he now is) it was as the world's most popular cannibal, Hannibal Lector in "The Silence of the Lambs."

But to return to Mr. Holmes. I must retreat to 1992. This was the time that Granada was struggling to bring their televised Holmesian adventures to the level of excellence of their earlier outings. Sadly, audience response and critical reviews had made this job increasingly difficult. In 1991 and as "The Casebook of Sherlock Holmes" was screened, it had been two years since the last Granada-Holmes film, and worse yet, the health of its star was greatly impaired. The earlier and problematic reception of "The Return of Sherlock Holmes" in

1988 and "The Hound of the Baskervilles" that same year had suggested that the initial magic of the thing was wearing thin.

But as I have said, it was the imperiled health, emotional welfare, and impaired ability to deliver his original incarnation of Sherlock Holmes that became Jeremy Brett's greatest enemy. Moreover, his bipolar history and perhaps not unrelated temperamental displays at times could not be hidden from the camera. Paradoxically, and as in the case eight years earlier, Brett himself was aware of channeling his own sadness over the death of his wife, if not his ensuing bouts with manic behavior into his work. Ergo, those criticisms of a more "over the top" Holmes may well have been part-and-parcel of this actor's mental and physiological condition. Like Stevenson's Mr. Hyde, his alter ego Dr. Jekyll became uncontrollably overwhelmed.

Another friend and confident has spoken candidly about Brett's decline, on screen and off. He said to me not long ago that he was not certain that the actor might have occasionally played his "bipolar card as an excuse for simple bad behavior." This remark was in due part the result of having dined with Brett, been in his company, even seen him in social settings wherein the genial and talented man became a rude and offensive companion, even to his nearest and dearest.

As for myself, up to my final meeting with Jeremy in Windsor, Ontario where he made a stop-over while plugging the PBS "Casebook" series, I had no personal reason to question his behavior. However, prior to crossing the Detroit River to join up with a colleague, I'd heard things. These included Brett's rudeness on tour, his disappointment of fans who'd been asked to dress in Victorian attire to have their pictures taken with "Sherlock Holmes" only to be rejected. And then the matter of "certain remarks."

When we greeted one another in Ontario at the riverfront Hiram Walker installation, I sensed a great deal of tension in Jeremy. Moreover, I watched him berate a waitress for not providing him with a drink, which, judging from his tone and demeanor, was the last thing he required.

Accompanying me was my older companion, a gentleman who prior to his retirement from the law had been of counsel to the Hiram Walker firm. To my surprise however, he had never seen Jeremy Brett as

Sherlock Holmes. My own history and my best descriptions of the series had made him curious.

But when Jeremy took to the stage, he was decidedly not Sherlock Holmes. Instead he seemed distracted, maudlin, and more eager to cite the state of world affairs, tinged by an allusion to the bygone death of his wife, and the bid, "but do not mourn for me." And throughout all of this, no Sherlock Holmes. But unlike my disappointment in Basil Rathbone's similar decision so long ago in my youth, here Brett did not fill in the artistic gaps with evidence of his wonderful career. Only upon agreeing to take a few questions did he re-orient himself back to Baker Street.

And then it happened. I'm not certain of exactly what the question was, but next thing I knew Brett was telling the audience about "my dear friend, Jean Conan Doyle." Then he went on about how she lived alone in London, was rather lonely, and "would love to hear from fans of her father's work." And if that wasn't enough, he then proceeded to ask the audience if they would write Jean, and then gave them her London address and telephone number!

Now I was aware of a great deal by then, including the fact that Jean was not as well as she had been, slept badly, and had been plagued recently by prank phone calls. Also that she employed no secretary, and with very few exceptions entertained no strangers at her door. All of which now seemed to hang in a degree of jeopardy, given Jeremy's plea for audience interaction.

I believe a brief clip from the "Casebook of Sherlock Holmes" was played, and after a couple of statements from the local PBS affiliate, the show was over.

As the audience milled about and Brett had already taken his leave, my companion and I retreated out a back door. Beyond this was a terrace, and below that, an extensive bit of foliage and well-tended grounds running down to the edge of the river.

My friend and I walked across the dewy lawn and faced the international waterway. He remarked on the program and asked me what I had thought of it? I replied rather guardedly, but still rather bothered by Jeremy's injudicious comments, couldn't hold back.

"Truthfully, I had a problem with it all" I said. "First of all, he never should have asked anyone to write to Dame Jean Conan Doyle. She's not well, and she's not lonely. It was the wrong thing to do."

And that's when, as if from the heavens close by, I heard the distinctive voice of God. And it sounded remarkably like a combination of Sherlock Holmes and Jeremy Brett. Suddenly I knew it was emanating from the nearby terrace behind where we stood, looking out toward the glimmering shoreline of Detroit.

"I don't think it really was a problem, Mark."

Turning about and looking up, there indeed was Jeremy Brett. He held a wine-glass in one hand and a cigarette in the other.

I faced that familiar ghost in the shadows and said, "well, Jeremy, I disagree. I think what you said was a problem, and I'll tell you why." And this said, I crossed around to the stone steps leading to the terrace and in moments stood face to face with my quarry.

I explained in calm tones that as we both undoubtedly knew, Jean had recently been unwell, and wasn't quite out of the woods yet. Also, that the last thing she needed was people writing or showing up at her door.

Exhaling a wisp of smoke, my companion pursed his lips and replied.

"Well I don't believe anyone will really write to her" he said. And that was that.

We may have said a bit more, I don't recall. All I do remember for certain was standing there on the terrace with the man I'd so admired for so many years. But here before me was not the world's greatest detective. Here was a brilliant actor, his skills sadly dulled by who-knew-what, who was more than capable, even as I'd heard and learned, to fly into a rage at the slightest offense. Add to this, hadn't I seen him lose it with an innocent member of the wait-staff scarcely an hour before?

"Well then, I'll see you in London, Jeremy" I said. I extended my hand. He took it. But did I know that it would be for the last time?

"See you in London, Mark" he repeated. And then I left.

Driving back to the Windsor-Detroit Bridge and Customs Authority, I felt an increasing sense of intuitive dread. Or was it only a sense of sadness at having to witness an obvious and disappointing performance from our friend Brett? *But no* said an inner voice, *this is different. And it's going to be bad, with rough weather ahead. Mark my words.*

About a week later I made one of my irregularly regular calls to London and to Jean. She was glad to hear from me, and I was pleased to learn she'd been on the road to recovery. We chatted about a few things and it was then I chanced to mention having seen our mutual friend a week ago.

She paused. 'Do you know, Mark, I have been hearing the strangest things about Jeremy and what he's been saying on his promotional tour." I bit my tongue. I wanted to tell her about his indiscreet remarks, but elected in that moment not to.

"What sort of things?" I asked, as casually as I could manage.

"Oh that people ought to write to me or call. He knows very well I wouldn't want that. I have only given him permission on one occasion to give my address, and it was to a professor who was writing a book. But to no one else."

I pondered what the better part of valor was just now. And then I thought, *in for a penny...*

It was then that I informed my friend that I too had heard Mr. Brett make such an overture to his audience in Windsor. Also that I shared my friend's displeasure at what he'd said. And it was then that I concluded by saying that I had every reason to believe that there was going to be trouble on account of what we'd discussed.

But I wasn't to know the full extent of that "trouble" for another two weeks or so. Strangely troubled by the entire affair, I'd decided to write Brett a letter, explaining my reason for upbraiding him (however carefully) on the matter of breeching what amounted to Jean's privacy.

The next call found me telling Jean that I couldn't help regretting the scene in Windsor. Also that what Brett had said might well have been fueled by his health, a bit of wine, or just the way he was.

Which only evoked Dame Jean's reply that "if so, he'd been repeating that performance at any number of stops on his trip to America."

"No Mark, he said it more than once" said the steely voice at the end of the transatlantic line. But it was not the tone of an elderly lady who felt abused, or of a lonely soul who wished to be left alone. It was the voice of a woman who had been a force to be reckoned with all her life. Adjutant to the Queen. Head of the Woman's Air Wing. And like her country's prime minister, an "iron lady" in her own right.

"I asked Jeremy about this when he got back in town" she continued.

"And when I bearded him with the question of whether he was giving out my private address, he replied by saying 'I suppose you heard that from Mark.' To which I said I had not. But that I had received other reports from other quarters."

I took this news in with a bit of a sour feeling, and then I decided to tell Jean that I'd regretted the entire messy scene and had decided just to attribute it to one man and his troubles. Also that I'd written Jeremy a letter, wishing him well, fibbing a bit to say it had been good to see him in Ontario, and that I looked forward to a future meeting. But as far as I could tell, I wasn't certain that he'd received it. Nor had he returned a telephone call in the same vein.

There was another pause. And then, "Oh Mark, he did receive your letter. He told me he took it and tore it into little pieces."

The feeling of sourness became something else. Something worse. *Sherlock Holmes had destroyed my attempt to offer an olive branch. And why? Over a much-perceived tiff over the daughter of Sir Arthur Conan Doyle. You couldn't, as they say, have made that up.*

Suffice it to say that among those various types of "straws capable of breaking a camel's back," my meeting with Jeremy Brett and what seemed now to be our final conversation had altered a great deal. And now, on behalf of running defense for my friend Jean, I had taken on

"Sherlock Holmes" and had earned myself his enmity as a result. And I continued to hear Jean's voice, *he said he tore it into little pieces.*

Seemingly then, I had touched more than a nerve that recent night in Windsor. And as far as I could tell, my instincts en route for home that evening had been correct. There was indeed trouble, but not brewing. It was here and on my doorstep. But why? As best as I could tell in mulling the matter over, my colleague Brett had obviously felt I had gone out of my way to sabotage him with the very woman whose respect he seemed to value greatly. But despite her own disavowal, he was prepared to make me the scape-goat. And just as I could recall any number of dramatized occasions when this man (or the one he was portraying) had turned his cold wrath against an inferior, or an enemy, now that cold blade was being aimed at me. And why? Simply because I had shared a confidence with the very person whose privacy I'd felt had been breached. Moreover, the friend whose own association remained very special to me.

It was probably then that I allowed myself to remember something Dame Jean had said to me, so many years earlier. *But you see, Mark, that's the way it is: in proportion my father was so much a bigger man than Sherlock Holmes. That is you to Jeremy.*

But all those years ago I had not suspected that an hour would arrive in which "Sherlock Holmes" would assail "Conan Doyle" over the one woman they both held in such high esteem. Ironically, for each of us Jean was "*the* Woman," in the parlance of "A Scandal in Bohemia."

It was a comfort, albeit a bit cold, I admit, that Dame Jean had not only understood my role in this *fracas,* but had thanked me for taking her part. And as far as I was concerned, and as I told her, I would have done and said exactly what I had weeks earlier. I simply had no control of what Jeremy Brett might or might not have to say about myself or anyone else. To date I had honored our association, and if he wished to end it over this, then so be it.

That then was the end. I cannot tell you that my own steely resolve in the wake of our falling out did not bother me. So much so in fact that I wrote to Brett once more. But no response. Stranger yet, on at least two occasions over the years to follow, I actually dreamed of standing before my new nemesis, if only to do my best to explain. But not entirely to apologize. I knew I had not been in the wrong. And yet, how to explain it? Or how to describe the great sense of discomfort I felt over time to come whenever someone would mention Brett, or worse, when I would decide to watch one of those excellent, iconic episodes from "The Adventures of Sherlock Holmes." Now however, seeing Holmes before me, a small voice managed to intrude, and to say *Sherlock Holmes has a problem with you. He holds a grudge. And there is nothing you can do about it.*

I suppose over the course of time I hoped that there would be the opportunity of my putting things right with Jeremy. But the chance of such a sorting-out never came. And not long ago, when I chanced to read a line from "His Last Bow," something about it evoked a mixture of pleasure, wonder, and disappointment. For now those well-remembered words of Holmes to his friend seemed to take on a newer, sadder meaning. So sad, in fact, that the Baker Street Irregulars have traditionally embraced them to signify the passing of its faithful members.

"Stand with me here upon the terrace, for it may be the last quiet talk that we shall ever have."

And as it chanced to happen, for Jeremy Brett and I, standing alone on that terrace in Ontario, it was indeed that. It was in effect, an eerie precursor of what would come to both of us.

Apart from a legion of other recollections I have set down in these pages, I find these last to be among my least favorite. Thinking this, as I swivel about to consider the summer-clad garden view beyond my library window, and then again, to view these well-stocked and lately perused shelves. There I know upon a lower level is a plastic boxed frame which contains a newspaper clipping. It is identified at its top in ink as being from *The Daily Telegraph*. It is taken from the publication's NEWS PAGE, and is dated Thursday, September 14, 1995.

The photograph which dominates the page is of a familiar face. But now it seems to reflect Jeremy Brett's many travails, as if the countenance of Sherlock Holmes had taken on a pinched aspect, like a soul plagued by an unending circle of displeasure. It reminded me of a strikingly similar photograph of Somerset Maugham taken in his later years. But even the photo was vastly overshadowed by the article's headline, which read:

Heart failure kills
Jeremy Brett,
alias Sherlock Holmes.

It was Jeremy's obituary, sent to me—could it be now, more than twenty years ago— by Jean Conan Doyle. I'd known at the time that given our histories, we'd both been sad on account of its message. But very like that *New York Times* review he'd kept and carried in his wallet, I had no doubt that in some strange but morbid way, Jeremy might have been honored by those fine and good hands which had clipped and then preserved this, his "final review" of sorts, and ironically, for me to see.

And even now there are still times that I look at that framed bit of newsprint, as I muse to myself that *there within this frame rests the obituary of Sherlock Holmes. And it was sent to you by the daughter of his creator.*

Still in a way as I must confess even now, something about my last encounter with "the true Sherlock Holmes" feels rather heart-breaking. But isn't that often the way when we sometimes view our heroes in the baser light where we ourselves tend to stand?

"Holmes" & "Sir Arthur"
Jeremy Brett and the author

Heart failure kills Jeremy Brett, alias Sherlock Holmes

By Dan Conaghan

Screen role: Jeremy Brett was seen as the definitive Sherlock Holmes

THE ACTOR Jeremy Brett, best-known for his definitive television portrayal of Sherlock Holmes, has died of heart failure, aged 59.

Brett, who had suffered heart problems for the past two years, died in his sleep at his home in Clapham, south London, early on Tuesday morning.

Edward Hardwicke, the actor who played his screen partner, Dr Watson, in the Granada Television series said: "He was a great friend and a really remarkable actor."

Hardwicke said his friend never received the recognition he deserved, adding: "The role of Sherlock Holmes is like that of Hamlet. Every generation brings something to it. Jeremy brought extraordinary energy to the part and made it his own."

Brett first played the detective in *A Scandal in Bohemia* in May 1984. There were 41 episodes and his last interpretation came last year, when Granada produced *The Cardboard Box* in its series, *The Memoirs of Sherlock Holmes*.

Jane Annakin, Brett's agent, said: "He worked the role for a 10-year period and, although he never really saw himself as Holmes, thoroughly enjoyed it."

The producer of the Holmes series, June Wyndham Davies, described Brett as "the definitive Holmes".

Earlier this year Brett appeared in the film *Mad Dogs and Englishmen*. His last performance was in a film dramatisation of Daniel Defoe's *Moll Flanders*, yet to be released.

He trained at the Central School of Speech and Drama and worked extensively in the theatre. Following a nervous breakdown after the death of his second wife, the actress Joan Sullivan, in 1986, he was re-admitted to hospital in March.

After collapsing with heart trouble while filming his last appearance as Holmes, he said: "I would be risking my heart, head and neck if I were to stick it on the block again playing Holmes."

A victim of depression in recent years, he made an appeal 10 days ago on Radio 4 on behalf of the Manic Depression Society.

Obituary: Page 17

"Jeremy's 'Final Notice'"

30
The Final Problem
(Being A Disquisition Upon Heroes, Their Images,
And Those Who Worship Them)

Hero worship is a strange thing indeed. Often I suppose it has much to do with who we are, where we are in life, and what we hope to be when we undertake its journeys. Small enough wonder then that a flip of the coin may find its reverse not only scarred, but of lesser (or even greater) value than once before.

In this memoir I have endeavored to remember many who are now gone, and by shining a light upon them, to see my own shadow as well. For the sake of such an exercise I have come to see such things as a Rorschach Test for my own thoughts and actions over the last fifty-three years.

I have succeeded, I think, in discerning which of those templates of my childhood, youth, young adulthood and now seniority have been the longest lasting? Quite evident as the answer to that may be to my wife or close friends, no one recognized these syntheses better than myself.

Therefore it is unlikely, even as I now clock seventy-four years of existence, that my childhood companion Peter Pan has taken his leave of me. Nor that what they call "maturity" has in any way exorcised those other friendly ghosts who have stood by my side for so long. Ergo, do not count upon the notion that King Arthur or Merlin or Sherlock Holmes or even James Bond will pull up stakes and move on without me,

And do not think that time and age may discourage the shades of Sir Arthur Conan Doyle or even Commander Ian Fleming from frequenting my chambers. No, for like friends they have shared quarters with me for far too long. Over many roads and terrains, local and not. Through luck and misfortune, adventure and tragedy.

And when at last the time for leaving perhaps arrives, I suspect my phantom friends and I will all go off together, retiring to the next stage or battlefield, leaving in our wake nothing more than a museum's worth of jumble and scores of sagging book-shelves in our Mad Hatter's collection.

I grew up learning to play by the rules as written, rather than those so recently revised. I have recognized the sodality of "Sherlockian" celebrations in many places by many persons. I have respected newer commentaries but always choose to retreat to the fifty-six stories and the quartet of novels which comprise the Sacred Canon. I have welcomed interest in my own work and have carried this to further points by not only studying Holmes' creator, but by soliciting those of his blood as I've sought to "become" him, however briefly. And I hope I have provided elucidation or entertainment to those who are at the heart or upon the cusp of loving the lore of Baker Street, which remains unchanged for me, in a Platonic kind of way.

In other words, I have been fortunate enough to love my favorite fantasy, and even to step into its byways. I have sought to go further than most, and perchance by seeking my Grail, gaining intimations of its nearness. Yes, all of this I have done, for good or for ill. And at the end of the day?

Despite my status and deeds, which may merit a minuscule footnote, possibly to be read or lost or re-discovered again, all that is truly important is that I have acted on my dreams. And for the sake of that, Sherlock Holmes has become very real to me.

I find myself reminded of Jeremy Brett's later comment to his friend Dame Jean Conan Doyle, when he said of his labors,

"But I've had a fascinating time playing him. I've danced in the moonlight with your father for ten years. The moonlight, not the sunlight —Holmes is a very dark character."

Brett may have inadvertently put his finger on the quick of the thing. For as he and a score of others have recognized (myself included) there is a certain strangeness attached to our subject as a whole. Its symptoms include Everest-like highs and cavernous lows. Friendship and enmity. Exultation and despair. Some have even called it the Doyle Curse. Fanciful, you may say? Ask anyone who has sat near the heart of the volcano and then think again.

Arthur Conan Doyle's creation of perhaps world literature's most realistic fictional characters has begotten a formula for adventure and excitement admired by a multitude, even to the point of emulation. Paradoxically perhaps, Sherlock Holmes became a bane of sorts to his creator, even to the point of Sir Arthur's need to kill Holmes, if only to liberate himself. But like Frankenstein's patchwork monster, the begetter became aware that while "the doll and its maker" were not the same, they were indeed one.

I have considered the "how?" and "why?" of my admiration for Holmes and Sir Arthur in light of my own life. In similar fashion, I have indulged in a good deal of sanctum musing over certain other of my personal heroes in this field. And as I have stated, my association with Jeremy Brett, as the detective's embodiment fell victim to what might be termed the "curse." As did an even more long-term relationship, the end-point of which involved not only who I was, but who I had become.

I began this recollection by describing my *entrée* into the world of Baker Street, courtesy of the kindness of a stranger named W.T. Rabe. He for me served as a surrogate parent in Sherlockian Lifemanship. His initial and successive interest in the melding and molding of my Doylean foundation remains unparalleled. Moreover, his personal image as a stern man of spirit, a jocular and clever gamesman, as well as a dominant and creative being did not elude me. Testament to his legacy, I cannot or will not apologize for following in Bill Rabe's footsteps in a number of ways. I loved Sherlock Holmes. I became a collector of his genre. I initiated a number of "Sherlockian" projects. I created a scion society. I became a member of the BSI. I became known as a good friend and at times, a fierce adversary. I became a university publicist, and made use of this as a base for my further undertakings, many of which became "press-worthy."

Over the course of nearly two decades I followed Rabe's lead. I began as his student and ended as his friend. And then, one night late in 1980, it all came apart.

Following the annual BSI dinner, we wound up in the lobby of the Algonquin Hotel. This was the very place where, fifteen years earlier, a boy had met a famous Scottish actor and learned to toast in the Gaelic way. Now however, my mentor and I sat in those aged armchairs and spoke about our respective lives.

I told Bill about my own last foray to Loch Ness, and of the odd lengths which some in the media had gone to cover my exploits. The subject of the Arthurian excavations in Glastonbury also came up, as did such Rabe-esque shenanigans as a mystery investigation at Detroit's Player's Club, or "The Last Houdini séance" at the magician's death room at the city's Harper- Grace Hospital.

I supposed that as I spoke and my companion listened, he might intuit what I felt I was saying: in other words, *I learned these things from you. How to handle the press. Generating publicity. Planting a piece in the next day's paper. Being a favorite radio interview guest. Or just going off on whatever self-interested romp I might imagine and finding others chiming in, wanting to join the party.*

But unnoted by me at first, something had short-circuited somewhere along the way of our conversation. Rabe seemed to go quiet just after we'd each shared some bit involving our respective collegiate administrations. I recall I was about to shift the subject to something else when Bill suddenly rose from his armchair. As if involuntarily taking his signal, I got up as well. I watched as he walked toward the elevator and pressed the button. This was the same elevator, I seemed to remember, that we had once shared upon an earlier and magically ghostly journey to this fairy tale city more than a dozen years ago.

I was in the midst of saying something when W.T. Rabe stepped ahead into the waiting car and de-pressed the button again. Looking back, I believe there could have been no more surgical means of cutting my words at midstream than the sight of those pneumatic doors closing. And before the serious presence of my long-time companion vanished, I saw his face, expressionless. And then he was gone. No nod. No gesture. Nothing at all.

I stood there frozen, initially wondering if this were a joke? But no, there'd been nothing like that afoot. Nor as I considered it, had there been anything in our conversation that had bordered on insult or offense. There'd been no raised voices, and no anger from the man seated across from me. Nothing more deafening, in fact, other than his unexpected exit.

I remember finally managing to un-root myself from that spot before the old elevator door. Puzzled? *Without a doubt.* Insulted? *No.* Hurt? *Yes. Yes, very much so.*

My last recollection is of grabbing my coat, gloves and scarf and entering into that stilled urban setting of snow-covered walkways, dismal alleys and vestiges of a bleak winter's night suddenly made bleaker in Old Gotham.

Hunkered down for the walk back to my own hotel many blocks away, I replayed the incidents of this final, mind-boggling phase of the evening. I began by envisioning our arriving at the old hotel, of our sitting down, of our talking about our wives, our jobs and the shortcomings of our respective academic fellow administrators. And then...

Oddly, I suppose it's the way my mind works, for on my solitary, silent walk something came into my head. It was a distant memory concerning the relationship between Zen masters and their disciples. As best as I could recall, this also had to do with an indication that at some point the pupil had completed his course. Yet I remained hazy over what happened then. Was the student dismissed? Did he embark upon his own way as a teacher? Did his former mentor now go about the business of finding another pliable youth to tutor? I didn't know.

But I also remembered what in Zen teaching was called the Dharma Transmission. This involved the establishment of the disciple within the great tradition and possibly as a teacher in his own right. As such, he was now a successor in an unbroken line of masters. But was this in any way where I now stood?

I asked myself many times over the course of many days to follow whether my tutelage under Bill Rabe as my Sherlockian "master" ended that night? Or did it, really? Or possibly if my perplexity at his veritable vanishing behind those elevator doors was somehow part of another lesson? Moreover, would our mutual recognition of that truth result in a resumption of our long friendship? Or is it a telling indication of what I had not done—had not learned—which explained why my childhood mentor and I would never see one another again.

All of this has remained a bit of a mystery to me which has endured across the bridge of many years. Yet in strangely typical fashion and while compiling this memoir, I chanced upon the seemingly bygone allusion that had set my mind to work on that sadly unusual winter's night when Rabe and I had parted. The key to it came from a slim volume entitled simply *Zen Buddhism* which had been given to me by a friend for my birthday forty-six years earlier. And there, one of its many aphorisms concerned a *koan* or lesson involving a student who visits his master. Wishing to impress him, he says *"There is no mind, there is no body, there is no Buddha. There is no better, there is no worse. There is no master and there is no student; there is no giving, there is no receiving. All that is real is Emptiness. None of these seeming things really exists."*

To which the master, quietly listening and smoking his pipe, says nothing. He merely picks up his staff and gives his pupil a tremendous whack. The youth recoils in anger.

"Since none of these things really exists" says the master, *"and all is Emptiness, where does your anger come from? Think about it."*

And I did think about it. And I have done. And I continue to do so, even now. But today and in retrospect, I am still left wondering. Was Rabe's response to me a lesson designed to evoke a reaction? Or was it something else? Or as the *koan* suggested, was it all nothing real at all?

Ultimately and like so much else Bill Rabe and I had shared, this constituted our final mystery, in the form of a dark valediction of sorts. That wintery evening in New York was in a way the full course of a circle that began on a much earlier snowy evening, when the boy not yet a man was astonishingly befriended by his olde, kindred spirit.

But the scene played out in the lobby of the Algonquin marked the last occasion I ever saw or spoke to Bill Rabe. He vanished, willfully enough, from my presence and my life. Sad to say our next communication would be many years later upon my old friend's final days. His friends were invited to write to him. And I did. And I took the time to say *"without you I could not have done any of this. You were my inspiration. I can only hope that the day will come when I might be as clever, and kind, and generous to some young person as you were to me. And for that, my friend, I do thank you. I am in your debt."*

The Zen tradition also has it that "when the student is ready, the master will appear." Looking back now to my own example, I have no doubt that the old axiom proved true. For when I'd unwittingly proclaimed myself ready Bill Rabe had seemingly answered the cosmic call. And for that I state here unreservedly, I'm more than glad.

Also and when The Amateur Mendicants needed a shepherd, Wilmer T. Rabe was there to guide and goad the flock. Moreover as good as the AMS might seem in the years to come, never again would it replicate some of those bygone days I was blessed to witness.

So then, when W.T. Rabe pulled up stakes to head northward to Lake Superior State College as its "Eccentric in Residence," he took with him more than a modicum of magic. But unwittingly perhaps, he also left a bit of that fairy-dust. Perhaps one day it will be my turn to pass it on?

31
L' Envoi

Serendipitously perhaps, the last time I saw my friend Jean Conan Doyle was upon the evening of the day I'd paid a call upon Sherlock Holmes. This involved my welcome response to an invitation from the wonderful character actor Douglas Wilmer to spend a long afternoon at his Suffolk home outside Woodstock.

As I mentioned at the beginning of this story, my first meeting with Douglas Wilmer was on the set of "Cromwell" in 1969. Many years later we touched base again concerning his sale of a Sidney Paget illustration. Now however, our purpose in meeting was only to discuss two subjects: Conan Doyle and Sherlock Holmes.

My casual conversation with Mr. Wilmer ranged from his earliest acting days to his being called into harness as Holmes in 1964. And there, snugly seated in his flat amidst what the actor called his "rural seclusion" we found a bit of common ground. Notwithstanding Richard Harris and Jeremy Brett, both of whom Wilmer had found less than admirable in their ways, he did have high praise for another. This was my friend Richard Lancelyn Green, who had produced a couple of Sherlockian-themed audio tapes in conjunction with the Sherlock Holmes Society of London. But even more interestingly, I thought, was the fact that the much younger incarnation of the later scholarly Holmesian collector and expert had once written Douglas Wilmer a fan letter.

"He was about eleven and wrote to me from his prep school, saying in his note that he would so 'like to meet the living spirit of Sherlock Holmes.'" Wilmer remembered. He then proceeded to tell me of how they had eventually later met. In Wilmer's autobiographical memoir *Stage Whispers,* he said "it was long after I met him as an adult that I connected the events. He never referred to it himself. I could hardly have had a more auspicious co-producer."

I found our mutual connection with Richard sadly moving. No, it would have been unlike my rather retiring friend to have made a later point of such an earlier fixation. And strangely as well, I mused, both my late colleague and I had made a long-ago connection with the famous actor, only to initiate a kind of adult-based association in the future.

As for Sherlock Holmes, there was no doubt that Douglas Wilmer has made a vital and longstanding contribution to the cinema-graphic history of the genre. His looks cannot be discounted as anything but an evocation of Paget's Holmes, and in his crisply blunt demeanor he was reminiscent of both Rathbone and the later Brett, but without the latter's penchant for the manic.

Interestingly as well, I have learned that within many quarters of Mr. Holmes's England, there is little debate over whether Douglas Wilmer was in fact "the finest Holmes of all time." Bold words those, but to anyone witnessing the man's performance or even listening to him expound, even as I happily did in incisive and out-of-character fashion, both inference and reason for the claim are strong.

Wilmer's memory of his early outing as the BBC's great detective over the course of thirteen installments were those of a rushed, low budgeted, and at the time, unprofessional attempt to redact Conan Doyle's stories. He was fonder by far of his co-star Nigel Stock, who was his Watson. But as for playing the sage of Baker Street, while it was a role he fancied and felt fit to perform, what had been lacking had been the proper frame for the as-yet-to-be-made masterpiece.

We spoke at length about the desire for authenticity, whether with Holmes or elsewhere. My recollection of our long-ago meeting on the set of "Cromwell' evoked a number of memories which did not reflect well upon Richard Harris, the star. In blunt terms, the older actor found Harris' antics and attitudes quite removed from his own standards, particularly when he began to "throw his weight around." Again, in *Stage Whispers,* Wilmer, playing Fairfax, Cromwell's general, wrote that Richard carried this to such paranoid lengths that he identified himself with his own idea of the character, regarding anyone opposing him in the plot of the film almost as an actual personal enemy. "And that, wrote the veteran performer of stage and screen, "very nearly out-methoded *Method.*"

And we spoke about a quiverful of other things which had nothing to do with Holmes. For instance, he pointed out that the Dark Age Sutton Hoo burial had been found not that far from nearby Woodstock. We also discovered a mutual liking for the works of Sax Rohmer, creator of the Dr. Fu Manchu series. Wilmer had played in a film of the same name with his co-star Christopher Lee which I'd remembered and remarked upon his portrayal of the Chinese king-villain's adversary Nayland Smith, as somewhat "Sherlockian." Correcting me, Wilmer altered that description to "a poor man's Holmes."

In terms of my own undertaking of the evolving role of Conan Doyle and my association with Dame Jean, Wilmer was interested in my relationship with Jeremy Brett. When asked I thought seriously about what *not* to say, and chose as the better part of valour to edit many of my perceptions to date. However I did chance to describe my final "closing" with Jeremy in Ontario, and the firestorm which had been begotten by what "Holmes" had gleaned from his conversation with Sir Arthur's daughter. I told him my regret at hearing that Brett had been so inflamed that he had admitted to tearing my letter into pieces.

For the sake of propriety and if not to denigrate the character of Mr. Brett to those who revere him, I won't repeat the balance of my conversation with Douglas Wilmer, or even of his opinion as to the "why?" Brett had reacted toward me as he had. On reflection however, some of this made sense and I could not remove the possibility as an option of sorts. Nevertheless, I could not then and cannot today divorce Brett's psychological and physiological conditions as factors which impeded his great talents. But no one could have known that better than dear Jeremy himself. So as is often said, perhaps it is best to remember better days, and God rest him, those times when the line of distinction between Holmes and Brett seemed wafer thin.

But a few additional words about Douglas Wilmer and Mr. Holmes. Meeting the famous actor for the first or even second time constituted a rare pleasure at the time, and does so even now. By virtue of his kindness and willingness to discuss both Arthur Conan Doyle and his fabled creation, I got to converse with a key embodiment of Holmes, adding to my roster at the time, which had begun with Basil Rathbone, continued with Christopher Plummer, and by then had included Jeremy Brett. And now Wilmer. Moreover, since our long ago visit I have acquired the DVD versions of Douglas Wilmer's televised dozen or so Sherlocks, and I must say in all honesty, they are crisp and authentic and for the lack of seeming over-produced or budgeted, they are like gorgeous little time-capsules in their own right.

In closing, here another emendation to the text. As I was pleased to relate in the Summer of 2015, Douglas Wilmer was 95 years old and like Holmes in his dotage, still an interested player in the peculiar game of "Sherlockian Pursuit." It wasn't all that long ago that I'd e-mailed him and received a very kind reply. And that is how I shall always remember him. Always the perfect English gentleman, he'd been kind to a 22-year-old fellow yet to find his way to Baker Street, and again to his much older incarnation decades later. And for that, I will always be in his debt.

Sadly perhaps for those who loved, knew or admired Douglas Wilmer, that excellent actor passed away in the Spring of 2016, succumbing at age 96 to pneumonia. Yes gone from us, but perhaps as I'd like to think, now to rejoin a majority of others, the company of many of whom was enriched by his presence.

As I began this chapter by saying, the evening of my day's pleasant meeting with Douglas Wilmer was my final meeting with my friend Jean. Moreover, my unwittingly final return to Cadogan Square proved to be perhaps the most difficult of any in memory. This no doubt was owing to the general atmosphere when I arrived. Jean was unwell, nervous, and already in the early grip of the malady which would decimate her former strength and independence. I too was a bit fatigued, and immediately regretted not postponing our appointment until the next day.

Originally we'd discussed my continuing the video-graphed "interview" I'd done with Wilmer earlier that evening with my friend. But on account of her general state, we decided to forego the visual dimension. Jean consented that our talk be recorded, but while my camera's lens cap was affixed.

How to describe a final meeting with a close friend or loved one? The line which comes to mind is that it beggars description, and so it did that night. Our visit was truncated to little more than an hour or so. In fact, so tense did we both feel that it was not until I was headed back for my hotel that the floodgate of memories were finally released.

Worse yet, when I left Jean's flat it was with an overburdened foreboding that it would be for the last time. Oddly, and hovering close even as I closed the door of Number 72 behind me, I found myself haunted by the echoes of other, better days over the course of nearly a decade. As I write these words, those memories are attested to in a physical sense by photographs and shelves of bulging scrapbooks and file folders. But that night, and like a parade of Dickensian spirits in flight, I felt their presence in a host of vignettes. *The first time I rang the bell as Dori and I stood upon the step, in anxious anticipation. Or my return to Jean's abode, to review the script for my "Evening." Or even my much later return, en route for Euston Station and the Night Train, bound for Inverness and a certain monster-haunted lake. Or even of now, as I remembered the small silver coin upon my watch-chain. That was a ten-penny piece Jean had given me whilst we'd been shopping. I smiled and told her I would wear it in her honour, even as Holmes had done with Irene Adler's token. She had liked that gesture very much.*

There were other recollections as well which had nothing to do with me. What about Michael Caine chancing to reside in an upper flat at Number 72 Cadogan Square while shooting "Without A Clue?" Yes, and Jean's description of her unexpected meeting with the famous actor in her building's small lift. And of her asking Caine what he was working on in the moment? And of the star's careful explanation: "a comedy" he said, diplomatically side-stepping the fact that he was in the midst of making a parody of Sir Arthur's greatest creation and admitting it to the true Daughter of Sherlock Holmes.

Last of all on that fateful night, I even allowed myself to imagine the first and other times when another actor named Jeremy Brett had paused upon Jean's threshold, no doubt nervously as had I. Both of us there, on the street where she lived and dramatic suitors of a sort, each hoping for a smile from "our fair lady."

And now, the rest seems to decline into silence.

Conan Doyle. Jean. Brett. Rabe. And a well-remembered legion of so many others. Over the course of passing years I have felt the tidal tug of each of them, reminding me that all were touchstones for what I thought, and to an extent, for who I became. Finally, by my convictions I am consoled that hopefully the day might come when we will meet again, either as unmet friends, or in a kind of glad reunion. Think me fanciful or not, but I like to put all of this within the context once described by C.S. Lewis in his book *The Last Battle*.

"All their life in this world and all their adventures in Narnia had only been the cover and the title page: now at last they were beginning chapter One of the Great Story which no one on earth had read: which goes on forever: in which every chapter is better than the one before."

With any luck, I've thought, that may apply to tales both "canonical" and "Conanical" as well as those of the magically Narnian kind.

And now we round the corner of that gaslit avenue with the end suddenly in sight

STAGE DIRECTION:

The set has gone to black. Now there is the sound of a distant trumpet, perhaps the skirl of a bag-pipe, possibly a drum-roll as the curtain is drawn to a close.

UNSEEN NARRATOR'S VOICE:

The vision begins as a waking dream. You are walking down what appears to be a London byway. Around you as you go a light mist rises, creeping catlike up the ebon trunks of the gas-lit lamps which flank your path. From somewhere in the near distance Big Ben strikes the hour. Your steps resound along the quiet avenue as you hasten, for you are expected down the way and your arrival is overdue. Somewhere out there in the shadows someone is waiting. And suddenly from a nearby point you hear the faint echo of two familiar voices, one of them your own. But it is the other, always compelling, which urges you into a forced march.

"See you in London, Mark" it says.
And in response you hear your own reply as you pick up your pace and advance..
"See you in London, Jeremy."
In London...
Yes, in London.
London.

FINIS

My Dear Watson:

I have completed the task as requested. You were correct in thinking that your old friend might find it a divertissement. As indeed and to my surprise, it was.

Like his namesake in the account you entitled "The Lion's Mane," I fear that Mr. McPherson has been stung by something which has assailed, if not irrevocably conquered him. However, the culprit in this instance may be more *Sherlockianus Extremis* than *Cyanea Capillata*, I am left with a curious sensation of wondering whether or not to feel accountable for the gentleman's rather chronic malady?

In any case, the story was as you promised, not without interest. Now however, it is time for me to attend to business at hand. Unlike your good self, my apian friends seem to require my personal and regular presence.

"Argumentum ab actoritate." Auf weidersein, my friend.

Holmes

An Authorial Addendum

To be a Sherlockian. This may signify many things to many persons.

For myself however, this condition has assumed the proportion of a mental landscape rather than a lifestyle or even casual pastime. Just so, the present memoir has been my attempt at describing many a journey through just such a labyrinthine terrain. And that mostly cerebral territory has been created out of dreaming, very like Coleridge's Xanadu. Yes, a place

> *"as holy and enchanted*
> *As e'er beneath a waning moon*
> *was haunted ..."*

And there I have willingly traversed boundaries of both time and space. Moreover, this device has been my way of remembering so many conversations, events, and most certainly, persons who have happily crossed my path.

Therefore and while shared, this memoir is now mine alone. For in it I have been able to describe only one "Sherlockian" or "Holmesian" or assuredly, one "Doylean" with complete fidelity. He has been by my side now for nearly seven decades. Willfully too, I followed Christopher Morley's literary advice and became "the man who made friends with himself." He is that same wide-eyed child who grew older, and in Conan Doyle's words, became "a boy who is half a man, and a man who is half a boy." In other words, I have grown old in the service of Never Land. Better yet, my alter ego has been that faithful and constant companion who began by being afraid of the bed-time shadows, if only to eventually find his way to sleep each night by daring himself to enjoy a new night-mare. And perhaps by this curious means of solitarily bearding the Dark Adversary, the tone was set.

In reviewing these words in the wake of their being written, I wonder how harshly I myself may be judged? It might be useless to fall back upon the sword of saying "you had to be there" or "remember this is only one (now older) man's crotchety opinion." For indeed this is another day and age. Much has changed, and often for the better. Yet memories recede into the fogs of one's past.

And while I might be criticized for eschewing social gatherings for the sake of being unsociable, this is not so. For instance, the BSI's males-only policy of former days has been altered. At last the like of my now late and old comrade Susan Rice annually populate the meeting rooms. For that I am mightily glad. Or perhaps I am now stuck in the place in which old wine is not comfortable in new wine skins? I do not know. Allow only, my corps of met, and unmet friends, to offer these views with respect for those who have gone before me, in a literal as well as a figurative manner.

Yes I have grown older, even as Sherlock Holmes in his dotage, yet as but one man among many who sought to know what others did not. And by such lights did we both create his own profession. Through such work did his fictive literary beacon unwittingly became a legend, while I was content enough simply to follow his legendary trail. And in the end, only to find myself more Quixote than Sir Nigel, but with quests aplenty in my timeworn quiver.

Obviously enough and with so much weather now at our backs, it is plain that Sherlock Holmes, his Watsonian and Doylean creators, if not their respectively contiguous worlds have tempered me more than a bit. These two stand at the vanguard of those real and unreal beings who have inspired me to lead a fantasy-based charge against the forces of reality. There have been others as well, I suppose. Yet I am left even today and so long after, still wondering whether my thoughts are in some part strange because I have read the "canonical" tales, or whether I read them because I myself was strange? In any event...

I believe that as Sherlockians some of us have danced with abandon on the edge of a peculiar abyss. And in looking downward we have risen to strange heights. We have seen things, heard things, done things. And all in the name of that one man who "never lived and so can never die." In his tracks we have followed, some of us, more intently than others of our herd. And why? Perhaps if only to discover that our journey's end was also its beginning.

For we have heard the familiar hunting call, and with that distant "view halloo" we have ventured from gaslit avenue to misty moor—and we have lived within the recesses of a thousand pages, each of which has seemingly sung as if to ourselves alone.

Here then is the good that is our Grail—and this that magic doorway we have willingly entered, if only "for the sake of the trust."

"For those with ears to hear, then let them listen."

Ave Atque Sherlock

Postscript To A Memoir

I have thought a good bit about how the present work ought to end. In this regard I've also tried to consider what it's "meet, right and proper" to say, before it is too late.

The other day I was reading in the bath (as is my wont) and my subject was a literary memoir by a chap named John Glassco. In his reminiscence *Memoirs of Montparnasse* he said something I found intriguing.

The once youthful memoirist wondered whether he should dare alter the truth of what he'd remembered of his longago's?

"After all, why change any of this?" he asked himself. "This young man is no longer myself: I hardly recognize him, even from his photographs and handwriting, and in my memory he is less like someone I have been than a character in a novel I have read."

But is this true of myself? For despite the passage of time I still feel my life vividly and as if within the present context. In great part as well, my love affair with Sherlock Holmes and his quasi-imaginary life and bygone world have left their indelible imprint upon me. And over the course of time that love has compelled me and impelled me to seek to better my understandings by seeing and touching and hearing what once upon a time, far, far away, was now tangible only upon the printed page.

Lightning Source UK Ltd.
Milton Keynes UK
UKHW011946120522
402896UK00001B/7